Productivity Measurement
in Regulated Industries

This is a Volume in
ECONOMIC THEORY, ECONOMETRICS, AND MATHEMATICAL
   ECONOMICS

A series of Monographs and Textbooks

Consulting Editor: KARL SHELL

A complete list of titles in this series appears at the end of this volume.

Productivity Measurement in Regulated Industries

Edited by **THOMAS G. COWING**

Department of Economics
State University of New York at Binghamton
Binghamton, New York

RODNEY E. STEVENSON

Graduate School of Business
University of Wisconsin — Madison
Madison, Wisconsin

 1981

ACADEMIC PRESS
A Subsidiary of Harcourt Brace Jovanovich, Publishers

New York   London   Toronto   Sydney   San Francisco

338.4561
P964 me

ACADEMIC PRESS, INC.
111 Fifth Avenue, New York, New York 10003

United Kingdom Edition published by
ACADEMIC PRESS, INC. (LONDON) LTD.
24/28 Oval Road, London NW1 7DX

Library of Congress Cataloging in Publication Data
Main entry under title:

Productivity measurement in regulated industries.

(Economic theory, econometrics, and mathematical
economics)
Papers presented at a conference, sponsored by the
National Science Foundation and the Graduate School of
Business at the University of Wisconsin--Madison, and
held Apr. 30--May 1, 1979.
Bibliography: p.
1. Industrial productivity--United States--Measure-
ment--Congresses. 2. Public utilities--United States--
Congresses. I. Cowing, Thomas G. II. Stevenson,
Rodney E. III. United States. National Science
Foundation. IV. Wisconsin. University--Madison.
Graduate School of Business.
HD56.P823   338.4'5613636'0973   80-1685
ISBN 0-12-194080-2

This book was prepared with the support of NSF
grant DAR-7716084. However, any opinions, findings,
conclusions, and/or recommendations herein are those of
the authors and do not necessarily reflect the views of NSF.

Contents

Part I   INTRODUCTION

1   Introduction: Productivity Measurement and Regulated Industries

Thomas G. Cowing and Rodney E. Stevenson

Part II   THEORETICAL FOUNDATIONS

2   The Theory of Total Factor Productivity Measurement in Regulated Industries

W. Erwin Diewert

Part III   REGULATED INDUSTRY STUDIES

3   U.S. Trunk Air Carriers, 1972–1977: A Multilateral Comparison of Total Factor Productivity

*Douglas W. Caves, Laurits R. Christensen,
and Michael W. Tretheway*

4   Regulation and the Structure of Technology in the Trucking Industry

*Ann F. Friedlaender, Richard H. Spady,
and S. J. Wang Chiang*

5   The Sources of Economic Growth in the U.S. Electric Power Industry

Frank M. Gollop and Mark J. Roberts

6 Capacity Expansion in the U.S. Natural-Gas Pipeline Industry

Varouj A. Aivazian and Jeffrey L. Callen

7 Comparative Measures of Total Factor Productivity in the Regulated Sector: The Electric Utility Industry

Thomas G. Cowing, Jeffrey Small, and Rodney E. Stevenson

8 The Measurement and Interpretation of Total Factor Productivity in Regulated Industries, with an Application to Canadian Telecommunications

Michael Denny, Melvyn Fuss, and Leonard Waverman

Part IV   POLICY IMPLICATIONS

13   Pollution Controls and Productivity Growth in Basic Industries

Robert W. Crandall

14   Motivations and Barriers to Superior Performance under Public Utility Regulation

Harry M. Trebing

References

List of Contributors

Numbers in parentheses indicate the pages on which the authors' contributions begin.

VAROUJ A. AIVAZIAN (145), *Faculty of Business, McMaster University, Hamilton, Ontario, Canada L8S 4M4*

JEFFREY L. CALLEN (145), *Faculty of Business, McMaster University, Hamilton, Ontario, Canada L8S 4M4*

DOUGLAS W. CAVES (47), *Department of Economics, University of Wisconsin – Madison, Madison, Wisconsin 53706*

S. J. WANG CHIANG (77), *Department of Civil Engineering, Massachusetts Institute of Technology, Cambridge, Massachusetts 02139*

LAURITS R. CHRISTENSEN (47), *Department of Economics, University of Wisconsin – Madison, Madison, Wisconsin 53706*

THOMAS G. COWING (3, 161), *Department of Economics, State University of New York at Binghamton, Binghamton, New York 13901*

ROBERT W. CRANDALL (347), *The Brookings Institution, Washington, D.C. 20036*

MICHAEL DENNY (179), *Department of Political Economy, Institute for Policy Analysis, University of Toronto, Toronto, Ontario, Canada M5S 1A1*

W. ERWIN DIEWERT (17), *Department of Economics, University of British Columbia, Vancouver, British Columbia, Canada V6T 1Y2*

ANN F. FRIEDLAENDER (77), *Department of Economics, Massachusetts Institute of Technology, Cambridge, Massachusetts 02139*

MELVYN FUSS (179), *Department of Political Economy, Institute for Policy Analysis, University of Toronto, Toronto, Ontario, Canada M5S 1A1*

FRANK M. GOLLOP† (107), *Department of Economics, University of Wisconsin – Madison, Madison, Wisconsin 53706*

† Present address: Department of Economics, Boston College, Chestnut Hill, Massachusetts 02167.

CHARLES F. HAYWOOD (283), *College of Business and Economics, University of Kentucky, Lexington, Kentucky 40506*

RAYMOND J. KOPP (249), *Resources for the Future, Washington, D.C. 20036*

M. ISHAQ NADIRI (219), *Department of Economics, New York University, and National Bureau of Economic Research, New York, New York 10003*

A. MEAD OVER, JR. (309), *Department of Economics, Williams College, Williamstown, Massachusetts 01267*

MARK J. ROBERTS† (107), *Department of Economics, University of Wisconsin — Madison, Madison, Wisconsin 53706*

MARK A. SCHANKERMAN (219), *Department of Economics, New York University, and National Bureau of Economic Research, New York, New York 10003*

JEFFREY SMALL (161), *Department of Economics, University of Wisconsin — Madison, Madison, Wisconsin 53706*

KENNETH R. SMITH (309), *College of Business and Public Administration, University of Arizona, Tucson, Arizona 85715*

V. KERRY SMITH (249), *Department of Economics, University of North Carolina, Chapel Hill, North Carolina 27514*

RICHARD H. SPADY‡ (77), *Department of Economics, Swarthmore College, Swarthmore, Pennsylvania 19081*

RODNEY E. STEVENSON (3, 161), *Graduate School of Business, University of Wisconsin — Madison, Madison, Wisconsin 53706*

HARRY M. TREBING (369), *Institute of Public Utilities, Graduate School of Business Administration, Michigan State University, East Lansing, Michigan 48824*

MICHAEL W. TRETHEWAY (47), *Department of Economics, University of Wisconsin — Madison, Madison, Wisconsin 53706*

LEONARD WAVERMAN (179), *Department of Political Economy, Institute for Policy Analysis, University of Toronto, Toronto, Ontario, Canada M5S 1A1*

† Present address: Department of Economics, Pennsylvania State University, University Park, Pennsylvania 16802.

‡ Present address: Bell Laboratories, Murray Hill, New Jersey 07974.

Preface

The measurement and analysis of aggregate productivity growth has been a major topic of interest since World War II. In contrast, the measurement of productivity advancement at the firm level is a relatively new area of interest, especially in the case of regulated industries. This volume, the result of a conference held at the University of Wisconsin, is meant to contribute to this new area of concern.

Many of the contributors are among the leading productivity measurement experts today, so this volume should be of interest to policy analysts, industry specialists, public utility regulators, and academic researchers alike. Following an introductory chapter, the papers in this volume are organized into three basic sections: theory, industry studies, and policy implications. In particular, the industry studies consist of ten papers and include such regulated industries as airlines, electric power, natural gas, telecommunications, commercial banking, and health care.

Productivity measurement is already an important issue in such regulated industries as electric power, railroads, and telecommunications and is likely to become even more important in the future in many other regulated industries. It is our sincere hope that this unique collection of papers will make a major contribution to this important area of policy interest.

Acknowledgments

This volume is the result of a conference, Productivity Measurement in Regulated Industries, sponsored by the National Science Foundation and the School of Business at the University of Wisconsin and held April 30–May 1, 1979, at Madison. We are deeply indebted to Larry Rosenberg of the National Science Foundation, not only for his enthusiastic participation in the conference but also for his patient support of a related research grant to us. We should also like to express our appreciation to a number of individuals who served as discussants at the conference: Donald Harmatuck, Charles Hulten, Knox Lovell, Larry Mannheim, Ned Nadiri, Paul Portney, Thomas Standish, Fred Sudit, and Bernie Tenenbaum. We are also grateful to Richard Hannsen, Dennis Ray, Diana Reese, and William Reed for their help in planning and conducting the conference. Finally, we should like to thank Vivian Carlip for her cheerful editorial assistance during the preparation of this volume and Frank Gollop and Charles Hulten for their comments on an early draft of the introductory chapter.

In addition to the conference, we have also been engaged in a research study on measuring productivity growth for electric utilities and have received the generous assistance of several individuals. We should especially like to thank our very capable research assistants during this project: William O'Neil, David Reifschneider, and Jeffrey Small at the University of Wisconsin, and Pete Parcells at the State University of New York at Binghamton.

Part I

INTRODUCTION

1

Introduction: Productivity Measurement and Regulated Industries

Thomas G. Cowing
Department of Economics
State University of New York
  at Binghamton
Binghamton, New York

Rodney E. Stevenson
Graduate School of Business
University of Wisconsin—Madison
Madison, Wisconsin

Productivity advancement has been a major contributing factor to economic growth in the postwar U.S. economy, especially in the regulated sector. Indeed, the regulated sector has typically led all other sectors in terms of measured productivity growth during this period.[1] More recently, however, productivity growth appears to have declined sharply in both regulated and nonregulated industries.

There are a number of reasons why the topic of productivity measurement in regulated industries is particularly appropriate as we enter the decade of the 1980s. From a policy perspective, the recent erosion in historical rates of productivity advancement in many regulated industries, along with rising fuel prices and interest rates, has spurred considerable interest within the regulated sector in increasing public utility performance. A wide range of

---

[1] Gollop and Jorgenson [1980] have recently estimated the following average annual rates of total factor productivity growth for the period 1948–1966: electric utilities, 5.6%; telephone, 3.4%; gas utilities, 3.2%; pipelines, 8.1%; airlines, 9.7%; trucking, 3.6%; and railroads, 5.1%. For their most recent period, 1966–1973, the growth rates were −0.4, 1.2, 0.4, 6.5, 3.5, −0.3, and 1.7%, respectively. See their Table 36.

3

procedures, including management audits, interfirm efficiency comparisons, and productivity-related rate adjustments have been discussed and, in some cases, instituted. Unfortunately, even though productivity advancement can serve as an effective offset against the pressures of inflation and resource shortages, little work has been done in developing accurate and reliable measures of regulated sector productivity, especially at the firm level.

From an analytical perspective, the problems of measuring productivity growth have been aided by relatively recent advances in three areas of economics: (i) the application of duality theory to measurement problems and the development of dual forms to the underlying production function, such as cost and profit functions; (ii) developments in aggregation theory and the related theory of index numbers; and (iii) the use of flexible-form econometric specifications, such as the translog and quadratic models, for estimating production technologies. The studies contained in this volume make several important contributions in bringing these developments to bear upon the basic problem of measuring and analyzing productivity growth for regulated firms.

Before introducing the individual studies, it may be useful to survey briefly two related aspects of the general problem of measuring productivity growth in the special case of regulated industries: first, general economic characteristics of regulated industries, particularly those characteristics that relate directly to productivity growth; and second, alternative methodologies or approaches to measuring productivity growth.

1. Economic Characteristics of Regulated Industries

There are several characteristics that are unique to many regulated industries and appear to have been closely related to the actual productivity performance of many of these industries over the past several decades. These characteristics can be classified generally as supply-related and demand-related factors.

On the supply side, there are three basic technological characteristics that are essential to understanding and measuring economic efficiency in the regulated sector. The first is the possible existence of scale economies, since most of the regulated industries are alleged to exhibit significant economies of scale in at least one major phase of production. Economies of scale are said to exist when an equiproportional expansion of all inputs leads to a greater than proportional expansion in output, or equivalently, when an increase in output at constant input prices leads to a less than proportional increase in total costs. Thus, average costs decline (increase) as output expands (contracts), and since larger firms would be able to produce at lower average costs than smaller firms, a competitive equilibrium is not sustainable.[2] The possible existence of economies of scale is also important for the accurate measurement of productivity growth since the results of scale effects and technical change are generally confounded in observed output–input changes over time. Thus, failure to account correctly for scale effects will lead to biased productivity measures in those regulated industries that are not characterized by constant returns to scale.

A second basic technological characteristic of any production process is technical change, which results when the maximum or efficient output that can be produced from any given bundle of inputs increases over time due to such things as experience, increased knowledge, new innovations, and, in general, better techniques for producing output. While technical change can either be disembodied or embodied in the form of newer (and more efficient) vintages of inputs, particularly capital, it is clear that many regulated industries are characterized by significant embodied technical change, such as occurs through the use of newer designs of more fuel-efficient aircraft, the introduction of automatic telephone switching equipment, and the development of more thermally efficient designs of steam electric turbines. An additional and complicating factor is that embodied technical change and scale economies may be highly interrelated in the form of new vintages of capital equipment that are both larger and more efficient.[3]

A third feature of many regulated industries is the relative capital intensity of the production technology. For example, telephone utilities, airlines, natural gas transmission companies, and electric power firms all require massive amounts of capital in the form of plant and equipment. This distinctive feature of the technology has several measurement implications. First, capital inputs are a significant component of total costs, so that careful attention must be given to measuring accurately their contribution to productivity growth. Unfortunately, however, capital is a difficult input to measure, and existing data on capital inputs are probably the least detailed and accurate relative to other inputs. Second, high levels of capital intensity increase the potential for measurement distortions if capacity utilization is not appropriately adjusted for. Third, as pointed out previously, technical change is often embodied in the capital input, so that close attention must be paid to accounting correctly for variations in the quality or efficiency of capital inputs.

[2] This model of "natural monopoly" is appropriate if economies of scale exist over the domain of market demand, and provides the rationale for the economic regulation of monopoly as a means of bringing about a more efficient resource allocation.

[3] For further discussion of this effect, referred to as "scale-augmenting" technical change, see Cowing [1970, 1974], Hughes [1971], and Stevenson [1980].

On the demand side, growth and pricing policies are important characteristics of many regulated industries. For example, in industries such as electric and gas utilities, telecommunications, airlines, and pipelines, annual growth rates in demand until recently have typically been significantly greater than for the manufacturing sector as a whole. Economic growth makes it possible for the benefits of both economies of scale and embodied technical change to be realized in the form of lower average costs. Pricing in the regulated sector has generally been carried out on the basis of average historical or embedded costs, rather than marginal costs, thus giving rise to potential allocative distortions, which must be taken into account when assessing productivity growth.

These characteristics, many of them unique to the special case of regulated industries, are crucial to productivity measurement using either cross-section or time-series data. Indeed, several of these characteristics have been responsible, in part, for some of the recent developments in productivity measurement, particularly those arising from the need to modify the traditional competitive model to permit accurate measurement of productivity growth for the case of regulated industries.

2. Productivity Measurement: An Overview of Recent Developments

Productivity is generally defined in terms of the efficiency with which inputs are transformed into useful output within the production process.[4] Thus, the earliest approach to productivity measurement was based upon ratios of a measure or index of aggregate output divided by the observed quantity of a single input, typically labor. These productivity ratios were usually normalized to some base year, resulting in a productivity index over time, and were used to measure aggregate productivity, that is, productivity for the entire economy. This index-number approach based upon the use of single or partial factor productivity measures had the advantage of computational simplicity and feasibility, given the general availability of the required aggregate labor input data, but made it difficult to identify the causal factors accounting for observed productivity growth. For example, the substitution of capital for labor, the introduction of more (labor) efficient vintages of capital, the realization of economies of scale, and the employment of better-trained manpower all show up in the form of increases over time in an index of output per man-hour.

A more comprehensive index-number approach to the measurement of

---

[4] An excellent survey of productivity theory can be found in Nadiri [1970]. A more recent discussion is contained in a National Academy of Sciences report [1979].

productivity is based on total factor productivity (TFP) measures, and has been used extensively by both Denison and Kendrick in their work at the aggregate level.[5] Early TFP indexes consisted of the ratio of two separate indexes, one for outputs and the second representing total input.[6] The output index or measure may be either a simple unweighted measure of relatively homogeneous outputs, such as kilowatt-hours of electricity, or else a weighted measure of heterogeneous joint outputs. At the firm level, the input measure should include all inputs used in the production process, e.g., labor, fuel, capital, materials, and supplies, and must include all phases of the production process, e.g. generation, transmission, and distribution in the case of electric utilities. TFP measures are a clear improvement over single-factor measures in that changes in the quantity and quality of *all* inputs can be accounted for, at least conceptually. However, the difficulties of disentangling technical change from the effects of scale economies and input substitution remain.

An alternative approach to measuring productivity involves the explicit specification of a production function and the direct linkage of productivity growth to key characteristics or parameters of this function. An additional benefit of this approach is that its econometric implementation yields parametric estimates of the production technology in the process of measuring productivity advancement. The pioneering paper in developing this approach is that of Solow [1957], who demonstrated that the rate of productivity growth could be identified with the rate of Hicks-neutral technical change, assuming constant returns to scale and competitive markets. This result clearly established the correspondence between the characteristics of a neoclassical technology and improvements in total factor productivity, at least under the maintained assumptions of a competitive equilibrium and Hicks-neutral technical change.[7]

A more recent development within the production function or neoclassical tradition, and one that has both theoretical and econometric implications for the measurement of productivity, is the cost-function model based upon duality theory and the early work of Shephard [1953, 1970], Uzawa [1964], and McFadden [1966, 1978]. The cost function represents a unique relationship between minimal cost and given output and input prices, that is, it

[5] See, for example, Denison [1962, 1967, 1974] and Kendrick [1961, 1973].

[6] The existence of separate aggregate output and input indexes requires that technical change be neutral and that the underlying transformation function be separable in outputs and inputs. For further discussion on this point, see Diewert [1976] and Caves *et al.* [1980]. However, as the latter paper points out, violation of these conditions does not necessarily preclude the measurement of TFP growth.

[7] An excellent discussion of the original Solow model, as well as a revised interpretation of aggregate TFP measurement, is contained in Hulten [1979].

represents the relationship between total cost and output for a cost-minimizing firm facing competitive input markets. Perhaps the most basic result of duality theory is that production and cost functions are dual to each other in that the cost function is an equivalent and equally fundamental specification of the underlying production technology to that of the production function, under the assumption of cost minimization. In addition, the cost function can be used to relate such technological characteristics as scale economies, input substitution, and technical change to observed changes in total factor productivity, as shown by a number of the studies included in this volume. Thus, the cost-function model represents a powerful and flexible econometric tool for measuring total factor productivity, especially at the firm level and where the required assumptions of exogenous output and input prices and cost-minimizing behavior are tenable.

Paralleling these theoretical developments in duality theory has been related work in the development of more general and flexible specifications of a neoclassical technology—such as the translog, quadratic, and generalized Leontief models—which require fewer restrictions than the older Cobb–Douglas and constant elasticity of substitution (CES) specifications. Given these developments, it is not surprising that recent productivity studies, especially those at the firm level and including a number in this volume, have been based largely upon the use of flexible specifications of a neoclassical cost function.

Another recent theoretical development has occurred in the area of index-number theory and is related to a basic problem that has confronted productivity analysis from the very beginning, namely, the problem of output and input aggregation. Based largely upon the recent work of Diewert [1976, 1978a] and others in the area of "exact" or "superlative" index numbers, it has been shown that there is a unique correspondence between the type of index used to aggregate over outputs and inputs and the structure of the underlying technology.[8] Thus, any given index number implies a particular structure for the underlying production technology, so that considerable care must be taken in the selection of the appropriate aggregation or index procedure. Unfortunately, it is also true that the more complex types of index numbers are required under the assumption of more flexible, and hence more general, specifications of the technology. The basic importance of this work lies in the linkage of the two approaches to TFP measurement, index number and neoclassical production and cost function,

---

[8] For example, the Laspeyres indexing procedure, used in many of the earlier productivity studies, has been shown to be exact for, or imply, a linear production function in which all inputs are perfect substitutes in the production process. Similarly, the Törnqvist index, a discrete approximation to the more general Divisia index, implies a homogeneous translog production function.

in that the problems of selecting an appropriate production function and a suitable index number have been shown to be dual to each other.

Another recent area of development in productivity analysis for which several papers, both in and related to this volume, should be regarded as pioneering consists of a number of amendments to the early Solow model, based upon the assumption of a competitive equilibrium, which are necessary if this approach is to be applied to the case of regulated industries.[9] For example, economies of scale may exist in such industries as natural-gas transmission, telephone, railroads, and electric power. Thus, while the competitive equilibrium condition of constant returns to scale, assumed in Solow's model, may be acceptable at more aggregate levels of productivity analysis, it is not likely to be generally appropriate for the case of regulated industries or firms.

A second necessary amendment to the original Solow model involves the assumption of neutral technical change since there is no a priori reason for believing that nonneutral or input-biased technical change may not be important. Indeed, most recent empirical studies of regulated industries have found strong evidence of biased technical change.[10] Fortunately, these two amendments to account for the possibilities of economies of scale and biased technical change can be easily accommodated within a cost-function model.

Another amendment that may be important for several regulated industries and has been given some thought in several studies prior to this volume is related to the possible impact of the regulatory environment upon the resource allocation decisions of the regulated firm.[11] This recent work draws upon the earlier insight of the Averch–Johnson [1962] model, which showed that rate-base regulation involving a rate-of-return constraint on the earned return to capital could induce allocative inefficiency, and hence costs above those for the unregulated cost-minimizing firm. This implies that cost- and profit-function models for the regulated firm must be amended to take account of the possible impact of rate-of-return regulation. Since several studies have indicated that significant economic inefficiency due to the so-called A–J effect may exist, this amendment appears to be important when measuring productivity growth in regulated industries.[12] Similar amendments to account for other types of constraints upon firm behavior, such as environmental restrictions, may also be necessary, as suggested by several of the papers in this volume.

---

[9] See also Caves *et al.* [1980].

[10] For example, see Stevenson [1980].

[11] See Cowing [1978, 1979], Fuss and Waverman [1977], and Stevenson [1976].

[12] For example, see Spann [1974], Courville [1974], Petersen [1975], and Cowing [1978].

Finally, the Fuss *et al.* paper in this volume points out a fourth area in which further amendments to the competitive model may be needed, namely, to account for possible distortions from nonmarginal cost pricing on the part of joint-output regulated firms. Although marginal cost pricing is generally required as a necessary condition for economic efficiency, with due adjustment for second-best problems and revenue and other side constraints, there is no guarantee that the prices or rates established by regulatory commissions will correspond to the appropriate marginal costs. Given price discrimination so that prices do not equal marginal costs in a joint-output model, it can be shown that allocative distortions at the firm level will result and must be taken into account if productivity growth is to be measured correctly with the cost-function model.

Thus, a number of amendments to the original Solow model are required, some of which can be included within the competitive cost-function framework and several of which may require the derivation of restricted cost- and profit-function models. In either case, the result is likely to be more accurate estimates of total factor productivity growth for the special case of regulated industries.

3. An Introduction to the Studies

The papers included in this volume can be divided into three major areas of productivity research interest: (1) the general theory of productivity measurement, including the special case of regulated industries; (2) the estimation or assessment of productivity growth and technological structure for individual regulated industries, such as airlines, trucking, electric power, natural gas, telecommunications, banking, and health care; and (3) the policy implications of economic efficiency and productivity growth. The first area is covered by a single paper, that by Diewert, and lays out the theoretical foundation and implications for the empirical measurement of productivity. The second group of ten papers—those by Caves, Christensen and Tretheway; Friedlaender, Spady, and Chiang; Gollop and Roberts; Aivazian and Callen; Cowing, Small, and Stevenson; Denny, Fuss, and Waverman; Nadiri and Schankerman; Kopp and Smith; Haywood; and Smith and Over—presents the analysis and results of applying a variety of alternative productivity measurement techniques to a number of regulated industries. The volume concludes with a third group of two papers—those by Crandall and Trebing—which examine some of the policy implications connected with both regulatory constraints and regulated industry structure, and the resulting impact upon economic performance and productivity growth.

In the first paper, Diewert reviews those aspects of duality theory that are relevant to the measurement of total factor productivity for the case of a competitive firm. Four alternative approaches are presented: (i) the econometric estimation of production and cost functions; (ii) the use of Divisia indexes; (iii) the use of exact index numbers; and (iv) nonparametric methods for measuring technical progress. Each of these approaches is then applied to the special case of a rate-of-return regulated firm, and the necessary assumptions required for each case, regulated as well as competitive, are derived. Diewert also shows in general that two kinds of shadow price information are required in order to measure TFP within his joint-output regulated firm model, shadow output prices involving the monopoly markup, and a shadow input price for capital that includes the allowed rate of return. The informational requirements for measuring TFP for a regulated firm using each of three different approaches—(ii), (iii), and (iv)—are also derived.

The next two papers, the first group of empirical studies, involve productivity studies of two of the regulated U.S. transportation industries, commercial airlines and trucking. In their study, Caves, Christensen, and Tretheway estimate the growth and relative levels of total factor productivity for the 11 U.S. trunk airlines over the period 1972–1977. Using an index-number approach and disaggregated measures of both passenger and freight service (output) and five categories of inputs, they find wide variations in measured growth rates for trunk airlines over this recent period. Their results appear to be consistent with those of several other studies of airline efficiency, and also indicate little statistical relationship between TFP growth rates and such traditional measures of airline performance as average stage length, system size, and system load factor. Friedlaender, Spady, and Chiang estimate the technological structure of a basic segment of the U.S. trucking industry, commercial carriers of general commodities, using cross-section data for 1972 and a translog cost-function model that includes hedonic measures of six operating characteristics. The results of this study indicate that operating characteristics have a major impact upon trucking costs and that to the extent that regulation, and changes in the nature of regulation, affect these characteristics, it appears that regulation may serve to reduce productivity and increase costs in the trucking industry.

The second group of empirical papers highlight two of the traditional public utility industries, electric power and natural gas, and include studies by Gollop and Roberts; Aivazian and Callen; and Cowing, Small, and Stevenson. The main objective of the Gollop–Roberts paper is to identify the sources of postwar economic growth for firms of varying size in the U.S. electric-power industry. They employ a translog cost-function model that includes factor-augmenting technical change, and apply the model to 11 electric utilities for each of the years in the 1958–1975 period. Evidence of a dramatic decline in productivity growth, especially after 1970, is found, and this result is traced to a reduced rate of technical change as well as reduced scale economies. They conclude that the single most important driving force behind this result is increased fuel prices. In contrast to the econometric studies that constitute much of this volume, Aivazian and Callen use a simulation approach to account for the dynamics of capacity expansion in the postwar U.S. interstate natural-gas transmission industry. Two variants of the Chenery–Manne–Srinivasan model are used, representing unregulated and regulated firms, respectively, in which two basic characteristics of the industry are introduced, namely, rapidly growing demand and indivisibilities in capacity expansion. Each model is solved dynamically, and the results are then compared to actual data for 28 major interstate natural-gas pipeline companies. The results indicate that the unregulated cost-minimizing model has a better predictive record, indicating that the economic inefficiency induced by regulation may not be significant. The purpose of the third paper in this group, that by Cowing, Small, and Stevenson, is to develop several alternative measures of TFP for regulated firms and to evaluate the relative performance of each of these measures. Cross-section firm data for 81 U.S. electric utilities covering the period 1964–1975 are used to evaluate the relative performance of three productivity measures: a Laspeyres TFP index, a Divisia TFP index, and a competitive translog cost-function measure. Cowing, Small, and Stevenson also demonstrate the potential magnitude of the A–J-induced productivity measurement bias.

The third group of empirical papers consists of two papers on the Canadian and U.S. telecommunications industries. In the first paper, Denny, Fuss, and Waverman use Bell Canada data for the period 1952–1976 to measure the biases that are introduced when conventional Divisia TFP indexes are used without regard to the effects caused by several characteristics unique to many regulated industries, namely, nonconstant returns to scale, rate-base regulation, and price discrimination. Using duality theory, they demonstrate that these biases can be accounted for, so that real TFP growth can be accurately measured. Their results indicate that the effects of scale economies are the single most important component of economic growth, accounting for over 60% of the total and increasing over time, while the effects of non-marginal cost pricing and technical change were of lesser and approximately equal importance in the Canadian telephone industry. The second paper, by Nadiri and Schankerman, also focuses upon the relative contributions of technical change and scale economies in observed economic growth, using a translog cost function and AT&T data for the period 1947–1976. A unique aspect of this study is the inclusion of a measure of research and development expenditures as an explicit input in the production process. Their results indicate that although scale economies accounted for between 80 and 90% of growth during the early postwar period 1947–1956, technical change played an increasingly important role during the later years 1957–1976. Thus, there appear to be some interesting differences in the structure of TFP growth over the postwar period between the U.S. and Canadian telephone industries.

The final group of three empirical papers attempts to expand the scope of productivity measurement for regulated industries to include several industries that although formally regulated are not usually included as public utilities, such as banking and health care, and to include other forms of regulation, such as environmental restrictions. The purpose of the first paper in this group, by Kopp and Smith, is to examine empirically the implications of environmental regulations concerning both air and water pollution for the measurement of productivity change. Since detailed data on many pollutants are not generally available at either the firm or industry level, this study uses a kind of simulation analysis in the form of "pseudo-data" generated by a large-scale linear programing process analysis model of the steel-making process developed at Resources for the Future. Their results, based on single-factor productivity measures, indicate that in general the regulation of effluent discharges does have an impact upon measured productivity and that this impact may be more complex than previously assumed. The Haywood paper contains a discussion of several ways in which regulation in the commercial banking industry affects both banking productivity and technology, especially innovation in new technologies. In particular, the impact of state restrictions affecting multioffice banking on the diffusion of computer technologies is analyzed. Haywood also outlines several new types of banking regulations that have come into being since the late 1960s and discusses their probable impact upon commercial banking performance. The final paper, by Smith and Over, investigates the extent and nature of technical change in the production of ambulatory medical care, that is, in a doctor's office. The basic problem confronted in this study is that ambulatory medical care output is essentially unobservable, so that indirect measures of output based upon patient characteristics and medical tasks performed have to be used. Their results indicate that institutional and regulatory constraints upon the use of inputs, in particular the health practitioner, have a significant and negative impact upon productivity.

The third major group of studies, on policy implications, includes papers by Crandall and Trebing. The basic thesis of the Crandall paper is that current pollution control policy is deliberately inefficient because political goals have been substituted for the goal of economic efficiency. Crandall argues that the results of these political goals are inimical to economic efficiency, and that a significant part of the recent decline in U.S. productivity growth can be traced to the use of inefficient pollution control regulations. Recent evidence from a variety of U.S. industries is presented to support this claim.

In his paper, Trebing examines a number of public policies, institutional practices, and structural features that affect efficiency and productivity growth in the public utility industries, especially since 1968. The adequacy of current regulatory efforts at both state and federal levels is assessed in some detail, followed by a series of recommendations designed to improve performance in the public utility sector. Trebing concludes that regulatory reform and increased competition can be used effectively to improve economic performance and promote public welfare.

Part II

THEORETICAL FOUNDATIONS

2

The Theory of Total Factor Productivity Measurement in Regulated Industries

W. Erwin Diewert

Department of Economics
University of British Columbia
Vancouver, British Columbia, Canada

1. Introduction

A change in total factor productivity is usually interpreted as: (i) the rate of change of an index of outputs divided by an index of inputs (Jorgenson and Griliches [1967, p. 253]) or (ii) a rate of shift in a production function (Tinbergen [1942] or Solow [1957, p. 312]).

In Section 2 we outline various methods that have been used to measure total factor productivity in competitive industries. We shall interpret a change in total factor productivity as a shift in an underlying production function or production possibilities set, i.e., definition (ii) above, but we shall also see that definition (ii) reduces to definition (i) under appropriate assumptions.

In Section 3, we discuss the microeconomics of the Averch–Johnson [1962] model of the regulated firm. In particular, we decompose the usual Averch–Johnson constrained profit maximization problem into two stages. In the first stage, the regulated firm minimizes the variable cost of producing a fixed

17

output vector assuming that a vector of capital inputs is given. This minimization problem yields the joint cost function. In the second stage, the usual regulated firm's profit maximization problem is solved, except that variable cost is replaced by the joint cost function.

In Section 4, we show how the results of Section 3 can be used to estimate econometrically the technology of a regulated firm. At the same time, we show how a statistical test for competitive behavior and a test for classical monopolistic behavior can be obtained. The material in this section is related to the pioneering work of Courville [1974], Spann [1974], Cowing [1978, 1979], Gollop and Karlson [1978a], and Appelbaum [1979].

In Section 5, we use the results of Sections 2 and 3 to show how the exact-index-number approach to the measurement of total factor productivity (Diewert [1976, 1980]; Christensen et al. [1980]) can be modified to deal with the case of a regulated firm, provided that information on the elasticity of scale and on the elasticities of demand that the regulated monopolist faces is available—a somewhat tenuous assumption.

In Section 6, we indicate how the Farrell [1957], Afriat [1972], Hanoch and Rothschild [1972] nonparametric approach to production function estimation can be extended to the problem of measuring technical progress in a regulated industry, i.e., without making any specific parametric assumptions about the functional form of the underlying production function.

In Section 7 we offer some concluding comments.

At this point, we should indicate a few of the limitations of the present paper: (i) We do not explore why or how technical change takes place or how it may be induced.[1] (ii) We do not discuss various controversies that are associated with the measurement of total factor productivity (e.g., see Nadiri [1970], Jorgenson and Griliches [1972], and Usher [1974]. (iii) Models alternative to the Averch–Johnson model of the regulated firm are not discussed.[2] However, in spite of these limitations and others, we hope that the present paper will indicate how the problem of measuring total factor productivity or technical progress in regulated industries can be approached.

2. The Measurement of Total Factor Productivity in Competitive Industries

2.1   Approach 1: The Econometric Estimation of Cost and Production Functions

This approach to the measurement of technical change needs little elaboration. If data on output produced during period t, y^t, and inputs use during

---

[1] For discussions and references to the literature, see Salter [1960], Nadiri [1970], and Binswanger [1974b].

[2] For alternative models, see Bailey and Malone [1970], Bailey [1973], and Baumol and Klevorick [1970].

period t, $x^t \equiv (x_1^t, x_2^t, ..., x_J^t)$, are available, then we need only assume a convenient functional form for the production function f and estimate the parameters that characterize f using the regression equation

$$y^t = f(x^t, t) + \text{error.} \qquad (1)$$

A convenient measure of technical change during period t is $\partial \ln f(x^t, t)/\partial t$, the percentage change in output due to an increment of time. It is useful to assume a functional form for f that can provide a second-order approximation to an arbitrary twice-continuously-differentiable production function.[3] An example of such a functional form is the translog (see Christensen *et al.* [1971]).

If the producer faces the positive vector of input prices $w^t \equiv (w_1^t, w_2^t, ..., w_J^t) \gg 0_J$ during period t and behaves competitively with respect to inputs, then the producer's cost function C is defined as the solution to the following constrained cost minimization problem:

$$C(y^t, w^t, t) \equiv \min_x \{w^t \cdot x : f(x, t) \geq y^t, x \geq 0_J\}. \qquad (2)$$

Note that $w^t \cdot x \equiv \sum_{j=1}^{J} w_j^t x_j$ denotes the inner product between the vectors w^t and x.

Obviously, C is completely determined by f. Moreover, under certain regularity conditions C completely determines f, and we also have the following useful result (Shephard's lemma)[4]:

$$x^t = \nabla_w C(y^t, w^t, t), \qquad (3)$$

where $\nabla_w C(y^t, w^t, t) \equiv [\partial C/\partial w_1, \partial C/\partial w_2, ..., \partial C/\partial w_J]$ is the gradient vector of C with respect to the components of the input price vector w evaluated at (y^t, w^t, t). In other words, the producer's system of input demand equations can be obtained by differentiating the cost function with respect to input prices.

If we assume a functional form for the cost function and differentiate with respect to input prices, then upon adding errors to Eq. (3), the parameters that occur in the cost function can be estimated statistically. Again, it is useful to use a functional form for the cost function C that can provide a second-order approximation to an arbitrary cost function. Binswanger [1974a] implements this approach using a translog cost function and more recently, Berndt and Khaled [1979] use a generalized Box–Cox functional form for the cost function, which has the translog and several other functional forms as special cases. The advantage of this second approach to the measurement of technical progress over the first approach suggested above, ie., using (i), is that the system of equations (3) has many more degrees of freedom in a statistical sense than the single equation (1). The disadvantage of the second

---

[3] Such functional forms are termed "flexible." See Diewert [1974] and Lau [1974].

[4] See Shephard [1953, 1970], McFadden [1978], and Diewert [1978b].

approach is that it requires the assumption of competitive behavior on the part of the producer with respect to inputs.

We turn now to a method for measuring shifts in a production function that apparently does not require any assumptions about the functional form of the production function.

2.2 Approach 2: Divisia Indexes

The Divisia [1926, p. 40] index is frequently used in the measurement of total factor productivity. We outline Solow's [1957] derivation of the index.[5]

Suppose that a linearly homogeneous, concave, nondecreasing in inputs x production function $F(x, t)$ is given. Let $y(t) \equiv F(x(t), t)$ be output at time t and let $x(t) \equiv [x_1(t), x_2(t), \ldots, x_J(t)]$ be the vector of inputs used at time t. If the production function exhibits neutral technological change, then it can be written $F(x(t), t) = A(t)f(x(t))$ where $A(t)$ is a (cumulative) shift factor for the production function at time t. If we differentiate the identity $y(t) = A(t)f(x(t))$ with respect to time, divide by $y(t)$, and replace the terms $A(t)\,\partial f[x(t)]/\partial x_i$ by $w_i(t)$, the ith input price at time t, we obtain the identity[6]

$$\frac{\dot{A}(t)}{A(t)} = \frac{\dot{y}(t)}{y(t)} - \sum_{j=1}^{J} s_j(t)\frac{\dot{x}_j(t)}{x_j(t)}, \tag{4}$$

where a dot over a variable denotes a derivative with respect to time and the jth input share is defined as $s_j(t) \equiv w_j(t)x_j(t)/y(t)$.

If $\dot{A}(t)/A(t) = 0$, then $A(t)$ is a constant for all t and there is no exogenous shift in the production function. Alternatively, we say that there is no technical progress and therefore no increase in total factor productivity.

If we integrate (4) from time 0 to T, we obtain

$$\frac{A(T)}{A(0)} = \frac{y(T)/y(0)}{\exp\left[\int_0^T \sum_{j=1}^{J} s_j(t)[\dot{x}_j(t)/x_j(t)]\,dt\right]}, \tag{5}$$

and the denominator on the right-hand side of (5) is defined to be the Divisia index of input growth between time 0 and T, say $X(T)/X(0)$. Thus

$$\ln\left[\frac{X(T)}{X(0)}\right] = \int_0^T \sum_{j=1}^{J} s_j(t)\left[\frac{\dot{x}_j(t)}{x_j(t)}\right]dt. \tag{6}$$

The problem with the Divisia approach to the measurement of changes in total factor productivity is that economic data do not come in continuous-

---

[5] Solow assumed only one output. A treatment of the multiple-output case can be found in Richter [1966], Jorgenson and Griliches [1967], and Hulten [1973].

[6] This replacement is valid if the producer is paying inputs the value of their marginal products; i.e., it is valid if the producer is behaving competitively with respect to inputs.

time form $x(t)$, $w(t)$, $y(t)$; rather they come in discrete form x^t, w^t, y^t. Thus the continuous-time formula (6) has to be approximated using discrete-time data. It turns out that there are many ways to approximate (6) using discrete data, so that the Divisia approach does not yield unique estimates of total factor productivity when applied to discrete economic data.[7]

The above objection to the Divisia approach explains why it will not be pursued further in the present chapter. However, this objection is certainly not a fatal one, and the Divisia approach to the measurement of total factor productivity in regulated industries is presented in some detail in several other chapters in this volume, particularly in the contributions by Gollop and Roberts; Denny, Fuss and Waverman; and Nadiri and Schankerman. The reader is referred to these chapters for a thorough presentation of the Divisia approach.

Finally, we note that the restriction that there be only a single output is not essential to either the Divisia approach or Approach 1: both approaches can be reworked in the multiple-output context.

2.3 Approach 3: Exact Index Numbers

We now consider the case of a multiple-output firm, which necessitates some new notation.

Let $x \equiv (x_1, \ldots, x_J) \geq 0_J$ denote a nonnegative vector of variable inputs and $w \equiv (w_1, \ldots, w_J) \gg 0_J$ denote the corresponding positive vector of input prices. In addition, let $y \equiv (y_1, \ldots, y_I) \geq 0_I$ denote a nonnegative vector of outputs and $p \equiv (p_1, \ldots, p_I) \gg 0_I$ denote the corresponding positive vector of output prices. Finally, we let $k \equiv (k_1, \ldots, k_N) \geq 0_N$ denote a nonnegative vector of "fixed" inputs (or capital stock components) and let $r \equiv (r_1, \ldots, r_N) \gg 0_N$ be the corresponding vector of positive rental prices.

The firm's production possibilities set at time t is the set of feasible output and input combinations that the firm can produce and use, and we denote it by S^t.

The firm's variable cost function at time t is defined as the solution to the variable cost minimization problem

$$C(w, y, k, t) \equiv \min_x \{w \cdot x : (y, x, k) \in S^t\}. \tag{7}$$

If S^t is a closed nonempty subset of the nonnegative orthant in Euclidean $(I + J + N)$-dimensional space, then it can be shown that C is a nonnegative function that is concave and linearly homogeneous in w for fixed y, k, t.[8] If, in

---

[7] See for example the discussion in Diewert [1980].

[8] This concavity property means: if $w^1 \gg 0_J$, $w^2 \gg 0_J$, $0 \leq \lambda \leq 1$, y and k are such that there exists an x such that $(y, x, k) \in S^t$, then $C(\lambda w^1 + (1 - \lambda)w^2, y, k, t) \geq \lambda C(w^1, y, k) + (1 - \lambda)C(w^2, y, k, t)$.

addition, S^t has a free disposal property,[9] then C will be nondecreasing in w for fixed y, k, t,[10] nondecreasing in y for fixed w, k, t, and nonincreasing in k for fixed w, y, t. If, in addition, S^t is a convex set,[11] then $C(w, y, k, t)$ will be a convex function[12] in y, k for fixed w, t. Finally, if, in addition, S^t is a cone[13] (so that the technology exhibits constant returns to scale), then $C(w, y, k, t)$ will be linearly homogeneous in y, k for fixed w, t.[14] If S^t is a closed, nonempty, convex subset of the nonnegative orthant that has the free disposal property, then it can be shown that the variable cost function C defined by (7) completely describes the producer's production possibilities set S^t.[15]

If $C(w, y, k, t)$ is differentiable with respect to the components of the variable input price vector w, then again, Shephard's lemma holds [*recall* (3)]:

$$x^t = \nabla_w C(w^t, y^t, k^t, t), \tag{8}$$

where $x^t \geq 0_J$ denotes the variable cost-minimizing input vector, $w^t \gg 0_J$ denotes the vector of variable input prices during period t, $y^t \geq 0_I$ denotes the vector of outputs produced by the firm during period t, and $k^t \geq 0_N$ denotes the vector of capital stocks used by the firm during period t.

Suppose that the firm could sell output i during period t at a price $p_i^t > 0$ for $i = 1, 2, \ldots, I$, and suppose that the user cost or rental price for the nth component of the firm's capital stock was $r_n^t > 0$ for $n = 1, 2, \ldots, N$. Denote the vectors of output prices and capital user costs as $p^t \equiv (p_1^t, \ldots, p_I^t)$ and $r^t \equiv (r_1^t, \ldots, r_N^t)$, respectively. If the firm is a competitive profit-maximizing firm, then the observed vector of outputs and inputs (y^t, x^t, k^t) during period t will be a solution to the profit-maximization problem

$$\max_{y,x,k} \{p^t \cdot y - w^t \cdot x - r^t \cdot k : (y, x, k) \in S^t\} = p^t \cdot y^t - w^t \cdot x^t - r^t \cdot k^t. \tag{9}$$

Moreover, it can be shown that if the variable cost function $C(w^t, y^t, k^t, t)$ is differentiable with respect to the components of y and k, then the following relations hold for the profit-maximizing firm[16]:

$$p^t = \nabla_y C(w^t, y^t, k^t, t) \tag{10}$$

---

[9] If $(y^1, x^1, k^1) \in S^t, 0_I \leq y^2 \leq y^1, x^2 \geq x^1$, and $k^2 \geq k^1$, then $(y^2, x^2, k^2) \in S^t$ also.

[10] That is, if there exists an x such that $(y, x, k) \in S^t$ and $w^2 \geq w^1 \gg 0_J$, then $C(w^2, y, k, t) \geq C(w^1, y, k, t)$.

[11] That is, if $(y^1, x^1, k^1) \in S^t$, $(y^2, x^2, k^2) \in S^t$, $0 \leq \lambda \leq 1$, then $\lambda(y^1, x^1, k^1) + (1 - \lambda) \cdot (y^2, x^2, k^2) \in S^t$ also.

[12] A function f is a convex function iff $-f$ is a concave function.

[13] S^t is a cone iff $z \in S^t, \lambda \geq 0$ implies $\lambda z \in S^t$.

[14] That is, if there exists an x such that $(y, x, k) \in S^t, w \gg 0_J, \lambda \geq 0$, then $C(w, \lambda y, \lambda k, t) = \lambda C(w, y, k, t)$.

[15] The variable-cost function is a special case of a variable-profit function: see Gorman [1968], Diewert [1973], Lau [1976], and McFadden [1978] for discussions and proofs of the above results.

[16] See Diewert [1974, p. 140] or Lau [1976].

and

$$r^t = -\nabla_k C(w^t, y^t, k^t, t). \tag{11}$$

A proof of (10) and (11) can be constructed along the following lines. Define the set of output and capital vectors that belong to the technology set S^t when the input vector is fixed at $x \geq 0$, as $S^t(x) \equiv \{(y, k) : (y, x, k) \in S^t\}$. Then we can decompose the competitive firm's profit-maximization problem into two parts, where the first part involves the minimization of variable costs $w \cdot x$, given a vector of outputs y to produce and the availability of a vector of capital services k. In the second stage, the producer maximizes profits $p \cdot y - C(w, y, k, t) - r \cdot k$ with respect to y and k. Thus assuming that y^t, x^t, k^t solves (9), we have

$$p^t \cdot y^t - w^t \cdot x^t - r^t \cdot k^t = \max_{y,x,k}\{p^t \cdot y - w^t \cdot x - r^t \cdot k : (y, x, k) \in S^t\}$$

$$= \max_{y,k}\{p^t \cdot y - C(w^t, y, k, t) - r^t \cdot k : (y, k) \in S^t(x^t)\}$$

$$= p^t \cdot y^t - C(w^t, y^t, k^t, t) - r^t \cdot k^t. \tag{12}$$

If (y^t, k^t) belongs to the interior of $S^t(x^t)$, then the first-order necessary conditions for the maximization problem (12) imply that (10) and (11) hold.

Note that the above proof for (10) and (11) does not require S^t to be a convex set nor does it require that S^t be a cone (i.e., that constant returns to scale prevail).

In what follows, we shall assume that the relations (8)–(11) hold (so that in particular, we are assuming that capital is freely variable during period t).

Assume that the firm's variable cost function C is the following (time-modified) translog variable cost function[17]:

$$
\begin{aligned}
\ln C(w^t, y^t, k^t, t) \equiv{}& \alpha_0 + \sum_{j=1}^{J} (\alpha_j \ln w_j^t) + \frac{1}{2}\sum_{j=1}^{J}\sum_{k=1}^{J} (\alpha_{jk} \ln w_j^t \ln w_k^t) \\
&+ \sum_{i=1}^{I} (\beta_i \ln y_i^t) + \frac{1}{2}\sum_{i=1}^{I}\sum_{h=1}^{I} (\beta_{ih} \ln y_i^t \ln y_h^t) + \sum_{n=1}^{N} (\gamma_n \ln k_n^t) \\
&+ \frac{1}{2}\sum_{n=1}^{N}\sum_{m=1}^{N} (\gamma_{nm} \ln k_n^t \ln k_m^t) + \delta_0 t + \tfrac{1}{2}\delta_{00} t^2 \\
&+ \sum_{i=1}^{I}\sum_{j=1}^{J} (\varepsilon_{ij} \ln y_i^t \ln w_j^t) + \sum_{i=1}^{I}\sum_{n=1}^{N} (\gamma_{in} \ln y_i^t \ln k_n^t) \\
&+ \sum_{j=1}^{J}\sum_{n=1}^{N} (\phi_{jn} \ln w_j^t \ln k_n^t) + \sum_{i=1}^{I} (\rho_{it} \ln y_i^t) + \sum_{j=1}^{J} (\psi_{jt} \ln w_j^t) \\
&+ \sum_{n=1}^{N} (\xi_{nt} \ln k_n^t), \tag{13}
\end{aligned}
$$

[17] It can provide a second-order approximation to an arbitrary variable-cost function.

where $\alpha_{jk} = \alpha_{kj}$, $\beta_{ih} = \beta_{hi}$, and $\gamma_{nm} = \gamma_{mn}$. In order to ensure that C is linearly homogeneous in w, we require that the following restrictions be satisfied:

$$\sum_{j=1}^{J} \alpha_j = 1, \qquad \sum_{k=1}^{J} \alpha_{jk} = 0 \qquad \text{for} \quad j = 1, 2, \ldots J,$$

$$\sum_{i=1}^{I} \varepsilon_{ij} = 0 \qquad \text{for} \quad j = 1, 2, \ldots, J,$$

$$\sum_{n=1}^{N} \phi_{jn} = 0 \qquad \text{for} \quad j = 1, 2, \ldots, J$$

and

$$\sum_{j=1}^{J} \psi_j = 0.$$

It should be noted that although the above translog variable cost function can provide a second-order approximation to an arbitrary twice-continuously-differentiable variable cost function, the approximation need not be close for all w, y, and k vectors. Moreover, the translog variable cost function defined by (13) need not be well behaved as any component of y^t or k^t approaches zero, because in this case the right-hand side of (13) will approach plus or minus infinity and hence the variable cost $C(w^t, y^t, k^t, t)$ will approach plus infinity or zero. Thus one should not use the translog variable cost function in empirical applications where any of the components of y^t or k^t are zero.

Before proceeding, it is necessary to note the following result: If $f(z) \equiv a_0 + \Sigma_{m=1}^{M} a_m z_m + \frac{1}{2} \Sigma_{m=1}^{M} \Sigma_{n=1}^{M} a_{mn} z_m z_n$ is a quadratic function in the vector of variables $z \equiv (z_1, z_2, \ldots, z_M)$, then the following identity is true[18]:

$$f(z^1) - f(z^0) = \frac{1}{2}[\nabla_z f(z^1) + \nabla_z f(z^0)] \cdot (z^1 - z^0). \tag{14}$$

We now suppose that the producer is engaging in profit-maximizing behavior during periods t and t^* and that the producer's variable cost function is defined by (13). Upon noting that $\ln C$ is a quadratic function in time and the logarithms of prices and quantities, we may apply (14) in order to obtain the identity

---

[18] On the other hand, Diewert [1976, p. 138] and Lau [1979a] show that if f satisfies the functional equation (14), then f is quadratic.

$$\ln C(w^t, y^t, x^t, t) - \ln C(w^r, y^r, x^r, t^*)$$

$$= \frac{1}{2} \sum_{j=1}^{J} \left[w_j^t \frac{\partial \ln C}{\partial w_j}(w^t, y^t, x^t, t) + w_j^{t*} \frac{\partial \ln C}{\partial w_j}(w^r, y^r, x^r, t^*) \right] \ln \frac{w_j^t}{w_j^{t*}}$$

$$+ \frac{1}{2} \sum_{i=1}^{I} \left[y_i^t \frac{\partial \ln C}{\partial y_i}(w^t, y^t, x^t, t) + y_i^{t*} \frac{\partial \ln C}{\partial y_i}(w^r, y^r, x^r, t^*) \right] \ln \frac{y_i^t}{y_i^{t*}}$$

$$+ \frac{1}{2} \sum_{n=1}^{N} \left[k_n^t \frac{\partial \ln C}{\partial k_n}(w^t, y^t, x^t, t) + k_n^{t*} \frac{\partial \ln C}{\partial k_n}(w^r, y^r, x^r, t^*) \right] \ln \frac{k_n^t}{k_n^{t*}}$$

$$+ \frac{1}{2} \left[\frac{\partial \ln C}{\partial t}(w^t, y^t, x^t, t) + \frac{\partial \ln C}{\partial t}(w^r, y^r, x^r, t^*) \right] [t - t^*]. \tag{15}$$

Define the *impact effect* on variable cost due to technical change (or to unexplained shifts in the production function or production possibilities set S^t) at time t as $\tau^t \equiv \partial \ln C(w^t, y^t, x^t, t)/\partial t$; i.e., τ^t is the percentage change in variable cost at time t that cannot be explained by changes in inputs or outputs or changes in variable input prices. If there is technological progress (i.e., the production possibilities set S^t is growing larger as time t increases), then τ^t will be negative.[19] Thus we should normally expect τ^t to be negative. If we substitute the definition of τ^t into the identity (15), let $t = 1$, $t^* = 0$, and make use of the competitive equilibrium relations (8), (10), and (11), we obtain the following formula (after some rearrangement and upon exponentiating both sides)[20]:

$$e^{[i\tau^1 + \tau^0]/2}$$

$$= \frac{\left\{ \dfrac{w^1 \cdot x^1}{w^0 \cdot x^0} \right\} \displaystyle\prod_{n=1}^{N} \left\{ \dfrac{k_n^1}{k_n^0} \right\}^{\{r_n^1 k_n^1/w^1 \cdot x^1 + r_n^0 k_n^0/w^0 \cdot x^0\}/2}}{\displaystyle\prod_{j=1}^{J} \left[\dfrac{w_j^1}{w_j^0} \right]^{\{w_j^1 x_j^1/w^1 \cdot x^1 + w_j^0 x_j^0/w^0 \cdot x^0\}/2} \displaystyle\prod_{i=1}^{I} \left[\dfrac{y_i^1}{y_i^0} \right]^{\{p_i^1 y_i^1/w^1 \cdot x^1 + p_i^0 y_i^0/w^0 \cdot x^0\}/2}} .$$

$$\tag{16}$$

The right-hand side of (16) is equal to an implicit quantity index in the variable inputs, x,[21] times a quantity index in the capital inputs, k, divided by

[19] Ohta [1974] discusses the relationship between measures of technological progress based on time derivatives of the production function versus time derivatives of the corresponding cost function.

[20] We also use the identities $w^t \cdot x^t = C(w^t, y^t, k^t, t)$ for $t = 0$ and 1.

[21] Diewert [1976] defines the implicit Törnqvist quantity index to be $\tilde{Q}_0(w^0, w^1, x^0, x^1) \equiv w^1 \cdot x^1/w^0 \cdot x^0 \prod_{j=1}^{J} [w_j^1/w_j^0]^{\{s_j^1 + s_j^0\}/2}$ where $s_j^t \equiv w_j^t x_j^t/w^t \cdot x^t$ for $t = 0, 1$.

a quantity index in the outputs, y.[22] Thus if the right-hand side of (16) is less than 1 (so that real output grew faster than real input going from period 0 to period 1), then $\frac{1}{2}[\tau^1 + \tau^0] < 0$ and we conclude that there was technological progress between period 0 and period 1.

The advantage of the present approach to measuring changes in total factor productivity (or shifts in the technology) over the Divisia approach is that we obtain an explicit formula (16) that is suitable for discrete data. The disadvantage of the present approach is that we must assume a specific functional form for the producer's variable cost function, namely, (13). However, since the translog functional form (13) is "flexible," this may not be too severe a disadvantage.

The present approach also has advantages over approach 1: (i) no econometric estimation is required, and (ii) the present approach can deal with an arbitrarily large number of inputs and outputs. The disadvantage of the present approach over approach 1 is that we must assume competitive behavior.

Approach 3 is a straightforward modification of Diewert's [1976, 1980] approach.[23] For discussions of the aggregation problems which occur in practical applications of approach 3, see Vartia [1976, 1978] and Diewert [1978a, p. 890] for a discussion of the two-stage aggregation-over-goods problem, and Diewert [1980, pp. 495–498] and Hulten [1978] for a discussion of the aggregation-over-sectors problem.

Note that to implement empirically the Divisia approach to measuring changes in total factor productivity, we have to numerically approximate continuous-time integrals [such as the right-hand side of (6)] with discrete data. On the other hand, approach 3 leads to an exact formula that is suitable for discrete data, but the formula is contingent on the assumption that the producer's variable cost function be of the translog functional form. Since it is unlikely that the producer's technology can be precisely represented by means of a translog variable cost function over the relevant (w, y, k) range, it must be conceded that the exact index-number approach as well as the econometric and Divisia approaches all involve approximation errors.

We now turn to an approach that in sharp contrast to the previous three methods, involves no approximation errors at all.

---

[22] If S^t is a cone, so that the technology exhibits constant returns to scale, then $C(w, y, k, t)$ is linearly homogeneous in y and k and we find that $w^t \cdot x^t = C(w^t, y^t, k^t, t) = p^t \cdot y^t - r^t \cdot k^t$. In this case, we find that the right-hand side of (16) reduces to $\tilde{Q}_0(w^0, w^1, x^0, x^1)/Q_0(u^0, u^1, z^0, z^1)$ where $\ln Q_0(u^0, u^1, z^0, z^1) = \frac{1}{2}\sum_{k=1}^{I+N}[(u_k^1 z_k^1/u^1 \cdot z^1) + (u_k^0 z_k^0/u^0 \cdot z^0)] \ln[z_k^1/z_k^0]$ and the $(I + N)$-dimensional vectors $u^t \equiv [p^t, -r^t]$ and $z^t \equiv [y^t, k^t]$ for $t = 0, 1$. Q_0 is the Törnqvist quantity index. We require $w^t \gg 0_J$, $y^t \gg 0_I$, and $k^t \gg 0_N$ for $t = 0, 1$..

[23] In Diewert [1980], a variable-profit function is used in place of the variable-cost function C and constant returns to scale are assumed.

2.4   Approach 4: A Nonparametric Method for the Measurement of Technical Progress

In order to simplify matters, let us revert to the notation used in Section 2.1, so that $y^t \geq 0$ is the amount of output produced by a firm during period t and $x^t \equiv (x_1^t, \ldots, x_J^t) \geq 0_J$ is the vector of inputs used during period t for $t = 1, 2, \ldots, T$.

Suppose that for each period t, the firm's production function $f^t(x)$ is continuous, nondecreasing, and concave for $x \geq 0_J$. If there is *no technical regress*, then the period specific production functions f^t are such that $f^t(x) \geq f^r(x)$ for all $x \geq 0_J$ if $t > r$; i.e., the maximal output that can be produced by the input vector x during period t, $f^t(x)$, is equal to or greater than the maximal output that can be produced by the same input vector x during a prior period r, $f^r(x)$.

Define the free disposal convex hull of the first t input vectors as

$$S(x^1, x^2, \ldots, x^t) \equiv \{x : x \geq \sum_{i=1}^t \lambda_i x^i, \lambda_i \geq 0, \sum_{i=1}^t \lambda_i = 1\}. \tag{17}$$

Following Farrell [1957] and Afriat [1972], we can define the inner approximation period t production function $\tilde{f}^t$ over the set $S(x^1, \ldots, x^t)$ as

$$\tilde{f}^t(x) \equiv \max_{\lambda_1 \geq 0, \ldots, \lambda_t \geq 0} \left\{ \sum_{i=1}^t \lambda_i y^i : \sum_{i=1}^t \lambda_i x^i \leq x, \sum_{i=1}^t \lambda_i = 1 \right\} \tag{18}$$

for $t = 1, 2, \ldots, T$. Note that for each t and x, (18) is a linear-programming problem.

The following (nonstatistical) tests allow us to determine whether the given firm data are consistent with increasing total factor productivity over time.

TEST 1   (Diewert and Parkan [1979, p. 41]): If $y^t = \tilde{f}^t(x^t)$ for $t = 1, 2, \ldots, T$, then the given data $\{(x^t, y^t) : t = 1, 2, \ldots, T\}$ are consistent with the efficiency hypothesis (i.e., the firm produces a maximal amount of output for a given input vector) and with the hypothesis of no technological regress for some family of production functions $\{f^t : t = 1, 2, \ldots, T\}$ where f^t is continuous, nondecreasing, and concave over the domain set $S(x^1, x^2, \ldots, x^t)$.[24] On the other hand, if $y^t < \tilde{f}^t(x^t)$ for any t, then the given data are not consistent for any family of continuous, nondecreasing, and concave production functions $\{f^t\}$ satisfying the no-technological-regress assumption.

Geometrically, the above test at stage t forms the free disposal convex hull in $(J + I)$-dimensional space of the first t data points $\{(x^i, y^i) : i = 1, 2, \ldots, t\}$ and then checks whether (x^t, y^t) is on or below the frontier of this set. Since

---

[24] In fact, f^t can be taken to be $\tilde{f}^t$ defined by (18).

we are assuming no technological regress, each of the first t data points (x^i, y^i), $i = 1, 2, \ldots, t$, should belong to the production possibilities set for period t, $S^t \equiv \{(x, y) : y \geq 0, x \in S(x^1, x^2, \ldots, x^t), y \leq f^t(x)\}$, and since f^t is nondecreasing and concave by hypothesis, the free disposal convex hull in $J + I$ space of the first t data points should form an (inner) approximation to the true production possibilities set S^t. If the efficiency hypothesis is true, then (x^t, y^t) should be on the boundary of both S^t and the inner approximation to S^t and thus we should have $y^t = \tilde{f}^t(x^t)$.

TEST 2   If we want to assume that the true period t production function f^t satisfies the additional property of linear homogeneity (so that the true period t production possibilities set S^t is a cone), then we can modify Test 1 into Test 2 simply by dropping the constraints $\Sigma_{i=1}^t \lambda_i = 1$ from (17) and (18).[25]

The above tests yield a sequence of estimated production functions $\tilde{f}^t$, and when the tests pass, these estimated production functions can be used to measure the shifts in the firm's production function over time.[26]

This approach to measuring shifts in the production function has advantages and disadvantages compared to the three previous approaches. The biggest advantage of the present approach is that it does not require any restrictive assumptions about the functional form of the firm's production function. (This is why it is called a nonparametric approach.) Some disadvantages of the present approach are: (i) it does not work if there is technological regress, and (ii) it is computationally more complex than the other procedures since it is necessary to solve T linear programs.

This completes our summary of the various technical methods that have been used (or could be used) to measure shifts in a production function or, equivalently, changes in total factor productivity in general. In the following section, we consider some of the problems that are specific to modeling the behavior of firms in regulated industries and then, in subsequent sections, we shall discuss how the general approaches to the measurement of changes in total factor productivity can be adapted to the case of a regulated firm.

3.   The Microeconomics of the Averch–Johnson Model of the Regulated Firm

Recall the notation introduced in Section 2.3. We shall use the same notation in the present section, except that we suppress the time index t for now, so that we can focus on the static allocation problem faced by a regulated

---

[25] See Diewert and Parkan [1979] for the details.

[26] A reasonable single number that would summarize the shift from one period to the next would be $\tilde{f}^t(x^{t-1})/\tilde{f}^{t-1}(x^{t-1})$. These numbers could be computed for periods $t = 2, 3, \ldots, T$.

monopolist. We shall consider only the Averch–Johnson [1962] model of firm behavior under regulation.[27]

We assume that the regulated monopolist's basic constrained profit maximization problem is

$$\max_{y,x,k,p} \{ p \cdot y - w \cdot x - r \cdot k : (i)\,(y, x, k) \in S ; (ii)\, p = g(y);$$

$$(iii)\, p \cdot y - w \cdot x - r \cdot k \leq e \cdot k \}, \tag{19}$$

where $y \geq 0_I$ is an I-dimensional vector of outputs produced by the firm, $p \gg 0_I$ is a positive vector of output prices, $x \geq 0_J$ is a J-dimensional vector of variable inputs used by the firm, $w \gg 0_J$ is a positive vector of variable input prices, $k \geq 0_N$ is an N-dimensional vector of variable capital inputs used by the firm, $r \gg 0_N$ is a positive vector of competitive user costs or rental rates for capital services, S is the firm's production possibilities set,[28] $p = g(y)$ means $p_i = g_i(y_1, y_2, \ldots, y_I)$ for $i = 1, 2, \ldots, I$ where g_i is the ith inverse demand function that the monopolist is facing,[29] and $e \gg 0_N$ is a positive vector of excess profit rates that the regulated firm is allowed to earn on its use of each component of capital; i.e., the firm is allowed to expense the nth type of capital services at a rental price of $r_n + e_n \equiv s_n$ for $n = 1, 2, \ldots, N$, where s_n is a "fair rate of return" rental rate set by the regulators.[30]

In words, we assume that the regulated monopolist attempts to maximize profits subject to three sets of constraints: (i) the output and input combination chosen must be technologically feasible; (ii) the output vector supplied must be demanded; and (iii) the profits earned by the firm must satisfy a regulatory constraint.

If the regulatory constraint is not binding, then we can drop it and we are left with a standard monopolistic profit maximization problem, i.e., drop (iii) from (19) in order to obtain the monopoly maximization problem.

We shall find it convenient to decompose the regulated monopolist's maximization problem (19) into two stages. In the first stage, we minimize variable cost, and in the second stage, we maximize profits subject to constraints (ii) and (iii). Thus we first define the firm's variable cost function as in Section 2.3[31]:

$$C(w, y, k) \equiv \min_x \{ w \cdot x : (y, x, k) \in S \}. \tag{20}$$

---

[27] Actually they considered only the one-output–one-variable-input–one-type-of-capital case, whereas we allow for an arbitrary number of goods.

[28] The set S could depend on components of the capital stock that are fixed during the period of time under consideration.

[29] If the monopolist behaves competitively with respect to the ith output, then the function $g_i(y)$ is identically equal to a constant, say p_i^*.

[30] Because of differences in depreciation rates, the r_n will usually differ across types of capital.

[31] Given $w \gg 0_J$, $y \geq 0_I$, and $k \geq 0_N$, if there is no x such that $(y, x, k) \in S$, then we define $C(w, y, k) \equiv +\infty$.

Theorem 1: Let $w \gg 0_J, r \gg 0_N$, and $e \gg 0_N$ be given, and suppose that the production possibilities set S is a nonempty, closed set that satisfies the free disposal property mentioned in footnote 9.[32] Suppose that $y^* \geq 0_J$, $x^* \geq 0_J$, $k^* > 0_N$, and $p^* = g(y^*)$ solves the regulated monopolist's profit-maximization problem (19).[33] Then $w \cdot x^* = C(w, y^*, k^*)$ where C is defined by (20) and y^*, k^* is a solution to the following profit-maximization problem

$$\max_{y,k} \{ y \cdot g(y) - C(w, y, k) - r \cdot k : y \cdot g(y) - C(w, y, k)$$
$$- r \cdot k \leq e \cdot k, y \geq 0_I, k \geq 0_N \}. \tag{21}$$

The point of the above theorem is that solutions to the "simpler" constrained maximization problem (21) yield solutions to the more complicated constrained maximization problem (19).

Assuming that the regulatory constraint in (21) is binding [i.e., the constraint $y \cdot g(y) - C(w, y, k) - r \cdot k \leq e \cdot k$ holds as an equality] and the nonnegative constraints $y \geq 0_I$, $k \geq 0_N$ are not binding (i.e., the optimal solution values satisfy the strict inequalities $y \gg 0_I$ and $k \gg 0_N$), then the first-order necessary conditions for (21) are (assuming that C and g are continuously differentiable around the optimal values)

$$[g(y) + \nabla g(y)y - \nabla_y C(w, y, k)][1 - \lambda] = 0_I, \tag{22a}$$

$$-\nabla_k C(w, y, k) - r - \lambda[-\nabla_k C(w, y, k) - r - e] = 0_N, \tag{22b}$$

$$y \cdot g(y) - C(w, y, k) - r \cdot k - e \cdot k = 0, \tag{22c}$$

where $\nabla g(y)$ is an $I \times I$ matrix of partial derivatives of the vector of inverse demand functions g. We can define a markup vector as

$$m(y) \equiv -\nabla g(y)y.$$

Usually, $m(y) \geq 0_I$ for an equilibrium y. Using an argument due to Zajac [1972, p. 128], it can be shown that the optimal Lagrange multiplier λ^* will satisfy the inequalities $0 \leq \lambda^* < 1$.

Actually, it is possible to establish sharper bounds on λ^* by adapting a technique due to Bailey [1973, pp. 72–75]. At the same time, we can show that it will generally not be profitable for the fair rate-of-return constrained monopolistic firm to make completely unproductive purchases of capital equipment, i.e., to "pad" its rate base. We outline Bailey's technique below.

Consider the following constrained maximization problem, which is a

---

[32] Actually, we require only free disposability with respect to k.
[33] $k^* > 0_N$ means $k^* \geq 0_N$ but $k^* \neq 0_N$.

generalization of (21):

$$\max_{y,k,j}\{y \cdot g(y) - C(w, y, k) - r \cdot (k + j) : y \cdot g(y) - C(w, y, k)$$

$$-r \cdot (k + j) \leq e \cdot (k + j), \; y \geq 0_I, \; k \geq 0_N, \; j \geq 0_N\}. \tag{23}$$

The above maximization problem differs from (21) in that we have introduced the nonnegative vector $j \geq 0_N$ into the regulatory constraint. In the maximization problem (23), the firm is now allowed to rent a vector of capital services $(k + j)$ and use part of it productively (k) to produce the output vector y and waste the rest of it (j). The only reason for using this wasted capital (or junk) is to enlarge (or pad) the rate base; i.e., by including this unproductive capital in the aggregate capital, the firm can make the regulatory constraint less binding. However, the following theorem shows that it will not generally be profitable for the regulated firm to pad.

THEOREM 2: Let $w \gg 0_J$, $r \gg 0_N$, and $e \gg 0_N$ be given and suppose that the production possibilities set S is a nonempty, closed set that satisfies the free disposal assumption of footnote 9. Define the firm's variable cost function C by (20) and assume that $y^* \gg 0_I$, $k^* \gg 0_N$, and $j^* \geq 0_N$ are a solution to (23) and that the regulatory constraint is binding at this solution; i.e., $y^* \cdot g(y^*) - C(w, y^*, k^*) - r \cdot (k^* + j^*) = e \cdot (k^* + j^*)$. Assume also that C is differentiable with respect to the components of y and k at the point w, y^*, k^*: i.e., the gradient vectors $\nabla_y C(w, y^*, k^*)$ and $\nabla_k C(w, y^*, k^*)$ exist. Finally, assume that $-\nabla_k C(w, y^*, k^*) \gg 0_N$ (so that the shadow price of each type of capital is positive at the solution to (23), i.e., $\partial C(w, y^*, k^*)/\partial k_n < 0$ for $n = 1, 2, \ldots, N$ so that increasing the nth type of capital above k_n^* leads to a decrease in variable cost). Then

(i) λ^*, the Lagrange multiplier for the regulatory constraint in the constraint maximization problem (23), satisfies the following bounds: $0 \leq \lambda^* \leq \min_n\{r_n/(r_n + e_n) : n = 1, 2, \ldots, N\} < 1$;

(ii) $j^* = 0_N$ (thus padding is not profitable, and

(iii) the optimal Lagrange multiplier for the regulatory constraint in (23), λ^*, is also equal to the optimal Lagrange multiplier for the regulatory constraint in the earlier constrained maximization problem (21) and thus the λ that occurs in (22) satisfies the bounds given in (i) above.

Since Theorem 2 shows that the optimal Lagrange multiplier λ^* for the constrained maximization problem (21) will satisfy the inequalities $0 \leq \lambda^* < 1$ under the stated regularity conditions, we can evaluate equations (22) at an optimal solution y^*, k^*, λ^* and rewrite them [noting that $(1 - \lambda^*)^{-1}$ is a well-defined positive number)

$$p^* - m^* = \nabla_y C(w, y^*, k^*), \tag{24}$$

$$r - \lambda^*(1 - \lambda^*)^{-1}e = -\nabla_k C(w, y^*, k^*), \tag{25}$$

$$e \cdot k^* = p^* \cdot y^* - C(w, y^*, k^*) - r \cdot k^*, \tag{26}$$

where $p^* \equiv g(y^*)$ is the equilibrium output price vector and $m^* \equiv -\nabla g(y^*)y^*$ is the equilibrium markup vector. If S satisfies the free disposal property of footnote 9, then $\nabla_y C(w, y^*, k^*) \geq 0_I$ and $-\nabla_k C(w, y^*, k^*) \geq 0_N$. If $m^* \gg 0_I$ and λ^* is such that $0 < \lambda^* < 1$, then it can be seen that the shadow output price vector $p^* - m^* \ll p^*$ (so that, generally, "too little" output will be produced) and the shadow capital user cost vector $r - \lambda^*(1 - \lambda^*)^{-1}e \ll r$ (so that "too much" capital will be used by the regulated monopolistic firm).

It is perhaps useful to make the last two statements more precise. The problem with a regulated firm that satisfies the relations (24)–(26) is that it will not be as efficient as a competitive firm with the same technology that faces output prices p^* and input prices w, r, in the sense that the competitive firm will produce higher profits. Let us see why this is so. Define (social) profits as a function of y and k as $\pi(y, k) \equiv p^* \cdot y - C(w, y, k) - r \cdot k$. Note that social profits evaluated at the regulated equilibrium are $\pi(y^*, k^*) = p^* \cdot y^* - C(w, y^*, k^*) - r \cdot k^*$. The vector of partial derivatives of π with respect to outputs evaluated at the regulated equilibrium is $\nabla_y \pi(y^*, k^*) = p^* - \nabla_y C(w, y^*, k^*) = m^*$ using (24). Thus if the ith markup m_i^* is positive, social profits can be increased by increasing the production of the ith output above the initial regulated level. Similarly, the vector of partial derivatives of π with respect to capital service inputs evaluated at the regulated equilibrium is $\nabla_k \pi(y^*, k^*) = -\nabla_k C(w, y^*, k^*) - r = -\lambda^*(1 - \lambda^*)^{-1}e$ using (25). Thus if $0 < \lambda^* < 1$ and $e_n > 0$, then social profits can be increased by decreasing the nth capital input.

For geometric treatments of the one-output–one-variable-input–one-capital case, see Baumol and Klevorick [1970], Zajac [1970], and Bailey [1973].

Armed with the above results, we may now turn to our main problem: the measurement of changes in total factor productivity for a regulated firm.

4. The Econometric Approach: The Estimation of Variable Cost Functions

The essence of our suggested econometric approach to the problem of measuring shifts in technology is to assume differentiable functional forms for the variable cost function C and the inverse demand functions g and to use Eq. (8), (24), and (25). Rewriting these equations (after adding time superscripts) and adding errors yields the following system of estimating equations:

$$x^t = \nabla_w C(w^t, y^t, k^t, t) + \text{errors}, \tag{27}$$

$$p^t = m^t + \nabla_y C(w^t, y^t, k^t, t) + \text{errors}, \tag{28}$$

$$r^t = \beta_t e^t - \nabla_k C(w^t, y^t, k^t, t) + \text{errors}, \tag{29}$$

where $m^t \equiv \nabla g(y^t) y^t$ is the markup vector for period t and the scalar $\beta_t \equiv \lambda_t/(1 - \lambda_t)$ is an unknown coefficient that must be estimated for each period t. Once β_t is determined, the Lagrange multiplier for period t can be defined as $\lambda_t \equiv \beta_t/(1 - \beta_t)$. Note that the same coefficient β_t appears on the right-hand side of each of the N equations in (29). The hypothesis that capital is being used efficiently can be tested by testing the hypothesis: $\beta_t = 0$ for $t = 1$, $2, \ldots, T$.

With respect to Eq. (28), a simple way of proceeding would be to assume that the markup vector m^t equals a constant vector $\alpha \equiv (\alpha, \alpha_2, \ldots, \alpha_I)$ for all time periods $t = 1, 2, \ldots, T$. This is consistent with the producer exploiting the system of inverse demand functions $p_i^t = \gamma_i(t) + \alpha_i \ln y_i^t$ for $i = 1, 2, \ldots, I$ and $t = 1, 2, \ldots, T$, or it is consistent with the producer being a markup monopolist. A simple test for competitive behavior in output markets suggests itself; i.e., test whether $\alpha = 0_I$.[34] On the other hand, alternative functional forms for the inverse demand functions $g_i(y)$ can be assumed. In this case, we replace the terms m^t that occur in (28) by $-\nabla g(y^t) y^t$, and we estimate the unknown parameters that characterize the functions g_i.[35]

There remains the problem of choosing a functional form for $C(w, y, k, t)$. C should be chosen so that: (i) C is linearly homogeneous in w; (ii) C can provide a second-order approximation to an arbitrary function of (w, y, k, t) that is linearly homogeneous in w; (iii) the derivatives of C with respect to the components of w, y should be linear in the unknown parameters that characterize C; (iv) if certain restrictions on the parameters of C are true, then C can also provide a second-order approximation to an arbitrary function of (w, y, k, t) that is linearly homogeneous in w and also linearly homogeneous in (y, k); and (v) C should not contain more unknown parameters than are necessary in order to meet the restrictions inherent in (i)–(iv).

Let us define the $(I + N)$-dimensional vector of quantities z as (y, k). Then

---

[34] For further discussion, see Diewert [1978b, pp. 79–82]. For closely related approaches, see Appelbaum [1979] and Appelbaum and Kohli [1979].

[35] Assuming that each $g_i(y)$ equals a linear function of y will work nicely.

a functional form for C that meets the above criteria is[36]:

$$C(w, z, t) \equiv \sum_{j=1}^{J} \sum_{k=1}^{J} \alpha_{jk} w_j^{1/2} w_k^{1/2} \left[\sum_{m=1}^{M} z_m \right]$$

$$+ \sum_{m=1}^{M} \sum_{n=1}^{M} \beta_{mn} \left[\tfrac{1}{2} z_m^2 + \tfrac{1}{2} z_n^2 \right]^{1/2} \left[\sum_{j=1}^{J} w_j \right]$$

$$+ \sum_{j=1}^{J} \sum_{m=1}^{M} \gamma_{jm} w_j z_j + \sum_{j=1}^{J} \delta_j w_j t \left[\sum_{m=1}^{M} z_m \right]$$

$$+ \sum_{m=1}^{M} \varepsilon_m z_m t \left[\sum_{j=1}^{J} w_j \right] + \sum_{m=1}^{M} \phi_m z_m^2 \left[\sum_{j=1}^{J} w_j \right], \qquad (30)$$

where $M \equiv I + N$ and the unknown parameters satisfy the following restrictions:

$$\alpha_{jj} = 0, \quad j = 1, \dots, J; \qquad \beta_{mm} = 0, \quad m = 1, \dots, M; \qquad \sum_{j=1}^{J} \delta_j + \sum_{m=1}^{M} \varepsilon_m = 0,$$

$$(31)$$

$$\alpha_{jk} = \alpha_{kj}, \quad 1 \leq j, k \leq J; \qquad \beta_{mn} = \beta_{nm}, \quad 1 \leq m, n \leq M. \qquad (32)$$

The restrictions in (31) can be imposed without loss of generality [and in fact, similar restrictions must be imposed if we attempt to estimate the unknown parameters which occur in (30) using econometric techniques]. The symmetry restrictions (32) can be tested statistically if we estimate the system of equations (27)–(29).

The hypothesis of a constant technology (or no change in total factor productivity over time) can be tested by testing whether the following restrictions are satisfied[37]:

$$\delta_j = 0, \quad j = 1, \dots, J; \qquad \varepsilon_m = 0, \quad m = 1, \dots, M. \qquad (33)$$

Finally, the hypothesis of constant returns to scale can be tested by statistically testing whether the following restrictions are valid:

$$\phi_m = 0, \quad m = 1, \dots, M. \qquad (34)$$

The above procedure assumes that we know x^t, p^t, r^t, w^t, y^t, k^t, and e^t for each time period t. Standard econometric techniques can be used if we

---

[36] The functional form defined by (30) is similar to the functional forms for variable-profit functions defined in Diewert [1973] and the reader is referred there for further discussion.

[37] Since the restrictions in (31) have been imposed already, there are only $J + M - 1$ additional independent restrictions in (33).

assume that the conditional distribution of (x^t, p^t, r^t) is multivariate normal, given w^t, y^t, k^t, m^t, e^t, and t. Note that x^t, p^t, and r^t do not appear on the right-hand side of Eq. (27)–(29).

Note also that $C(w^t, y^t, k^t, t) = w^t \cdot \nabla_w C(w^t, y^t, k^t, t)$, since $C(w, y, k, t)$ is linearly homogeneous in w. Thus once we have econometrically estimated the unknown parameters that occur in Eq. (27)–(29), we can calculate estimates for $C(w^t, y^t, k^t, t)$ and $\partial \ln C(w^t, y, k^t, t)/\partial t$ and other measures of technical progress.

The present approach to measuring shifts in technology has the disadvantage of being unimplementable if the number of observations T is small relative to the number of goods $I + J + N$, if we assume a functional form for C that can provide a second-order approximation to an arbitrary variable cost function. The approach to be discussed in the following section does not suffer from this disadvantage.

For alternative econometric approaches, see Courville [1974], Spann [1974], Cowing [1978, 1979], Gollop and Karlson [1978a], and the other chapters in this volume.

5. The Exact Index Number Approach to the Measurement of Total Factor Productivity

The exact-index-number approach can readily be implemented (recall Section 2.3) provided that we know the correct shadow prices of output and of capital services.

However, the approach does not appear to be implementable unless we know the markup vector $m^t \equiv -\nabla g(y^t) y^t$ for each time period t (or unless we are willing to assume that it is 0_I, as in Cowing [1978, 1979]). Thus in the remainder of this section we assume that we know the markup vector m^t for each time period t. Given m^t and the observed selling price vector for outputs in period t, p^t, we can calculate the correct shadow price vector for outputs in period t as [recall (24)]

$$\tilde{p}^t \equiv p^t - m^t, \qquad t = 0, 1, \ldots, T. \tag{35}$$

If the regulatory constraint is binding and we have nonconstant returns to scale, then it appears that we *still* cannot apply the exact index number approach even if we know the markup m^t. This is because we generally will not know the value λ_t of the Lagrange multiplier for the constrained monopolist's profit-maximization problem (21) in period t. In order to implement the exact-index-number approach [i.e., obtain a formula like (16)], we require that the functional form for C be the translog functional form defined by (13) and that the relations $p^t = \nabla_y C(w^t, y^t, k^t, t)$ and $r^t = -\nabla_k C(w^t, y^t, k^t, t)$ hold for $t = 0, 1$ [recall Eq. (10) and (11)]. However, instead of (10) and (11), we have $p^t - m^t = \nabla_y C(w^t, y^t, k^t, t)$ and $r^t - \lambda_t(1 - \lambda_t)^{-1}e^t = -\nabla_k C(w^t, y^t, k^t, t)$ for $t = 0, 1$ [recall Eq. (28) and (29) without the error terms].

However, if we knew λ_t, then the correct shadow price vector for capital services in period t can be calculated as

$$\tilde{r}^t = r^t - \lambda_t(1 - \lambda_t)^{-1}e^t, \quad t = 0, 1, \ldots, T. \tag{36}$$

If we compare (24) and (25) with (10) and (11), it can be seen that the procedure outlined in Section 2.3 can be applied in the present context: all we need to do is replace the price vectors p^t and r^t that occur in Section 2.3 by the correct shadow price vectors $\tilde{p}^t$ and $\tilde{r}^t$ defined above by (35) and (36), respectively. In particular, formula (16) will be valid if we replace p^0, p^1, r^0, and r^1 by $\tilde{p}^0$, $\tilde{p}^1$, $\tilde{r}^0$, and $\tilde{r}^1$, respectively.[38]

Therefore the exact-index-number approach to the measurement of changes in total factor productivity can be implemented provided that we know the period t markup vector m^t and the Lagrange multiplier λ_t for the constrained monopolist's period t profit-maximization problem (21).

In empirical applications we may have some a priori information on the markup vectors m^t, but it is unlikely that information on λ_t would be available. However, this difficulty can be solved provided that information on returns to scale is available.

Define the *elasticity of cost* with respect to outputs and capital service components (or the *inverse scale elasticity*) in period t as

$$1 + \varepsilon_t \equiv \partial \ln C(w^t, \lambda y^t, \lambda y^t, t)/\partial \lambda|_{\lambda=1}$$

$$= y^t \cdot \nabla_y \ln C(w^t, y^t, k^t, t) + k^t \cdot \nabla_k \ln C(w^t, y^t, k^t, t).$$

If $\varepsilon_t < 0$, then the technology exhibits locally increasing returns to scale; if $\varepsilon_t = 0$, then the technology exhibits constant returns to scale; if $\varepsilon_t > 0$, then the technology exhibits locally decreasing returns to scale or locally increasing variable costs. If we use the fact that $C(w^t, y^t, k^t, t) = w^t \cdot x^t$, we can rewrite the definition of $(1 + \varepsilon_t)$

$$w^t \cdot x^t(1 + \varepsilon_t) = y^t \cdot \nabla_y C(w^t, y^t, k^t, t) + k^t \cdot \nabla_k C(w^t, y^t, k^t, t)$$

$$= y^t \cdot (p^t - m^t) - k^t \cdot (r^t - \lambda_t(1 - \lambda_t)^{-1}e^t), \tag{37}$$

where we have used (24) and (25). If we substitute (26), $e^t \cdot k^t = p^t \cdot y^t - w^t \cdot x^t - r^t \cdot k^t$, into (37) and solve for λ_t, we find that

$$\lambda_t = 1 - e^t \cdot k^t [w^t \cdot x^t \varepsilon_t + m^t \cdot y^t]^{-1}. \tag{38}$$

---

[38] It should be noted that the procedure outlined in this section is closely related to Allen's [1981] procedures for measuring total factor productivity in the context of monopolistic behavior.

Thus if the inverse scale elasticity ε_t and the markup vector m^t are known for all periods t, then λ_t can be calculated using (38), the shadow price vectors $\tilde{p}^t$ and $\tilde{r}^t$ can be calculated using (35) and (36), and formula (16) can be used to measure shifts in the technology if we replace the price vectors p^t and r^t by the shadow price vectors $\tilde{p}^t$ and $\tilde{r}^t$. Note that if the technology exhibits constant returns to scale, then $\varepsilon_t = 0$ for all t and the λ_t can be calculated using (38), provided that we know the markup vectors m^t.

Finally, if we assume that the regulated producer behaves competitively in output and input markets, and that the regulatory constraint is not binding, then we can apply formula (16) immediately without further adjustments. For an example of a study that uses essentially this approach, see Caves, Christensen, and Swanson [1980].

6. The Nonparametric Approach to the Measurement of Total Factor Productivity

Recall the tests and techniques outlined in Section 2.4. Since these techniques did not make any assumption about profit-maximizing behavior on the part of the producer, they can be applied in the present context, provided that we generalize these tests to cover the multiple-output case. The required generalization has been done in Diewert and Parkan [1979], and we shall not repeat that analysis here.

However, from Section 3, we know that the regulated monopolist should be minimizing variable costs. Thus in the present section, we indicate how the nonparametric approach can be adapted to make use of this information.

Let the data (w^t, x^t, y^t, k^t) be given with $w^t \gg 0_J$, $x^t > 0_J$, and $k^t > 0_N$ for $t = 1, 2, \ldots, T$. We assume that the production possibilities set in period t is a closed nonempty set S^t that has the following property: if $(y, x, k) \in S^t$, then $y \geq 0_I$, $x \geq 0_J$, and $k \geq 0_N$. The interpretation of y, x, and k is the same as in *Section* 3.

The period-t variable-input production possibilities set for a given $y \geq 0_I$ and $k \geq 0_N$ is defined as

$$L^t(y, k) \equiv \{x : (y, x, k) \in S^t\}. \tag{39}$$

We say that the family of production possibilities sets $\{S^t : t = 1, 2, \ldots, t\}$ satisfies the *no-technological-regress* assumption if $m \leq t$ implies $S^m \subset S^t$; i.e., S^m is a subset of S^t.

We note two lemmas that will be useful later.

LEMMA 1: If $S^m \subset S^t$ and $(y^t, x^t, k^t) \in S^t$, then

$$L^m(y^t, k^t) \subset L^t(y^t, k^t). \tag{40}$$

LEMMA 2:   Suppose S^t has the free disposal property of footnote 9. Let $(y^1, x^1, k^1) \in S^t$. If $x^2 \geq x^1$, $k^2 \geq k^1$, and $y^1 \geq y^2 \geq 0_I$, then

$$L^t(y^1, k^1) \subset L^t(y^2, k^2) \qquad (41)$$

and x^1 and x^2 both belong to $L^t(y^1, k^1)$ and $L^t(y^2, k^2)$.

The proofs of the above lemmas are immediate consequences of definitions. We assume that the producer is minimizing variable cost in each period. Thus we have

$$w^t \cdot x^t = \min_x \{w^t \cdot x : (y^t, x, k^t) \in S^t\}$$

$$\equiv C(w^t, y^t, k^t, t)$$

$$= \min_x \{w^t \cdot x : x \in L^t(y^t, k^t)\}. \qquad (42)$$

For our first test in this section, we shall place minimal regularity conditions on the production possibilities sets S^t. Subsequent tests will strengthen these regularity conditions. We must first define an index set for each period. For $t = 1, 2, \ldots, T$, define the set

$$M_t \equiv \{m : m \text{ is an integer, } 1 \leq m \leq t, \text{ and } m \text{ is such that } k^m \leq k^t \text{ and } y^m \geq y^t\}.$$

$$(43)$$

Note that $t \in M_t$ for all t. Now we can define the following linear programming problems for $t = 1, 2, \ldots, T$:

$$\min_{\lambda_m} \left\{ \sum_{m \in M_t} \lambda_m w^t \cdot x^m : \lambda_m \geq 0, \sum_{m \in M_t} \lambda_m = 1 \right\} \equiv C^{t*}. \qquad (44)$$

Note that $C^{t*} \leq w^t \cdot x^t$ since $t \in M_t$.

TEST 3   If $C^{t*} = w^t \cdot x^t$ for $t = 1, 2, \ldots, T$, then the given data $\{(w^t, x^t, y^t, k^t) : t = 1, 2, \ldots, T\}$ are consistent with variable-cost-minimizing behavior for some family of production possibilities set S^t, which satisfies the no-technological-regress assumption, where each S^t is a closed nonempty set that has the free disposal property, and is such that $L^t(y^t, k^t)$ is a convex set (call these *Conditions I* on $\{S^t : t = 1, \ldots, T\}$). In this case, we can define an inner approximation to the set $L^t(y^t, k^t)$ by

$$\tilde{L}^t(y^t, k^t) \equiv \left\{ x : x \geq \sum_{m \in M_t} \lambda_m x^m, \lambda_m \geq 0, \sum_{m \in M_t} \lambda_m = 1 \right\}.^{39} \qquad (45)$$

---

[39] An inner approximation to the true S^t can be obtained by taking the free disposal hull of the sets $\tilde{L}^1(y^1, k^1)$, $\tilde{L}^2(y^2, k^2)$, $\ldots$, $\tilde{L}^t(y^t, k^t)$, provided that S^t satisfies the free disposal property.

On the other hand, if $C^{t*} < w^t \cdot x^t$ for any t, then the given data are not consistent with variable-cost-minimizing behavior for any family of production possibilities sets $\{S^t\}$ satisfying Conditions I above.

We note that Conditions I are consistent with increasing returns to scale when all inputs and outputs are varied.

In the next test, we assume that the sets S^t are convex and thus increasing returns to scale are ruled out. In order to generate Test 4, it is first necessary to define the following linear programming problems for $t = 1, 2, \ldots, T$:

$$\min_{\lambda_1, \ldots, \lambda_t} \left\{ \sum_{m=1}^{t} \lambda_m w^t \cdot x^m : \sum_{m=1}^{t} \lambda_m y^m \geq y^t, \sum_{m=1}^{t} \lambda_m k^m \right.$$
$$\left. \leq k^t, \lambda_m \geq 0, \sum_{m=1}^{t} \lambda_m = 1 \right\} \equiv C^{t**}. \tag{46}$$

Note that $C^{t**} \leq w^t \cdot x^t$.

TEST 4   If $C^{t**} = w^t \cdot x^t$ for $t = 1, 2, \ldots, T$, then the given data are consistent with variable-cost-minimizing behavior for some family of production possibilities sets $\{S^t : t = 1, 2, \ldots, T\}$ that satisfy the no-technological-regress assumption, where each S^t is a closed nonempty convex set that has the free disposal property (call these *Conditions II* on $\{S^t\}$). In this case, we can define an inner approximation to the true S^t as

$$\tilde{S}^t \equiv (y, x, k) : x \geq \sum_{m=1}^{t} \lambda_m x^m, k \geq \sum_{m=1}^{t} \lambda_m k^m, 0_I \leq y$$
$$\leq \sum_{m=1}^{t} \lambda_m y^m, \lambda_1 \geq 0, \ldots, \lambda_t \geq 0, \sum_{m=1}^{t} \lambda_m = 1 \Big\}. \tag{47}$$

On the other hand, if $C^{t**} < w^t \cdot x^t$ for any t, then the given data are not consistent with variable-cost-minimizing behavior for any family of production possibilities sets satisfying Conditions II above.

If we add the additional property of constant returns to scale to Conditions II (so that in addition, each S^t is a cone), then we can modify Test 4 into Test 5.

TEST 5   is precisely Test 4, except that we drop the restriction $\Sigma_{m=1}^{t} \lambda_m = 1$ from (46) and 47), and we add the additional hypothesis to Conditions II that S^t is a cone for each t (call the resulting conditions *Conditions III*).

The tests outlined in this section could be useful in "screening" data. If Test 3 in particular fails (so that $C^{t*} < w^t \cdot x^t$ for some t), then the raw data are not consistent with variable-cost minimization from a strict point of view. One might argue that the hypothesis of variable-cost-minimizing behavior should not be rejected unless C^{t*} is *significantly* less than $w^t \cdot x^t$. However, such a statistical testing procedure has not been worked out as yet.

If Tests 4 or 5 pass, then the sets $\tilde{S}^t$ defined by (47) can be used to provide an approximate measure of shifts in the true production possibilities sets S^t. A reasonable measure for the shift in the production possibilities set from period $t - 1$ to period t is the greatest proportion $\tau_t^* \geq 1$ by which the output vector for period $t - 1$, y^{t-1}, can be increased, given that the producer uses the period t technology set S^t and given the period $t - 1$ inputs vectors x^{t-1} and k^{t-1}. If we replace the true sets S^t by the inner approximations $\tilde{S}^t$ defined by (47) and ask what is the greatest proportion $\tilde{\tau}_t \geq 1$ by which y^{t-1} can be increased given the period t set $\tilde{S}^t$ and the input vectors x^{t-1} and k^{t-1}, then it is easy to show that $\tilde{\tau}_t$ is the solution to the following linear-programming problem:

$$\tilde{\tau}_t \equiv \max_{\tau_t, \lambda_1, \ldots, \lambda_t} \left\{ \tau_t : \tau_t y^{t-1} \leq \sum_{m=1}^t \lambda_m y^m, \sum_{m=1}^t \lambda_m x^m \leq x^{t-1}, \right.$$

$$\left. \sum_{m=1}^t \lambda_m k^m \leq k^{t-1}, \sum_{m=1}^t \lambda_m = 1, \lambda_1 \geq 0, \lambda_2 \geq 0, \ldots, \lambda_t \geq 0 \right\} \geq 1. \qquad (48)$$

Since $\tau_t = 1$, $\lambda_1 = 0$, $\lambda_2 = 0, \ldots, \lambda_{t-2} = 0$, $\lambda_{t-} = 1$, $\lambda_t = 0$ is a feasible solution for (48). The linear-programming problem (48) can be defined for $t = 2, 3, \ldots, T$. We note that $\tau_t^* \geq \tilde{\tau}_t \geq 1$ for $t = 2, 3, \ldots, T$. Thus if $\tilde{\tau}_t > 1$, then we can definitely conclude that S^t is bigger than S^{t-1} so that there has been an outward shift in the production possibilities set going from period $t - 1$ to period t, and that the true proportional shift in outputs τ_t^* at the period $t - 1$ input quantities is equal to or greater than the number $\tilde{\tau}_t$, which we can calculate from observable data by solving the linear program in (48). Note that the sequence of shift factors $\tilde{\tau}_2, \tilde{\tau}_3, \ldots, \tilde{\tau}_T$ is an appropriate generalization to the multiple-output case of the shift factors we suggested for the output case, $\tilde{f}^t(x^{t-1})/\tilde{f}^{t-1}(x^{t-1})$ for $t = 2, 3, \ldots, T$ (recall footnote 26).

To conclude this section, we note some advantages and disadvantages of the present approach over the exact-index-number approach. The exact approach has the advantage of being computationally simple but it has two major disadvantages: (i) the technology has to be representable by a translog variable cost function of the form (13), and (ii) we require information on the markup vectors m^t and the Lagrange multipliers λ_t (or alternatively, on inverse returns to scale ε_t) in the case of a regulated monopoly. On the other hand, the nonparametric approach is completely flexible with respect to the underlying technology and it does not require information on m^t, λ_t, or ε_t. These are major advantages. The disadvantages of the nonparametric approach are: (i) it is computationally more demanding in that various linear programming problems have to be solved, and (ii) the measures of the shifts in technology that the nonparametric approach generates, the $\tilde{\tau}_t$, are only lower bounds to the true shifts, the τ_t^*. However, there is still much to be said for the nonparametric approach. In the future, we shall probably see this method applied in a routine manner once the appropriate programming software becomes readily available.

7. Conclusion

We have provided a brief survey of existing techniques for measuring changes in total productivity (i.e., for measuring unexplained shifts in the production possibilities set) for a regulated firm that is subject to a rate-of-return constraint. However, rate-of-return regulation is only one form of regulation. There are a large number of regulatory constraints that we have not even mentioned, e.g., environmental regulations, zoning restrictions, building codes, health standards, safety regulations, and a host of other regulatory constraints designed to restrict competition (or "protect" the public interest) such as restrictions on cable-television companies.[40]

Even in the context of the Averch–Johnson model of the regulated firm, several topics require further research: (i) The construction of the appropriate user costs r^t and excess returns e^t for capital is a nontrivial task.[41] (ii) We have not discussed how one could measure the welfare losses (or gains) due to regulatory constraints.[42] (iii) We have not discussed what an "optimal" form of regulation would be.[43] On the third topic, we note that if the technology is subject to constant returns to scale, then a monopolistic firm can be made to behave almost like a competitive firm if we give the monopolist an appropriate subsidy for each of his outputs [equal to m $\equiv -\nabla g(y)y$, to use the notation of Section 3] and then tax his profits at a rate close to unity. Of course, there are problems with this proposal (production may not be subject to constant returns and it is difficult for the regulators to know what the appropriate subsidy vector should be), but these problems do not seem to justify the lack of discussion of alternatives to rate-of-return regulation.

[40] In some cases, we may be able to model the effects of changes in these types of regulations by making the firm's production possibilities set S^t depend explicitly on various regulatory variables in period t, say v^t. We could then attempt to implement a variant of the econometric approach of Section 4, where C would now be an explicit function of v^t as well, $C(w^t, y^t, k^t, v^t, t)$.

[41] A user cost of capital depends not only on the appropriate depreciation and interest rates but also on the corporate profit and property taxes that the firm faces. For references and discussions about the recent controversies in this area, see Stiglitz [1976] and King [1977].

[42] See Sheshinski [1971] on this topic. However, his treatment is not entirely satisfactory, due to the partial equilibrium nature of his model.

[43] There is some discussion of this topic in Baumol and Klevorick [1970] and in Leland [1974].

Appendix: Proofs of Theorems

Proof of Theorem 1:   Suppose that $w \cdot x^* \neq C(w, y^*, k^*)$. Then since (y^*, x^*, k^*, p^*) is a solution to (19), we have $(y^*, x^*, k^*) \in S$ and thus x^* is feasible for the minimization problem $\min_x \{w \cdot x = (y^*, x, k^*) \in S\} \equiv C(w, y^*, k^*)$. Thus

$$w \cdot x^* > C(w, y^*, k^*) \equiv w \cdot \bar{x}, \tag{A1}$$

where $(y^*, \bar{x}, k^*) \in S$. The structure of the maximization problem (19), along with the inequality (A1), implies

$$p^* \cdot y^* - w \cdot \bar{x} - r \cdot k^* > p^* \cdot y^* - w \cdot x^* - r \cdot k^* \tag{A2}$$

$$\leq e \cdot k^*. \tag{A3}$$

Now increase each component of k^* by the factor $1 + \alpha$ where $\alpha > 0$, so that the following constraint is satisfied:

$$p^* \cdot y^* - w \cdot \bar{x} - r \cdot (1 + \alpha)k^* = e \cdot (1 + \alpha)k^*$$

$$> e \cdot k^* \qquad \text{since} \quad e \gg 0_N, \quad k^* > 0_N, \quad \text{and} \quad \alpha > 0$$

$$\geq p^* \cdot y^* - w \cdot x^* - r \cdot k^* \qquad \text{using (A3).} \tag{A4}$$

The inequality (A4) shows that $(y^*, \bar{x}, (1 + \alpha)k^*, p^*)$ is a feasible solution for (19), which gives rise to a higher profit level than our solution (y^*, x^*, k^*, p^*). This contradiction implies that our *supposition* is false, and thus

$$w \cdot x^* = C(w, y^*, k^*). \tag{A5}$$

The rest of the theorem follows readily, since it is clear that (y^*, k^*) is a feasible solution for (21). If (y^*, k^*) is not the optimal solution to (21), then it is easy to show that (y^*, x^*, k^*, p^*) cannot be the optimal solution to (19), a contradiction. Thus (y^*, k^*) is optimal for (21).

Proof of Theorem 2:   Form the Lagrangian for (23); i.e., define

$$L(y, k, j, \lambda) \equiv y \cdot g(y) - C(w, y, k) - r \cdot (k + j) + \lambda[e \cdot (k + j) - y \cdot g(y)$$

$$+ C(w, y, k) + r \cdot (k + j)].$$

Note that the gradient vector of the constraint function with respect to j is $e + r \gg 0_N$. Thus the Mangasarian–Fromovitz constraint qualification condition (see Mangasarian [1969, pp. 172–173]) is satisfied and there will exist $\lambda^* \geq 0$ such that λ^* and the solution $y^* \gg 0_I$, $k^* \gg 0_N$, and $j^* \geq 0_N$ to (23) satisfies the Kuhn–Tucker conditions

$$[g(y^*) + \nabla g(y^*)y^* - \nabla_y C(w, y^*, k^*)][1 - \lambda^*] = 0_I,$$

$$[-\nabla_k C(w, y^*, k^*) - r][1 - \lambda^*] + \lambda^* e = 0_N,$$

$$-r + \lambda^*(e + r) \leq 0_N; \quad j^* \geq 0_N; \quad (-r + \lambda^* e + \lambda^* r) \cdot j^* = 0.$$

From the third set of Kuhn–Tucker conditions, we have $\lambda^*(e + r) \leq r$ or $\lambda^* \leq r_n/(e_n + r_n)$ for $n = 1, 2, \ldots, N$, which proves (i). Suppose now that the nth component of j^*, j_n^*, is positive. Then we must have $-r_n + \lambda^*(e_n + r_n) = 0$ or $\lambda^* = r_n/(e_n + r_n)$. Now substitute this last equation into the nth component of the second set of Kuhn–Tucker conditions above and we find that

$$-\frac{\partial C}{\partial k_n}(w, y^*, k^*) = r_n - \frac{\lambda^* e_n}{1 - \lambda^*} = r_n - r_n = 0,$$

which contradicts our assumption that $-\partial C(w, y^*, k^*)/\partial k_n > 0$. Thus $j_n^* = 0$ for each n or $j^* = 0_N$, which proves (ii). Part (iii) now follows since (23) reduces to (21) when we set $j = 0_N$.

Proof of Test 3: Suppose that the producer is engaging in variable-cost-minimizing behavior for some family $\{S^t\}$ which satisfies Conditions 1. Define M_t as in (43). By (42), $(y^m, x^m, k^m) \in S^m$ for all m. Thus

$$x^m \in L^m(y^m, k^m) \qquad \text{for} \quad m \in M_t. \tag{A6}$$

By the no-technological-regress assumption, $S^m \subset S^t$ for $m \in M_t$ (using also the definition of M_t). Thus by Lemma 1 and (A6),

$$x^m \in L^t(y^m, k^m) \qquad \text{for} \quad m \in M_t. \tag{A7}$$

Since $m \in M_t$, by the definition of M_t, $y^m \geq y^t$ and $k^m \leq k^t$. Thus by Lemma 2 and (A7),

$$x^m \in L^t(y^t, k^t) \qquad \text{for} \quad m \in M_t. \tag{A8}$$

Since $L^t(y^t, k^t)$ is a convex set by assumption, then $\sum_{m \in M_t} \lambda_m x^m \in L^t(y^t, k^t)$ for all $\lambda_m \geq 0$ such that $\sum_{m \in M_t} \lambda_m = 1$. Thus $\sum_{m \in M_t} \lambda_m x^m$ is a feasible solution for the cost-minimization problem in (42) and thus we must have $w^t \cdot x^t \leq C^{t*}$. Since we also have $C^{t*} \leq w^t \cdot x^t$, we must have $w^t \cdot x^t = C^{t*}$.

Proof of Test 4: Suppose that the producer is engaging in variable-cost-minimizing behavior for some family $\{S^t\}$ that satisfies Conditions II. By

(42), $(y^m, x^m, k^m) \in S^m$ for all m. If $m = 1, 2, \ldots t$, then $S^m \subset S^t$ by the no-technological-regress assumption. Thus

$$(y^m, x^m, k^m) \in S^t \quad \text{for} \quad m = 1, 2, \ldots, t. \tag{A9}$$

Let $\lambda_1^* \geq 0,\ \lambda_2^* \geq 0, \ldots, \lambda_t^* \geq 0$ solve (46). Then since S^t is a convex set, we have, using (A9),

$$\sum_{m=1}^{t} \lambda_m^*(y^m, x^m, k^m) = \left(\sum_{m=1}^{t} \lambda_m^* y_m, \sum_{m=1}^{t} \lambda_m^* x^m, \sum_{m=1}^{t} \lambda_m^* k^m \right) \in S^t. \tag{A10}$$

From (46), we have $\Sigma_{m=1}^{t} \lambda_m^* y^m \geq y^t$ and $\Sigma_{m=1}^{t} \lambda_m^* k^m \leq k^t$. Thus by the free disposal property of S^t and (A10), we have $(y^t, \Sigma_{m=1}^{t} \lambda_m^* x^m, k^t) \in S^t$. Thus $\Sigma_{m=1}^{t} \lambda_m^* x^m$ is a feasible solution for the cost-minimization problem (42) and thus $w^t \cdot x^t \equiv C(w^t, y^t, k^t) \leq w^t \cdot (\Sigma_{m=1}^{t} \lambda_m^* x^m) \equiv C^{t**}$. We have already noted that $C^{t**} \leq w^t \cdot x^t$, so we must have $C^{t**} = w^t \cdot x^t$ for $t = 1, 2, \ldots, T$.

The fact that $\tilde{S}^t$ is an inner approximation to S^t follows readily from (A9), the convexity of S^t, and the free disposal property of S^t.

Proof of Test 5:   Similar to the proof of Test 4 above.

ACKNOWLEDGMENTS

My thanks to Tom Cowing, Charles Hulten, and M. I. Nadiri for extremely helpful comments.

Part III

REGULATED INDUSTRY STUDIES

3

U.S. Trunk Air Carriers, 1972–1977: A Multilateral Comparison of Total Factor Productivity

Douglas W. Caves

Laurits R. Christensen

Michael W. Tretheway

Department of Economics
University of Wisconsin — Madison
Madison, Wisconsin

1. Introduction

By any reasonable definition of productivity growth, the U.S. air-transport industry has had one of the strongest records of any U.S. industry in the post–World War II period. The Bureau of Labor Statistics (BLS) estimates of output per unit of labor input indicate that air-transport productivity in 1977 was more than eight times as high as in 1947.[1] Kendrick's [1973] estimate of output relative to an index of capital and labor input was four times as high in 1966 as in 1948. Using a narrower definition of productivity growth, Gollop and Jorgenson [1980] estimated that air-transport productivity was 2.7 times higher in 1973 than in 1947. In all three of these investigations, only petroleum pipelines had more rapid productivity growth than the air-transport industry.

[1] U.S. Bureau of Labor Statistics [1978].

The rapid productivity growth of the U.S. air transport industry is universally acknowledged, but little is known about the productivity performance of the individual carriers that constitute the industry. The industry includes five distinct categories of carriers: (1) trunk; (2) local service; (3) supplemental; (4) all-cargo; and (5) intrastate and commuter. The trunk carriers dominate the statistics of virtually any aspect of the industry. For example, in 1975 the trunk carriers accounted for 86% of the revenue passenger-miles produced by all types of carriers. In this paper we estimate the growth and relative levels of productivity for the trunk carriers for the period 1972–1977, using an index-number approach. We also investigate the sources of growth and differences in levels of productivity, using regression analysis.

We restrict our study to the 11 trunk carriers during a relatively short time period because extensive data development has been necessary to accomplish even this limited objective. Nevertheless, the years chosen for study are of considerable interest since they represent the closing of an epoch. The two principal epochs in the postwar period are pre- and post-1959, the first year in which jet aircraft were widely used in commercial service. Since 1959 several generations of commercial jet aircraft have been developed. The most recent generation, the wide-bodied jets, became an important segment of trunk-carrier fleets only during the 1970s. Both the pre- and post-1959 epochs have been characterized by rigid regulation of the industry by the Civil Aeronautics Board (CAB), under the authority of the Civil Aeronautics Act of 1938. A new epoch for the U.S. air-transport industry began with the passage of the Airline Deregulation Act of 1978, which legislated the phasing out of CAB authority over routes by 1981 and over rates by 1983. It is too early to be able to compare performance pre- and post-1978 but the methodology that we develop in this paper will facilitate such a comparison when the necessary data become available.

Two previous studies of the trunk carriers provide indications of their relative levels of productivity. Using data from a three-month period in 1961, Gordon [1965] studied the relative cost levels of the trunk carriers. Douglas and Miller [1974] compared actual and predicted cost per unit of output based on pooled cross-section data from 1962 to 1970. These two studies suggest that there are substantial differences in productivity among the trunk carriers.

Comparisons of productivity over time are often based on index-number procedures. Recent developments in economic theory have improved our knowledge about which index-number procedures are most attractive for making productivity comparisons. The distinguishing feature of these new procedures is that they possess many of the properties considered desirable in classical index-number analysis, and in addition they represent exactly production structures that have attractive properties. Caves and Christensen [1980c] have proposed a procedure for making productivity comparisons among a cross section or within a combined time series and cross section of firms. The methodology they developed is used in this paper to provide estimates of the relative levels of total factor productivity (TFP) for the 11 trunk carriers during the six-year period 1972–1977. These estimates are then examined for their association with characteristics of the individual trunk carriers.

2. Methodology

Christensen and Jorgenson [1970] proposed the following index of total factor productivity:

$$\ln \text{TFP}_k - \ln \text{TFP}_l = \sum_i \left(\frac{R_{ik} + R_{il}}{2}\right) \ln\left(\frac{Y_{ik}}{Y_{il}}\right) - \sum_i \left(\frac{W_{ik} + W_{il}}{2}\right) \ln\left(\frac{X_{ik}}{X_{il}}\right),$$

(1)

where k and l are adjacent time periods, the Y_{ij} are output indexes, the X_{ij} are input indexes, the R_{ij} are output revenue shares, and the W_{ij} are input cost shares. Diewert [1976] showed that (1) can be derived from a homogeneous translog transformation function that is separable in outputs and inputs, and exhibits neutral differences in technology. Caves and Christensen [1980c] have shown that separability and neutrality are not required to derive (1) from a homogeneous translog transformation function.

The subscripts k and l in (1) can be interpreted as time periods or as firms. In this paper we allow them to represent both firms and time periods—11 firms and 6 time periods, for a total of 66 time-differentiated firm observations. The direct use of (1) for comparisons of air-carrier productivity would result in 2145 binary comparisons—the number of possible ways of choosing 2 of the 66 observations to compare. Unfortunately, there is no guarantee of transitivity in such comparisons. For example, in 1977 firm k might be found to be more productive than firm l and less productive than firm m; yet a direct comparison of l and m might indicate that m is less productive than l. This lack of transitivity is possible because weights R_{ij} and W_{ij} specific to the two firms in question are used. The traditional solution to this problem has been to use weights that are not specific to the individual observation. The disadvantage of this solution is that the comparisons lose characteristicity—they are no longer based on economic conditions specific to the two entities being compared.[2]

[2] The term characteristicity appears to have been coined by Drechsler [1973].

It is impossible to achieve transitivity and complete characteristicity simultaneously. However, Caves and Christensen [1980c] have proposed the following compromise formula for binary comparisons:

$$\ln \text{TFP}_k - \ln \text{TFP}_l = \sum_i \frac{R_{ik} + \bar{R}_i}{2} \ln\left(\frac{Y_{ik}}{\tilde{Y}_i}\right)$$

$$- \sum_i \frac{R_{il} + \bar{R}_i}{2} \ln\left(\frac{Y_{il}}{\tilde{Y}_i}\right) - \sum_i \frac{W_{ik} + \bar{W}_i}{2} \ln\left(\frac{X_{ik}}{\tilde{X}_i}\right)$$

$$+ \sum_i \frac{W_{il} + \bar{W}_i}{2} \ln\left(\frac{X_{il}}{\tilde{X}_i}\right), \tag{2}$$

where a bar over a variable indicates the arithmetic mean and a tilde over a variable indicates the geometric mean. The use of (2) for binary comparisons results in transitive multilateral comparisons that retain a high degree of characteristicity. The weights used to compute the productivity comparisons reflect the economic conditions faced by all economic entities (through $\bar{R}_i$ and $\bar{W}_i$), but at the same time more than half of each weight is specific to k or l.

Equation (2) can be derived directly from a translog transformation structure by taking the difference between each firm's transformation function and the function resulting from averaging arithmetically the transformation functions across all observations. This procedure, in effect, uses the geometric average level of productivity as the norm. Equation (2) can also be derived in an alternative manner as follows. Consider a representative firm that produces the geometric means of the outputs ($\tilde{Y}_i$) from the geometric means of the inputs ($\tilde{X}_i$). Such a firm will be in equilibrium when its revenue and cost shares are equal to the arithmetic means ($\bar{R}_i$ and $\bar{W}_i$) computed over the full set of observations being considered. Transitive comparisons are achieved by using this representative firm as the basis for making all possible binary comparisons, i.e., any two firms are compared with each other by comparing them both with the representative firm.

The use of revenue shares as weights in (2) implies that the structure of production exhibits constant returns to scale and that the prices of the outputs are proportional to their marginal costs (Caves et al. [1980]). Relaxation of these assumptions would require extensive econometric estimation. We believe that the assumptions are reasonable first approximations in that previous investigators have: (1) failed to find evidence against constant returns to scale for trunk air carriers; and (2) concluded that rigid regulation of air fares has resulted in service competition such that marginal costs have risen to the regulated fares (Douglas and Miller [1974]).

3. Data

In this section we provide a description of the sources and methods used in the construction of our data set, along with tables of the most important variables. The primary source of our data is the CAB's Form 41 report filed annually by each air carrier. Some of these data are summarized and reported in the CAB's biennial *Handbook of Airline Statistics*. However, to complete this study it was necessary to use thousands of pages of the original Form 41 reports, which are available only in the CAB's Public Reference Room. Many of the Form 41 data are reported for time periods of different lengths, and for individual "operations" of the air carrier. A large effort was required to transform these raw data to represent system-wide operations on an annual basis.

We omit an annual observation for a carrier if it experienced a "major" strike in that year. For the six-year period under study, there were six strikes of 25 days or less, but there were only three strikes of longer duration. These ranged from 45 days to 236 days.[3] We omit from our analysis the four observations affected by these major strikes: Northwest, 1972; TWA, 1973; National, 1974 and 1975. The level of productivity for these years would be of some interest, but we do not have the data that would be required to reflect the diminished employment of inputs during the strike and the period of recovery.

We distinguish three categories of passenger service and two categories of freight service. The passenger categories are scheduled first-class service, scheduled coach-class service, and charter service. Indexes in each category are based on revenue passenger-miles (RPM). The two freight service indexes are ton-miles of revenue freight (RTM) and ton-miles of mail. The five indexes for each carrier are presented in Table 1, where all values shown are relative to Delta Airlines in 1977.[4] The proportions of each carrier's total revenue accounted for by the five output categories are presented in Table 2, along with the total revenue realized.

[3] The number of days of the strikes were

National	236	1974–1975	Continental	25	1975	Northwest	3	1975
Northwest	95	1972	United	16	1975	TWA	1	1976
TWA	45	1973	National	6	1976	Braniff	1	1974.

[4] The actual output figures for Delta in 1977 are

	Million RPM	Million RTM
First class	1,613.0	
Coach	17,506.7	
Charter passenger	322.9	
Freight		206.9
Mail		81.9

TABLE 1

Output Indexes for Trunk Carriers, 1972–1977[a]

	AM	BR	CN	DL	EA	NA	NW	PA	TW	UN	WE
				First class passenger-miles							
1972	1.716	0.358	0.351	0.961	1.203	0.399		0.974	1.451	1.890	0.221
1973	1.793	0.410	0.339	1.080	1.078	0.428	0.446	1.005		1.874	0.247
1974	1.767	0.453	0.372	1.441	1.194		0.482	0.837	1.303	1.814	0.202
1975	1.557	0.417	0.385	1.202	1.082		0.410	0.696	1.167	1.437	0.217
1976	1.413	0.408	0.321	1.057	1.023	0.302	0.395	0.726	1.083	1.407	0.251
1977	1.351	0.400	0.316	1.000	0.981	0.341	0.394	0.809	1.072	1.356	0.273
				Coach class passenger-miles							
1972	0.948	0.245	0.268	0.614	0.827	0.281		1.026	1.130	1.265	0.318
1973	1.015	0.276	0.292	0.759	0.865	0.298	0.416	1.022		1.371	0.340
1974	1.007	0.305	0.289	0.788	0.899		0.480	0.854	1.092	1.394	0.360
1975	1.049	0.321	0.328	0.830	0.938		0.503	0.785	1.090	1.366	0.380
1976	1.188	0.357	0.325	0.909	1.019	0.273	0.578	0.848	1.174	1.572	0.418
1977	1.283	0.392	0.382	1.000	1.093	0.324	0.598	0.925	1.264	1.688	0.453
				Charter passenger-miles							
1972	3.842	1.813	1.625	0.273	1.871	0.007		7.499	6.669	5.443	0.204
1973	3.294	1.280	0.396	0.038	1.803	0.005	2.909	12.175		6.478	0.367
1974	3.093	1.216	0.051	0.072	0.934		2.439	11.929	5.240	6.078	0.378
1975	3.780	1.003	0.161	0.081	0.386		1.610	10.131	4.748	6.082	0.324
1976	4.769	0.800	0.269	0.949	0.120	0.013	1.590	12.541	5.962	8.060	0.354
1977	4.123	1.096	0.325	1.000	0.139	0.059	1.687	10.884	5.794	9.048	0.660
				Freight ton-miles							
1972	2.782	0.430	0.959	0.785	0.966	0.338		4.637	2.627	3.086	0.263
1973	2.742	0.430	0.722	0.916	1.058	0.380	1.308	4.748		3.246	0.262
1974	2.492	0.439	0.833	0.888	0.949		1.552	4.901	2.638	3.112	0.355
1975	2.332	0.416	1.082	0.810	1.034		1.940	4.373	2.253	2.660	0.412
1976	2.540	0.422	1.065	0.940	0.933	0.306	2.301	4.571	2.256	2.792	0.527
1977	2.932	0.452	1.225	1.000	1.027	0.341	2.220	4.741	2.343	2.918	0.618
				Mail ton-miles							
1972	1.191	0.420	0.280	0.871	0.836	0.209		3.214	2.147	2.041	0.266
1973	1.203	0.419	0.277	0.836	0.723	0.227	1.088	2.880		2.009	0.273
1974	1.289	0.445	0.288	0.803	0.678		1.162	2.527	2.245	1.969	0.269
1975	1.339	0.448	0.319	0.834	0.743		1.159	2.647	1.654	1.806	0.286
1976	1.398	0.450	0.269	0.933	0.800	0.194	1.264	2.332	1.719	1.894	0.318
1977	1.457	0.487	0.282	1.000	0.847	0.216	1.322	2.323	1.732	1.983	0.362

[a] Delta (1977) = 1.000.

The following abbreviations are used throughout: AM—American; BR—Braniff; CN—Continental; DL—Delta; EA—Eastern; NA—National; NW—Northwest; PA—Pan American; TW—Trans World; UN—United; WE—Western.

TABLE 2

Revenue Shares and Total Revenue for Airline Outputs

	AM	BR	CN	DL	EA	NA	NW	PA	TW	UN	WE
				First class passenger							
1972	0.168	0.144	0.132	0.160	0.143	0.155		0.102	0.138	0.142	0.071
1973	0.163	0.148	0.123	0.147	0.123	0.152	0.116	0.105		0.132	0.072
1974	0.160	0.147	0.133	0.169	0.130		0.110	0.097	0.125	0.126	0.060
1975	0.143	0.136	0.125	0.145	0.118		0.093	0.092	0.118	0.110	0.059
1976	0.123	0.127	0.116	0.125	0.110	0.126	0.081	0.092	0.107	0.097	0.061
1977	0.115	0.118	0.098	0.113	0.098	0.129	0.080	0.095	0.103	0.089	0.062
				Coach class passenger							
1972	0.717	0.717	0.741	0.759	0.775	0.781		0.658	0.722	0.727	0.866
1973	0.715	0.729	0.767	0.778	0.794	0.781	0.712	0.645		0.735	0.862
1974	0.725	0.740	0.768	0.761	0.807		0.728	0.619	0.736	0.752	0.872
1975	0.734	0.754	0.778	0.788	0.823		0.738	0.616	0.747	0.767	0.870
1976	0.754	0.770	0.783	0.798	0.836	0.814	0.741	0.614	0.760	0.775	0.867
1977	0.763	0.775	0.796	0.804	0.843	0.812	0.753	0.633	0.769	0.782	0.856
				Charter passenger							
1972	0.022	0.046	0.037	0.004	0.020	0.000		0.050	0.035	0.031	0.006
1973	0.020	0.031	0.011	0.001	0.018	0.000	0.043	0.074		0.035	0.009
1974	0.021	0.029	0.002	0.001	0.010		0.032	0.085	0.030	0.032	0.008
1975	0.026	0.026	0.005	0.001	0.005		0.028	0.082	0.034	0.037	0.008
1976	0.026	0.020	0.006	0.008	0.001	0.001	0.022	0.096	0.036	0.042	0.007
1977	0.021	0.021	0.006	0.007	0.001	0.002	0.021	0.081	0.036	0.044	0.011
				Freight service							
1972	0.077	0.069	0.074	0.059	0.047	0.052		0.144	0.076	0.079	0.043
1973	0.084	0.067	0.082	0.056	0.050	0.054	0.097	0.140		0.076	0.041
1974	0.079	0.062	0.082	0.053	0.042		0.102	0.161	0.081	0.073	0.046
1975	0.081	0.061	0.078	0.051	0.043		0.112	0.167	0.079	0.070	0.050
1976	0.081	0.063	0.082	0.055	0.041	0.049	0.131	0.163	0.077	0.070	0.052
1977	0.088	0.058	0.085	0.055	0.041	0.047	0.117	0.160	0.073	0.072	0.055
				Mail service							
1972	0.016	0.024	0.016	0.019	0.014	0.012		0.046	0.028	0.021	0.014
1973	0.018	0.024	0.018	0.018	0.015	0.013	0.032	0.037		0.022	0.015
1974	0.015	0.022	0.015	0.015	0.011		0.028	0.037	0.028	0.018	0.013
1975	0.015	0.023	0.014	0.014	0.011		0.029	0.043	0.022	0.016	0.013
1976	0.015	0.020	0.013	0.015	0.012	0.010	0.026	0.035	0.020	0.016	0.013
1977	0.013	0.028	0.014	0.021	0.016	0.011	0.029	0.031	0.020	0.013	0.016
				Total revenue (billions of dollars)							
1972	1.338	0.367	0.353	0.873	1.146	0.365		1.272	1.392	1.714	0.366
1973	1.476	0.423	0.383	1.104	1.232	0.410	0.572	1.400		1.909	0.406
1974	1.622	0.524	0.440	1.327	1.440		0.745	1.477	1.673	2.152	0.469
1975	1.698	0.570	0.502	1.391	1.536		0.791	1.557	1.713	2.078	0.501
1976	1.994	0.650	0.515	1.602	1.737	0.429	0.956	1.616	1.919	2.522	0.586
1977	2.256	0.759	0.637	1.856	1.944	0.532	1.034	1.846	2.157	2.821	0.669

TABLE 3

Input Indexes for Trunk Carriers, 1972–1977[a]

	AM	BR	CN	DL	EA	NA	NW	PA	TW	UN	WE
					Labor						
1972	1.268	0.385	0.338	0.950	1.217	0.279		1.027	1.302	1.700	0.369
1973	1.338	0.411	0.331	1.015	1.270	0.287	0.418	1.199		1.701	0.385
1974	1.305	0.421	0.344	1.025	1.183		0.431	1.138	1.285	1.764	0.368
1975	1.311	0.414	0.361	0.998	1.172		0.422	1.028	1.221	1.754	0.374
1976	1.306	0.414	0.346	1.023	1.204	0.278	0.420	0.952	1.254	1.744	0.393
1977	1.330	0.416	0.385	1.000	1.116	0.275	0.407	0.906	1.253	1.689	0.382
					Aircraft						
1972	1.422	0.309	0.304	0.757	0.923	0.228		1.029	1.268	1.774	0.279
1973	1.375	0.313	0.325	0.858	1.097	0.207	0.715	0.990		2.047	0.304
1974	1.276	0.325	0.365	0.901	1.120		0.758	0.960	1.485	1.908	0.302
1975	1.175	0.349	0.366	0.975	1.145		0.842	0.855	1.306	1.932	0.328
1976	1.186	0.377	0.397	1.036	1.226	0.237	0.929	0.902	1.309	1.840	0.334
1977	1.228	0.388	0.376	1.000	1.280	0.225	0.900	0.864	1.314	1.859	0.373
				Ground property and equipment							
1972	1.099	0.213	0.311	0.642	0.822	0.198		1.498	1.122	1.822	0.250
1973	1.119	0.259	0.448	0.904	0.970	0.330	0.458	1.942		2.451	0.297
1974	1.091	0.274	0.448	0.983	0.912		0.472	1.785	1.185	1.866	0.372
1975	1.123	0.274	0.426	0.991	0.845		0.460	1.600	1.118	1.798	0.362
1976	1.186	0.286	0.398	0.963	0.830	0.327	0.432	1.481	1.024	1.751	0.342
1977	1.342	0.304	0.416	1.000	1.032	0.308	0.442	1.452	0.958	1.823	0.348
					Fuel						
1972	1.306	0.377	0.371	0.813	1.049	0.272		1.245	1.445	1.676	0.325
1973	1.353	0.391	0.360	1.019	1.101	0.361	0.628	1.214		1.689	0.337
1974	1.162	0.400	0.307	0.890	0.942		0.599	1.020	1.294	1.491	0.311
1975	1.185	0.412	0.334	0.911	0.994		0.606	0.959	1.217	1.426	0.323
1976	1.236	0.418	0.307	0.951	1.024	0.285	0.631	0.928	1.199	1.522	0.352
1977	1.280	0.450	0.353	1.000	1.053	0.316	0.647	0.928	1.239	1.586	0.386
					Materials						
1972	1.363	0.411	0.379	0.833	1.137	0.478		1.561	1.566	1.478	0.384
1973	1.562	0.419	0.383	0.939	1.207	0.487	0.587	1.587		1.546	0.376
1974	1.525	0.508	0.387	0.933	1.292		0.645	1.622	1.619	1.565	0.395
1975	1.490	0.519	0.422	0.909	1.280		0.673	1.590	1.541	1.534	0.409
1976	1.570	0.518	0.386	0.934	1.310	0.370	0.736	1.470	1.565	1.700	0.440
1977	1.638	0.544	0.424	1.000	1.316	0.435	0.722	1.627	1.636	1.741	0.468

[a] Delta (1977) = 1.000.

TABLE 4

Cost Shares and Total Cost

	AM	BR	CN	DL	EA	NA	NW	PA	TW	UN	WE
					Labor share						
1972	0.411	0.380	0.387	0.419	0.451	0.289		0.378	0.382	0.431	0.408
1973	0.410	0.402	0.396	0.434	0.453	0.353	0.309	0.394		0.409	0.418
1974	0.392	0.356	0.357	0.416	0.391		0.280	0.354	0.347	0.415	0.392
1975	0.390	0.347	0.346	0.401	0.380		0.266	0.346	0.354	0.407	0.376
1976	0.395	0.340	0.363	0.409	0.383	0.352	0.261	0.350	0.361	0.404	0.379
1977	0.394	0.337	0.372	0.405	0.388	0.343	0.266	0.346	0.369	0.394	0.371
					Aircraft share						
1972	0.192	0.168	0.152	0.173	0.140	0.143		0.154	0.172	0.192	0.155
1973	0.164	0.145	0.145	0.151	0.143	0.100	0.222	0.130		0.201	0.148
1974	0.132	0.114	0.146	0.129	0.132		0.183	0.099	0.142	0.155	0.116
1975	0.115	0.113	0.130	0.130	0.130		0.190	0.091	0.124	0.152	0.115
1976	0.101	0.103	0.135	0.118	0.122	0.097	0.180	0.089	0.111	0.120	0.099
1977	0.104	0.104	0.122	0.122	0.135	0.088	0.180	0.088	0.112	0.131	0.116
					Ground property and equipment share						
1972	0.026	0.020	0.030	0.026	0.025	0.022		0.038	0.027	0.034	0.024
1973	0.022	0.020	0.036	0.027	0.023	0.029	0.025	0.041		0.040	0.024
1974	0.018	0.015	0.028	0.022	0.017		0.018	0.029	0.018	0.024	0.023
1975	0.018	0.015	0.025	0.022	0.015		0.017	0.028	0.018	0.023	0.021
1976	0.025	0.019	0.031	0.027	0.020	0.030	0.020	0.036	0.022	0.028	0.025
1977	0.022	0.016	0.024	0.022	0.019	0.021	0.016	0.028	0.016	0.023	0.019
					Fuel share						
1972	0.105	0.117	0.132	0.103	0.105	0.102		0.109	0.116	0.113	0.115
1973	0.107	0.117	0.126	0.118	0.104	0.116	0.140	0.116		0.112	0.118
1974	0.140	0.157	0.157	0.161	0.146		0.204	0.182	0.178	0.147	0.160
1975	0.165	0.167	0.184	0.191	0.171		0.209	0.174	0.190	0.162	0.186
1976	0.162	0.203	0.178	0.193	0.171	0.192	0.215	0.175	0.183	0.183	0.187
1977	0.174	0.219	0.194	0.202	0.180	0.200	0.230	0.171	0.193	0.192	0.201
					Materials share						
1972	0.266	0.315	0.299	0.279	0.280	0.444		0.321	0.305	0.230	0.298
1973	0.296	0.316	0.296	0.270	0.276	0.402	0.304	0.320		0.238	0.292
1974	0.319	0.357	0.312	0.272	0.314		0.315	0.336	0.315	0.259	0.310
1975	0.312	0.359	0.316	0.255	0.304		0.318	0.361	0.314	0.256	0.303
1976	0.319	0.335	0.293	0.253	0.305	0.330	0.324	0.350	0.323	0.265	0.310
1977	0.307	0.324	0.287	0.249	0.279	0.348	0.307	0.367	0.311	0.260	0.292
					Total cost (billions of dollars)						
1972	1.375	0.351	0.340	0.802	1.092	0.289		1.306	1.381	1.730	0.346
1973	1.536	0.386	0.376	1.011	1.272	0.351	0.560	1.441		1.894	0.374
1974	1.672	0.491	0.428	1.187	1.440		0.709	1.669	1.797	2.110	0.441
1975	1.834	0.549	0.509	1.353	1.616		0.805	1.677	1.882	2.299	0.514
1976	2.010	0.625	0.533	1.494	1.750	0.454	0.919	1.699	1.975	2.614	0.574
1977	2.311	0.720	0.633	1.721	2.045	0.536	1.007	1.901	2.278	2.899	0.686

TABLE 5

Categories of Labor Used to Form Labor Index

---

1. General management personnel
2. Pilots, copilots, and other flying operations flight personnel
3. Passenger service flight personnel
4. Maintenance labor
5. General aircraft and traffic handling personnel
6. Aircraft control personnel
7. Passenger handling personnel—traffic servicing
8. Passenger handling personnel—reservations and sales
9. Cargo handling personnel
10. Trainees and instructors
11. Communications personnel
12. Record-keeping personnel, lawyers, and law clerks
13. Traffic solicitors
14. Purchasing personnel
15. Hotel, restaurant, food service, and other personnel

We distinguish the following five categories of input: labor; aircraft; ground property and equipment; fuel; and materials. Quantity indexes for each input are shown in Table 3, where all values are shown relative to Delta in 1977. The proportions of each carrier's total cost accounted for by the five input categories are presented in Table 4, along with the annual levels of total cost.

The labor input indexes are constructed from the 15 categories of labor shown in Table 5. The annual reports filed by the carriers with the CAB indicate the number of employees and the compensation which they received, in each of the 15 categories.[5] In order to compute a single index of real labor input for each carrier we adapt formula (2) as follows:

$$\ln L_k - \ln L_l = \sum_{i=1}^{15} \frac{W_{ik} + \overline{W}_i}{2} \ln\!\left(\frac{L_{ik}}{\tilde{L}_i}\right) - \sum_{i=1}^{15} \frac{W_{il} + \overline{W}_i}{2} \ln\!\left(\frac{L_{il}}{\tilde{L}_i}\right), \quad (3)$$

where L_{ij} is the number of employees in the ith category for the jth (time-differentiated) carrier, L_j is the aggregate index of labor input for the jth

---

[5] The carriers do not report any information on number of hours worked by employees. We have been forced to assume that there are no differences across carriers in the number of hours worked per year within a category. Information we have received from the Airline Pilots Association indicates that this is a reasonable assumption for the "pilots" category. We note that our results are not affected by differences in average hours worked across labor categories. We have allowed for differences across years in the number of hours worked per employee per year by using National Income and Product Accounts data on the number of hours worked per employee for the aggregate Air Transport sector.

carrier, and the W_{ij} are the compensation shares. This procedure provides transitive indexes with a high degree of characteristicity.

Our treatment of ground property and equipment is based on Christensen and Jorgenson [1969]. We begin by using the perpetual inventory method to estimate the real stock of ground property and equipment. We use historical real-investment data with geometrically declining weights to estimate the stock for each carrier for each year.[6] We assume that the flow of capital services is proportional to the stock. Finally, we estimate the annual cost of using ground property and equipment by imputing interest and depreciation expenses, adjusted for income taxes, property taxes, and capital gains.

It is not feasible to use the perpetual inventory method to construct indexes of aircraft in use by the airlines. Historical investment data are available, but the airlines typically sell their aircraft before their useful lifetimes are exhausted. Hence, use of the perpetual inventory method would require acquisition and retirement accounts by type of aircraft.

We employ an alternative procedure for aircraft, which is based on detailed aircraft counts. We assume that the flow of capital services for an aircraft in a given category is independent of its age.[7] This implies that the flow of capital services from any category of aircraft is proportional to the number of aircraft in that category employed by the carrier. We have obtained data by carrier and year for the following eight categories of aircraft: (1) propeller-driven (miscellaneous older types); (2) two-engine narrow-bodied jet (DC9 and B737); (3) early three-engine narrow-body jets B727-100); (4) recent three-engine narrow-body jet (B727-200); (5) four-engine narrow-body jets (DC8 and B707); (6) three-engine wide-body jet (L1011); (7) three-engine wide-body jet (DC10); (8) four-engine wide-body jet (B747).

Construction of an index of real capital input from the eight categories of aircraft requires weights that reflect the annual capital cost of each type of aircraft. A substantial number of the trunk carriers' aircraft are on long-term leases. We estimate the annual cost of each type of aircraft from the

---

[6] We use benchmarks from 1945. In constructing our real investment series, we consolidated the investment series and benchmarks for any predecessor or acquired firms.

[7] CAB, *Aircraft Operating Cost and Performance Report* [1977], reports average utilization of various aircraft types in hours per day for the year 1976. Representative values, along with the year in which the aircraft type was introduced are given in the following tabulation:

B707-100B	1961	8.01
DC9-10	1965	6.09
DC8-61	1967	7.67
B747	1970	6.68
DC10-10	1971	8.05
L1011	1972	6.96

lease data available to us. Thus, for each carrier in each year, we estimate the total capital cost for each aircraft type as the product of the estimated lease payment times the number of airplanes. The total aircraft capital cost is then computed as the sum across the eight categories of aircraft.

In principle an index of real capital input from aircraft could be computed from Eq. (3) using airplane counts with weights based on estimated lease values. This turns out to be infeasible because each air carrier employs only a subset of the eight categories of aircraft, and (3) is undefined if there are any zero quantities. However, the price dual to (3) is well-defined because there is a positive lease value for each type of aircraft, even if the quantity is zero. Thus we use the following formula to compute the price of aircraft services, p, for each carrier in each year:

$$\ln p_k - \ln p_l = \sum_{i=1}^{8} \frac{W_{ik} + \overline{W}_i}{2} \ln\left(\frac{p_{ik}}{\tilde{p}_i}\right) - \sum_{i=1}^{8} \frac{W_{il} + \overline{W}_i}{2} \ln\left(\frac{p_{il}}{\tilde{p}_i}\right), \qquad (4)$$

where p_{ij} is the annual lease value of aircraft of the ith type and w_{ij} is the jth carrier's share of total imputed aircraft capital cost attributed to aircraft of type i. Finally, we obtain the quantity index of aircraft services for each carrier as the ratio of total imputed annual aircraft costs to the price index of aircraft capital services computed from (4).

Since virtually all fuel used by the trunk carriers during the 1972–1977 period was jet fuel, gallons of fuel consumed provides a satisfactory index of fuel input. The CAB provides figures for gallons consumed and the corresponding expenditure.

The trunk carriers use a wide variety of inputs other than labor, capital, and fuel. We refer to them as "materials." The cost of materials is readily obtainable as operating expenses not attributable to labor, capital, or fuel. We estimate quantity indexes of materials by applying a price deflator to expenditures on materials.[8]

The five input indexes in Table 3 are all presented relative to Delta Airlines in 1977. Some of these indexes have no interpretation in terms of their absolute magnitudes. However, we note that in 1977 Delta employed 30,976 persons; had an aircraft inventory consisting of 21 L1011s, 92 B727-200s, and 53 DC9s; had an estimated stock of ground property and equipment of $208,083,000 in 1977 dollars; consumed 980.4 million gallons of jet fuel; and spent $428,836,000 in 1977 dollars on other inputs—the largest single category being food ($64,200,000).

---

[8] The price index used was a discrete time Divisia index of seven separate National Income and Product Account deflators.

4. Productivity

Using Eq. (2), we compute TFP indexes for the 11 trunk carriers. These indexes, normalized so that the level of TFP for Delta in 1977 is 1.000, are presented in Table 6 along with their percentage rates of growth.[9] In Table 7 we rank the trunk carriers by their level of TFP in 1977. We also include in the table their 1972 rank, and the average annual percentage growth from 1972 to 1977.[10] The wide disparity in growth rates over the 1972–1977 period resulted in substantial changes in the ranking of the firms. For example, between 1972 and 1977 Northwest rose from sixth to second, Western rose from eight to third, TWA fell from second to eighth, and National fell from fifth to seventh. In terms of TFP growth the trunks fall into three distinct categories. Three carriers achieved very high growth rates of productivity: Delta (5.2%), Northwest (4.7%), and Western (4.7%). Two carriers achieved productivity growth that was much lower than average for the trunk carriers: TWA (1.0%) and Pan Am (0.7%). The remaining six carriers fall in the relatively narrow range of 2.1–3.3% per year.

American, Eastern, and United each experienced a decline in TFP for a single year in the 1973–1975 period. Continental's TFP declined in both 1973 and 1974, and Pan Am had negative TFP growth for all three years 1973 – 1975. By 1975, Pan Am had fallen from first to fourth in level of TFP. However, Pan Am experienced very high productivity growth of 13.6% in 1976 to regain the top rank.

Our methodology for computing productivity does not require the assumption that inputs and outputs are separable or that productivity differences are neutral. If we impose these assumptions, our estimates of productivity are not altered; however, under these assumptions we can interpret the terms on the right hand side of (2) as indexes of aggregate output and aggregate input. These indexes and their rates of growth are presented in Table 8.

Table 8 indicates a wide range of output levels and growth rates for the trunk carriers. Observe that the two years of modest TFP growth, 1973 and 1975, were quite different in terms of input and output growth. It is also worth noting that although growth of output was modest in the recession

---

[9] We adopt the convention that growth is continuously compounded and therefore compute percentage growth rates and percentage differences as the difference between natural logarithms times 100. For example, United's productivity index is 1.056 in 1977 and 0.896 in 1972. We take the difference of the natural logs of 1.056 and 0.896, divide by 5 (the number of years), and multiply by 100 to obtain 3.3%.

[10] For Northwest we impute a level of productivity for 1972 based on the 4.7% per year growth rate experienced in the 1973–1977 period.

TABLE 6

Total Factor Productivity for Trunk Airlines, 1972–1977, Indexes and Growth Rates[a]

	AM	BR	CN	DL	EA	NA	NW	PA	TW	UN	WE
1972	0.872	0.770	0.918	0.773	0.802	0.879		1.069	0.951	0.896	0.872
1973	0.865	0.804	0.905	0.805	0.763	0.884	0.916	1.038		0.916	0.909
1974	0.895	0.808	0.888	0.880	0.811		0.986	0.961	0.893	0.943	0.963
1975	0.918	0.810	0.962	0.887	0.822	0.893	0.988	0.933	0.918	0.906	0.989
1976	0.982	0.860	0.986	0.944	0.831		1.068	1.069	0.963	0.997	1.039
1977	1.010	0.903	1.043	1.000	0.893	1.001	1.106	1.110	1.001	1.056	1.101
					Growth rates (%)						
1973	−0.8	4.3	−1.4	4.1	−5.0	0.6		−3.0		2.2	4.2
1974	3.4	0.5	−1.9	8.9	6.0		7.3	−7.7		2.9	5.8
1975	2.5	0.2	8.0	0.8	1.4		0.3	−3.0	2.8	−3.9	2.6
1976	6.8	6.1	2.4	6.2	1.1		7.8	13.6	4.7	9.6	5.0
1977	2.8	4.8	5.7	5.8	7.2	11.4	3.5	3.8	3.9	5.7	5.7
				Average annual growth rate 1972–1977 (%)							
	2.9	3.2	2.5	5.2	2.1	2.6	4.7[b]	0.7	1.0	3.3	4.7

[a] Delta (1977) = 1.000.
[b] Computed for 1973–1977.

TABLE 7

Trunk Carriers Ranked by 1977 Level of Productivity

	1977		1972		Average annual growth of productivity 1972–1977	
	Rank	Level	Rank	Level	Rank	% Growth
PA	1	1.110	1	1.069	11	0.7
NW	2	1.106	6	0.874[a]	2	4.7[a]
WE	3	1.101	8	0.872	3	4.7
UN	4	1.056	4	0.896	4	3.3
CN	5	1.043	3	0.918	8	2.6
AM	6	1.010	7	0.872	6	2.9
NA	7	1.001	5	0.879	7	2.6
TW	8	1.001	2	0.951	10	1.0
DL	9	1.000	10	0.773	1	5.2
BR	10	0.903	11	0.770	5	3.2
EA	11	0.893	9	0.802	9	2.1

[a] Extrapolated to 1972 at 1973–1977 rate of growth.

year of 1974, the carriers were able to achieve gains in TFP by reducing inputs.

Our estimates of TFP can be compared with more traditional indicators of airline productivity. In 1976 the CAB issued a report entitled "Productivity and Cost of Employment, System Trunks, Calendar Years 1974 and 1975." In this report the CAB compared the 11 trunk carriers on the basis of (1) revenue ton-miles per employee, and (2) available ton-miles per employee. We present these indexes for all six years, 1972–1977 in Table 9. In Table 10 we present the 1977 rankings of these two productivity indexes. Although there are some similarities with our rankings in Tables 6 and 7, there are some major differences. We have found that in 1975 Pan Am's productivity exceeded that of Delta by only 5.1% (Table 6). However, Pan Am's revenue ton-miles per employee exceeded Delta's by 43.6% and Pan Am's available ton-miles per employee exceeded Delta's by 38.5% (Table 9). These crude measures of productivity indicate that in 1975 Pan Am had the second-highest and Delta the second-lowest levels of productivity. In contrast, the TFP estimates in Table 6 place Pan Am fourth and Delta eight. In none of the years did revenue ton-miles per employee and available ton-miles per employee produce identical rankings. For example, Braniff in 1977 ranks ninth on the basis of revenue ton-miles per employee but fourth on the basis of available ton-miles per employee.

TABLE 8

Aggregate Output and Input for Trunk Airlines, 1972–1977, Indexes and Growth Rates[a]

	AM	BR	CN	DL	EA	NA	NW	PA	TW	UN	WE
					Output						
1972	1.148	0.287	0.319	0.660	0.892	0.284		1.292	1.312	1.480	0.303
1973	1.209	0.313	0.318	0.777	0.910	0.301	0.496	1.340		1.585	0.326
1974	1.190	0.342	0.314	0.841	0.934		0.558	1.184	1.251	1.585	0.342
1975	1.204	0.347	0.360	0.845	0.949		0.575	1.076	1.206	1.501	0.362
1976	1.321	0.373	0.352	0.929	0.989	0.268	0.651	1.167	1.277	1.696	0.404
1977	1.403	0.406	0.405	1.000	1.050	0.319	0.664	1.225	1.353	1.803	0.444
					Growth rates (%)						
1973	5.1	8.7	-0.3	16.3	2.0	5.9		3.6		6.8	7.3
1974	-1.6	8.9	-1.2	7.9	2.6		11.8	-12.4		0.0	4.7
1975	1.2	1.7	13.6	0.5	1.5		3.0	-9.6	-3.6	-5.4	5.7
1976	9.3	7.2	-2.3	9.5	4.1		12.5	8.2	5.7	12.2	10.9
1977	6.0	8.4	14.1	7.3	6.0	17.6	2.0	4.9	5.7	6.1	9.4
					Average annual growth rate 1972–1977 (%)						
	4.0	7.0	4.8	8.3	3.3	2.3	7.3[b]	-1.1	0.6	3.9	7.6

Input

	Input										
1972	1.317	0.372	0.347	0.854	1.112	0.323		1.209	1.380	1.652	0.348
1973	1.398	0.389	0.351	0.965	1.192	0.340	0.541	1.291		1.730	0.359
1974	1.329	0.423	0.354	0.956	1.153		0.566	1.232	1.400	1.681	0.355
1975	1.312	0.429	0.374	0.953	1.155		0.582	1.153	1.313	1.656	0.366
1976	1.344	0.434	0.357	0.985	1.190	0.300	0.610	1.092	1.327	1.701	0.389
1977	1.389	0.450	0.388	1.000[a]	1.176	0.319	0.600	1.104	1.351	1.708	0.403
	Growth rates (%)										
1973	6.0	4.4	1.1	12.2	7.0	5.3		6.6		4.6	3.2
1974	-5.0	8.3	0.8	-0.9	-3.4		4.5	-4.6		-2.9	-1.0
1975	-1.3	1.5	5.6	-0.3	0.2		2.8	-6.6	-6.4	-1.5	3.1
1976	2.5	1.2	-4.7	3.2	3.0		4.7	-5.5	1.0	2.6	5.9
1977	3.2	3.6	8.4	1.6	-1.2	6.2	-1.5	1.1	1.8	0.4	3.7
Average annual growth rate 1972–1977 (%)											
	1.1	3.8	2.2	3.2	1.1	-0.3	2.6[b]	-1.8	-0.4	0.7	3.0

[a] Delta (1977) = 1.000.
[b] Computed for 1973–1977.

TABLE 9

Ratio of Revenue and Available Ton-Miles to Employees for Trunk Airlines, 1972–1977, Indexes and Growth Rates[a]

	AM	BR	CN	DL	EA	NA	NW	PA	TW	UN	WE
					Revenue ton–miles index						
1972	1.023	0.878	1.144	0.727	0.755	1.113		1.523	1.137	0.948	0.920
1973	0.994	0.882	1.087	0.825	0.731	1.134	1.469	1.359		1.003	0.954
1974	1.014	0.938	1.066	0.852	0.793		1.617	1.330	1.097	0.985	1.052
1975	1.027	0.967	1.210	0.879	0.828		1.750	1.360	1.099	0.935	1.103
1976	1.134	1.043	1.197	0.936	0.841	1.056	2.008	1.547	1.144	1.051	1.185
1977	1.124	1.101	1.226	1.000	0.922	1.214	2.015	1.600	1.164	1.143	1.304
					Growth rates (%)						
1973	−2.9	0.5	−5.1	12.6	−3.3	1.9		−11.4		5.6	3.6
1974	1.9	6.1	−2.0	3.2	8.2		9.6	−2.2		−1.8	9.8
1975	1.3	3.1	12.7	3.1	4.3		7.9	2.3	0.2	−5.2	4.7
1976	9.8	7.5	−1.1	6.2	1.5		13.8	12.8	4.0	11.7	7.2
1977	−0.8	5.4	2.5	6.6	9.2	13.9	0.3	3.4	1.8	8.4	9.5
				Average annual growth rate 1972–1977 (%)							
	1.9	4.5	1.4	6.4	4.0	1.7	7.9[b]	1.0	0.5	3.7	7.0

Available ton-miles index

Year											
1972	1.160	0.943	1.297	0.819	0.756	1.291	1.930	1.495	1.184	0.992	0.884
1973	1.113	0.949	1.366	0.910	0.747	1.362	1.922	1.355	1.189	1.022	0.932
1974	1.039	1.041	1.167	0.868	0.735			1.309	1.200	0.937	0.982
1975	1.094	1.115	1.278	0.915	0.817		2.085	1.345	1.175	0.924	1.031
1976	1.096	1.183	1.201	0.966	0.804	1.311	2.292	1.443	1.175	0.986	1.119
1977	1.075	1.251	1.218	1.000	0.864	1.451	2.338	1.480	1.179	1.065	1.230
						Growth rates (%)					
1973	−4.1	0.6	5.1	10.4	−1.2	5.3		−9.8		3.0	5.3
1974	−6.9	9.2	−15.7	−4.7	−1.5		−0.4	−3.5		−8.7	5.2
1975	5.2	6.9	9.1	5.3	10.6		8.2	2.8		−1.5	4.9
1976	0.2	5.9	−6.2	5.4	−1.6		9.5	7.0	−2.1	6.5	8.2
1977	−2.0	5.6	1.4	3.4	7.2	10.2	2.0	2.6	0.3	7.7	9.5
Average annual growth rate 1972–1977 (%)	−1.5	5.7	−1.3	4.0	2.7	2.3	4.8[b]	−0.2	−0.1	1.4	6.6

[a] Delta (1977) = 1.000.
[b] Computed for 1973–1977.

TABLE 10

Trunk Carriers Ranked by Revenue Ton-Miles per Employee and Available Ton-Miles per Employee, 1977

| | 1977 RTM/E[a] | | 1977 ATM/E[b] | | 1972–1977 Average annual growth rates | | TFP Rankings | |
| | | | | | | | 1977 | 1972–1977 |
	Rank	Level	Rank	Level	RTM/E	ATM/E	Level	Rate of growth
NW	1	2.015	1	2.338	7.9[c]	4.8	2	2
PA	2	1.600	2	1.480	1.0	−0.2	1	11
WE	3	1.304	5	1.230	7.0	6.6	3	3
CN	4	1.226	6	1.218	1.4	−1.3	5	8
NA	5	1.214	3	1.451	1.7	2.3	7	7
TW	6	1.164	7	1.179	0.5	−0.1	8	10
UN	7	1.143	9	1.065	3.8	1.4	4	4
AM	8	1.124	8	1.075	1.9	−1.5	6	6
BR	9	1.101	4	1.251	4.5	5.7	10	5
DL	10	1.000	10	1.000	6.4	4.0	9	1
EA	11	0.922	11	0.864	4.0	2.7	11	9

[a] RTM/E = revenue ton-miles per employee.
[b] ATM/E = available ton-miles per employee.
[c] Extrapolated at 1973–1977 rate of growth.

There are problems with both the input and output measures used by the CAB. Obviously "employees" provides a very crude measure of total input, but there are also problems with using "ton-miles" as the measure of output. This measure treats first class, coach class, and charter service as equivalent, and it treats ton-miles of freight as equivalent to ton-miles of mail. Furthermore, the use of ton-miles assumes that one freight ton-mile is equivalent in cost to ten passenger-miles. For the trunk carriers as a group in 1977, revenue per ton-mile of freight was only 4.8 times the revenue per coach class passenger-mile. This suggests that freight ton-miles are given far too much weight in the CAB measure of output. In Table 11 we illustrate the carrier-by-carrier deviation between revenue ton-miles and our output index, and between employees and our input index. We find that the deviations quite often fall in the ten to twenty percent range.

5. Analysis of Differences in Productivity

Numerous factors might account for the substantial differences we have found among levels and growth rates of TFP for the trunk carriers. Although it is beyond the scope of this paper to conduct a full study of the structure

TABLE 11

Comparison of Aggregate Output and Aggregate Input with CAB Output and Input Measures[a]

	AM	BR	CN	DL	EA	NA	NW	PA	TW	UN	WE
Revenue ton-miles index/aggregate output index										
1972	1.066	1.044	1.124	0.999	0.989	1.013		1.184	1.074	1.059	0.998
1973	1.051	1.022	1.058	1.016	0.996	1.022	1.133	1.190		1.059	0.994
1974	1.043	1.014	1.087	0.993	0.982		1.134	1.223	1.081	1.055	1.008
1975	1.042	1.011	1.108	0.998	0.993		1.165	1.221	1.058	1.049	1.013
1976	1.051	1.009	1.110	0.995	1.001	1.015	1.173	1.206	1.062	1.049	1.018
1977	1.061	1.014	1.113	1.000	1.001	0.999	1.167	1.196	1.059	1.051	1.026
Available ton-miles index/aggregate output index										
1972	1.208	1.121	1.275	1.126	0.990	1.176		1.163	1.119	1.107	0.960
1973	1.177	1.099	1.329	1.120	1.018	1.228	1.489	1.187		1.080	0.971
1974	1.068	1.126	1.191	1.011	0.910		1.347	1.204	1.173	1.004	0.941
1975	1.110	1.165	1.170	1.039	0.980		1.388	1.208	1.155	1.037	0.947
1976	1.016	1.144	1.114	1.027	0.957	1.259	1.339	1.124	1.091	0.984	0.961
1977	1.014	1.152	1.106	1.000	0.938	1.195	1.354	1.106	1.072	0.979	0.968
Number of employees index/aggregate input index										
1972	0.908	0.916	0.902	1.062	1.051	0.801		0.831	0.898	1.001	0.946
1973	0.914	0.931	0.881	0.991	1.040	0.798	0.707	0.909		0.967	0.947
1974	0.920	0.874	0.906	1.025	1.003		0.691	0.884	0.881	1.010	0.923
1975	0.931	0.846	0.881	1.007	0.985		0.658	0.837	0.884	1.017	0.908
1976	0.911	0.832	0.914	1.003	0.990	0.858	0.624	0.833	0.894	0.995	0.893
1977	0.953	0.831	0.947	1.000	0.970	0.824	0.641	0.829	0.910	0.970	0.866

[a] Delta (1977) = 1.000.

of airline costs, we believe it is worthwhile to carry out some preliminary analysis. We begin by examining the relationships between productivity and three variables—output, average stage length, and load factor—which have been considered important in several previous investigations of airline costs.

In 1977 the largest carrier, United, had an output level that was nearly six times as great as the smallest carrier, National. Furthermore, the rates of growth of output for the trunk carriers over the 1972–1977 period ranged from −1.1% per year for Pan Am, to 8.3% per year for Delta. We investigate the extent to which these differences in size and growth rates are associated with differences in productivity levels and growth rates. In Table 12a we rank the carriers by their 1977 levels of output; in addition we indicate output levels in 1972 and growth of output, 1972–1977. In the last two columns of this table we present the rankings for TFP levels in 1977 and TFP growth rates from 1972 to 1977. The largest carriers do not have the highest productivity—the three largest carriers rank fourth, sixth, and eighth

TABLE 12a

Trunk Carriers Ranked by 1977 Level of Aggregate Output

	Output				Growth of output 1972–1977		TFP rankings 1972–1977	
	1977		1972			Annual	1977	Rate of
	Rank	Level	Rank	Level	Rank	growth (%)	Level	growth
UN	1	1.803	1	1.480	7	3.9	4	4
AM	2	1.403	4	1.148	6	4.0	6	6
TW	3	1.353	2	1.312	10	0.6	8	10
PA	4	1.225	3	1.292	11	−1.1	1	11
EA	5	1.050	5	0.892	8	3.3	11	9
DL	6	1.000	6	0.660	1	8.3	9	1
NW	7	0.664	7	0.461[a]	3	7.3	2	2
WE	8	0.444	9	0.303	2	7.6	3	3
BR	9	0.406	10	0.287	4	7.0	10	5
CN	10	0.405	8	0.319	5	4.8	5	8
NA	11	0.319	11	0.284	9	2.3	7	7

[a] Extrapolated to 1972 at 1973–1977 rate of growth.

in TFP in 1977. Furthermore, the five smallest carriers include three of the five most productive airlines. This indication of no relationship between size and performance is consistent with previous investigations, which have generally accepted the hypothesis of constant returns to scale.[11] On the other hand, there does seem to be some relationship between growth of output and growth of TFP. During the 1972–1977 period, Delta, Western, and Northwest were the leaders in both categories. Furthermore, TWA and Pan Am have shown the lowest growth in both output and TFP.

We summarize the relationships between TFP and output by reporting two bivariate regressions in Table 12b. In these regressions we pool observations across firms and years. The first regression shows a positive but statistically insignificant relationship between natural logarithms of TFP and output. The second regression shows a positive and highly significant relationship between growth of TFP and growth of output.[12]

Previous discussions of the relative performance of individual air carriers have invariably attributed considerable importance to differences in route

[11] There are indications of scale economies for the local service airlines. However, it is generally agreed that the trunk carriers have all achieved sufficient size to have fully exploited scale economies. For example, see Snow [1977].

[12] The bivariate regression of TFP on output can be derived from a specification in which total cost is a function of output and factor prices. A positive coefficient on output corresponds to positive scale economies.

TABLE 12b

Bivariate Regressions of TFP on Output (OP) [a]

$$\ln \text{TFP}_{it} = -0.067 + 0.031 \ln \text{OP}_{it}$$
$$(0.014) \quad (0.020)$$
$$\ln \text{TFP}_{it} - \ln \text{TFP}_{i,t-1} = 0.572(\ln \text{OP}_{it} - \ln \text{OP}_{i,t-1})$$
$$(0.053)$$

[a] Standard errors in parentheses.

structure. The cost of serving differing configurations of city pairs may vary for several reasons, but average stage length (miles between each takeoff and landing) is generally considered the leading indicator of route structure. There is substantial agreement that average cost declines with increasing stage length. For example, **Douglas and Miller [1974, p. 148]** found a highly significant relationship between operating costs per available ton-mile and the log of average stage length.

In Table 13a we present average stage length in 1972 and 1977 and the average annual percentage change in average stage length from 1972 to 1977. There appears to be a fairly strong relationship between TFP level and average stage length. Pan Am was first in both categories in 1977, the three carriers with the shortest average stage length in 1977 were the three

TABLE 13a

Trunk Carriers Ranked by Average Stage Length in 1977

	Average stage length				Growth of average stage length 1972–1977		TFP rankings	
	1977		1972				1977	1972–1977
	Rank	Miles	Rank	Miles	Rank	Annual growth (%)	Level	Rate of growth
PA	1	1410	1	1143	1	4.2	1	11
TW	2	902	2	956	10	−1.2	8	10
AM	3	779	3	731	7	1.3	6	6
UN	4	663	4	708	11	−1.3	4	4
WE	5	645	6	581	4	2.1	3	3
NW	6	637	5	591[a]	5	1.6	2	2
NA	7	582	10	488	2	3.5	7	7
CN	8	581	7	540	6	1.5	5	8
BR	9	554	9	489	3	2.5	10	5
EA	10	519	8	504	9	0.6	11	9
DL	11	446	11	417	8	1.3	9	1

[a] Extrapolated to 1972 at 1973–1977 rate of growth.

TABLE 13b

Bivariate Regressions of TFP on Average Stage Length (ASL) [a]

$$\ln TFP_{it} = -1.147 + 0.165 \ln ASL_{it}$$
$$(0.222) \quad (0.034)$$
$$\ln TFP_{it} - \ln TFP_{i,t-1} = 0.620(\ln ASL_{it} - \ln ASL_{i,t-1})$$
$$(0.258)$$

[a] Standard errors in parentheses.

trunks with the lowest levels of TFP in 1977. There also appears to be a positive, but weaker relationship between growth of TFP and growth of average stage length. The bivariate regressions in Table 13b confirm these impressions.

Finally, we consider the possible relationship between productivity performance and system load factor, which can be taken as an indicator of capacity utilization. The a priori expectation is that higher load factor is associated with higher TFP. In Table 14a we present the trunk carriers' load factors in 1972 and 1977 and their average rates of increase of load factor over this period. Eight carriers had 1977 load factors within the

TABLE 14a

Trunk Carriers Ranked by Passenger Load Factor[a]

	Passenger load factor				Load factor growth 1972–1977		TFP rankings	
	1977		1972				1977	1972–1977 Rate of
	Rank	Level	Rank	Level	Rank	Annual growth (%)	Level	growth
UN	1	0.609	6	0.546	4	2.2	4	4
AM	2	0.597	5	0.548	5	1.7	6	6
TW	3	0.588	4	0.564	7	0.8	8	10
PA	4	0.583	1	0.605	11	−0.8	1	11
WE	5	0.574	3	0.582	9	−0.3	3	3
DL	6	0.572	9	0.503	3	2.6	9	1
EA	7	0.564	2	0.584	10	−0.7	11	9
CN	8	0.559	7	0.533	6	1.0	5	8
BR	9	0.516	8	0.514	8	0.0	10	5
NW	10	0.495	10	0.421[b]	2	3.2	2	2
NA	11	0.475	11	0.393	1	3.8	7	7

[a] Revenue passenger-miles divided by available seat-miles (includes first class, coach, and charter).
[b] Extrapolated to 1972 at 1973–1977 rate of growth.

range 0.55–0.61. The other three carriers had considerably lower load factors, within the range 0.47–0.52. Changes in load factors ranged from −0.8% per year for Pan Am to +3.8% per year for National. There appears to be a clear positive relationship between the rates of growth of TFP and load factors, but not between their levels. The bivariate regressions in Table 14b indicate positive correlations in both cases, but only in the growth rates regression is the relationship statistically significant.

Tables 12–14 indicate positive correlations, of varying degrees of significance, between TFP and output, average stage length, and load factor. The correlations are positive between both levels and growth rates. In the first two columns of Table 15 we report the results of multiple regressions which include all three regressors from Tables 12 a,b–14a,b. In the levels regression we find that output is not significant, and its sign is now negative. The coefficient on average stage length is larger than in the bivariate regression and highly significant. The coefficient on load factor is reduced in size and no longer significant. Thus, average stage length appears to be the only one of the three regressors in the multiple regression with a clear association with the level of TFP.

In the bivariate regressions using growth rates, all three regressors had significant positive coefficients. In the multiple regression, the coefficients of all three regressors are reduced in size; output and load factor retain their statistical significance, but average stage length is not significant. Thus we have a levels regression in which average stage length appears to be the key predictor of TFP, and a growth rates regression in which output and load factor appear to be the key regressors.

The disparity in findings from the levels and growth rates regressions may be reconciled by modifying both analyses to correspond to a general econometric model. Econometricians have recognized (e.g., Mundlak [1961]) that it is important in the analysis of panel data (cross sections of time series) to allow for effects related to each time period and to each cross-section unit. Here these effects represent differences in TFP associated with firms and with time that are not accounted for by differences in output, average stage

TABLE 14b

Bivariate Regressions of TFP on Load Factor (LF)[a]

$$\ln \mathrm{TFP}_{it} = 0.072 + 0.247 \ln \mathrm{LF}_{it}$$
$$(0.083) \quad (0.136)$$
$$\ln \mathrm{TFP}_{it} - \ln \mathrm{TFP}_{i,t-1} = 0.452(\ln \mathrm{LF}_{i,t} - \ln \mathrm{LF}_{i,t-1})$$
$$(0.119)$$

[a] Standard errors in parentheses.

TABLE 15

Multiple Regressions of TFP on Output (OP), Average Stage Length (ASL), and Load Factor (LF) [a]

			Analysis of covariance regressions [Eq. (5)]				
	Levels (1)	Growth rates (2)	Levels (3)	Growth rates (4)	Levels ($\gamma_i = 0$) (5)	Levels CAP index (CAP) included (6)	Growth rates CAP index (CAP) included (7)
α	−1.164 (0.278)	—	0.045 (0.478)	—	−1.092 (0.226)	0.039 (0.475)	—
β_{OP}	−0.029 (0.022)	0.507 (0.060)	0.377 (0.040)	0.457 (0.064)	−0.029 (0.018)	0.424 (0.050)	0.480 (0.067)
β_{ASL}	0.182 (0.040)	0.079 (0.158)	0.028 (0.080)	−0.059 (0.150)	0.176 (0.033)	0.011 (0.080)	−0.088 (0.151)
β_{LF}	0.165 (0.139)	0.219 (0.076)	0.241 (0.067)	0.185 (0.075)	0.071 (0.115)	0.207 (0.069)	0.159 (0.077)
δ_{1972}			−0.049 (0.013)	−0.038 (0.025)	−0.140 (0.029)	−0.049 (0.013)	−0.044 (0.025)
δ_{1973}			−0.068 (0.012)	−0.062 (0.021)	−0.132 (0.029)	−0.068 (0.012)	−0.065 (0.021)
δ_{1974}			−0.061 (0.011)	−0.054 (0.017)	−0.120 (0.029)	−0.059 (0.011)	−0.055 (0.017)
δ_{1975}			−0.048 (0.010)	−0.042 (0.014)	−0.108 (0.029)	−0.046 (0.010)	−0.043 (0.014)
δ_{1976}			−0.023 (0.009)	−0.019 (0.009)	−0.052 (0.028)	−0.020 (0.009)	−0.018 (0.009)
γ_{PA}			−0.024 (0.090)	—	0	−0.020 (0.089)	—
γ_{NW}			0.297 (0.032)	—	0	0.308 (0.032)	—
γ_{WE}			0.394 (0.045)	—	0	0.376 (0.046)	—
γ_{UN}			−0.195 (0.047)	—	0	−0.171 (0.048)	—
γ_{CN}			0.409 (0.041)	—	0	0.396 (0.041)	—
γ_{AM}			−0.130 (0.050)	—	0	−0.117 (0.050)	—
γ_{TW}			−0.123 (0.064)	—	0	−0.106 (0.064)	—
γ_{NA}			0.465 (0.043)	—	0	0.425 (0.050)	—
γ_{BR}			0.283 (0.038)	—	0	0.265 (0.039)	—
γ_{EA}			−0.135 (0.019)	—	0	−0.124 (0.020)	—
β_{CAP}			—	—	—	−0.062 (0.040)	−0.064 (0.051)

[a] Standard errors in parentheses.

length, or load factor. Such effects can be captured by using either fixed or random effects models (see Mundlak [1978]). We specify a fixed-effects model (analysis of covariance):

$$\ln \text{TFP}_{it} = \alpha + \sum_{t=1972}^{1976} \delta_t + \sum_{i=1}^{10} \gamma_i + \beta_{\text{OP}} \ln \text{OP}_{it}$$

$$+ \beta_{\text{ASL}} \ln \text{ASL}_{it} + \beta_{\text{LF}} \ln \text{LF}_{it}, \tag{5}$$

where the δ_t are the effects associated with years prior to 1977, and the γ_i are the effects associated with firms other than Delta. Hence, α represents the intercept for Delta in 1977. The levels regression of (5) is obtained by appending a classical additive disturbance term. The model (5) can also be estimated in growth rate form. We achieve this by differencing (5) and then adding a disturbance term. In the differenced version the γ_i and α drop out of the equation. The results of these two regressions are presented in the third and fourth columns of Table 15.

The growth rates regressions in columns two and four of Table 15 are quite similar. The coefficients on output and load factor have approximately the same size and significance. Growth of average stage length is not significant in either regression. The δ_t indicate differences in level of TFP, for all carriers, between year t and 1977. For example, the level of TFP in 1972 is estimated to be 3.8% below the level in 1977. This regression can be interpreted as explicitly controling for the level of TFP in each year and implicitly controlling for the level of TFP for each carrier.

The level form of (5) in column three of Table 15 provides estimates which are very similar to those of the time-differenced form in column four. This suggests that most of the difference between the first two regressions in Table 15 is due to the fact that the growth rate regression represents a model that implicitly contains firm binary variables while the level regression does not. This is confirmed by the level regression with the γ_i constrained to be zero, which is presented in the fifth column of Table 15. With the firm effects suppressed, the coefficients on OP, ASL, and LF are similar both in size and significance to those of the level regression in column one.

Note that the strong effect of average stage length found by Douglas and Miller [1974, p. 178] was in a regression similar to column five of Table 15. Their dependent variable was total operating costs per available ton-mile, which can be viewed as a proxy for the inverse of TFP. The regressors were average stage length, available ton-miles (a proxy for output), market density, and binary variables for the years 1963–1970. Average stage length had a negative coefficient with a t ratio of 6.7. The output and market density variables were not significant. The similarity of their results and our own is remarkable, especially since the time periods did not overlap. Thus it would not be surprising if including firm binary variables in the Douglas and Miller regression rendered insignificant the coefficient on average stage length.

The analysis of covariance results in the third and fourth columns of Table 15 indicate that over the 1972–1977 period there has only been a modest growth of TFP that cannot be explained by the growth of output and load factor. The estimates of average annual TFP growth not explained by output and load factor growth are 1.0% and 0.8%, respectively, which correspond to the estimates of -0.049 and -0.038 for δ_{1972}.·

The question remains as to why there is such a strong relationship between TFP and output. The set of plausible explanations includes economies resulting from the filling of excess capacity and economies resulting from larger firm size—often referred to as short-run and long-run scale economies, respectively. There is anecdotal evidence that the trunk air carriers had excess capacity to fill in 1972 due to large purchases of jumbo jets. We are not aware of any prior evidence of economies due to firm size.

The significance of load factor in the first two columns of Table 15 tends to confirm that filling of excess capacity is at least a partial explanation for the growth of TFP in the 1972–1977 period. However, load factor does not provide a complete picture of capacity utilization, since it only indicates the utilization of seats on existing flights. Trunk carriers have great latitude in the number of flights they schedule. It is possible that some carriers showed large gains in TFP by scheduling more flights without having to purchase or lease additional flight equipment. If so, we would expect the partial correlation of TFP and aircraft capacity to be negative. We investigate this expectation by rerunning the third and fourth columns of Table 15 with the inclusion of a variable to represent aircraft capacity. We have used the flight equipment index discussed above as the capacity variable.[13] The results are presented in the last two columns of Table 15. The capacity variable (CAP) has the expected negative sign in both the level and time differenced regressions. The inclusion of CAP results in increases in the coefficients on OP and decreases in the coefficients on LF; ASL remains insignificant. The coefficients on the time binary variables change little, but the coefficients on the firm binary variables are generally reduced in absolute value. Although some of these reductions are substantial, there remain large unexplained differences in TFP across the trunk carriers.

The regressions containing a capacity index suggest that filling excess capacity may be an important factor in the performance of the trunk air carriers in the 1972–1977 period. Further research into this possibility and the possibility of economies of firm size would clearly be desirable.

[13] We performed a limited amount of experimentation with other indicators of capacity and obtained similar results.

6.   Summary and Concluding Remarks

We have compared the 11 U.S. trunk air carriers on the basis of levels and rates of growth of outputs, inputs, and total factor productivity. Annual estimates have been presented for the years 1972–1977. We have found wide variations among the carriers for all of these measures. The largest carrier, United, had an output index in 1977 that was nearly six times as large as that of the smallest carrier, National. The most productive and least productive carriers in 1977 were Pan Am and Eastern, respectively. These carriers were similar in size, having the fourth and fifth largest indexes of output, but Pan Am's TFP index was 22% higher than Eastern's. The average annual growth of productivity ranged from a low of 0.7% for Pan Am to a high of 5.2% for Delta.

We have investigated whether the large differences in levels and growth are associated with differences in total output, average stage length, system load factor, and capacity. Contrary to previous studies, we have not found evidence of a statistically significant relationship between average stage length and productivity performance. We have found, however, that TFP is positively related to output and load factor. We have also found weak evidence of a negative relationship between TFP and capacity, which is consistent with the view that the positive relationship between TFP and output results from the filling of excess capacity. We believe that our regression analysis has shed some light on the determinants of TFP in the air-transport industry, but further research is needed.

One interpretation of our results is that the differences in levels of TFP reflect differences in managerial efficiency. This interpretation is consistent with the conclusion of Gordon [1965], who found large differences in cost among the trunk carriers after adjusting for differences in route structure and fleet composition. In fact there is a surprisingly close relationship between Gordon's findings, which were based on data from 1961, and our productivity level rankings. Gordon's estimates indicated that six of the trunks could add more than four points to their rate of return by better control of costs.[14] These six carriers turn out to be those ranked fifth through tenth in level of TFP in 1977. Three of the four carriers that Gordon found to be relatively more efficient are at the top of our rankings—Northwest, Western, and Continental. The exceptional case is Eastern, which Gordon found to have the least to gain from better cost control, but which we found to have the lowest level of productivity in 1977.

Beginning in 1977, regulation of U.S. airlines has been considerably relaxed. President Carter has appointed to the CAB persons who favor a

---

[14] Pan Am was not included in Gordon's study.

larger role for market forces in the air transport industry. In 1978 the passage of the Airline Deregulation Act added the force of law to the movement toward extensive deregulation. These developments appear to have been a leading factor in the surge of output growth by the airlines in 1978 and 1979. Anecdotal evidence indicates that carriers have moved to substantially higher levels of productivity. Such a result is predicted by the regression results we have reported. As data become available, we intend to update our estimates and to study further the relationships among TFP, individual carrier characteristics, and the degree of regulation.

ACKNOWLEDGMENTS

The authors wish to thank Dean Amel, Lynda Borucki, and Judy Todes for proficient research assistance and Gary Chamberlain, John Geweke, and Joe Swanson for helpful discussions. We are also indebted to Jack Calloway, Jerry Coffee, Vida David and her staff, Carl Hintze and Frank Lewis, all of the CAB for access to worksheets and Form 41 reports, and to Jack Cergol of the Airline Pilots Association for discussions of labor practices.

4

Regulation and the Structure of Technology in the Trucking Industry

Ann F. Friedlaender

Department of Economics
Massachusetts Institute of Technology
Cambridge, Massachusetts

Richard H. Spady[†]

Department of Economics
Swarthmore College
Swarthmore, Pennsylvania

S. J. Wang Chiang

Department of Civil Engineering
Massachusetts Institute of Technology
Cambridge, Massachusetts

1. Introduction and Overview

The appropriate form and extent of regulation in the trucking industry is currently a subject of considerable debate. While much of the discussion has focused upon the potential market structure of the trucking industry in a deregulated environment or the impact of deregulation upon the rates and service levels offered to small, rural communities,[1] an equally important subject is the extent to which regulation affects the costs and productivity of firms in this industry. If, for example, it can be demonstrated that current regulatory practices are associated with higher costs or fuel usage than would

[†] Present address: Bell Laboratories, Murray Hill, New Jersey 07974.
[1] See, for example, National Research Council [1978].

exist in their absence, this would indicate that regulation imposes a dead-weight burden upon society. Similarly, if certain regulatory structures are associated with lower measures of total factor productivity than others, it would indicate that such structures may encourage an inefficient utilization of factors and thus lower levels of output and productivity than would exist in their absence. Thus, regardless of the impact of regulation upon market structure and small shippers, it is important to know how regulation affects productivity and the costs of carrying commodities and whether productivity would be higher or trucking costs would be significantly lower in a de-regulated environment.

Although there is a considerable literature on the relationship between regulation and market structure and the relationship between regulation and service to rural shippers,[2] there has been virtually no analysis of the relationship between regulation and trucking costs or productivity. The reason for this difference in analytical effort is relatively clear. The questions of market structure and service to rural shippers are largely linked to questions of scale economies. If the trucking industry is not subject to economies of scale,[3] then regulation should not be needed to ensure competitive markets or competitive treatment with respect to service to shippers in relatively small isolated communities. Thus, by focusing on the question of scale economies, it is possible to answer many questions related to the impact of trucking regulation. In contrast, the link between regulatory restrictions and trucking costs or productivity is considerably less direct. Consequently, whether regulation imposes social costs by encouraging the use of in-efficient techniques is a question that has remained unexplored.

In analyzing the relationship between regulation and trucking costs or productivity, it is important to consider the relationships among factor utilization, operating characteristics, and costs or output. To take the simplest case first, it may be that regulation changes the production possi-bilities sets firms face in some easily characterizable way—the simplest being that the firm produces x percent less output for any combination of inputs. A somewhat more complicated case is where the percentage loss in output

---

[2] See, for example, Friedlaender and Spady [1980]; Roberts [1977].

[3] Or, more precisely, is not a natural multiproduct monopoly; see Baumol [1977a], Baumol *et al.* [1977], Faulhaber [1975], and Sharkey and Telser [1978]. Trucking is certainly a multiple-output industry since a firm generally handles a wide variety of shipments by size and distance. Our inclusion of summary measures of such variables in the cost function is an attempt to model output mix differences without requiring data on shipment distribution by size and distance, which are not available. The errors incurred in such an approach are likely to be small if firms with similar average shipment characteristics have similar shipment mixes.

is a function of the operating characteristics of the firms—for example, the the average length of haul.

These two cases can be usefully modeled as changes in total factor productivity. As we shall see, however, deregulation of the trucking industry brings us to a third case: many firms will presumably produce both new goods (such as special express services) and new combinations of old goods (combining special commodity operations with long-distance general freight, for example, or even simply providing additional services to avoid empty backhauls). While it is conceptually possible to estimate changes in total factor productivity after deregulation, it is unlikely that any estimates of these changes can be made on the basis of currently available data.

The technology of general freight trucking may be substantially altered by deregulation, resulting in increased prices and marginal costs for some services but not others. It is useful to refer to such changes as "cost changes," rather than productivity changes, since firms will not generally be producing easily comparable goods.

Our strategy in this paper is to examine three cross-section samples of common carriers of general commodities; firms in these samples generally carry similar commodities, but differ widely with respect to certain operational characteristics likely to be affected by deregulation. If it is possible to characterize this wide range of carriers by a single technology that takes differences in operating characteristics into account, then it would seem possible to make reasonably confident predictions concerning industry structure after deregulation. For example, it may be that all segments of the industry face increasing returns to scale, or would if, for example, load factor were increased. On the other hand, if we find that even this relatively homogeneous portion of the industry is characterized by very disparate technologies, then evaluation of the effects of deregulation must proceed more cautiously. While we shall be able to characterize the effects of some forms of partial deregulation, the effects of the more radical forms that would allegedly result in major innovations can be at best a matter of informed speculation.

The organization of this paper is as follows: In Section 2 we discuss alternative specifications of the technology of this industry. In Section 3 we then present definitions of the variables entering the neoclassical cost function we have specified and explain the division of relevant U.S. firms into three samples. In Section 4 we discuss difficulties associated with measuring total factor productivity; in Section 5 we discuss the estimated cost function for the three samples and examine the relationship between regulation and trucking costs. In Section 6 we provide a brief summary.

2. The Specification of a Technology for Common Carriers of General Commodities

The trucking industry is highly segmented. In terms of ton-miles, approximately half of the industry is unregulated and comprises the following types of carriers: private carriage; carriage of exempt (primarily agricultural) commodities; and local and intrastate operations. The other half of the industry is regulated by the Interstate Commerce Commission (ICC), which controls rates, routes, entry, and mergers of these carriers. However, the regulated carriers are not homogeneous, and this half of the industry can be divided into two parts. The first consists of carriers whose operations are limited to either a specific commodity (such as household goods, petroleum, and autos) or to specific services for a small number (usually less than 10) of customers. These carriers are almost exclusively engaged in carrying shipments of truckload (TL) size or greater, where a truckload is arbitrarily defined by the ICC as five tons. While they obviously form an important segment of the trucking market because of their specialized nature, wide diversities exist in the type of goods hauled by these carriers and thus in the commodity-specific technologies they employ. Hence it is highly unlikely that a meaningful technology can be described across specialized-commodity carriers.

In contrast, since common carriers of general commodities carry a wide range of manufactured goods in relatively small shipment sizes, there is reason to think that their technology might be relatively homogeneous. In particular, common carriers of general commodities are primarily engaged in less-than-truckload (LTL) activities (on a tonnage basis, roughly one-half of their traffic is LTL) that require labor-intensive consolidation operations in local terminals. These operations of general-commodity carriers present certain technological similarities that one would not expect to find in analyzing the behavior of specialized-commodity truckload carriers who might be variously hauling steel bars or paper towels. Consequently, this paper will focus upon the technology of common carriers of general commodities.

Although all general-commodity carriers are permitted to carry all types of commodities and are characterized by a large amount of LTL activity, they face rigid restrictions concerning routes, gateways, and the geographical areas over which they operate. In addition, they have a "common carrier obligation" to serve all customers requesting service at ICC-approved rates. Consequently, the market environment, output levels, and operating characteristics of these firms are largely determined by the regulatory restrictions under which they operate. Since there are wide differences in the operating authorities granted to these carriers, there are also wide differences in their route structures and operating characteristics with respect to shipment size, length of haul, load factor, and so forth. Hence one of the major questions we shall address in the ensuing analysis is to what extent these carriers, which are generally perceived to have a relatively homogeneous technology, can be characterized by a single technology, or to what extent differences in market environments lead to differences in technology.

In earlier studies (Friedlaender [1978], Spady and Friedlaender [1978]) we found that the failure to model differences in operating characteristics could lead to spurious inferences of economies of scale in this industry, while models incorporating such differences as quality differences in the Fisher–Shell [1972] simple repackaging model not only had significantly higher values for their likelihood functions but also had different implications concerning elasticities of factor substitution and demand. In particular, we found that a neoclassical cost function of the form

$$C = C(y, w) \tag{1}$$

was inferior to the function

$$C = C[\psi(y, t,), w], \tag{2}$$

where y is ton-miles, w a vector of factor prices, t a vector of summary measures of shipment characteristics and load factors, and ψ a function of the form

$$\psi(y, t) = y \cdot \phi(t). \tag{3}$$

A translog functional form was assumed for (1), (2), and $\phi(t)$. In addition, the factor share equations implied by the two models were estimated simultaneously with the cost equations using iterated Zellner efficient estimation, yielding full information maximum likelihood (FIML) estimators if y, t, and w are exogenous. Since shipment characteristics and load factors are determined by route structure and demand conditions, the common carrier obligations and the limited operating rights of these firms make this a realistic assumption.

While the specification given by (2) is clearly superior to (1), the performance of the factor-share equations in this model is, from an informal goodness-of-fit point of view, disappointing; R^2s are uniformly below 0.06. This is not too surprising since (2) implies that the elements of the t vector—shipment characteristics and vehicle load—do not directly affect optimal factor intensities. A generalization of (2), embodying a suggestion of McFadden [1978], is to specify that there is a continuum of technologies, each corresponding to a different value of the t vector and of the usual neoclassical form given by (1). This continuum can be expressed as

$$C = C(y, w; t). \tag{4}$$

Using a translog functional form for (4) yields:

$$\ln C = \alpha_0 + \sum_i \alpha_i \ln w_i + \sum_j \beta_j \ln t_j + \gamma_y \ln y$$

$$+ \frac{1}{2} \sum_i \sum_l A_{il} \ln w_i \ln w_l + \sum_i \sum_j B_{ij} \ln w_i \ln t_j$$

$$+ \sum_i C_{iy} \ln w_i \ln y + \frac{1}{2} \sum_j \sum_m D_{jm} \ln t_j \ln t_m$$

$$+ \sum_j E_{jy} \ln t_j \ln y + \frac{1}{2} F_{yy} (\ln y)^2 + \varepsilon_C, \tag{5}$$

where ε_C represents a disturbance term. Applying Shephard's lemma, the corresponding factor share equations are

$$\frac{w_i x_i}{C} = \alpha_i + \sum_l A_{il} \ln w_l + \sum_j B_{ij} \ln t_j + C_i \ln y + \varepsilon_i, \tag{6}$$

where ε_i is again a disturbance. Note that the effects of shipment characteristics and the load factor on factor *shares* are given by the B_{ij}s.

Our procedure is to estimate Eq. (5) and (6) jointly using FIML and imposing the constraint that $C(y, w, t)$ be homogeneous of degree one in w. This requires that

$$\sum_i \alpha_i = 1, \tag{7a}$$

$$\sum_i A_{il} = 0, \qquad A_{il} = A_{li}, \tag{7b}$$

$$\sum_i B_{ij} = 0, \tag{7c}$$

$$\sum_i C_i = 0. \tag{7d}$$

Imposing homogeneity in w is appropriate even under the approximation interpretation of the translog function since the translog approximation to a homogeneous function is still homogeneous.

3. Sample Construction and Variable Definitions

Although the specification given in (5) and (6) incorporates differences in operating characteristics directly into the cost function, it is important to recognize that interfirm differences in these variables are sufficiently large to suggest that common carriers of general commodities cannot be characterized by a single technology. The most obvious characteristic differentiating these firms is the geographical range of their operations: some firms operate in contiguous portions of only two or three states and perform an essentially local carriage service, while others are truly transcontinental. We therefore divided common carriers of general commodities into three groups according to their geographical operations as defined by the ICC. Specifically, the first sample consists of carriers operating primarily withinin any one of several small subregions of the northeastern and central United States, while the second consists of carriers operating in the much larger subregions of the south and west or across the boundaries of the subregions in the northeast. The third sample consists of interregional and transcontinental carriers. The northeast, regional, and interregional samples include 154, 161, and 47 firms, respectively.[4]

The data for the three samples for which we estimated (5) and (6) are taken from *Trinc's Blue Book of the Trucking Industry* [1973], which summarizes motor carrier reports to the ICC for operations in calendar year 1972. With only minor alterations we employed these data to define the variables entering (5) and (6) as in Spady and Friedlaender [1978].

Total costs for each firm are calculated as ICC operating costs plus a 12% opportunity cost for capital, with the item "carrier operating property—net" (of depreciation) taken as a measure of the quantity of capital. These costs were then divided into four parts—labor costs, fuel expenditures and fuel taxes, purchased transportation, and other expenditures. The last category consists mostly of the imputed opportunity cost of capital, and depreciation and maintenance of capital items; thus, these expenditures were assumed to be payments for capital services.

Firm-specific factor prices for labor and capital were obtained by defining the former as labor costs per employee and the latter as capital service payments per unit of capital. Firm-specific prices for fuel and purchased transportation cannot be calculated, however, since only indirect quantity measures (for example, rented vehicle-miles; but vehicle characteristics vary greatly) are available. Consequently, we estimated regional prices for these factors.[5]

Table 1 presents definitions for the six components of the t vector. The data on terminals are taken from the 1973 edition of *National Highway and Airway Carriers and Routes*.

As average length of haul (ALH) increases, the proportion of costly and labor-intensive pickup, consolidation, and delivery operations falls, so that high values of ALH will be associated with lower costs and small labor

---

[4] See Chiang [1979] for a discussion of their geographical distribution.

[5] See Spady and Friedlaender [1978] for a description of the methodology used to estimate these factor prices. A copy of the estimates will be made available upon request.

TABLE 1

Definitions of Operating Characteristics[a]

t_1 = ALH	Average length of haul, defined as total ton-miles divided by total tons
t_2 = AVLOAD	Average load per vehicle, defined as total ton-miles divided by total vehicle-miles
t_3 = LTL	Percentage of freight in less-than-truckload lots, defined as total LTL tons divided by total tons
t_4 = AVSIZE	Average shipment size, defined as tons per shipment
t_5 = INSURANCE	Unit insurance cost, defined as insurance costs per ton-mile
t_6 = TERMINAL	Terminal density, defined as ton-miles per terminal

[a] Components of the t vector.

shares, ceteris paribus. Similarly, greater vehicle loads, representing operations in traffic lanes of greater density and operating authorities or route structures which are consistent with fewer empty or light backhauls, should be associated with lower costs, although the directions of any deviations from proportional factor reduction are not certain a priori.

The proportion of tons shipped in LTL lots (LTL) and average shipment size (AVSIZE) are both attempts to measure the distribution of shipments by size. In general, one would expect that small average shipment sizes and high LTL proportions would be associated with higher costs and high labor intensities, with other factor intensities shifting so that decreases in shipment size or increases in LTL proportion would have effects in the same direction.

The remaining two components of the t vector—insurance cost per ton-mile and ton-miles per terminal—are not direct measures of shipment characteristics or load factors. Since insurance costs reflect, among other factors, the fragility and value of the transported commodities, we included this variable in an attempt to measure interfirm differences in commodity mix. In some earlier studies this variable was found to influence costs to an extent beyond that which one would expect from its relative importance in total costs (insurance costs are about 1.5% of the total), or from any plausible assessment of the possible bias induced by its inclusion (cf. Spady and Friedlaender [1978, Table 1, p. 167]). However, we find below that in the specification represented by Eq. (5), this variable is without substantial effect.

The rationale for including ton-miles per terminal as an exogeneous operating characteristic is also less than clearcut. On the one hand, it is evident that costs are affected by route network configurations and by traffic density, which are partially captured by this variable. On the other hand, however, since we estimate a long-run cost function, the number of terminals is presumably under the control of the firm and hence is not an exogenous variable. Nevertheless, it seems useful to include this variable on balance since it is important to incorporate some measure of network density into the analysis.

In constructing the samples used in this analysis, we found that not all of the firms listed in Trinc's could be included. About half, for example, were not required by the ICC to report all the information necessary to calculate the t-vector data. In addition, during the sample period, the ICC did not require consolidated reports from wholly owned subsidiaries. Thus it was necessary to limit our samples to firms that met the following four conditions:

(1)   They purchased some of all four factors, but no more than 10% of their costs was for purchased transportation. (The first restriction affects firms reporting either no fuel or no purchased transportation costs; a firm reporting no purchased transportation is probably not in a long-run cost-minimizing position. Firms that rent most of their vehicles do so from subsidiaries set up for tax and regulatory purposes. Due to an ICC ruling allowing the deduction of such expenses as current costs, a firm that establishes such a subsidiary can artifically lower its operating ratio, which was a primary regulatory target in the early 1970s. Subsequent ICC rulings required that the operations of such subsidiaries be reported.)

(2)   They reported an average salary of $8000/year or more per employee. (Some firms implicitly reported salaries as low as $2000, presumably because they counted owner/operators whose trucks they rented as employees, even though they did not directly pay them any wages.)

(3)   They had a calculated price of capital of less than 10.[6] [Due to reasons related to (1) above, a few carriers report almost no operating property, as it is presumably owned by subsidiaries. Note that carrier

---

[6] The price of capital has been calculated as expenditures for capital services divided by book value, net of depreciation, of carrier operating property. This price is certainly subject to considerable measurement error, since the data are insufficiently detailed to separate nonfuel material expenditures (pencils, etc.) from capital maintenance expenditures (truck parts, etc.). Moreover, carrier operating property net is probably a poor measure of capital services, and, for the reason given in the text, possibly underreported. To deal at least with the last problem, our rule is to exclude calculated "prices" that fall very far away from typical values. The rule of excluding observations with values over 10 is equivalent to excluding values over eight standard deviations from the (final) sample mean since the mean is about 2 and the standard deviation 1 for each sample. While this is obviously a rough procedure, it seems no worse than its dual, which is to subtract capital costs including maintenance from total costs to obtain variable costs, and to include carrier operating property net as a capital measure in a short-run cost function.

For a consideration of the biases introduced by measurement error in the factor prices, see Spady and Friedlaender [1978, footnote 13].

operating property is the value of the property that the firm owns, *not* its equity in that property.

(4) They had no other "obvious" error in the data. (For instance, one firm reported an average load of 92 tons.)

4. Trucking Costs and Total Factor Productivity

In terms of policy, a crucial issue is whether regulation encourages trucking firms to adopt a form of organization that is inherently inefficient, i.e., with a lower level of total factor productivity than would exist in a deregulated environment. Thus if it could be demonstrated that regulated firms had higher costs or lower levels of output than unregulated firms for given technology, factor inputs, factor prices, and operating characteristics, one could conclude that regulation fosters inefficiency.

Unfortunately, however, while there is an abundance of data on the regulated sector of the trucking industry, no data exist for the costs of operations for the unregulated sectors of the industry. Thus it is impossible to make direct comparisons between the regulated and unregulated sectors of the industry.

Nevertheless, as we have previously indicated, regulated trucking firms are subject to wide differences in the route and commodity restrictions under which they must operate. This suggests that it may be possible to determine whether productivity is higher or lower in certain kinds of regulatory environments. Suppose, for example, that the regulated trucking industry could be segmented into type "A" and type "B" carriers, whose technology could be characterized by the cost function

$$C^i(y, w, t, T) = g^i(T)C(y, w; t), \qquad i = A, B. \tag{8}$$

That is, the technologies of the two types of carriers are identical except for a multiplicative constant representing a pure productivity effect.

If (8) holds, then we can be reasonably confident that the technology embodied in the common cost function $C(y, w; t)$ will hold over a wide variety of operating conditions, and thus would (we hope) also hold after deregulation which effects changes in the t vector. Moreover, the $g^i(T)$s can be interpreted as (Hicks-neutral) productivity effects induced by differences in regulatory environments.

On the other hand, if (8) can be decisively rejected on the basis of the data, little inference could be drawn concerning differences in aggregate efficiency between the two segments. While one segment might have lower costs for identical outputs, input prices, and operating characteristics, it would be impossible to ascribe these differences to differences in market or regulatory environments as long as the technologies are different. To ascribe such cost differentials to regulation would be akin to comparing trucking costs to barge costs and arguing that since barges are largely deregulated and have lower costs, trucking costs would fall in the advent of regulation.

This indicates that a crucial question to resolve is whether different segments of the trucking market have identical or separate technologies. If the three different types of general commodity carriers do indeed have a common technology, it should be possible to estimate differences in aggregate efficiency among these market segments, which could then be used to draw inferences concerning the impact of different regulatory environments upon aggregate efficiency.[7]

Unfortunately, however, there is reason to suspect that these market segments do have different technologies. The northeast carriers are mostly firms that were in existence when trucking regulation was first instituted in 1935. These carriers are largely geared to relatively short-haul, high-density service. In contrast, the regional carriers tend to be carriers in the south and west, whose operating authorities cover wider, more dispersed geographical areas. Finally, the interregional carriers have operating authorities that are transcontinental in scope.

In view of these differences in operating authorities, one would expect to find wide differences in operating characteristics and organization. These are shown in Table 2. Indeed, while the northeast carriers have a mean average length of haul of 120 miles and an average load of 7.5 tons, the transcontinental carriers have an average length of haul of 674 miles and an average load of 14.7 tons. Associated with these differences in operating characteristics are concomitant differences in output: the average ton-miles of carriers in the northeast is 21.0 million while that of the interregional carriers is 931.6 million. In view of such differences in operations and the scale of output, it would be surprising to find that technology was homogeneous across these types of carriers.

To examine the question of technological differences, we have estimated the equations represented by (5) and (6) jointly using FIML methods. This requires deleting one factor share equation, since the disturbances of the factor share equations sum to zero and thus have a singular covariance matrix; FIML is invariant to the equation dropped (see Barten [1969] or Berndt and Savin [1975]). In this context, imposition of (7a)–(7d) is easily achieved by choosing the price of the factor whose equation is deleted as

---

[7] In principle, this analysis could also be extended to include specialized-commodity carriers. Since, however, specialized-commodity carriers perform truckload services and thus do not engage in consolidation or terminal activities, their technology is different from those of general-commodity carriers. Thus no comparisons can be made between the aggregate efficiency of truckload and LTL carriers.

TABLE 2

Means and Standard Deviations for Costs, Revenues, and Ton-Miles for Common Carriers of General Commodities, by Type of Carrier

Variable	Abbreviation	Unit	Northeast		Regionals		Interregionals	
			Mean	Standard deviation	Mean	Standard deviation	Mean	Standard deviation
Average length of haul	ALH	miles	120.014	65.0765	185.566	94.044	673.957	284.170
Average load per vehicle	AVLOAD	tons	7.5316	3.3825	10.0812	3.1381	14.6831	2.6325
Proportion of freight in LTL lots	LTL	LTL ton/total tons	0.4829	0.1988	0.5109	0.1733	0.3657	0.1234
Average shipment size	AVSIZE	tons/shipment	1.2783	1.4102	0.8837	0.7028	1.3378	1.9265
Insurance	INSUR	insurance cost/ton-mile	0.0035	0.0038	0.0025	0.0018	0.0009	0.0004
Ton-miles per terminal	TERMINAL	ton-miles/no. of terminals	na	na	na	na	18209.8	15923.9
Ton-miles	TM	millions	20.955	30.708	57.241	86.751	931.628	1010.780
Total cost	TCOST	$ millions	4.198	4.584	8.090	10.169	68.449	72.673
Revenues	REV	$ millions	4.418	4.873	8.787	11.397	72.928	79.363
Number of firms			154		161		47	

numéraire; the coefficients on the terms containing this factor's price can then be calculated from (7a)–(7d).

In addidion, to make our results easier to interpret, we have standardized each variable to have a mean value of 1.0; that is, we have divided the raw measure of each variable in each sample by its sample arithmetic mean. In the approximation interpretation of the translog function, this standardization is equivalent to taking the sample mean of (y, w, t) as the point of approximation.

When all coefficients in (5) and (6) are estimated, this standardization does not affect the results. If ton-miles/terminal is included in the vector of operating characteristics, there are 66 coefficients to be simultaneously estimated after (7a)–(7d) are imposed by normalization; since there are 154 and 161 firms, respectively, in the northeast and regional samples, this poses no problem.

However, there are only 47 firms in the interregional sample. This situation is not as bad as it first appears, however, since 30 of the coefficients appear in at least one factor share equation, leaving 47 observations of the cost function to estimate the 36 coefficients that appear only in the cost function. However, since this leaves just 11 degrees of freedom for an estimation method whose desirable properties are only asymptotic, we decided to impose as a priori restrictions on Eq. (5) the additional coefficient restriction

$$D_{jm} = 0, \qquad j, m = 1, \ldots, 6, \tag{9}$$

that is, that the coefficients on terms of the form $\ln t_j \ln t_m$ be constrained to zero. This eliminates 21 coefficients that appear only in the cost equation, leaving effectively 32 degrees of freedom for the remaining 15 coefficients. One way of viewing (5) with (9) imposed is:

$$\ln C(y, w; t) = \ln g(t; y, w) + \ln h(y, w), \tag{10}$$

where $h(y, w)$ is a neoclassical cost function and $g(t; y, w)$ is Cobb–Douglas for given y and w and homogeneous of degree zero in w. While estimating (5) with (9) imposed no longer provides a second-order approximation to an arbitrary $C(y, w; t)$, it is equivalent to specifying (10) with a translog functional form for $h(y, w)$. Thus (10) retains the advantage of modeling the effect of t on costs and factor shares, although it means sacrificing some of the flexibility of the general translog function.

Since the TERMINAL variable is available on a reliable basis only for the interregionals, the "best" model for this sample cannot be estimated for the other two samples. Thus, for the purpose of testing whether (5) can be restricted to (8), that is, whether the three samples can be described by a common cost function except for a disembodied productivity effect, we estimated the model given by (5) using the five common components of the

TABLE 3

Logs of Likelihood Functions for Five-Component t-Vector Models

Sample	Log of likelihood function
Northeast	1208.497
Regional	1251.433
Interregionals	420.458
Total	2880.388
Pooled: all samples[a]	2604.291
Pooled: regionals and northeast	2393.094

Test 1: all samples can be pooled:
$$2(2880.388 - 2604.291) = 552.356 = \chi^2(128 \text{ d.f.})$$
Test 2: northeast and regionals can be pooled:
$$2(2459.930 - 2393.094) = 131.980 = \chi^2(64 \text{ d.f.})$$

[a] Different intercepts estimated for different samples.

t vector. Note that we do not impose the restriction $D_{jm} = 0$ on the interregional sample at this point.

Table 3 presents the likelihood-function values and shows that not only is the hypothesis that (8) holds for all three samples rejected, but the hypothesis that the regional and northeast samples can be adequately described by (8) is also rejected (at the 0.005 level).[8] Possibly in view of the strong restrictions implied by (8) this is not surprising, but it does indicate that simple models do not adequately represent the differences between even the relatively similar northeast and regional carriers. Moreover, a detailed examination of the results suggests no simple alternative to (8).

Thus we are left with the rather unfortunate conclusion that regulated trucking firms operating under different regulatory environments are organized in such a way as to engender different technologies. But if technologies are different, comparisons of aggregate efficiency cannot be made. Thus while the types of carriers show wide differences in costs, these differences cannot be ascribed to differences in regulation per se.

---

[8] Note that the estimated productivity difference between samples when (8) is imposed is less than 2% and has t statistic of less than 1 in all cases.

5.   Regulation and Carrier Costs

While we cannot confidently attribute cost differences among the different types of general commodity carriers to differences in their regulatory environments, it is nevertheless possible to assess the probable impact of changes in regulatory practices upon the costs of each type of carrier and show that costs would generally be lower if regulatory restrictions were reduced. In this section we therefore analyze the estimated cost structure of the three types of carriers and consider the impact that relaxing regulation may have upon carrier costs.

It is important to note, however, that considerable caution should be used in any analysis that relates regulation to trucking costs. This is true for several reasons. First, while it is likely that regulation has a decided impact upon the operating characteristics of trucking firms, it is unclear how this impact can be quantified. Thus whether an elimination of all route, commodity, and backhaul restrictions would lead to a 5, 10, or 50% increase in average load or average length of haul is unknown. Consequently, although it is possible to quantify the impact of changing operating conditions upon costs, it is impossible to relate these changes directly to changes in the regulatory environment. Second, wide differences exist in the structure of technology within the regulated trucking industry. Hence changes in operating characteristics will have widely differing impacts on different types of carriers, making it difficult to characterize the relationships between costs and operating characteristics that exist within the industry. Third, even within segments of the industry that can be characterized by a common technology, significant nonseparabilities exist with respect to operating characteristics, output, and factor utilization. Hence while it is possible to estimate the impact upon costs of changing, say, the average load for a given type of carrier facing given factor prices, producing at a given output level, and having given other operating characteristics, it is not generally possible to characterize the impact of this change upon all firms in this segment of the trucking industry or upon the trucking industry per se. Consequently, generalizations about the relationship between regulation, operating characteristics, and trucking costs or productivity cannot generally be made.

Nevertheless, by using the generalized cost functions embodied in Eqs. (5) and (10), which include operating characteristics in addition to the conventional arguments of factor prices and output, it is possible to obtain some insights into the quantitative relationships between costs and operating characteristics. To the extent that some of these characteristics should be related to regulatory practices, it is then possible to obtain some insights into the impact of regulation upon trucking costs.

The estimated cost functions for each of the three trucking samples are given in the Appendix. In what follows we concentrate upon the impact of operating characteristics upon costs, scale economies, and factor utilization, drawing upon the empirical results shown in Tables A1 and A2 in the Appendix.

5.1 The Relation between Costs
and Operating Characteristics

Since the technology specified by Eqs. (5) or (10) is nonhomothetic, global characterization of the relationship between costs and operating characteristics is not generally possible. Thus changes in costs with respect to operating characteristics will usually differ depending upon the level of factor prices, output, and/or other variables. The elasticity of costs with respect to operating characteristics can be given by

$$\frac{\partial \ln C}{\partial \ln t_i} = \beta_i + \sum_j B_{ji} \ln w_i + \sum_j D_{ji} \ln t_i + E_{i1} \ln y. \tag{11}$$

At mean factor prices, operating characteristics, and output levels, $\partial \ln C / \partial \ln t_i = \beta_i$. Hence the linear terms associated with operating characteristics reflect the elasticity of costs with respect to output for a "typical" firm, i.e., a firm operating at the mean. These are given in Table 4 and indicate that rather substantial cost reductions could occur with increase in average length of haul, average load, or average shipment size. The coefficients on these three characteristics are consistently of the expected sign and statistically significant, and relatively large. Thus a 10% increase in average load would reduce costs of the "typical" northeast, regional, and interregional carrier by 4.9, 2.3, and 5.8%, respectively. Somewhat higher cost reduction would be associated with increase in average length of haul and in average shipment size except in the case of northeast carriers.

In contrast, the direct effect of the other operating characteristics on costs is generally ambiguous or weak. The insurance variable is clearly insignificant, while LTL is significant and of the expected sign only in the northeast sample. Given the substantial effects of AVSIZE, it may be that this variable captures most of the total impact on costs of small shipment traffic.

In terms of regulatory policy, it is likely that average load is the operating characteristic most affected by current route and commodity restrictions. The operating authorities granted to carriers of general commodities are typically quite flexible with respect to commodities, but extremely rigid with respect to the routes and cities that can be served. Thus, for example, a

TABLE 4

Elasticity of Costs with Respect to Operating Characteristics at Mean Factor Prices, Operating Characteristics, and Output Levels

Coefficient	Variable	Northeast carriers		Regional carriers		Interregional carriers	
		Value	Standard error	Value	Standard error	Value	Standard error
β_1	t_1 (ALH)	−0.5112	0.0862	−0.6220	0.0706	−0.3804	0.1055
β_2	t_2 (AVLOAD)	−0.4897	0.0959	−0.2338	0.0893	−0.5799	0.2300
β_3	t_3 (LTL)	0.3327	0.1431	0.0140	0.1403	−0.1434	0.1506
β_4	t_4 (AVSIZE)	−0.2483	0.0931	−0.2656	0.0725	−0.4480	0.1648
β_5	t_5 (INSUR)	0.0074	0.0550	0.0244	0.0501	−0.0758	0.0808
β_6	t_6 (TERMINAL)	—	—	—	—	−0.0311	0.0766

firm operating in the northeast can have the authority to carry goods between Philadelphia and Buffalo, but not between Syracuse and either of these points. Consequently, trucking firms often are forced to use partially empty backhauls and to ship goods in lots that do not represent the full capacity of the vehicle. Thus if regulatory restriction on operating authorities were relaxed, it is likely that trucking firms could achieve higher loads and better use of equipment.

It is uncertain whether regulatory changes would affect other variables. Trucking firms clearly obtain large economies by using large shipment sizes and long lengths of haul. Thus in the absence of regulation, it is possible that trucking firms would tend to change their operations toward shippers who use larger shipment sizes and longer lengths of haul. Since, however, such changes in operations might reduce services to shippers who require small shipment sizes or shorter lengths of haul, it is not clear that these changes would represent a net gain to society. In contrast, increased use of backhauls and the resulting increases in average loads represent a clear social saving. We shall therefore address the cost savings that could arise from increased average loads.

While it is likely that regulation will cause average load to be lower than it would be otherwise, it is impossible to determine by how much all operating characteristics would change if all regulatory restrictions were removed. Consequently it seems useful to estimate the cost savings that could accrue if these characteristics were increased by 5, 10, and 20%, respectively. In performing this analysis, however, it is important to note that significant nonhomotheticities exist with respect to output, operating characteristics, and factor prices (cf. the Appendix). Hence characterizing the impact of operating characteristics upon the "typical" firm operating at mean values of the variables may not give a very accurate picture of these impacts for the range of firms within each sample. We have therefore analyzed the impact of increase in average load for carriers in each sample operating at different output levels and used weighted (by ton-miles) mean values of the other variables.

Table 5 presents the impact of an increase in average load on the costs of the "weighted-mean" firm in each sample and indicates a systematic tendency for small firms to obtain larger cost savings in percentage terms than large firms, whatever the type of carrier. Nevertheless, fairly wide variations exist in the response of different types of carriers to changes in these characteristics.

The costs of the northeast and regional carriers are, over the relevant range for each (5–200 and 5–500 million ton-miles, respectively), roughly equally responsive to changes in average load. The major difference is that the response of the northeast carriers is fairly insensitive to firm size, while the response of the regionals appears to be substantially greater among small

TABLE 5

Impact of Increase in Average Load on Cost of Weighted-Mean Trucking Firm, by Type of Carrier

Output (millions of ton-miles)	Northeastern				Regionals				Interregionals			
	Cost ($ thousands)	% Change in costs, AVLOAD increase of:			Cost ($ thousands)	% Change in costs, AVLOAD increase of:			Cost ($ thousands)	% Change in costs, AVLOAD increase of:		
		5%	10%	20%		5%	10%	20%		5%	10%	20%
5	648.74	−2.19	−4.07	−7.06	600.86	−3.43	−6.61	−12.30	144.26	−8.96	−16.76	−29.59
10	1348.59	−2.15	−3.99	−6.91	1158.04	−2.90	−5.61	−10.51	382.78	−8.16	−15.32	−27.24
20	2837.08	−2.11	−3.91	−6.76	2289.81	−2.38	−4.60	−8.67	973.64	−7.35	−13.85	−24.81
30	4407.70	−2.08	−3.86	−6.68	3452.63	−2.07	−4.01	−7.58	1648.38	−6.87	−12.98	−23.35
40	6040.12	−2.07	−3.83	−6.61	4645.17	−1.85	−3.59	−6.80	2374.03	−6.53	−12.35	−22.30
50	7723.19	−2.05	−3.80	−6.56	5864.98	−1.67	−3.26	−6.19	3134.70	−6.26	−11.87	−21.47
100	16704.11	−2.01	−3.72	−6.41	12307.77	−1.14	−2.23	−4.27	7228.10	−5.43	−10.34	−18.84
150	26375.72	−1.98	−3.67	−6.32	19215.19	−0.82	−1.62	−3.13	11554.65	−4.95	−9.43	−17.27
200	36562.30	−1.97	−3.64	−6.26	26498.39	−0.60	−1.19	−2.31	15977.14	−4.60	−8.79	−16.13
250	47169.32	−1.95	−3.61	−6.21	34103.75	−0.43	−0.85	−1.67	20440.42	−4.33	−8.28	−15.24
300	58136.19	−1.94	−3.59	−6.17	41994.63	−0.29	−0.57	−1.15	24917.01	−4.11	−7.86	−14.50
400	80989.21	−1.93	−3.56	−6.11	58531.13	−0.06	−0.13	−0.31	33854.84	−3.76	−7.20	−13.33
500	104887.10	−1.91	−3.53	−6.06	75954.21	0.11	0.21	0.34	42727.09	−3.48	−6.69	−12.40
750	168323.03	−1.89	−3.48	−5.97	122780.88	0.43	0.83	1.54	64492.35	−2.98	−5.75	−10.70
1000	236030.49	−1.87	−3.45	−5.91	173551.72	0.66	1.28	2.40	85617.73	−2.63	−5.07	−9.48
1500	381436.13	−1.84	−3.40	−5.82	284784.89	0.98	1.91	3.62	126076.08	−2.13	−4.11	−7.72
2000	537523.90	−1.83	−3.37	−5.76	406849.17	1.21	2.36	4.50	164464.04	−1.77	−3.43	−6.45
3000	874749.51	−1.80	−3.32	−5.67	677689.19	1.53	2.99	5.74	236267.55	−1.26	−2.45	−4.63
3500	1053785.63	−1.79	−3.30	−5.63	824663.62	1.65	3.23	6.22	270129.31	−1.07	−2.08	−3.93
4000	1238828.09	−1.78	−3.29	−5.61	978510.20	1.76	3.45	6.64	302848.27	−0.90	−1.75	−3.23

firms. In fact, for large regional carriers (over 400 million ton-miles), it appears that there would be no cost savings. (Since the largest carrier in the regional sample is at 635 million ton-miles, the *increases* in cost estimated for large hypothetical regional carriers should be disregarded, because such firms could presumably always choose to operate with current load factors.)

The effect of average load on costs among the interregionals varies widely by firm size. For example, small interregional carriers with an output level of 300 million ton-miles would enjoy cost reductions of 14.5% if average load increased by 20%, while large interregional carriers with an output of 2 billion ton-miles would only enjoy cost reductions of 6.5% under similar increases in average load. In contrast, a 20% increase in average load would reduce the costs of the northeast carriers by about 6% regardless of the size of the firm.

Thus to the extent that relaxation of regulatory restrictions would lead to increases in average load, it appears that small carriers within any market segment would enjoy differential cost reductions, but that the interregional carriers would enjoy relatively more benefits than regional or northeast carriers. To the extent that current regulatory restrictions particularly limit the operations of small firms operating in small geographical areas, deregulation will result in relatively greater increases in average load for such firms with consequent additional cost reductions.

In conclusion then, it appears that fairly substantial cost reductions could accrue from a relaxation of route or commodity restrictions that would lead to an increase in average load. While it is of course impossible to predict the precise change in these variables that would be occasioned by deregulation, an increase in average load of 10% would appear to be relatively modest. Such an increase could lead to cost reductions of about 4% among the northeast carriers, and ranging from 0 to 6% among the regional carriers and from 2 to 10% among the interregional carriers.[9] Larger increases in this variable would lead to concomitant cost reductions. Thus it appears that route and commodity restrictions that prevent full use of equipment cause trucking costs to be significantly higher than they would be if these regulations were relaxed.

5.2 Regulation, Operating Characteristics, and Returns to Scale

Since the technology specified by (5) is nonhomothetic even for fixed operating characteristics, global characterization of returns to scale is not possible. A good local measure of returns to scale which generalizes to the

---

[9] Note that the largest northeast carrier had an output of approximately 200 million ton-miles while the largest regional carrier had an output of approximately 700 million ton-miles.

multiple-output case (see Panzar and Willig [1977]) is the elasticity of cost with respect to output, $\partial \ln C / \partial \ln y$. From (5), this is given by

$$\frac{\partial \ln C}{\partial \ln y} = \gamma_y + \sum_i C_{iy} \ln w_i + \sum_j E_{jy} \ln t_j + F_{yy} \ln y. \qquad (12)$$

Thus local returns to scale depend not only on factor prices but also on technological conditions.

At mean factor prices, operating conditions, and output levels, $\partial \ln C / \partial \ln y = \gamma_y$; our estimates (standard errors) of γ_y are 1.0864 (0.0376), 1.0759 (0.0273), and 0.8969 (0.0501) for the northeastern, regional, and interregional carriers, respectively. Thus, a hypothetical firm with sample mean characteristics faces declining returns to scale for the northeastern and regional samples, and increasing returns to scale in the interregional sample.

Table 6 presents estimates of the E_{jy}'s and F_{yy} for the three samples. While the positive values of F_{yy} for the northeast and regional samples indicate (asymmetric) U-shaped average cost curves, the negative value of F_{yy} for the interregionals indicates an inverse-U-shaped average cost curve. Moreover, since γ_y is less than one by a statistically significant margin, it would seem

TABLE 6

Estimated Cost Elasticities at Mean Factor Prices, by Type of Carrier, 1972[a]

Parameter	Region		
	Northeast	Regional	Interregional
γ_y	1.0864	1.0759	0.8969
	(0.0376)	(0.0273)	(0.0501)
E_{1y}(ln ALH)	0.0365	−0.0467	−0.0932
	(0.0504)	(0.0606)	(0.0600)
E_{2y}(ln AVLOAD)	0.0128	0.1604	0.2602
	(0.0562)	(0.0705)	(0.0957)
E_{3y}(ln LTL)	0.1434	0.0681	−0.2664
	(0.0679)	(0.0722)	(0.0819)
E_{4y}(ln AVSIZE)	0.0014	0.0086	−0.3223
	(0.0447)	(0.0454)	(0.0868)
E_{5y}(ln INSUR)	0.0035	0.0388	−0.0413
	(0.0271)	(0.0283)	(0.0581)
E_{6y}(ln TERMINAL)	—	—	0.0990
			(0.0338)
F_{yy}(ln y)	0.0248	0.0533	−0.0880
	(0.0347)	(0.0256)	(0.0320)

[a] Standard errors are in parentheses.

that the interregionals face increasing returns to scale. However, this is not so for two reasons.

First, no firm in the sample corresponds (paradoxically) very closely to the hypothetical firm of the sample mean: when $\partial \ln C/\partial \ln y$ is calculated for each firm, only 14 of 47 have values less than one. Furthermore, of these 14, 6 fall between 0.95 and 1.0, 6 between 0.90 and 0.95, and 2 between 0.87 and 0.90; also, only 1 falls more than two estimated standard errors below 1.0, and 6 fall within one estimated standard error of 1.0. Thus the hypothesis of constant returns to scale cannot be rejected for the overwhelming majority of the sample.

Second, the role of the TERMINAL variable is ambiguous. In at least the "quasi long run" in which terminals are fixed, an increase in ton-miles also increases ton-miles/terminal, which in turn increases costs at the sample mean. Thus in the "medium run" $\partial \ln C/\partial \ln y = \gamma_y + E_{6y} = 0.8969 + 0.0990 = 0.9959$ at the sample mean.

Although the question of the existence of economies of scale cannot be totally resolved for the interregional carriers, the econometric evidence presented in Table 6 clearly indicates that northeast and regional carriers are not subject to increasing returns to scale. Thus on balance, it seems reasonable to conclude that the possibility of scale economies is generally unlikely in the common carrier trucking market.

The effects of factor prices on $\partial \ln C/\partial \ln y$, though generally statistically significant, are minor. The largest and most consistent of these effects in the three samples is that of wages: high-wage firms have high values of $\partial \ln C/\partial \ln y$, that is, $C_{1y} > 0$. In the interregional sample, for example, $C_{1y} = 0.0220 \ (0.0061)$, so that a wage rate 20% above the sample mean increases $\partial \ln C/\partial \ln y$ by 0.004. Thus we can effectively ignore the impact of factor prices on economies of scale.

While the previous discussion indicated that increases in average load reduced costs for all types of carriers, note that such increases generally serve to increase the elasticity of cost with respect to output. This means that increases in average load will, ceteris paribus, tend to make trucking firms more subject to decreasing returns to scale. Thus changes in the regulatory environment that led to increases in average load would also tend to make the cost structure of the interregional carriers more competitive, thus negating a commonly cited rationale for regulation.

5.3   Elasticities of Factor Substitution and Demand

Table 7 presents estimated Allen–Uzawa partial elasticities of substitution and elasticities of demand at the sample mean for each of the three samples.[10]

[10] Neoclassical production theory requires that $C(y, w; t)$ be concave in w for all y and t. In the approximation interpretation of the translog function, the properties of the underlying

TABLE 7

Factor Demand Elasticities and Allen–Uzawa Partial Elasticities of Substitution, by Type of Carrier

	Labor	Fuel	Capital	Purchased transportation
		Northeast carriers		
Labor	—	−0.1715	0.9309	1.4606
		(0.2166)	(0.0396)	(0.6481)
Fuel		—	0.1510	4.3218
			(0.1137)	(3.1307)
Capital			—	1.3452
				(0.4686)
Own price elasticity	−0.3552	−0.0960	−0.6011	−1.4871
	(0.0271)	(0.1527)	(0.0244)	(0.3958)
		Regional carriers		
Labor	—	−0.0137	0.9023	0.0718
		(0.1584)	(0.0363)	(0.5282)
Fuel		—	0.3430	−0.1367
			(0.0947)	(2.2702)
Capital			—	1.2317
				(0.3589)
Own price elasticity	−0.2960	−0.0987	−0.5946	−0.4378
	(0.0247)	(0.1006)	(0.0221)	(0.3031)
		Interregionals		
Labor	—	0.5419	0.9405	−0.1226
		(0.2621)	(0.0433)	(0.5753)
Fuel		—	0.3188	−0.1770
			(0.0917)	(0.9586)
Capital			—	3.2215
				(0.8716)
Own price elasticity	−0.3091	−0.3995	−0.7510	−0.8849
	(0.0366)	(0.1671)	(0.0262)	(0.3383)

function are generally only preserved at the point of approximation, which in our case is the sample mean. The estimated cost functions are concave at the point of approximation for all three samples. Moreover, concavity holds for nearly all points in the samples. Upon examination we found that the exceptions consisted entirely of observations for which the estimated elasticity of fuel demand was greater than −0.05. Since, heuristically, the violation of the concavity condition occurs when elasticities of substitution are large (in absolute value) compared to elasticities of demand, it seems appropriate to view these violations as benign given the plausibility of the estimate of the fuel demand elasticity and the comparatively large estimates of the standard errors of the relevant elasticities of substitution.

The estimated elasticities of Table 7 in general accord with prior expectations. Capital and purchased transportation are substitutes in all three samples. Purchased transportation is also a substitute for labor and fuel in the northeastern sample (although the estimated standard errors are relatively large), but not in the other samples; these differences may arise from the fact that rented vehicles may or may not include fuel and/or driver. Labor and capital have an elasticity of substitution of approximately one in all three samples, while the elasticity of fuel–labor substitution is roughly zero for the northeast and regional carriers. The apparent substitutability of fuel for labor among the interregionals is a paradox unless large vehicles are fuel-inefficient and firms substitute heavily loaded large vehicles for small vehicles as driver wages increase. The comparatively "high" elasticity of demand for fuel among the interregionals probably derives from the long-haul nature of their operations. The elasticities of demand for labor and capital are roughly the same in all three samples, while the variations in the demand elasticity of purchased transportation may derive from differences in its composition as outlined above, or from defects in the procedure used to estimate its price.

The elasticity of demand for factor i with respect to technological condition j at the sample mean is given by

$$\beta_j + B_{ij}/\alpha_i; \tag{13}$$

while the corresponding expression for the elasticity of factor demand with respect to output is

$$\gamma_y + C_{ij}/\alpha_i. \tag{14}$$

These elasticities and their standard errors are presented in Table 8.

The most important elasticities for our purposes are those corresponding to AVLOAD. As might be expected, the savings engendered by an increase in AVLOAD occur through savings in all factors (as opposed, for instance, to the case of AVSIZE where almost no fuel is saved), with somewhat greater than proportional savings in fuel. The small cost savings that accrue to increases in AVLOAD among the northeast carriers as calculated in the preceding section are due to the large positive value of D_{22} [the coefficient on $(\ln \text{AVLOAD})^2$ in the cost function; see the Appendix], an effect that does not occur among the regionals and which is constrained not to occur among the interregionals through the imposition of $D_{jm} = 0$. Thus, for the northeastern carriers, cost reductions caused by increasing AVLOAD are quickly exhausted; just as the point estimate of $\partial \ln C/\partial \ln \text{AVLOAD}$ of -0.49 cannot be used to calculate effects over a large range, the elasticities of Table 8 must be interpreted cautiously. Nevertheless, changes in operating characteristics have important effects on relative factor intensities. Thus, a

TABLE 8

Elasticities of Cost and Factor Demand with Respect to Operating Characteristics[a]

	Cost	Labor	Fuel	Capital	Purchased transportation
		Northeast Carriers			
ALH	−0.5112	−0.5837	−0.1273	−0.4609	−0.2034
	(0.0862)	(0.0871)	(0.0844)	(0.0927)	(0.4014)
AVLOAD	−0.4897	−0.4752	−0.6504	−0.4943	−0.5075
	(0.0959)	(0.0968)	(0.0919)	(0.1032)	(0.1994)
LTL	0.3327	0.3932	0.1745	0.2680	0.1075
	(0.1431)	(0.1439)	(0.1408)	(0.1483)	(0.2383)
AVSIZE	−0.2483	−0.2886	−0.1215	−0.2056	−0.1218
	(0.0931)	(0.0937)	(0.0909)	(0.0965)	(0.2267)
INSUR	0.0074	0.0037	0.0015	0.0182	−0.0252
	(0.0550)	(0.0554)	(0.0534)	(0.0582)	(0.1407)
Ton-miles	1.0864	1.1130	0.9980	1.0512	1.0771
	(0.0376)	(0.0378)	(0.0365)	(0.0406)	(0.1016)
		Regional Carriers			
ALH	−0.6220	−0.6973	−0.3540	−0.5457	−0.4092
	(0.0706)	(0.0745)	(0.0721)	(0.0756)	(0.3124)
AVLOAD	−0.2338	0.2333	−0.3891	−0.1764	−0.5680
	(0.0893)	(0.0941)	(0.0907)	(0.0940)	(0.1882)
LTL	0.0140	0.0505	0.0569	−0.0089	−0.4352
	(0.1403)	(0.1442)	(0.1413)	(0.1456)	(0.2382)
AVSIZE	−0.2656	−0.2967	−0.0511	−0.2468	−0.1934
	(0.0725)	(0.0764)	(0.0729)	(0.0777)	(0.2341)
INSUR	0.0244	0.0104	0.0256	0.0522	0.0015
	(0.0501)	(0.0524)	(0.0513)	(0.0532)	(0.1654)
Ton-miles	1.0759	1.1004	1.0367	1.0264	1.1705
	(0.0273)	(0.0288)	(0.0278)	(0.0296)	(0.1117)
		Interregional Carriers			
ALH	−0.3804	−0.4678	−0.2163	−0.3453	−0.1363
	(0.1055)	(0.0650)	(0.0629)	(0.0975)	(0.3587)
AVLOAD	−0.5799	−0.4664	−0.5959	−0.5090	−2.0709
	(0.2300)	(0.1301)	(0.1270)	(0.1946)	(0.5086)
LTL	−0.1434	0.0931	0.4584	−0.0864	−3.4654
	(0.1506)	(0.1442)	(0.1121)	(0.1460)	(1.2482)
AVSIZE	−0.4480	−0.4091	0.0789	−0.4399	−1.4506
	(0.1648)	(0.1550)	(0.1114)	(0.1563)	(0.6950)
INSUR	−0.0758	−0.1181	−0.1511	−0.0840	0.4724
	(0.0808)	(0.0803)	(0.0581)	(0.0822)	(0.7656)
TERMINAL	−0.0311	−0.0781	−0.1155	−0.1149	0.9672
	(0.0766)	(0.0774)	(0.0559)	(0.0743)	(0.4650)
Ton-miles	0.8969	0.9349	0.9269	0.9041	0.4465
	(0.0501)	(0.0490)	(0.0409)	(0.0483)	(0.3301)

[a] At sample mean; standard error in parentheses.

deregulation policy that increases AVLOAD would especially realize savings in fuel and purchased transportation.

6.   Summary and Conclusions

While the evidence regarding the relationships between regulation and trucking costs on productivity is admittedly somewhat inferential, it is certainly consistent with the hypothesis that regulation serves to reduce efficiency and increase costs. In particular, we have found clear evidence that trucking costs would be lower if average loads were increased, with cost savings concentrated in the areas of purchased transportation and fuel. In view of the efforts to obtain energy efficiencies, the fuel savings associated with increases in average load are particularly significant. Thus these findings indicate that resource costs associated with trucking activities would be reduced if regulatory restrictions concerning routes and commodities were relaxed to enable increased use of backhauls and higher loads.

While these findings are certainly suggestive, they do not lend themselves to broad generalizations concerning the impact of regulation upon trucking costs and productivity. This is true for two principal reasons. First, the link between regulatory policy and operating characteristics is sufficiently tenuous that it is not possible to quantify by how much these characteristics could be expected to change in the advent of regulatory change. Second, the technologies of the different segments of the trucking industry are sufficiently different that they do not lend themselves to comparisons of aggregate efficiency across different regulatory environments. Thus, while different segments of the trucking industry have widely differing costs, it is not clear whether these differences can be attributed to regulation or to the market environment in which they operate.

Nevertheless, this paper has clearly demonstrated that operating characteristics have a major impact upon trucking costs. From a methodological viewpoint, this indicates that efforts to analyze the costs of the industry without considering operating characteristics may lead to serious bias in the estimated coefficients. From a policy viewpoint, it suggests that the interrelationships between regulation and these variables are of crucial importance. Thus if the relationship between regulatory policy and the trucking firms' choice of these variables can be quantified, we would have gone a long way toward fully understanding the impact of regulation upon trucking costs. This paper has shown that considerable efficiencies can be obtained by increased loads. At the very least this should encourage regulators to adopt policies that would encourage more efficient equipment use and hence lower costs.

Appendix

TABLE A1

Coefficient Estimates for Technology Model, Northeast and Regional Carriers

Coefficient[a]	Variable[b]	Northeast carriers Value	Northeast carriers Standard error	Regional carriers Value	Regional carriers Standard error
α_0	constant	8.6919	0.0595	9.7507	0.0391
α_1	w_1 (labor)	0.5902	0.0057	0.5929	0.0056
α_2	w_2 (fuel)	0.0401	0.0014	0.0454	0.0011
α_3	w_3 (capital)	0.3358	0.0057	0.3259	0.0054
α_4	w_4 (purchased transportation)	0.0339	0.0038	0.0358	0.0033
β_1	t_1 (ALH)	-0.5112	0.0862	-0.6220	0.0706
β_2	t_2 (AVLOAD)	-0.4897	0.0959	-0.2338	0.0893
β_3	t_3 (LTL)	-0.3327	0.1431	0.0140	0.1403
β_4	t_4 (AVSIZE)	-0.2483	0.0931	-0.2656	0.0725
β_5	t_5 (INSUR)	0.0074	0.0550	0.0244	0.0501
γ_y	y (output)	1.0864	0.0376	1.0759	0.0273
A_{11}	$\frac{1}{2}(w_1)^2$	0.0322	0.0158	0.0659	0.0143
A_{12}	$w_1 w_2$	-0.0277	0.0050	-0.0273	0.0042
A_{13}	$w_1 w_3$	-0.0137	0.0079	-0.0189	0.0070
A_{14}	$w_1 w_4$	0.0092	0.0130	-0.0197	0.0113
A_{22}	$\frac{1}{2}(w_2)^2$	0.0346	0.0060	0.0388	0.0046
A_{23}	$w_2 w_3$	-0.0114	0.0015	-0.0097	0.0014
A_{24}	$w_2 w_4$	0.0045	0.0042	-0.0018	0.0037
A_{33}	$\frac{1}{2}(w_3)^2$	0.0212	1.0079	0.0259	0.0070
A_{34}	$w_3 w_4$	0.0039	0.0053	0.0027	0.0042
A_{44}	$\frac{1}{2}(w_4)^2$	-0.0177	0.0133	0.0189	0.0110
B_{11}	$w_1 t_1$	-0.0427	0.0089	-0.0447	0.0097
B_{12}	$w_1 t_2$	0.0086	0.0096	0.0003	0.0114
B_{13}	$w_1 t_3$	0.0357	0.0101	0.0216	0.0136
B_{14}	$w_1 t_4$	-0.0237	0.0067	-0.0184	0.0097
B_{15}	$w_1 t_5$	-0.0022	0.0048	-0.0083	0.0063
B_{21}	$w_2 t_1$	0.0154	0.0021	0.0122	0.0019
B_{22}	$w_2 t_2$	-0.0064	0.0023	-0.0071	0.0022
B_{23}	$w_2 t_3$	-0.0063	0.0025	0.0019	0.0027
B_{24}	$w_2 t_4$	0.0051	0.0016	0.0097	0.0019
B_{25}	$w_2 t_5$	-0.0004	0.0012	0.00005	0.0012
B_{31}	$w_3 t_1$	0.0169	0.0089	0.0249	0.0094
B_{32}	$w_3 t_2$	-0.0015	0.0096	0.0187	0.0111
B_{33}	$w_3 t_3$	-0.0217	0.0101	-0.0075	0.0132
B_{34}	$w_3 t_4$	0.0144	0.0067	0.0061	0.0094
B_{35}	$w_3 t_5$	0.0036	0.0048	0.0090	0.0061
B_{41}	$w_4 t_1$	0.0104	0.0060	0.0076	0.0057
B_{42}	$w_4 t_2$	-0.0006	0.0064	-0.0120	0.0068
B_{43}	$w_4 t_3$	-0.0076	0.0067	-0.0161	0.0081

(Continued)

Coefficient[a]	Variable[b]	Northeast carriers		Regional carriers	
		Value	Standard error	Value	Standard error
B_{44}	$w_4 t_4$	0.0043	0.0045	0.0026	0.0057
B_{45}	$w_4 t_5$	−0.0011	0.0032	−0.0008	0.0037
C_{1y}	$w_1 y$	0.0157	0.0038	0.0145	0.0038
C_{2y}	$w_2 y$	−0.0035	0.0009	−0.0018	0.0008
C_{3y}	$w_3 y$	−0.0118	0.0038	−0.0161	0.0037
C_{4y}	$w_4 y$	−0.0003	0.0025	0.0034	0.0023
D_{11}	$\frac{1}{2}(t_1)^2$	0.3716	0.1636	0.0419	0.1892
D_{12}	$t_1 t_2$	−0.5550	0.1455	−0.4445	0.1311
D_{13}	$t_1 t_3$	−0.1485	0.1276	0.0675	0.1485
D_{14}	$t_1 t_4$	0.2405	0.0822	0.1301	0.1176
D_{15}	$t_1 t_5$	−0.0361	0.0569	−0.1210	0.0802
D_{22}	$\frac{1}{2}(t_2)^2$	0.7874	0.1878	−0.0699	0.2030
D_{23}	$t_2 t_3$	−0.0900	0.1582	0.0426	0.1769
D_{24}	$t_2 t_4$	−0.4934	0.1124	0.0056	0.1419
D_{25}	$t_2 t_5$	−0.0150	0.0658	−0.1945	0.1033
D_{33}	$\frac{1}{2}(t_3)^2$	0.5234	0.1875	−0.5860	0.3100
D_{34}	$t_3 t_4$	0.0160	0.0822	−0.1377	0.1640
D_{35}	$t_3 t_5$	−0.1398	0.1120	0.0781	0.0786
D_{44}	$\frac{1}{2}(t_4)^2$	0.0562	0.0505	0.2748	0.0983
D_{45}	$t_4 t_5$	−0.2054	0.0708	0.1234	0.0583
D_{55}	$\frac{1}{2}(t_5)^2$	0.0266	0.0248	−0.0164	0.0580
E_{1y}	$t_1 y$	0.0365	0.0504	−0.0467	0.0606
E_{2y}	$t_2 y$	0.0128	0.0562	0.1604	0.0705
E_{3y}	$t_3 y$	0.1434	0.0699	0.0681	0.0722
E_{4y}	$t_4 y$	0.0014	0.0447	0.0086	0.0454
E_{5y}	$t_5 y$	0.0035	0.0271	0.0388	0.0283
F_{yy}	$\frac{1}{2}(y)^2$	0.0248	0.0347	0.0533	0.0256

Northeast carriers[c]

	R^2	RMSE
Cost equation	0.9533	0.2074
Labor equation	0.3974	0.0392
Fuel equation	0.3312	0.0095
Capital equation	0.1766	0.0393
Purchased transportation equation	0.1013	0.0261

Regional carriers[d]

	R^2	RMSE
Cost equation	0.9743	0.1823
Labor equation	0.2693	0.0442
Fuel equation	0.4391	0.0086
Capital equation	0.2211	0.0431
Purchased transportation equation	0.1619	0.0262

[a] As defined in Eq. (2).
[b] We have omitted ln for convenience.
[c] Log of likelihood function = 1208.497.
[d] Log of likelihood function = 1251.433.

TABLE A2

Coefficient Estimates for Technology Model for the Interregional Carriers[a]

Coefficient[b]	Variable[c]	Value	Standard error
α_0	Constant	11.7986	0.0698
α_1	w_1 (labor)	0.5795	0.0114
α_2	w_2 (fuel)	0.0625	0.0036
α_3	w_3 (capital)	0.3002	0.0101
α_4	w_4 (purchased transportation)	0.0577	0.0161
β_1	t_1 (ALH)	-0.3804	0.1055
β_2	t_2 (AVLOAD)	-0.5799	0.2300
β_3	t_3 (LTL)	-0.1434	0.1506
β_4	t_4 (AVSIZE)	-0.4480	0.1648
β_5	t_5 (INSUR)	-0.0758	0.0808
β_6	t_6 (TERMINAL)	-0.0311	0.0766
γ_y	y (output)	0.8969	0.0501
A_{11}	$\frac{1}{2}(w_1)^2$	0.0645	0.0201
A_{12}	$w_1 w_2$	-0.0166	0.0094
A_{13}	$w_1 w_3$	-0.0103	0.0075
A_{14}	$w_1 w_4$	-0.0376	0.0174
A_{22}	$\frac{1}{2}(w_2)^2$	0.0336	0.0103
A_{23}	$w_2 w_3$	-0.0128	0.0013
A_{24}	$w_2 w_4$	-0.0043	0.0033
A_{33}	$\frac{1}{2}(w_3)^2$	-0.0154	0.0063
A_{34}	$w_3 w_4$	0.0385	0.0079
A_{44}	$\frac{1}{2}(w_4)^2$	0.0033	0.0195
B_{11}	$w_1 t_1$	-0.0506	0.0163
B_{12}	$w_1 t_2$	0.0658	0.0348
B_{13}	$w_1 t_3$	0.1371	0.0217
B_{14}	$w_1 t_4$	0.0225	0.0257
B_{15}	$w_1 t_5$	-0.0245	0.0133
B_{16}	$w_1 t_6$	-0.0272	0.0112
B_{21}	$w_2 t_1$	0.0103	0.0053
B_{22}	$w_2 t_2$	-0.0010	0.0109
B_{23}	$w_2 t_3$	0.0376	0.0069
B_{24}	$w_2 t_4$	0.0330	0.0080
B_{25}	$w_2 t_5$	-0.0047	0.0042
B_{26}	$w_2 t_6$	-0.0053	0.0036
B_{31}	$w_3 t_1$	0.0105	0.0147
B_{32}	$w_3 t_2$	0.0212	0.0310
B_{33}	$w_3 t_3$	0.0171	0.0194
B_{34}	$w_3 t_4$	0.0024	0.0223
B_{35}	$w_3 t_5$	-0.0025	0.0119
B_{36}	$w_3 t_6$	-0.0252	0.0100
B_{41}	$w_4 t_1$	0.0298	0.0232
B_{42}	$w_4 t_2$	-0.0861	0.0492
B_{43}	$w_4 t_3$	-0.1918	0.0307

(*Continued*)

TABLE A2 (*Continued*)

Coefficient[b]	Variable[c]	Value	Standard error
B_{44}	$w_4 t_4$	-0.0579	0.0359
B_{45}	$w_4 t_5$	0.0317	0.0189
B_{46}	$w_4 t_6$	0.0576	0.0159
C_{1y}	$w_1 y$	0.0220	0.0061
C_{2y}	$w_2 y$	0.0019	0.0019
C_{3y}	$w_3 y$	0.0021	0.0053
C_{4y}	$w_4 y$	-0.0260	0.0085
E_{1y}	$t_1 y$	-0.0932	0.0600
E_{2y}	$t_2 y$	0.2602	0.0956
E_{3y}	$t_3 y$	-0.2665	0.0819
E_{4y}	$t_4 y$	-0.3223	0.0868
E_{5y}	$t_5 y$	-0.0413	0.0581
E_{6y}	$t_6 y$	0.0990	0.0338
F_{yy}	$\frac{1}{2}(y)^2$	-0.0880	0.0320

	R^2	RMSE
Cost equation	0.9811	0.1818
Labor equation	0.8537	0.0315
Fuel equation	0.4598	0.0102
Capital equation	0.1790	0.0286
Purchased transportation equation	0.8035	0.0451

[a] Log of likelihood function $= 407.964$.
[b] As defined in Eq. (2).
[c] We have omitted ln for convenience.

5

The Sources of Economic Growth in the U.S. Electric Power Industry

Frank M. Gollop †

Mark J. Roberts ‡

Department of Economics
University of Wisconsin—Madison
Madison, Wisconsin

The electric power industry in the United States has experienced tremendous economic growth over the postwar period. Among the 51 industries studied by Gollop and Jorgenson [1980] for the 1947–1973 period, electric utilities rank sixth, having an average annual rate of growth in output exceeding the rates reported for all agriculture, mining, service, and government sectors and all but one manufacturing industry.[1] More precisely, kilowatt-hours sold to ultimate consumers by privately owned electric utilities have increased at an average annual rate of 8.4% per firm over the 1950–1975 period.[2] Growth in the stocks of labor, capital, and fuel inputs,

---

† Present address: Department of Economics, Boston College, Chestnut Hill, Massachusetts.

‡ Present address: Department of Economics, Pennsylvania State University, University Park, Pennsylvania.

[1] Gollop and Jorgenson [1980, Table 35]. The industries with average annual rates of growth greater than that found in electric utilities are air transportation, telephone and telegraph, gas utilities, chemicals, and radio and television broadcasting.

[2] This growth rate was constructed from data reported in the 1950 and 1975 editions of *Statistics of Privately Owned Utilities*.

the changing postwar composition of each firm's labor hours, capital stock, and fuel mix, and gains due to economies of scale and technical change have each contributed to this growth. The primary objective of this paper is to quantify the contribution of each of these sources to the economic growth experienced by firms of varying size in the electric power industry.

The model developed for this paper is a generalization of the sectoral model of production and technical change recently introduced by Gollop and Jorgenson [1980]. They begin with a production function for each industrial sector, giving output as a function of capital, labor, intermediate inputs, and time. Consistent with earlier productivity research, Gollop and Jorgenson [1980] assume production exhibits constant returns to scale. While perhaps suitable for an industry-wide study relying on national income data, this assumption is particularly inappropriate for a productivity study at the firm level in the electric power industry. Christensen and Greene [1976], for example, not only find that nearly three-fourths of industry output in 1955 was produced by utilities having significant unexploited scale economies but also conclude that by 1970, despite the marked increase in average firm size, this figure had only fallen to one-half of total industry output.[3] The implication is clear. A study of the industry's performance must treat economies of scale and technical change as distinct sources of economic growth.

The model of production and technical change developed in Section 1 incorporates the separable contributions of scale economies and technical change. The industry's technology is characterized in terms of a factor minimal cost function. Production cost is a function of input prices, output, and time. Constant returns to scale becomes a testable, rather than a maintained, hypothesis of the model of economic growth.

While this model provides a useful framework in which to measure the contributions of each source of growth, our secondary objective is to analyze the sources and structure of technical change. In particular, we wish to determine whether the rate of technical change can be allocated among components uniquely associated with individual inputs and, if so, which inputs are the dominant mediums of technical change. This requires that the model of production be respecified in terms of a factor-augmentation model of technical change. The structure of the model, adapted from a model developed by Gollop and Jorgenson (Gollop [1974]), is described in Section 2, and the necessary and sufficient conditions implied by factor-augmenting technical change are identified.[4] Factor-specific augmentation coefficients

---

[3] Christensen and Greene [1976, p. 673].

[4] Discussions and applications of factor-augmenting technical change in the context of translog models have appeared previously in the economics literature. See Berndt and Jorgenson [1975], Berndt and Wood [1975], Woodland [1976], and Wills [1979].

become the basis for the allocation of technical change among its source components. In addition, given the factor-augmentation characterization of production, the structure of technical change can be evaluated. Necessary and sufficient parametric restrictions consistent with Hicks, Harrod, Solow, and Leontief neutralities are identified.

The models described in Sections 1 and 2 are applied to a pooled time-series cross-section analysis of economic growth over the 1958–1975 period for 11 electric utilities. The sample utilities vary in size while having otherwise similar production characteristics. The estimating model and data are described in Sections 3 and 4, respectively. Results of all hypothesis tests and inferences based directly on the estimated parameters are reported in Section 5. Most important, the rate of change in each firm's total production cost over the 18-year period is decomposed into seven source components: the rates of growth in the stock prices of labor hours, capital stock, and fuel, the contributions of the changing composition of each firm's capital stock and fuel mix,[5] gains due to scale economies, and the rate of technical change. Applying the model of exponential factor-augmenting technical change permits the further decomposition of each firm's rate of technical change into components that can be associated with labor, capital, and fuel inputs.

1. Model of Economic Growth

The appropriate structure of a model of economic growth for an individual firm is specified by the microeconomic theory of production. Given a set of input prices, the firm chooses a particular combination of labor, capital, and intermediate inputs for each level of output and presumably alters the composition of that mix in response to changing input prices. In addition, technical change can differentially augment individual inputs, thus affecting how the firm reacts to changes in relative factor prices. As a general model, microeconomic theory requires a model of production with no restrictions on either the particular form of technical change or the marginal rates of substitution among the arguments of the production function.

Given the results of duality theory,[6] this general model of production and technical change applied to the electric power industry can be represented by

---

[5] The data required to distinguish the growth contributions of particular categories of labor (e.g., production, supervisory, and clerical) are unavailable. As a result, as explained in Section 4, our analysis of the growth in the price of labor input is restricted to the growth in the stock price of labor hours.

[6] See Baumol [1977b, pp. 364–373], Diewert [1974], and Varian [1978, pp. 118–135] for excellent discussions of duality theory.

a factor minimal cost function G for each electric utility:

$$C = G(p_L, p_K, p_F, Q, T),\qquad(1)$$

where production cost (C) is a function of the input prices of labor (p_L), capital (p_K), and fuel (p_F), the level of output (Q), and time (T).[7] Following Christensen and Greene [1976], the model maintains that factor markets are competitive and that each utility is compelled to supply all electric power demanded at any given price. Thus input prices and output are treated as exogenous variables while input levels are endogenous. We emphasize, however, that constant returns to scale is not a maintained hypothesis. Average cost is a function of output.

Logarithmically differentiating the cost function (1) with respect to time decomposes the rate of growth of total cost into its source components:

$$\frac{d\ln C}{dT} = \left[\frac{\partial \ln C}{\partial \ln p_L}\frac{d\ln p_L}{dT} + \frac{\partial \ln C}{\partial \ln p_K}\frac{d\ln p_K}{dT} + \frac{\partial \ln C}{\partial \ln p_F}\frac{d\ln p_F}{dT}\right]$$
$$+ \frac{\partial \ln C}{\partial \ln Q}\frac{d\ln Q}{dT} + \frac{\partial \ln C}{\partial T}.\qquad(2)$$

The rate of growth of total cost can be expressed as the cost elasticity weighted average of rates of growth of input prices, plus the scale weighted rate of growth of output, plus the rate of cost reduction due to technical change.

The logarithmic partial derivatives appearing in (2) have particular economic interpretations. Applying Shephard's lemma, the elasticity of cost with respect to the price of each input equals the corresponding input's share (v_i) in total cost:

$$\frac{\partial \ln C}{\partial \ln p_i}(p_L, p_K, p_F, Q, T) = \frac{p_i X_i}{C} \equiv v_i \qquad (i = L, K, F).\qquad(3)$$

The elasticity of cost with respect to output (v_Q) can be interpreted as a measure of static or scale economies

$$\frac{\partial \ln C}{\partial \ln Q}(p_L, p_K, p_F, Q, T) \equiv v_Q.\qquad(4)$$

If v_Q equals unity, cost proportionally responds to changes in firm output; this condition characterizes constant returns to scale. If v_Q is less (greater) than unity, cost increases less (more) than proportionally with increases in output, implying the existence of scale economies (diseconomies). Regardless of its value, v_Q isolates the change in cost that is independent of technical

[7] Intermediate inputs other than fuel are relatively unimportant in the industry's production process and are therefore excluded from the analysis.

change and changes in input prices. Finally, the rate of technical change can be defined in terms of the partial elasticity of cost with respect to time. The rate of technical change (v_T) equals the negative of the rate of growth of total cost with respect to time, holding output and the prices of all inputs constant

$$-\frac{\partial \ln C}{\partial T}(p_L, p_K, p_F, Q, T) \equiv v_T. \tag{5}$$

Given this characterization of economic growth, the change in total cost holding input prices constant (W) can be viewed as the sum of static and dynamic sources of economic growth:

$$W = \frac{\partial \ln C}{\partial \ln Q}\frac{d \ln Q}{dT} + \frac{\partial \ln C}{\partial T} = v_Q \frac{d \ln Q}{dT} - v_T,$$

where

$$W \equiv \frac{d \ln C}{dT} - \left[v_L \frac{d \ln p_L}{dT} + v_K \frac{d \ln p_K}{dT} + v_F \frac{d \ln p_F}{dT} \right]. \tag{6}$$

The expression for W is a Divisia index number; it equals the sum of the contributions of scale economies and technical change to economic growth. A principal objective of this paper is first to measure W and then to decompose it into its static and dynamic components.

While the above continuous model of production provides the foundation for this study, application of the model requires that it be extended to incorporate price and quantity data at discrete points in time. For this purpose, we consider the translog cost function, a second-order approximation to the cost function G defined in (1):

$$C = \exp[\alpha_0 + \sum_i \beta_i \ln p_i + \beta_Q \ln Q + \beta_T T$$

$$+ \frac{1}{2}\sum_i \sum_j \gamma_{ij} \ln p_i \ln p_j + \sum_i \gamma_{iQ} \ln p_i \ln Q$$

$$+ \sum_i \gamma_{iT} \ln p_i T + \frac{1}{2}\gamma_{QQ}(\ln Q)^2 + \gamma_{QT} \ln QT + \frac{1}{2}\gamma_{TT}T^2]. \tag{7}$$

Taking the logarithmic partial derivative of (7) with respect to each input price and applying Shephard's lemma (3), the behavioral equations take the form

$$v_i = \beta_i + \sum_j \gamma_{ij} \ln p_j + \gamma_{iQ} \ln Q + \gamma_{iT} T \qquad (i,j = L, K, F). \tag{8}$$

Using (4) and (5), the logarithmic partial derivatives with respect to output and time are, respectively,

$$v_Q = \beta_Q + \sum_i \gamma_{iQ} \ln p_i + \gamma_{QQ} \ln Q + \gamma_{QT} T, \tag{9}$$

$$-v_T = \beta_T + \sum_i \gamma_{iT} \ln p_i + \gamma_{QT} \ln Q + \gamma_{TT} T. \tag{10}$$

Substituting these expressions into equation (6) yields an expression for W in terms of the translog parameters:

$$W = \left[\beta_Q + \sum_i \gamma_{iQ} \ln p_i + \gamma_{QQ} \ln Q + \gamma_{QT} T \right] \frac{d \ln Q}{dT}$$

$$+ \left[\beta_T + \sum_i \gamma_{iT} \ln p_i + \gamma_{QT} \ln Q + \gamma_{TT} T \right]. \tag{11}$$

The dependent variables in the three equations in (8) are input shares of total cost and as a result must sum to unity. The estimated translog cost function will satisfy this condition if and only if

$$\sum_i \beta_i = 1 \quad \text{and} \quad \sum_i \gamma_{ij} = \sum_i \gamma_{iQ} = \sum_i \gamma_{iT} = 0 \quad (j, i = L, K, F). \tag{12}$$

Modeling the growth contributions of scale economies and technical change in terms of discrete data requires considering the translog cost function at two points in time, say T and $T - 1$. Given (6), the average contribution $\overline{W}$ of these two sources of growth over the period $T - 1$ to T can be expressed as the difference between successive logarithms of total cost less a weighted average of the differences between successive logarithms of input prices:

$$\overline{W} \equiv [\ln C(T) - \ln C(T - 1)] - \sum_i \bar{v}_i [\ln p_i(T) - \ln p_i(T - 1)], \tag{13}$$

where, applying the quadratic approximation lemma,[8]

$$\overline{W} = \bar{v}_Q [\ln Q(T) - \ln Q(T - 1)] - \bar{v}_T$$

and

$$\bar{v}_i = \tfrac{1}{2} [v_i(T) + v_i(T - 1)] \quad (i = L, K, F),$$

$$\bar{v}_Q = \tfrac{1}{2} [v_Q(T) + v_Q(T - 1)],$$

$$\bar{v}_T = \tfrac{1}{2} [v_T(T) + v_T(T - 1)].$$

The expression $\overline{W}$ is a Törnqvist index number measuring the average

---

[8] See Diewert [1976, p. 118].

contribution of scale economies and technical change to economic growth. It can be measured in terms of price and quantity data at each point in time. The decomposition of $\overline{W}$ into its two source components requires an estimating model. An important part of that model is the parametric expression for the index number $\overline{W}$ which, from (11), takes the form

$$
\overline{W} = \left\{ \beta_Q + \sum_i \gamma_{iQ} \left[\frac{\ln p_i(T) + \ln p_i(T-1)}{2} \right] + \gamma_{QQ} \left[\frac{\ln Q(T) + \ln Q(T-1)}{2} \right] \right.
$$

$$
\left. + \gamma_{QT} \left[\frac{T + (T-1)}{2} \right] \right\} [\ln Q(T) - \ln Q(T-1)]
$$

$$
+ \left\{ \beta_T + \sum_i \gamma_{iT} \left[\frac{\ln p_i(T) + \ln p_i(T-1)}{2} \right] + \gamma_{QT} \left[\frac{\ln Q(T) + \ln Q(T-1)}{2} \right] \right.
$$

$$
\left. + \gamma_{TT} \left[\frac{T + (T-1)}{2} \right] \right\}. \tag{14}
$$

The cost function (7), the behavioral equations (8), the output and time derivatives (9) and (10), and the expression for W form the basis for the model of factor-augmenting technical change developed in Section 2. The econometric model developed in Section 3 is based on these same equations and the Törnqvist index number $\overline{W}$.

2.   Factor Augmentation

While measuring the sources of economic growth and, in particular, isolating the contributions of scale economies and technical change are important productivity issues, productivity analysis suggests two additional questions. First, can the rate of technical change be allocated into components uniquely associated with individual inputs? Second, presuming an affirmative answer to the first question, which inputs are the dominant mediums of technical change?

Both questions focus on the structure of technical change. Analyzing the former requires a model of factor-augmenting technical change that can be derived as a restricted form of the general model introduced in Section 1; evaluating the latter requires identifying restrictions appropriate to a variety of neutrality hypotheses. The two objectives of this section are to restructure the general model of technical change into a factor-augmentation model and to identify the parametric restrictions consistent with factor augmentation and with each form of neutral technical change, that is, Hicks, Harrod, Solow, and Leontief neutralities.

We begin by considering a model of production maintaining factor-augmenting technical change. We adapt a model developed by Gollop and Jorgenson (Gollop [1974]) in which inputs and input prices are defined in terms of efficiency units.[9] Stated more precisely, the number of efficiency units E_i of each input is measured as the product of the input level and its corresponding augmentation coefficient,

$$E_i(T) = X_i A_i(T) \qquad (i = L, K, F), \qquad (15)$$

where A_i represents a factor specific augmentation function of a single argument, time. Since the ith input has price p_i and since it comprises $A_i(T)$ efficiency units, the price of the ith efficiency unit is $p_i/A_i(T)$.

Given factor augmentation, the cost function G in (1) can be respecified as a function H of output and efficiency input prices

$$C = H\left[\frac{p_L}{A_L(T)}, \frac{p_K}{A_K(T)}, \frac{p_F}{A_F(T)}, Q\right]. \qquad (16)$$

We assume that each augmentation function A_i is a translog function of time[10]

$$A_i(T) = \exp[\eta_i T + \tfrac{1}{2}\phi_i T^2] \qquad (i = L, K, F). \qquad (17)$$

Given (17), the translog approximation[11] to the factor-augmented cost function (H) in (16) becomes

$$C = \exp[\alpha_0 + \sum_i \beta_i \ln p_i - \sum_i \beta_i \eta_i T + \beta_Q \ln Q$$

$$+ \frac{1}{2}\sum_i \sum_j \gamma_{ij} \ln p_i \ln p_j - \frac{1}{2}\sum_i \sum_j \gamma_{ij}\eta_i \ln p_j T$$

$$+ \sum_i \gamma_{iQ} \ln p_i \ln Q - \sum_i \gamma_{iQ}\eta_i \ln QT$$

$$+ \tfrac{1}{2}\gamma_{QQ}(\ln Q)^2 + \tfrac{1}{2}\gamma_{TT}T^2], \qquad (18)$$

where

$$\gamma_{TT} = -\sum_i \beta_i \phi_i + \sum_i \sum_j \gamma_{ij}\eta_i\eta_j.$$

The general model of production and technical change described in Section 1

---

[9] See Dixit [1976, pp. 16–42] for an excellent discussion of augmentation coefficients and efficiency units.

[10] Though the second-order expansion of $A_i(T)$ formally has an intercept term, it is set equal to zero, i.e., $A_i(T)$ is indexed to unity when $T = 0$.

[11] Since the translog function is a second-order approximation, all terms involving higher order expressions are set equal to zero.

includes the cost function (7), behavioral conditions (8), and the expression (11) for W representing the sum of the growth contributions of scale economies and technical change. The model of production maintaining factor-augmenting technical change has an analogous structure. The necessary conditions for producer equilibrium corresponding to (18) are formed by taking the logarithmic partial derivative of (18) with respect to each efficiency input price

$$v_i = \beta_i + \sum_j \gamma_{ij} \ln p_j + \gamma_{iQ} \ln Q - \left(\sum_j \gamma_{ij}\eta_j\right) T \qquad (i,j = L, K, F). \quad (19)$$

The parametric representation of W is formed by substituting the logarithmic partial derivatives of the factor-augmented cost function (18) with respect to output (v_Q) and time ($-v_T$) into the expression (6) so that

$$
\begin{aligned}
W = & \left[\beta_Q + \sum_i \gamma_{iQ} \ln p_i + \gamma_{QQ} \ln Q - \left(\sum_i \gamma_{iQ}\eta_i\right) T\right] \frac{d \ln Q}{dT} \\
& - \left[\sum_i \beta_i\eta_i + \sum_i \left(\sum_j \gamma_{ij}\eta_j\right) \ln p_i \right. \\
& \left. + \left(\sum_i \gamma_{iQ}\eta_i\right) \ln Q - \gamma_{TT}T\right] \qquad (i,j = L, K, F).
\end{aligned}
$$
$$(20)$$

While the accounting identity still implies a set of restrictions on the translog parameters

$$\sum_i \beta_i = 1 \quad \text{and} \quad \sum_i \gamma_{ij} = \sum_i \gamma_{iQ} = 0 \qquad (i,j = L, K, F), \quad (21)$$

it is important to note that there are no necessary restrictions on the augmentation parameters η_L, η_K, and η_F.

Since the model of factor-augmenting technical change (16) is a restricted form of the more general model (1), one would expect that there is some identifiable set of restrictions distinguishing the two translog models (7) and (18). Comparing the fixed parameters in the two models of technical change reveals that the first- and second-order time parameters in the general model (7) (i.e., $\beta_T, \gamma_{LT}, \gamma_{KT}, \gamma_{FT}$, and γ_{QT}) are replaced by the parameters η_L, η_K, and η_F in the factor-augmentation model (18). More precisely, the substitutions are of the form[12]

$$\beta_T = -\sum_j \beta_j\eta_j, \qquad \gamma_{iT} = -\sum_j \gamma_{ij}\eta_j, \qquad \gamma_{QT} = -\sum_j \gamma_{jQ}\eta_j \qquad (i,j = L, K, F).$$
$$(22)$$

---

[12] These restrictions are derived by evaluating the first- and second-order partial time derivatives of the models (7) and (18) at the point of expansion ($\ln p_L = \ln p_K = \ln p_F = \ln Q = T = 0$).

The accounting identity restrictions (21) indicate that only two of the three parameters γ_{LT}, γ_{KT}, and γ_{FT} are independent. Consequently, four independent parameters in the general model of production and technical change are respecified in terms of already-included second-order parameters and three new parameters. There is thus one "factor-augmentation" restriction for the translog cost function. This restriction becomes an econometrically testable hypothesis in Section 3.

Our objective, recall, is not simply to specify a model of factor-augmenting technical change but to use the model to decompose the rate of technical change into its source components. This analysis requires that an additional restriction be imposed on the factor-augmentation model. The parameter γ_{TT} in (18) is currently a function of the six first- and second-order coefficients η_L, η_K, η_F, ϕ_L, ϕ_K, and ϕ_F. The second-order parameters ϕ_i ($i = L, K, F$) cannot be econometrically identified. Consequently, the desired decomposition of technical change can proceed if and only if γ_{TT} can be expressed in terms of the first-order parameters alone. This requires that factor augmentation be of the first-order exponential form

$$A_i(T) = \exp[\eta_i T] \qquad (i = L, K, F). \tag{23}$$

In terms of the translog model described in Eqs. (18)–(20), this characterization leads to the single restriction

$$\gamma_{TT} = \sum_j \left(\sum_i \gamma_{ij} \eta_i \right) \eta_j \qquad (i, j = L, K, F). \tag{24}$$

We refer to (24) as the "first-order factor-augmentation" restriction.

Given this form of technical change, the rate of cost reduction due to technical change [the logarithmic partial derivative of (18) with respect to time] takes the form

$$-v_T = -\left(\sum_i \beta_i \eta_i \right) - \sum_i \left(\sum_j \gamma_{ij} \eta_j \right) \ln p_i$$

$$- \left(\sum_i \gamma_{iQ} \eta_i \right) \ln Q + \sum_i \left(\sum_j \gamma_{ij} \eta_j \right) \eta_i T \qquad (i, j = L, K, F). \tag{25}$$

Given that restrictions (22) and (24) are a reasonable characterization of technical change, the rate of technical change in (25) can be allocated among components associated with each input. The contribution of technical change through labor input, for example, can be expressed as

$$-\eta_L \left[\beta_L + \sum_i \gamma_{iL} \ln p_i + \gamma_{LQ} \ln Q - \left(\sum_i \gamma_{iL} \eta_i \right) T \right] \qquad (i = L, K, F). \tag{26}$$

The contributions through capital and fuel inputs are defined symmetrically. Referring to Eqs. (19) makes clear that the bracketed expression in (26) is always positive. Consequently, the sign associated with the direct effect is determined by the sign of the corresponding η_i. The sum of the three expressions equals $-v_T$ in (25).

Our second objective in developing this factor-augmentation model is to evaluate the structure of technical change. The critical parameters are η_L, η_K, and η_F. If any η_i equals zero, the corresponding augmentation coefficient defined in (23) equals unity. It necessarily follows that technical change does not augment the ith input. If, however, η_i is greater (less) than zero, $A_i(T)$ is greater (less) than unity and technical change augmenting the ith input is a positive (negative) source of the firm's economic growth. Moreover, restrictions on the first-order parameters η_L, η_K, and η_F identify four alternative structures of neutral technical change:

$$\text{Hicks neutrality:} \quad \eta_L = \eta_K = \eta_F, \tag{27}$$

$$\text{Harrod neutrality:} \quad \eta_K = \eta_F = 0, \tag{28}$$

$$\text{Solow neutrality:} \quad \eta_L = \eta_F = 0, \tag{29}$$

$$\text{Leontief neutrality:} \quad \eta_L = \eta_K = 0. \tag{30}$$

The models of technical change described in Sections 1 and 2 form the basis for our analysis of the sources of economic growth in the electric power industry. The factor-augmentation model introduced in this section focuses on the components of technical change and its structure. Implementation of our methodology requires an estimating model suitable to data observed at discrete points in time. Such a model is derived in Section 3.

3. Estimation Model

In this section we develop an econometric model based on the general model of production and technical change described in Section 1. As shown in Section 2, the factor-augmentation model can be considered a restricted form of the more general model.

Construction of the estimation model begins with adding a random disturbance to each of the input share equations (8), the expression for W in (11), and the cost function (7). The error terms are ε_L, ε_K, ε_F, ε_W, and ε_C, respectively. Since the cost shares v_L, v_K, and v_F sum to unity at every observation, the cost function parameters must satisfy the restrictions identified in (12). Consequently, the three disturbances ε_L, ε_K, and ε_F must sum to zero.

We assume that the vector of error terms from all equations for each firm has mean zero and variance-covariance matrix $\Sigma \otimes I$. The elements of the 5×5 matrix Σ are the variance of each equation and the covariance between each pair of equations. This is the familiar contemporaneous covariance specification proposed by Zellner [1962].

While the value shares v_L, v_K, and v_F can be observed directly from price and quantity data, the variable W is not directly observable. Consequently, we use the Törnqvist index number $\overline{W}$ defined in Eq. (13)

$$\overline{W} \equiv [\ln C(T) - \ln C(T - 1)] - \sum_i \bar{v}_i [\ln p_i(T) - \ln p_i(T - 1)].$$

Since

$$\bar{v}_i = \tfrac{1}{2}[v_i(T) + v_i(T - 1)] \qquad (i = L, K, F),$$

the estimating equations can be written in the form

$$\bar{v}_i = \beta_i + \sum_j \gamma_{ij} \overline{\ln p_j} + \gamma_{iQ} \overline{\ln Q} + \gamma_{iT} \overline{T} + \bar{\varepsilon}_i, \qquad (i, j = L, K, F),$$

$$\overline{W} = \left[\beta_Q + \sum_i \gamma_{iQ} \overline{\ln p_i} + \gamma_{QQ} \overline{\ln Q} + \gamma_{QT} \overline{T} \right]\!\!\left[\ln Q(T) - \ln Q(T - 1) \right]$$

$$+ \left[\beta_T + \sum_i \gamma_{iT} \overline{\ln p_i} + \gamma_{QT} \overline{\ln Q} + \gamma_{TT} \overline{T} \right] + \bar{\varepsilon}_W,$$

(31)

$$\overline{\ln C} = \alpha_0 + \sum_i \beta_i \overline{\ln p_i} + \beta_T \overline{T} + \beta_Q \overline{\ln Q}$$

$$+ \tfrac{1}{2} \sum_i \sum_j \gamma_{ij} \overline{\ln p_i \ln p_j} + \sum_i \gamma_{iQ} \overline{\ln p_i \ln Q} + \sum_i \gamma_{iT} \overline{\ln p_i T}$$

$$+ \gamma_{QT} \overline{\ln QT} + \tfrac{1}{2} \gamma_{QQ} \overline{\ln Q^2} + \tfrac{1}{2} \gamma_{TT} \overline{T^2} + \bar{\varepsilon}_C$$

where the overlined variables represent the average values for the two periods T and $T - 1$. In general, for any variables X and Y,

$$\overline{XY} = \tfrac{1}{2}[X(T)Y(T) + X(T - 1)Y(T - 1)].$$

Note that the average disturbances still satisfy the accounting identity

$$\bar{\varepsilon}_L + \bar{\varepsilon}_K + \bar{\varepsilon}_F = 0;$$

one of the average share equation disturbances depends on the remaining two. It necessarily follows that the variance-covariance matrix of average disturbances in the ith estimating equation for each firm is

$$
\text{Var}\begin{pmatrix} \bar{\varepsilon}_i(2) \\ \bar{\varepsilon}_i(3) \\ \vdots \\ \bar{\varepsilon}_i(N) \end{pmatrix} = \sigma_{ii}\begin{bmatrix} \frac{1}{2} & \frac{1}{4} & 0 & \cdots & 0 \\ \frac{1}{4} & \frac{1}{2} & \frac{1}{4} & \cdots & 0 \\ 0 & \frac{1}{4} & \frac{1}{2} & \cdots & 0 \\ \vdots & \vdots & \vdots & & \vdots \\ 0 & 0 & 0 & \cdots & \frac{1}{2} \end{bmatrix}
$$

$$
= \sigma_{ii}\Omega \qquad (i = L, K, F, W, C),
$$

where Ω is a Laurent matrix. Similarly, the covariance between the ith and jth equations for each firm can be written as $\sigma_{ij}\Omega$.

Since the form of the covariance matrix of average disturbances is the same for each equation (as is the pattern of cross equation correlation), the covariance matrix of the vector of average disturbances for each firm has the Kronecker product form

$$
\text{Var}\begin{pmatrix} \bar{\varepsilon}_L \\ \bar{\varepsilon}_K \\ \bar{\varepsilon}_F \\ \bar{\varepsilon}_W \\ \bar{\varepsilon}_C \end{pmatrix} = \Sigma \otimes \Omega.
$$

Although the disturbances are autocorrelated, the data can be transformed to eliminate the autocorrelation. Using a procedure outlined in Gollop and Jorgenson [1979], we transform each firm's data so that the covariance matrix of transformed disturbances has the required form $\Sigma \otimes I$.

We jointly estimate the $\bar{v}_L, \bar{v}_K, \bar{v}_F, \overline{W}$, and $\overline{\ln C}$ equations as a multivariate regression system using a modification of Zellner's method for seemingly unrelated regressions. At the first stage, all five equations (31) are estimated with the restrictions in (12) imposed. The resulting residuals are then used to estimate Σ. Since the estimated Σ will be singular, one of the three cost-share equations is deleted prior to the second stage. This method provides parameter estimates that are invariant to the choice of the equation to be dropped without requiring that maximum likelihood estimates be formed. Fifteen parameters are estimated directly and six additional ones are computed from the restrictions in (12).

Having estimated the complete econometric model, the single factor-augmentation restriction resulting from (22) is tested. We evaluate this hypothesis using an F test based on the sum of squared residuals. If the hypothesis cannot be rejected, we proceed to test this hypothesis jointly with the single first-order factor-augmentation restriction (24). If, in turn, this hypothesis cannot be rejected, we test it jointly with each set of restrictions consistent with Hicks, Harrod, Solow, and Leontief neutrality. More important, failing to reject the hypothesis that technical change can be characterized by a first-order augmenting form permits us to allocate the rate of technical change among components uniquely related to each input. The parameter estimates for both the unrestricted and augmentation models and all test statistics are reported in Section 5.

4. Data Base

The development of the data set required for this study is guided by the model of production and technical change described in Section 1. Since the necessary conditions for producer behavior are an important part of that model, the firm rather than the plant is the relevant unit of observation. Producers make input decisions on the basis of technical and market conditions facing the complete system, not isolated plants.

Our model of economic growth likewise establishes a set of criteria by which sample firms can be selected. Our model assumes that input prices and output are exogenous and that the technical properties of the production function are represented by the fixed parameters of the cost function. Consequently, our sample of firms must be limited to those that have adopted a similar technology and exist in substantially similar market and regulatory environments.

Engineering considerations[13] and past empirical research[14] suggest that technologies vary considerably across fuel types. A sample neglecting to distinguish firms by dominant fuel use would violate the assumption of a homogeneous technology. We therefore limit our attention to firms relying mainly on coal; in particular, we consider only utilities with 65% or more of their fuel expenditures allocated to the purchase of coal.[15] We focus on coal not only because coal has been the industry's dominant fuel throughout the postwar period but also because coal-fired generation is expected to take on even greater significance in the near future.

[13] For a discussion of the technical differences due to fuel choice, see Boyes [1976], n. 6, and Cowing [1970].

[14] Gollop and Karlson [1978b] find that the estimated sets of production parameters differ significantly among sets of firms grouped by regions defined by the dominant use of a particular fuel.

[15] Our ultimate objective is to select a set of firms which, relative to any other group of firms, best exhibits a homogeneous set of production, market, and regulatory characteristics. Our 65% coal constraint is the first of the elements in a set of selection criteria. Had we further tightened this constraint, we would have excluded firms that satisfied all other constraints listed later in the text.

To further ensure that our sample firms do not exhibit significantly different technologies, we examine each firm's asset structure. We exclude those utilities that are engaged primarily in either transmission or distribution. On the basis of reported book values, our sample is restricted to firms participating in generation, transmission, *and* distribution activity and, of this group, to those whose generating stock is at least equal to one-third of total capital assets.

We also exclude firms that are publicly owned, participate as members of larger holding companies, make significant purchases in wholesale power markets,[16] and, relative to other utilities, serve a nontypical mix of residential, commercial, industrial, and wholesale consumers. Not accounting for these characteristics could result in a sample that includes firms that face a significantly different set of regulatory constraints and market conditions.

Applying these technological, market, and regulatory criteria to the complete set of electric power companies results in a sample of 11 utilities: Carolina Power and Light, Cincinnati Gas and Electric, Cleveland Electric Illumination Co., Consumers Power, Duke Power, Illinois Power, Pennsylvania Power and Light, Potomac Electric Power, Ohio Edison, South Carolina Electric and Gas, and Wisconsin Electric Power. The firms vary considerably in size, enabling us to contrast the source contributions of technical change and scale economies to productivity growth at different scales of operation. Duke Power is the largest, with net generation in 1975 equal to 46.3 billion kilowatt-hours (kWh); South Carolina Gas and Electric is the smallest, with 1975 net generation equal to 10.3 billion kWh. Our sample includes annual observations on data for each of these eleven utilities for the complete 1958–1975 period.[17]

Implementation of our model of economic growth requires annual measures of firm output and detailed annual price and quantity data for each input. We measure annual output for each firm as total net generation (in kWh) as reported in the Federal Power Commission's annual editions of *Statistics of Privately Owned Electric Utilities in the United States* (hereafter, *Statistics*).

Constructing appropriate measures of input prices and quantities is less straightforward. Denison [1974], Jorgenson and Griliches [1967], and others argue persuasively that growth accounting requires that inputs be measured in quality-adjusted units. Stated equivalently, each input price should measure the price per quality-adjusted unit of the corresponding input. The growth in real labor input between two points in time may not equal the

---

[16] None of our sample utilities purchases more than 11% of its needs on the wholesale market.

[17] Our data set begins with 1958 because the average numbers of full- and part-time workers by firm (data required by our model) are not reported for earlier years.

observed growth in the unweighted sum of total hours worked; the growth in the price per quality-adjusted unit of labor input may not equal the reported growth in the ratio of total labor compensation to total hours worked. The composition of the labor force may have changed; that is, the quality of the stock of labor input may have increased or decreased. It follows that input and input price variables used in growth accounting must be measured in quality-adjusted units.

The model of production introduced in Section 1 specifies cost as a function of output, time, and the prices of *aggregate* labor, capital, and fuel inputs. To incorporate measures based on quality-adjusted units, the model must maintain that each input is an aggregate of individual inputs or, stated in dual form, that each input price is a function of the prices of its components:

$$p_i = p_i(p_{i1}, p_{i2}, \ldots, p_{iM_i}) \qquad (i = L, K, F). \tag{32}$$

We assume that each price function, (32), is homogeneous of degree one in the component input prices; by construction, the value of each input aggregate equals the sum of the values of the corresponding input components.

The rate of growth of the price of each aggregate input can be expressed as an elasticity-weighted average of the rates of growth of the prices of its components

$$\frac{d \ln p_i}{dT} = \sum_{l=1}^{M_i} \frac{\partial \ln p_i}{\partial \ln p_{il}} \frac{d \ln p_{il}}{dT} \qquad (i = L, K, F). \tag{33}$$

Given linear homogeneity, the elasticity weights in (33) can be replaced with cost shares

$$\frac{d \ln p_i}{dT} = \sum_{l=1}^{M_i} v_{il} \frac{d \ln p_{il}}{dT} \qquad (i = L, K, F), \tag{34}$$

where each share weight equals the component input's share in the value of the corresponding input aggregate. The expressions for p_L, p_K, and p_F derived from the expressions in (34) are Divisia price indexes of labor, capital, and fuel, respectively.

A set of arguments parallel to those developed in Section 1 leads to expressions for each aggregate input price in terms of data at discrete points in time:

$$\ln p_i(T) - \ln p_i(T - 1) = \sum_{l=1}^{M_i} \bar{v}_{il} [\ln p_{il}(T) - \ln p_{il}(T - 1)] \qquad (i = L, K, F),$$

$$\tag{35}$$

where the weights $\bar{v}_{il}$ equal average value shares of the individual inputs in total payments to the corresponding input aggregate. The resulting indexes p_L, p_K, and p_F are Törnqvist price indexes.

We apply the expressions in (35) to construct price indexes for inputs used by each firm. This is consistent with the requirements of growth accounting. Moreover, it enables us to identify the contribution of each input's changing quality to economic growth. Accounting for the changing composition of each aggregate input leads to the now familiar result that each input's contribution to economic growth is the sum of two components: the growth in the aggregate input's stock plus the growth in the aggregate input's quality. Stated equivalently, the rate of growth in each input price is the sum of the growth rate of the price of the input stock less the rate of growth in the aggregate input's quality,

$$\frac{d \ln p_i}{dT} = \frac{d \ln p_i^s}{dT} - \frac{d \ln q_i}{dT} \qquad (i = L, K, F), \qquad (36)$$

where p_i^s and q_i are price and quality indexes, respectively, of the stock of the ith input. This result can be derived directly from the expressions in (34) by adding and subtracting $d \ln p_i^s / dT$ to the right-hand terms in (34):

$$\frac{d \ln p_i}{dT} = \frac{d \ln p_i^s}{dT} - \sum_j v_{ij} \left[\frac{d \ln p_i^s}{dT} - \frac{d \ln p_{ij}}{dT} \right] \qquad (i = L, K, F) \qquad (37)$$

so that, following the discussion in Jorgenson and Griliches (1967),

$$\frac{d \ln q_i}{dT} = \sum_j v_{ij} \left[\frac{d \ln p_i^s}{dT} - \frac{d \ln p_{ij}}{dT} \right] \qquad (i = L, K, F). \qquad (38)$$

The corresponding expressions relevant to discrete data can be derived from (35), yielding:

$$\ln p_i(T) - \ln p_i(T - 1) = \left[\ln p_i^s(T) - \ln p_i^s(T - 1) \right]$$
$$- \left[\ln q_i(T) - \ln q_i(T - 1) \right] \qquad (i = L, K, F), \quad (39)$$

where

$$\ln q_i(T) - \ln q_i(T - 1) = \sum_j \bar{v}_{ij} \{ \left[\ln p_i^s(T) - \ln p_i^s(T - 1) \right]$$
$$- \left[\ln p_{ij}(T) - \ln p_{ij}(T - 1) \right] \} \qquad (i = L, K, F). \quad (40)$$

By rewriting the Törnqvist indexes in (35) in terms of (39) and (40) the growth in the price of each input stock and the growth in each input's quality can be identified as distinct sources of economic growth. The separable contributions of each are measured and reported in Section 5.

The construction of the aggregate price indexes defined in (35) requires detailed price and quantity data for each firm's individual inputs. Much of our data comes directly from the Federal Power Commission *Statistics* and *Steam-Electric Plant Construction Costs and Annual Production Expenses*. The latter source lists the annual amount and unit cost of each type of fuel used at the major generating stations of each of our sample firms. Equation (35) for fuel is applied to these data to construct a Törnqvist price index (p_F) for fuel across our eleven firms over the 1958–1975 period. An index of the price of fuel stocks (required to decompose the growth in p_F into its stock price and quality components) is constructed for each utility from the same data. Expenditures by fuel type are first converted to constant 1972 dollars. The constant dollar expenditures are summed across fuels within each firm at each point in time and an index of constant dollar expenditures is formed for each utility. The index of fuel stock price (p_F^s) for each firm equals the ratio of the utility's current dollar fuel expenditures to constant dollar expenditures at each year. The quality index (q_F) for each firm is determined from (40).

Federal Power Commission reports do not provide sufficient detail to distinguish among distinct categories of labor. Consequently, we are forced to maintain that the changing composition of each company's labor force makes no contribution to economic growth. We measure the price of labor input in each firm as the average annual labor expenditure per employee in that firm. Labor expenditures, as reported in *Statistics*, are the sum of salaries, wages, and employee pensions and benefits. Labor input is the sum of full-time employees plus one-half the number of reported part-time laborers.

In contrast to labor input, considerable data are available to distinguish capital stock by asset type. Typically, applied economic research measures capital input by reported book value or, when focusing only on generation, by megawatt capacity. The former accounts neither for the different vintages and asset types of investment comprising capital stock nor for economic decay. The latter makes no adjustment for generators with identical megawatt ratings but different capital–fuel ratios; moreover, it is inappropriate for our purposes since we need to incorporate transmission and distribution equipment in addition to generation plant and equipment in our measure of capital input. Appropriate measures of capital input and price must capture differences in both asset and vintage mix of the capital stock.

Our measure of capital input and its input price p_K are constructed according to the methods described in Christensen and Jorgenson (1969).[18] We

---

[18] Our measures of X_K and p_K are a subset of similar measures constructed for each of 136 electric utilities in each year 1950–1975. The complete data set was generated jointly with L. Christensen and R. Stevenson of the University of Wisconsin.

begin by distinguishing among seven asset classes: fossil steam, nuclear, hydroelectric, other internal combustion generation, transmission, distribution, and general plant. The capital stock K_k in each period for each asset type is constructed using the perpetual inventory method of capital accumulation. Investment data reported for the 1950–1975 period in *Statistics* are converted to real stock additions by the use of 1966 acquisition prices[19] extrapolated over 1950–1975 using the *Handy–Whitman Index of Utility Construction Costs*. Capital decay for each asset type is assumed to follow the 1.5 declining balance pattern[20]; service lives are determined from engineering estimates.[21]

Input prices p_{Kk} for capital in each asset class are constructed according to the definitions applied in Caves *et al.* [1980]. Each p_{Kk} is a marginal price, a function of capital gains, service lives, tax policy, and the firm's opportunity cost of capital. The service price of capital input p_K is formed from the p_{Kk} and K_k by the Törnqvist indexing procedure described in (35). An index of the capital stock price (p_K^s) is formed by constructing a Törnqvist index of asset acquisition prices using capital stock shares as weights. The indexes of input and stock prices (p_K and p_K^s, respectively) are used to generate an index of capital quality q_K.

The input price, stock price, and quality indexes constructed for labor, capital, and fuel inputs serve three important functions in this study. First, the stock price and quality indexes identify the unique contributions of changing stock prices and the changing composition of input stocks to movements in production costs. Second, the input price indexes are important variables determining the value of $\overline{W}$ that represents the sum contribution of scale economies and technical change to economic growth. Third, the input price indexes together with indexes of total cost, $\overline{W}$, output, and time complete the data set required by the econometric model described in Section 3.

5. Findings

Parameter estimates for the unrestricted model of production and technical change described in Section 1 are reported in Table 1. The estimates describe the maintained model from which estimates of scale economies and technical

---

[19] For a complete description of the sources of asset acquisition prices, see Christensen *et al.* [1980a].

[20] The individual decay patterns (δ_k) are defined by the 1.5 declining balance method—i.e., $\delta_k = 1.5/T_k$ where T_k is the service life of the kth asset type.

[21] Engineers at the Wisconsin Public Service Commission kindly provided us with asset-specific service life estimates.

TABLE 1

Unrestricted Model of Production and Technical Change[a]

Parameter	Estimate	Parameter	Estimate
α_0	−0.0669 (0.0139)	γ_{FL}	−0.0344 (0.0053)
β_K	0.5705 (0.0037)	γ_{FF}	0.1502 (0.0061)
β_L	0.1410 (0.0031)	γ_{FQ}	0.0346 (0.0058)
β_F	0.2885 (0.0037)	γ_{FT}	0.0612 (0.0063)
β_Q	0.7746 (0.0246)	γ_{LL}	0.1551 (0.0117)
β_T	−0.0024 (0.0175)	γ_{LQ}	−0.0039 (0.0049)
γ_{KK}	0.2366 (0.0097)	γ_{LT}	−0.0602 (0.0053)
γ_{KL}	−0.1207 (0.0096)	γ_{QQ}	−0.0809 (0.0513)
γ_{KF}	−0.1158 (0.0055)	γ_{QT}	0.0233 (0.0283)
γ_{KQ}	−0.0307 (0.0057)	γ_{TT}	0.0258 (0.0303)
γ_{KT}	−0.0010 (0.0063)		

[a] Standard errors in parentheses.

change are derived and against which all scale and technical change hypotheses are evaluated. These hypotheses include constant returns to scale, homogeneity, factor-augmenting technical change, first-order exponential factor augmentation, and the alternative forms of neutral technical change. Results of these hypothesis tests and all inferences based directly on the estimated parameters are discussed in the first three subsections. The sources of economic growth over the 1958–1975 period for each of the sample utilities are identified in the final subsection.

5.1 Scale Economies

The elasticity of cost with respect to output measures static or scale economies. This elasticity, defined as v_Q in Section 1, is a function of input prices, output, and time. Given data at discrete points in time, the average scale elasticity $(\bar{v}_Q)$ between periods T and $T - 1$ is defined in terms of the translog parameters and the data at periods T and $T - 1$

$$\bar{v}_Q(T) = \tfrac{1}{2}[v_Q(T) + v_Q(T - 1)] = \beta_Q + \sum_i \gamma_{iQ} \overline{\ln p_i} + \gamma_{QQ} \overline{\ln Q} + \gamma_{QT} \bar{T}, \quad (41)$$

where $\overline{\ln p_i}$, $\overline{\ln Q}$, and $\bar{T}$ are defined in Section 3.

The two important scale hypotheses relevant for studies of economic growth are constant returns to scale $(\bar{v}_Q = 1)$ and homogeneity $(\bar{v}_Q = c$, where c is a constant). The former suggests that productivity analysis may ignore scale; the latter implies that, while scale economies may be an important source of economic growth, their contribution to any firm's productivity performance is insensitive to the firm's scale of operation, to changes in any input price, and even to particular periods in the firm's history.

The parametric restrictions consistent with each hypothesis can be derived directly from (41). If production everywhere exhibits constant returns, the scale elasticity is not a function of input prices, output, or time. Moreover, the elasticity equals unity. This set of conditions implies the following necessary and sufficient restrictions[22]:

$$\beta_Q = 1, \qquad \gamma_{LQ} = \gamma_{KQ} = \gamma_{QQ} = \gamma_{QT} = 0. \tag{42}$$

Homogeneity requires the same set of restrictions except that β_Q need not equal unity. The F test statistic corresponding to constant returns is 127.77; the critical $F(5,733)$ value is 3.04 at the 99% significance level. We therefore reject constant returns to scale and conclude that a study of economic growth in the electric power industry must not neglect the contribution of scale economies to productivity growth. We similarly reject homogeneity. The test statistic is 39.16; the critical $F(4,733)$ value at the 99% level is 3.34.

Given that the industry's technology cannot be characterized by homogeneity, economies of scale are a function of input prices, output, and time. Estimates for each firm can be determined directly from (41). Table 2 reports estimated average scale elasticities based on each utility's input prices and scale of operation at selected points in time. All estimates of $\bar{v}_Q$ are less than unity. They vary from 0.68 to 0.90, suggesting that the underlying technology exhibits substantial increasing returns at all scales of operation found in our sample.[23] On average, a 1% increase in output results approximately in an increase of 0.8% in total cost.

The parameters responsible for the variability in the scale estimates reported in Table 2 are identified in (41). Price effects are measured by γ_{LQ}, γ_{KQ}, and γ_{FQ}; output and time effects are modeled by γ_{QQ} and γ_{QT}, respectively. The estimates are reported in Table 1. Positive (negative) values indicate that increases in the corresponding variable lead to lower (higher) scale economies.[24] While $\hat{\gamma}_{QT} > 0$ and $\hat{\gamma}_{QQ} < 0$, neither is statistically signifi-

---

[22] Given the accounting restrictions (12), γ_{FQ} necessarily equals zero if $\gamma_{LQ} = \gamma_{KQ} = 0$.

[23] It is important to note that our estimates of scale economies are not inconsistent with the findings of Christensen and Greene [1976]. While they find evidence of minimal scale economies for the larger firms in their sample, their research focuses only on generation. Our data model each utility's complete production activity—generation, transmission, and distribution. While economies in generation may well be exhausted at a relatively small scale of operation, engineering considerations suggest that significant economies persist in both transmission and distribution. Since as much as two-thirds of the capital stock in some utilities is devoted to transmission and distribution, our estimate of scale economies would be expected to be higher than that estimated from a model studying generation alone.

[24] As $\bar{v}_Q$ approaches unity from below, scale economies decrease and the technology approaches constant returns to scale.

TABLE 2

Estimated Average Scale Elasticities[a]

Firm (ranked by 1972 size)	1972 net generation (million kWh)	1958– 1959	1961– 1962	1964– 1965	1967– 1968	1970– 1971	1972– 1973	1974– 1975
Illinois Power	10,230	0.836	0.819	0.798	0.790	0.771	0.774	0.785
South Carolina Electric & Gas	10,320	0.898	0.861	0.823	0.809	0.807	0.795	0.829
Cincinnati Gas & Electric	10,940	0.829	0.813	0.795	0.794	0.791	0.786	0.805
Wisconsin Electric Power	12,910	0.818	0.800	0.786	0.772	0.771	0.779	0.799
Cleveland Electric Illuminating Co.	15,400	0.793	0.773	0.761	0.757	0.758	0.754	0.783
Ohio Edison	17,270	0.774	0.750	0.740	0.736	0.737	0.736	0.777
Consumers Power	19,910	0.783	0.762	0.746	0.731	0.742	0.742	0.769
Potomac Electric	20,070	0.838	0.804	0.781	0.762	0.761	0.749	0.797
Pennsylvania Power & Light	20,520	0.779	0.767	0.758	0.741	0.738	0.721	0.739
Carolina Power & Light	22,530	0.834	0.800	0.776	0.753	0.743	0.730	0.759
Duke Power	40,570	0.752	0.725	0.709	0.688	0.684	0.682	0.707

[a] Evaluated at actual data.

cant. All other variables held constant, neither technical change nor changes in firm size have a statistically significant impact on the degree of scale economies. A change in wage rates similarly has no significant effect: $\hat{\gamma}_{LQ}$ is not statistically different from zero. Price changes for capital and fuel inputs, however, do lead to input combinations along expansion paths that exhibit statistically different degrees of scale economies: $\hat{\gamma}_{KQ}$ and $\hat{\gamma}_{FQ}$ are both significant at the 99% level. Increases in the price of capital inputs move firms to expansion paths characterized by greater scale economies ($\hat{\gamma}_{KQ} < 0$); increases in fuel prices result in lower scale economies ($\hat{\gamma}_{FQ} > 0$).

The relative magnitudes of the three price parameters determine the net effect of price changes on scale economies. Since $\hat{\gamma}_{FQ}$ exceeds both $\hat{\gamma}_{LQ}$ and $\hat{\gamma}_{KQ}$, a proportional increase in fuel prices has a greater effect on scale economies than does an equal proportional increase in either labor or capital prices. This finding is especially noteworthy since fuel accounts for less than 30% of total production costs. The important implication is clear: relative price movements in recent years have steadily lessened the contribution of scale economies to productivity growth in the electric power industry.

This conclusion is consistent with the pattern of scale elasticity estimates

TABLE 3

Estimated Average Scale Elasticities[a]

Firm (ranked by 1972 size)	Average net generation 1958–1975 (million kWh)	1958– 1959	1961– 1962	1964– 1965	1967– 1968	1970– 1971	1972– 1973	1974– 1975
Illinois Power	7534	0.800	0.788	0.785	0.783	0.786	0.791	0.812
South Carolina Electric & Gas	6296	0.831	0.816	0.814	0.810	0.820	0.823	0.852
Cincinnati Gas & Electric	7902	0.808	0.798	0.789	0.788	0.795	0.802	0.821
Wisconsin Electric Power Company	9823	0.797	0.783	0.778	0.776	0.782	0.767	0.782
Cleveland Electric Illuminating Co.	11,600	0.772	0.757	0.752	0.752	0.762	0.768	0.796
Ohio Edison	12,440	0.752	0.736	0.734	0.733	0.743	0.751	0.781
Consumers Power	15,360	0.759	0.746	0.743	0.742	0.748	0.750	0.768
Potomac Electric	11,500	0.786	0.770	0.765	0.765	0.774	0.778	0.812
Pennsylvania Power & Light	13,490	0.743	0.733	0.729	0.730	0.743	0.751	0.775
Carolina Power & Light	13,490	0.771	0.754	0.750	0.749	0.759	0.762	0.790
Duke Power	27,790	0.709	0.693	0.691	0.688	0.699	0.702	0.729

[a] Evaluated at actual price data; output and time fixed at mean values.

reported in Table 3. The estimates are formed holding each firm's output equal to its mean value over the 1958–1975 period; the time variable is set equal to its average 1966–1967 value, the midpoint in our sample period. Only input prices are allowed to vary. Consequently, observed differences in the reported estimates for each firm are wholly a function of net price effects. The expected pattern emerges. As prices of labor and capital increased relative to fuel prices in the early part of the period, the estimates of $\bar{v}_Q$ decline, suggesting increased scale economies. In later years, as fuel prices increased relative to any other input price, scale economies decrease. The sharp decline in scale economies between 1972–1973 and 1974–1975 is especially notable. All else constant, the reasonable expectation is that this trend has continued into the present and will continue into the foreseeable future.

5.2 Technical Change

Independent of scale effects, productivity growth is also a function of technical change. The rate of technical change v_T, as defined in Section 1, equals the negative of the rate of growth of total cost with respect to time, holding output and the prices of inputs constant:

$$v_T = -\frac{\partial \ln C}{\partial T}(p_L, p_K, p_F, Q, T). \tag{43}$$

Given data at discrete points in time, the average rate of technical change between periods T and $T - 1$ is defined in terms of the translog parameters and the data at periods T and $T - 1$:

$$\bar{v}_T(T) = \tfrac{1}{2}[v(T) + v(T - 1)]$$

$$= -[\beta_T + \sum_i \gamma_{iT} \overline{\ln p_i} + \gamma_{QT} \overline{\ln Q} + \gamma_{TT} \overline{T}]. \tag{44}$$

Estimated values of $\bar{v}_T$ for each firm are calculated from (44) and are reported in Table 4. The estimates are based on the parameter estimates listed in Table 1 and the actual data observed for each firm at each point in time. The rates of technical change vary across firms but the important pattern is unmistakable. Technical change declines consistently over the 18-year period. The average rate of technical change between 1958 and 1959 is 4.7%; this declines to -4.4% between 1974 and 1975. For many firms, retardation sets in by 1972. This pattern is consistent with the results reported by Gollop and Jorgenson [1980] for the aggregate electric power industry. They find that the industry's annual rate of technical change declines from nearly 4% in the 1957–1960 period to almost 2% between 1960 and 1966 and finally to -0.35% in the 1966–1973 period.[25] The implication of both investigations is clear: while technical change made substantial contributions to productivity growth prior to 1970, retardation characterized the decade of the 1970s.

Stated in terms of the dual cost function developed in this paper, the rate of technical change reflects a downward displacement of the average cost curve. The rate of cost reduction is itself a function of output, time, and input prices and, given (43) and (44), has the following direct representation in our estimating model:

$$\frac{\partial \overline{\ln C}}{\partial T} = \beta_T + \sum_i \gamma_{iT} \overline{\ln p_i} + \gamma_{QT} \overline{\ln Q} + \gamma_{TT} \overline{T}. \tag{45}$$

The effects of output and time on the rate of displacement require little explanation. The partial derivative of (45) with respect to time (γ_{TT}) measures the rate of change in the rate of cost reduction associated with technical change; the partial derivative with respect to output (γ_{QT}) captures the

[25] Gollop and Jorgenson [1980, p. 119].

TABLE 4

Estimated Average Annual Rates of Technical Change[a]

Firm (ranked by 1972 size)	1972 net generation (million kWh)	1958– 1959	1961– 1962	1964– 1965	1967– 1968	1970– 1971	1972– 1973	1974– 1975
Illinois Power	10,230	0.077	0.072	0.066	0.061	0.046	0.035	−0.000
South Carolina Electric & Gas	10,320	0.047	0.045	0.037	0.029	−0.001	−0.007	−0.051
Cincinnati Gas & Electric	10,940	0.050	0.039	0.044	0.036	0.017	0.001	−0.032
Wisconsin Electric Power	12,910	0.041	0.040	0.041	0.032	0.012	0.004	−0.017
Cleveland Electric Illuminating Co.	15,400	0.052	0.056	0.054	0.042	0.016	0.006	−0.040
Ohio Edison	17,270	0.069	0.067	0.065	0.057	0.037	0.021	−0.026
Consumers Power	19,910	0.024	0.023	0.022	0.011	0.001	−0.003	−0.034
Potomac Electric	20,070	0.026	0.025	0.020	0.007	−0.009	−0.021	−0.074
Pennsylvania Power & Light	20,520	0.080	0.077	0.072	0.052	0.016	−0.005	−0.037
Carolina Power & Light	22,530	0.037	0.038	0.029	0.017	−0.012	−0.025	−0.077
Duke Power	40,570	0.019	0.019	0.010	−0.004	−0.027	−0.049	−0.095

[a] Evaluated at actual data.

familiar Schumpeterian hypothesis. Only the price effects require detailed discussion.

Changing input prices affect the least cost combination of inputs and therefore may affect the rate of technical change. If, for example, technical change is capital-using, an increase in the price of capital not only encourages substitution of other inputs for capital but also makes the adoption of the capital-using innovation more costly. The result is a lower rate of cost reduction associated with technical change. If, however, technical change is capital-saving, an increase in the price of capital has the opposite effect on the rate of technical change. Substitution is still encouraged but now toward an input combination consistent with the capital-saving nature of technical change. Adopting the innovation, by economizing on a now more expensive input, increases the rate of cost reduction associated with technical change.[26]

We think it important to emphasize that these effects on the rate of technical change are achieved wholly because of changes in prices associated

[26] See Binswanger [1974b] for a good discussion of the relationship among biased technical change, changing input prices, and their effects on cost shares and input use.

with individual inputs. The input whose price has increased may itself not be a medium of technical change. Its marginal product may not be directly affected by the technical change. The sources of productivity growth may well be in other inputs substitutes and/or complements. Independent of any direct contribution associated with the input, an increase in its price may lead to a new combination of inputs. The resulting effect on technical change is a function of substitution possibilities and the factor-using/factor-saving nature of technical change.

The direction and magnitude of these price effects depend on the parameters γ_{LT}, γ_{KT}, and γ_{FT}. Each parameter represents the logarithmic second partial derivative of the translog cost function (7) with respect to time and the price of the corresponding input. Equivalently, each represents the logarithmic partial derivative of the rate of cost reduction due to technical change (45) with respect to the corresponding input price.

The parameter estimates reported in Table 1 suggest that the only statistically significant variability observed in Table 4 is associated with input prices. The rate of technical change is statistically insensitive to both firm size and time. Neither $\hat{\gamma}_{QT}$ nor $\hat{\gamma}_{TT}$ is significant at the 90% level. In contrast, two of the three price parameters identified in (44) are significant at the 99% level.

These estimates suggest that technical change is labor-saving, fuel-using, and capital-neutral: $\hat{\gamma}_{LT}$ is negative, $\hat{\gamma}_{FT}$ is positive, and $\hat{\gamma}_{KT}$ is not statistically different from zero.[27] An increase in the price of labor input leads to a greater (i.e., more negative) rate of cost reduction associated with technical change; an increase in the price of fuel leads to a reduced rate of technical change. The retarding effect of increased fuel prices is especially noteworthy since, once again, the effect of a fuel price increase exceeds the effect of an equal proportional increase in the price of either labor or capital input. This suggests that the net combined effect of recent price changes has been to shift rational producers to expansion paths exhibiting lower rates of technical change.

The magnitude of this net price effect is reflected in the estimates of $\bar{v}_T$ reported in Table 5. All output and time effects are held constant; the $\overline{\ln Q}$ and $\bar{T}$ variables appearing in (44) are held fixed at their mean values for

---

[27] Note that these results contrast with engineering observations, which suggest that technical change has been embodied in capital that is more thermally efficient than older vintages of capital stock. The implication is that technical change should be fuel-saving and capital-using, not fuel-using and capital-neutral as found in this investigation. The difference, of course, is that engineering estimates are based on ex ante designs while econometric estimates are based on ex post observations. It should also be reported that our results are consistent with the findings presented by Stevenson [1980]. He finds economic evidence that technical change in electric utilities has been fuel-using and labor- and capital-saving.

TABLE 5

Estimated Average Annual Rates of Technical Change[a]

Firm (ranked by 1972 size)	Average net generation 1958–1975 (million kWh)	1958–1959	1961–1962	1964–1965	1967–1968	1970–1971	1972–1973	1974–1975
Illinois Power	7534	0.041	0.046	0.056	0.062	0.063	0.059	0.034
South Carolina Electric & Gas	6296	0.001	0.016	0.028	0.032	0.016	0.021	−0.018
Cincinnati Gas & Electric	7902	0.018	0.018	0.035	0.037	0.031	0.025	−0.001
Wisconsin Electric Power Co.	9823	0.008	0.019	0.032	0.036	0.028	0.020	0.003
Cleveland Electric Illuminating Co.	11,600	0.020	0.035	0.045	0.043	0.030	0.029	−0.010
Ohio Edison	12,440	0.036	0.047	0.057	0.060	0.052	0.045	0.001
Consumers Power	15,360	−0.009	0.002	0.015	0.016	0.016	0.018	−0.008
Potomac Electric	11,500	−0.016	−0.001	0.009	0.011	0.008	0.007	−0.043
Pennsylvania Power & Light	13,490	0.044	0.051	0.057	0.052	0.031	0.023	−0.001
Carolina Power & Light	13,490	−0.007	0.008	0.015	0.019	0.005	0.003	−0.042
Duke Power	27,790	−0.019	−0.007	−0.002	−0.001	−0.020	−0.024	−0.062

[a] Evaluated at actual price data; output and time fixed at mean values.

each firm. Only input prices are allowed to vary. The resulting patterns are similar for each firm. Relative price movements in the early part of the 1958–1975 period led to increased rates of technical change; price changes in later years reduced the rate of technical change. The rapid rise in fuel prices beginning in 1973 had the expected result—a sharp decline in the rate of technical change and, consequently, productivity growth.

5.3 Factor Augmentation

A principal objective of this study is to identify the sources and structure of technical change in the electric power industry. In particular, we wish to determine whether the rate of technical change can be allocated among components uniquely associated with individual inputs and, if so, which inputs are the dominant mediums of technical change. This analysis of the structure of technical change involves testing six hypotheses: factor augmentation, exponential first-order augmentation, Hicks neutrality, Harrod neutrality, Solow neutrality, and Leontief neutrality. To control the overall level of significance for the complete set of six hypothesis tests, we set the overall level of significance at 0.06. We then allocate the overall level among the six tests, assigning a level of significance of 0.01 to each test. The probability of a false rejection for one test among the six tests is less than or equal to 0.06 by the Bonferroni inequality.

As explained in Section 2, conducting these hypothesis tests begins with respecifying the unrestricted model of production in terms of a factor-augmentation model of technical change. The model maintains that technical change augments individual inputs. Factor-specific augmentation coefficients model these effects. Production becomes a function of inputs defined in efficiency units; cost becomes a function of output and efficiency unit prices.

If factor-augmenting technical change makes no direct contribution to economic growth through a particular input, the augmentation coefficient corresponding to that input will not be a function of time. If technical change makes a positive (negative) contribution through an input, the corresponding augmentation coefficient will be a positive (negative) function of time.

The model of factor-augmenting technical change introduced in Section 2 is a restricted form of the general model of technical change developed in Section 1. Imposing the restrictions identified in (22) generates a factor-augmentation model having one less parameter than the unrestricted model of technical change. We test this single "factor augmentation" restriction. The F-test statistic is 0.52; the corresponding $F(1, 733)$ critical value is 6.66 at the 1% level of significance. As a result, we cannot reject the hypothesis that technical change affecting electric utilities has a factor-augmenting form.

Decomposing the rate of technical change into its source components requires an estimate of the augmentation coefficient associated with each input. Each augmentation coefficient, A_L, A_K, and A_F, is initially modeled as a translog function of time. As discussed above, the augmentation coefficients cannot be econometrically identified unless augmenting technical change takes the first-order exponential form. This leads to the first-order factor-augmentation restriction defined in (24). We test this restriction jointly with the factor-augmentation restriction described above. We cannot reject this joint hypothesis. The critical value for $F(2, 733)$ at the 1% level of significance is 4.62; the F-test statistic is 0.377. The functional form required for the total decomposition of technical change among its source components cannot be rejected when tested against a more general model of production and technical change.

We next evaluate whether the firms' histories exhibit evidence consistent with any of the first-order variants of neutral technical change. Restrictions implied by Hicks, Harrod, Solow, and Leontief neutralities are defined in

(27), (28), (29), and (30), respectively. Each hypothesized neutrality is modeled by two restrictions. Each of these hypotheses is tested jointly with the factor-augmentation and first-order factor-augmentation hypotheses discussed above. Consequently, each hypothesis test involves four restrictions. All four neutrality hypotheses are rejected. The F-test statistics for Hicks, Harrod, Solow, and Leontief neutralities are 153.15, 69.39, 153.48, and 103.18, respectively; the $F(4, 733)$ critical value at the 1% level is 3.34. While technical change in the electric power industry may well have an exponential first-order factor-augmenting structure, we find no statistical evidence suggesting that technical change can be represented by an input-neutral form.

We impose the first-order structure on the augmentation functions and estimate the parameters of the restricted model of production and technical change. The estimates are reported in Table 6. The critical parameters are η_L, η_K, and η_F. Each represents the rate of change in the corresponding augmentation function with respect to time. As discussed in Section 2, the signs of these estimated coefficients wholly determine the directions of the contributions to technical change associated with the corresponding inputs. Positive values indicate that technical change augments the corresponding inputs and makes a direct contribution to the rate of cost reduction due to technical change. Negative values indicate that the direct contributions associated with the corresponding inputs retard productivity growth.

The estimates of η_L, η_K, and η_F reported in Table 6 are all significant at the 1% level. Both η_K and η_L have positive values, suggesting that factor-augmenting technical change makes a direct contribution to productivity growth through capital and labor inputs. In contrast, the estimate of η_F

TABLE 6

Exponential First-Order Augmentation Model of Production and Technical Change[a]

Parameter	Estimate	Parameter	Estimate
α_0	-0.0677 (0.0144)	γ_{FL}	-0.0330 (0.0050)
β_K	0.5694 (0.0037)	γ_{FF}	0.1499 (0.0055)
β_L	0.1414 (0.0030)	γ_{FQ}	0.0329 (0.0053)
β_F	0.2892 (0.0034)	γ_{LL}	0.1502 (0.0113)
β_Q	0.7714 (0.0224)	γ_{LQ}	-0.0045 (0.0047)
γ_{KK}	0.2341 (0.0096)	γ_{QQ}	-0.0661 (0.0417)
γ_{KL}	-0.1172 (0.0094)	η_K	0.0516 (0.0167)
γ_{KF}	-0.1169 (0.0054)	η_L	0.3673 (0.0388)
γ_{KQ}	-0.0284 (0.0057)	η_F	-0.2956 (0.0350)

[a] Standard errors in parentheses.

has a negative value; augmentation of fuel input retards productivity growth. The signs of $\hat{\eta}_L$, $\hat{\eta}_K$, and $\hat{\eta}_F$ determine only the directions of the productivity contributions of technical change through the corresponding inputs. As indicated in Section 2, the magnitude of each contribution is a function of the complete set of parameter estimates and the data. In the next section, we evaluate the direct contributions associated with individual inputs.

5.4 Sources of Growth

The primary objective of this study is to quantify the sources of economic growth in the electric power industry. Stated in dual form, the rate of growth of total cost equals the sum of cost-share weighted rates of growth of the prices of input stocks, less the cost-share weighted rates of growth in input qualities, plus the contribution of scale economies, plus the rate of cost reduction associated with technical change. This last rate of cost reduction, moreover, equals the sum of the technical change contributions associated with individual inputs. The isolation and measurement of the separable contributions of changes in the stock prices of labor, capital, and fuel inputs and changes in the qualities of capital and fuel inputs are discussed in the data section. Measuring these contributions does not require econometric analysis; they follow directly from the observed data. In contrast, evaluating the contributions of scale economies and technical change requires an estimating model based on the theory of production and technical change described in Sections 1 and 2.

The results of this total decomposition are presented in Table 7. The table identifies the mean annual contribution of each source of economic growth to the average annual rate of growth in total cost in the 1958–1975 history of each of our sample utilities. Mean contributions calculated over the full sample are reported at the bottom of the table. The average annual rate of growth in *total* production cost ranges from 7.1% for Wisconsin Electric Power to 13.2% for Carolina Power & Light. The average rate of increase over the full sample is 9.9%.

The contribution of changes in each input's stock price is calculated as the product of the rate of growth in the stock price and that input's share in total cost. Not surprisingly, changes in input stock prices have universally made positive contributions to the rate of growth in each utility's total cost. The mean contributions of changing labor, capital, and fuel stock prices have been 0.8, 2.7, and 2.4%, respectively. Taken together, these sources, on average, account for 5.9 percentage points in the average annual 9.9% increase in production cost. What is notable is that the average contribution of fuel stock prices nearly equals the contribution associated with the price

TABLE 7

Sources of Growth of Total Cost: Average Annual Rates of Growth 1958–1975

Firm (ranked by 1972 output)	Average annual rate of growth of total cost	Source contributions									
		Input prices					Output	Technical change effect	Time		
		Labor	Capital		Fuel				Source contributions		
		Stock price	Stock price	Quality	Stock price	Quality	Scale effect		Labor	Capital	Fuel
Illinois Power	0.086	0.008	0.032	−0.0118	0.015	0.0006	0.063	−0.051	−0.071	−0.032	0.053
South Carolina Electric & Gas	0.124	0.006	0.028	−0.0100	0.025	0.0006	0.086	−0.013	−0.054	−0.031	0.072
Cincinnati Gas & Electric	0.090	0.008	0.027	−0.0085	0.021	0.0001	0.047	−0.024	−0.061	−0.031	0.068
Wisconsin Electric Power Co.	0.071	0.010	0.026	−0.0088	0.016	−0.0002	0.036	−0.024	−0.071	−0.028	0.075
Cleveland Electric Illuminating Co.	0.083	0.009	0.025	−0.0053	0.028	0.0002	0.041	−0.033	−0.069	−0.031	0.066
Ohio Edison	0.086	0.010	0.027	−0.0047	0.027	−0.0002	0.035	−0.049	−0.066	−0.033	0.051
Consumers Power	0.092	0.013	0.027	−0.0041	0.020	−0.0017	0.039	−0.013	−0.065	−0.028	0.081
Potomac Electric	0.115	0.007	0.027	−0.0079	0.030	0.0002	0.059	−0.002	−0.055	−0.030	0.082
Pennsylvania Power & Light	0.091	0.007	0.028	−0.0111	0.026	−0.0003	0.061	−0.046	−0.067	−0.033	0.054
Carolina Power & Light	0.132	0.005	0.027	−0.0028	0.027	0.0028	0.078	−0.009	−0.058	−0.030	0.079
Duke Power	0.115	0.004	0.028	−0.0074	0.025	0.0021	0.056	0.003	−0.051	−0.030	0.084
Mean	0.099	0.008	0.027	−0.0075	0.024	0.0004	0.055	−0.024	−0.063	−0.031	0.070

of capital stock. This occurs even though the share of fuel in production cost is roughly half the share of capital and fuel prices remained relatively stable in the early part of the sample period.

Changes in input qualities have reduced what would otherwise have been the rate of growth in total cost by an average rate equal to 0.71% per year. The changing composition of capital stock has reduced the rate of growth in total cost in each of the eleven utilities. The contributions range from −0.28% for Carolina Power & Light to −1.18% for Illinois Power. The average contribution over all utilities is −0.75% per year. The composition of fuel stocks, in contrast, has changed little. Changes in fuel quality have reduced the rate of growth in production cost in four utilities and increased its growth rate in seven firms. The average annual contribution across all utilities is 0.04%.

Recalling that the total contribution of changes in each input's price *per quality adjusted unit* equals the sum of that input's stock price and quality contributions, the average annual source contributions associated with labor, capital, and fuel quality adjusted prices are 0.80, 1.95, and 2.44%, respectively. Among inputs, increases in fuel input prices have contributed most to rising production cost over the full 1958–1975 period.

The contribution associated with the change in a utility's scale of operation between two points in time is defined in (6). It equals the product of the utility's rate of growth in output and its average scale elasticity between the two time periods. The average contribution from this source is 5.5%.

The remaining source of economic growth is technical change. It is defined as the *negative* of the partial derivative of the logarithm of cost with respect to time. The average annual rate of technical change has been positive in ten of the 11 industries listed in Table 7; that is, the effect of technical change has been to reduce the rate of growth in total cost. These annual contributions range from −0.2% for Potomac Electric to −5.1% for Illinois Power. Technical change has had a small retarding effect in Duke Power. On average, technical change has reduced the rate of growth in total production cost by 2.4 percentage points below what it would have been in the absence of technical change.

Given first-order exponential augmentation, the rate of technical change equals the sum of technical change contributions associated with individual inputs. This source decomposition is described in Eqs. (25) and (26). The results are reported in the last three columns of Table 7. Technical change reduces the rate of growth in cost through the positive augmentation of labor and capital inputs; it increases the rate of growth in production cost through the retardation of fuel input. In brief, technical change has increased the efficiency content of labor and capital inputs and reduced the marginal productivity of fuel. The average annual contributions to production cost of technical change through augmented labor, capital, and fuel inputs are -6.3, -3.1, and 7.0%, respectively.

Productivity growth is an important source of the economic growth described in Table 7. Formally defined, the rate of productivity growth v_G equals the negative of the rate of change in average production cost holding input prices constant

$$v_G = -\left.\frac{d\ln AC}{dT}\right|_{\underline{p}} \tag{46}$$

where AC equals average cost. Productivity studies that assume constant returns to scale treat productivity growth wholly in terms of technical change. This study, in contrast, treats scale economies (v_Q) *and* technical change (v_T) as distinct sources of productivity growth. The source decomposition follows directly from (6). The rate of growth in total cost holding input prices constant equals the sum of scale and technical change contributions:

$$\left.\frac{d\ln AC}{dT}\right|_{\underline{p}} = \frac{\partial\ln C}{\partial\ln Q}\frac{d\ln Q}{dT} + \frac{\partial\ln C}{\partial T} = v_Q\frac{d\ln Q}{dT} - v_T. \tag{47}$$

Subtracting the growth rate of output from both sides of (47) produces the relation between the rate of cost reduction associated with productivity growth and its two sources

$$\left.\frac{d\ln C}{dT}\right|_{\underline{p}} = \left(\frac{\partial\ln C}{\partial\ln Q} - 1\right)\frac{d\ln Q}{dT} + \frac{\partial\ln C}{\partial T} = (v_Q - 1)\frac{d\ln Q}{dT} - v_T \tag{48}$$

so that, given (46),

$$v_G = (1 - v_Q)\frac{d\ln Q}{dT} + v_T. \tag{49}$$

Holding input prices constant, the rate of reduction in average cost (productivity growth) equals the sum of the rates of change in average cost resulting from a *movement along* the average cost curve (scale economies) and a *shift* of the average cost curve (technical change). Under constant returns, v_Q equals unity, while under zero growth, $d\ln Q/dT$ equals zero. In either case, technical change becomes the sole source of productivity growth.

Given data at discrete points in time, the rate of productivity growth between periods T and $T - 1$ is defined in terms of the translog parameters and the data at periods T and $T - 1$:

$$\bar{v}_G(T) = [1 - \bar{v}_Q(T)][\ln Q(T) - \ln Q(T - 1)] + \bar{v}_T(T), \tag{50}$$

where $\bar{v}_Q$ and $\bar{v}_T$ are defined in terms of the translog parameters describing a first-order exponential model of factor augmentation. Table 8 reports the average annual rates of productivity growth for each firm over the full 1958–1975 period and within three subperiods. The growth rates are based on the translog parameter estimates listed in Table 6 and each utility's actual data.

The average annual rates of productivity growth over the full 18-year period are positive for every firm. The estimates, however, vary considerably across firms, ranging from 1.8% per year for Potomac Electric to 6.8% per year for Illinois Power. The average annual rate of productivity growth across the full sample of firms is 4.0%. Technical change is the dominant source of this productivity growth. The average annual rate of technical change across all utilities is 2.4%; that is, technical change accounts for three-fifths of the 4.0% rate of increase in productivity. Cost reductions resulting from scale economies account for the remaining 1.6% per year.

The important implications, however, are derived from the pattern of growth rates reported for the three subperiods 1958–1966, 1966–1973, and 1973–1975. Without exception, the average annual rate of productivity growth reported for each firm declines over time. While the productivity growth rates are all positive in both 1958–1966 and 1966–1973 periods, productivity performance in most firms declined by 50% between the two periods. The average annual rate of productivity growth calculated over all firms is 6.5% for the period 1958–1966; it drops to 3.3% for 1966–1973. The decline between 1966–1973 and 1973–1975 is even more substantial. With only one exception (Illinois Power), all rates of productivity growth in the latest subperiod are negative and the sample mean is −4.2% per year.

The decomposition of productivity growth into the contributions made by scale economies and technical change identifies the sources of this productivity decline. The contribution resulting from scale economies generally has been positive in every subperiod. Moreover, its average annual contribution remained constant over the 1958–1973 period; the average annual contribution to productivity growth equaled 1.8% in both the 1958–1966 and the 1966–1973 periods. By the 1973–1975 period, however, this positive contribution disappeared. The average annual contribution over all utilities equaled −0.1%. This resulted not from the exhaustion of scale economies (a hypothesis rejected earlier in this section) but from the fact that scale economies could make no contribution. On average, the annual rate of growth in output, $\ln Q(T) - \ln Q(T - 1)$ in (50), was approximately zero for the 1973–1975 period.

The principal cause of the overall decline in productivity growth, however, was the decline in technical change. The average annual rate of technical change declined from 4.7% in the 1958–1966 period to 1.5% during 1966–1973, and finally to −4.1% in the 1973–1975 subperiod. In the earliest period technical change, on average, accounted for slightly less than three-

TABLE 8

Contributions to Productivity Growth[a]

Firm (ranked by 1972 size)	1958–1975			1958–1966			1966–1973			1973–1975		
	Average annual rate of productivity growth	Average annual contribution		Average annual rate of productivity growth	Average annual contribution		Average annual rate of productivity growth	Average annual contribution		Average annual rate of productivity growth	Average annual contribution	
		Scale	Technical change		Scale	Technical change		Scale	Technical change		Scale	Technical change
Illinois Power	0.068	0.017	0.051	0.085	0.016	0.069	0.062	0.018	0.044	0.015	0.016	−0.001
South Carolina Electric & Gas	0.030	0.017	0.013	0.059	0.022	0.037	0.022	0.018	0.004	−0.057	−0.005	−0.052
Cincinnati Gas & Electric	0.036	0.012	0.024	0.056	0.011	0.045	0.032	0.016	0.016	−0.028	0.004	−0.032
Wisconsin Electric Power Co.	0.034	0.010	0.024	0.056	0.014	0.042	0.023	0.008	0.015	−0.023	−0.002	−0.021
Cleveland Electric Illuminating Co.	0.045	0.012	0.033	0.074	0.016	0.058	0.037	0.013	0.024	−0.043	−0.007	−0.036
Ohio Edison	0.061	0.012	0.049	0.086	0.014	0.072	0.059	0.017	0.042	−0.037	−0.016	−0.021
Consumers Power	0.025	0.012	0.013	0.049	0.019	0.030	0.014	0.008	0.006	−0.031	0.000	−0.031
Potomac Electric	0.018	0.016	0.002	0.048	0.022	0.026	0.015	0.019	−0.004	−0.088	−0.018	−0.070
Pennsylvania Power & Light	0.067	0.021	0.046	0.093	0.013	0.080	0.061	0.033	0.028	−0.024	0.008	−0.032
Carolina Power & Light	0.032	0.023	0.009	0.058	0.022	0.036	0.029	0.029	−0.000	−0.067	0.001	−0.068
Duke Power	0.019	0.022	−0.003	0.051	0.024	0.027	0.009	0.024	−0.015	−0.075	0.007	−0.082
Mean	0.040	0.016	0.024	0.065	0.018	0.047	0.033	0.018	0.015	−0.042	−0.001	−0.041

[a] Evaluated at actual data.

fourths of the substantial productivity advance experienced by electric utilities. By 1973–1975, technical retardation was responsible for almost all the decline in productivity growth.

6. Concluding Remarks

The single most important conclusion to be derived from this research is that the overall productivity performance of firms in the electric power industry has declined substantially over the 1958–1975 period. The average annual rate of total productivity growth across our sample of 11 utilities decreased from 6.5% in the 1958–1966 period to −4.2% in the 1973–1975 period.

Both sources of productivity growth contributed to this decline. Primary responsibility is assigned to technical change. Its average annual contribution decreased from 4.7% to −4.1% between the 1958–1966 and 1973–1975 periods. Remaining responsibility lies with a scale effect. It also contributed to the overall reduction in productivity growth. The average annual contribution associated with scale economies declined from 1.8% to nearly zero between the same two time periods.

The statistical results reported in Section 5 suggest that a single driving force has generated the rapid decline in productivity growth in the electric power industry. Equation (49) makes clear that the rate of productivity growth will decrease from any one of three causes: a decrease in scale economies, a decrease in the rate of growth of output ($d \ln Q/dT$), or a decrease in the rate of technical change (v_T).

In our model, scale economies and technical change are distinct functions of input prices, output, and time; the rate of growth of output is determined by demand conditions, primarily the market price of electricity. The sources of growth in production cost reported in Table 7 suggest that, among input price contributions, increasing fuel prices have been the dominant source of increased production cost. The decline in output growth observed in the 1973–1975 period is largely a result of higher market prices reflecting higher production costs due to rapidly rising fuel prices. In addition, our statistical results identify changes in relative input prices as the only statistically significant source of declining scale economies and technical change. Among these price effects, increasing fuel prices are found to have the largest impact, which, notably, is negative. In response to higher fuel prices, utilities have shifted to expansion paths exhibiting lower scale economies and reduced rates of technical change.

In short, changing input prices, primarily increasing fuel prices, have driven all three source components of productivity growth in adverse directions; that is, v_Q has increased while $d \ln Q/dT$ and v_T have both decreased. Unfortunately, we find no evidence that these adverse price effects for fuel can be countered by the more efficient use of fuel. If anything, the results of our augmentation model imply that technical change, while augmenting labor and capital inputs, has retarded the marginal productivity of fuel input.

The final conclusion is far from encouraging. Given that relative input prices in the electric power industry can be expected to continue their present trends, we cannot expect the industry's recent poor productivity performance to reverse itself in the near future.

ACKNOWLEDGMENTS

The model of factor augmentation described in this paper is an adaptation of a model developed by Gollop and Jorgenson (Gollop [1974]). The capital data used in this research were produced jointly with Laurits Christensen and Rodney Stevenson. We are grateful to the above individuals for their important contributions, to Tom Cowing, Erwin Diewert, and Knox Lovell for their valuable comments, to Carol Comfort and Gary Ferrier for able research assistance, and to the National Science Foundation and the University of Wisconsin Graduate School for research support.

6

Capacity Expansion in the U.S. Natural-Gas Pipeline Industry

Varouj A. Aivazian

Jeffrey L. Callen

Faculty of Business
McMaster University
Hamilton, Ontario, Canada

The regulatory environment could potentially affect total factor productivity in regulated industries in one of two major ways. First, regulation could at least partially determine the direction and rate of technological innovation in such industries. Second, regulation could alter the relationship between the growth in output and the input combinations needed to provide that output over time. The latter relationship, the dynamic analog of the Averch–Johnson effect, is the subject matter of this article.

One basic flaw in the extant empirical Averch–Johnson literature is its cavalier disregard for the dynamics of capacity expansion of public utilities. Chenery [1952] long ago argued that cost-minimizing firms facing growing demand and economies of scale would build plants with some "optimal" overcapacity. The indivisibilities upon which these scale economies are based and rapidly increasing demand are characteristics of the electrical generating and natural-gas pipeline industries, both of which are grist for the Averch–Johnson mill.[1] To the best of our knowledge not a single

[1] Except for the Callen [1978] and MacAvoy and Noll [1973] studies of the natural-gas pipeline industry and Vinod's [1972] study of the Bell System, the Averch–Johnson literature has

empirical Averch–Johnson paper recognizes these characteristics of postwar public utilities. Instead, cross-sectional data are employed in static long-run formulations of the Averch–Johnson hypothesis, the pretence being that the firm's optimal inputs are independent of capacity expansion.[2]

In this paper, we shall try to account for the dynamics of capacity expansion of regulated industries. Specifically, we shall study the postwar expansion of the U.S. interstate natural-gas pipeline industry, an industry whose basic technology can be described by a Cobb–Douglas engineering production function.[3]

In Section 1 we use one variant of what has become known as the Chenery–Manne–Srinivasan (C–M–S) model to show how an unregulated cost-minimizing pipeline industry would have expanded capacity in the face of exogenously growing demand for natural gas.[4] This variant of the C–M–S model is adjusted to include variable costs and it also takes into account the relative flexibility of horsepower capacity as compared to line-pipe capacity. In Section 2 we develop a regulated variant of the C–M–S model that preserves its fundamental tractability for empirical analysis. Regulation affects not only each firm's optimal input combinations but also the rate of capacity expansion. Section 3 contains a description of the data bases and the variable and parameter estimates used in the simulations. In Section 4, the optimal input combinations and capacity expansion rates of the cost-minimizing and regulated models are compared to actual data. The model that predicts the best is presumed to be the true underlying model of the natural-gas pipeline industry. In Section 5 we contrast our results with an earlier work by Callen [1978], which tested the Averch–Johnson hypothesis using the standard static methodology. Finally, in Section 6 we indicate the implications that our results may have for the measurement of total factor productivity in regulated industries.

1. The Cost-Minimizing Framework

1.1 Some Preliminary Assumptions

In the C–M–S model, demand is assumed to grow either linearly or geometrically over an infinite time horizon. Despite this heroic assumption, the C–M–S model is one of the few mathematically tractable intertemporal

---

centered most of its attention on electrical utilities. See, for example, Courville [1974], Cowing [1978], Hayashi and Trapani [1976], Peterson [1975], and Spann [1974], to name only a few.

[2] As we shall see below, this assumption is warranted (at capacity) for natural-gas pipelines which are subject to a Cobb–Douglas technology.

[3] The assumption of a Cobb–Douglas technology was used by Chenery [1949] for natural-gas transmission and by Cookenboo [1954] for oil pipelines.

[4] The case of linearly growing demand was first analyzed geometrically by Chenery [1952], algebraically by Manne [1961], and later extended to the geometric growth case by Srinivasan [1967]. Manne also analysed the case of uncertain growth.

economic models and thus lends itself to empirical analysis. The tractability of the C–M–S model stems from an optimal solution in which capacity is installed at equal points in time, called regeneration points. Recent generalizations of the model to include economic depreciation, embodied technological change, and variable costs have maintained the equal regeneration point property of the model, albeit at some expense to realism.[5]

Missing from the different variants of the C–M–S model, yet fundamental to Chenery's initial insights, is the fact that capacity expansion is not always as inflexible as the fixed regeneration point concept implies.[6] Where the technology requires more than one capacity input, the ultimate capacity of the system is limited by the most inflexible of these inputs. The fixed regeneration point argument applies to this input. However, capacity can be varied in a more continuous fashion by adding the relatively flexible capacity inputs to the inflexible "ultimate" capacity input. For example, in the case of natural-gas pipelines, the line-pipe may take months or years to construct and is clearly the most inflexible input. However, once the line-pipe is in the ground, horsepower capacity can be added fairly continuously to the line to build up capacity. In fact, the horsepower capacity may be so flexible relative to line-pipe capacity that the former can be treated as a variable input. The implications of this element of process flexibility, as Chenery pointed out, are twofold. First, the flexibility of horsepower capacity reduces substantially the capital cost of the pipeline. Second, the level of "optimal" overcapacity of the pipeline determined by the regeneration points will be greater than if all the inputs are inflexible.

To keep the equal regeneration point property of C–M–S model, we make the critical assumption that once each loop in the transmission system reaches its optimal long-run capacity, the pipeline is assumed to operate at this level forever. Therefore, the variable costs of operating the pipeline are constant once the capacity of the loop is attained.[7] Also, since the principal variable input into the transmission process, namely, compressor fuel, cannot be estimated accurately, variable costs are assumed to be proportional to either horsepower or line-pipe capacity.[8] Variable costs associated

[5] See Peck [1974] and Snow [1975].

[6] See Chenery [1952], especially p. 8].

[7] To maintain the equal regeneration point property and yet include variable costs in his model, Peck [1974] assumes that the machine operates forever at full capacity even before the demand warrants it. Clearly, this assumption is unnecessary. One need only assume that, once the capacity of the machine is reached, the machine operates at this constant rate forever. Thus, future capacity decisions are unaffected by previous capacity decisions.

[8] Natural-gas compressor–prime mover units are either reciprocating gas engines or centrifugal gas turbines. The latter consume a significantly greater amount of fuel per horsepower generated than the former, for a given horsepower capacity. Therefore, without an inventory of compressor types (for each firm) fuel consumption cannot be estimated. Nor is it reasonable to assume a representative inventory since the proportion of compressor–prime mover types differs dramatically among firms for which the data are available. See Jensen and Stauffer [1972, pp. 93–95].

with the line-pipe are minor so that almost all variable costs are horsepower related.

1.2 Optimal Input Combinations

Callen [1978] has shown that the natural-gas transmission process can be described by the Cobb–Douglas engineering production function

$$Q = AH^{0.27}K^{0.9}, \tag{1}$$

where Q is output measured in (billions of) cubic feet, H is horsepower, and K is the line-pipe measured in (thousands of) tons of steel. Thus, since each loop's inputs are assumed to operate at the cost-minimizing level forever once capacity is reached, the optimal input combinations at capacity must satisfy the condition

$$K/H = 0.9P_H/0.27P_K, \tag{2}$$

where P_H and P_K denote the rental values of H and K, respectively.[9] Prior to reaching capacity, horsepower capacity is added to the line-pipe in a continuous fashion as demand grows. It can be seen from the production function [Eq. (1)] that horsepower capacity is added proportionally to output, i.e., $H \propto Q^{1/0.27}$. At each new regeneration point, another loop is added to the pipeline system so that the system's intertemporal K/H ratio follows a sawtooth pattern. Clearly, at each regeneration point, the K/H ratio satisfies Eq. (2).

1.3 The Optimal Time Pattern of Capacity Expansion

We shall now proceed to determine the optimal time pattern for capacity expansion of the cost-minimizing firm subject to linearly growing demand.[10] Define X to be the constant time between regeneration points, $C(X)$ to be the total discounted cost of the pipeline looking forward from a point of regeneration, and $Z(X)$ to be the total discounted cost of a single loop of the

---

[9] The rental prices reflect the objective function of minimizing after-tax costs so that

$$P_K = (1 - t)P_{KV} + (r - td_K)P_{KF} \qquad \text{and} \qquad P_H = (1 - t)P_{HV} + (r - td_H)P_{HF},$$

where $P_{\cdot V}$ represents the variable costs per unit of either line-pipe or horsepower capacity, $P_{\cdot F}$ the fixed costs per unit of either line-pipe or horsepower capacity, r the firm's (weighted average) cost of capital, t the corporate tax rate, and d the depreciation rate for either line-pipe or horsepower capacity.

[10] The alternative assumption that demand is growing geometrically is unrealistic. Nevertheless, we would have used the geometric growth model as well, except that in many cases $r < g/1.17$ where g is the growth rate and r the cost of capital. Unfortunately, the reverse inequality is necessary for the geometric model to converge. On this point, see Peck [1974].

pipeline.[11] In the standard variants of the C–M–S model, $Z(X)$ is a simple power function. Incorporating process flexibility requires $Z(X)$ to take on the more complex form

$$Z(X) = \int_0^\infty e^{-rt}(BX^{1/1.17})\,dt - \int_0^x e^{-rt}(DX^{1/0.27})\,dt + \int_0^x e^{-rQ}(DQ^{1/0.27})\,dQ \tag{3}$$

so that

$$Z(X) = \frac{BX^{1/1.17}}{r} - \frac{DX^{1/0.27}(1 - e^{-rx})}{r} + D\int_0^x e^{-rQ}Q^{1/0.27}\,dQ, \tag{4}$$

where B and D are constants and r is the firm's discount rate.[12] The first term on the right-hand side of Eq. (4) is the total discounted cost of a single loop pipeline that follows the Cobb–Douglas technology of Eq. (1). This is the discounted cost of an inflexible pipeline for which total horsepower capacity is installed initially with the line-pipe and which operates continually at capacity. From this term, we net out the discounted cost of installing all the horsepower capacity and operating the pipeline at full capacity, from time zero to the regeneration point. Then we add back the flexible cost of operating the pipeline during this period, namely, the discounted cost of installing horsepower capacity continuously and operating the pipeline as warranted by the demand growth until the regeneration point. Once the regeneration point is reached this loop is assumed to operate at full capacity forever.

Since demand is growing linearly over an infinite horizon, so that the future from each regeneration point is identical, $C(X)$ must satisfy the recursive relationship[13]

$$C(X) = Z(X) + e^{-rx}C(X) \tag{5}$$

so that

$$C(X) = Z(X)/(1 - e^{-rx}). \tag{6}$$

Differentiating $C(X)$ with respect to X and setting the result equal to zero yields the first-order condition

$$(1 - e^{-rx})Z'(X) - re^{-rx}Z(X) = 0. \tag{7}$$

Equation (7) is then solved numerically for the optimal expansion time X.

---

[11] The term "total discounted cost" refers to the discounted cost of installed capacity and operating costs.

[12] $BX^{1/1.17}$ is the long-run cost function and $DX^{1/0.27}$ the variable cost portion of the short-run cost function derived from the Cobb–Douglas production function for natural gas transmission [Eq. (1)].

[13] This approach is due to Manne [1961].

2. The Regulatory Model

In the Averch–Johnson (A–J) literature, it is standard methodology to append a regulatory constraint to the cost-minimizing (or profit-maximizing) model in order to simulate the regulatory process. Aside from the fact that this approach may necessitate estimating some rather difficult to estimate parameters (for example, demand elasticities), the A–J assumption destroys the equal regeneration point property of the C–M–S model. To see this, it suffices to note that in the typical regulatory constraint formulation, prior period capacity decisions affect future potential revenues, so that the past and future do not appear identical at each regeneration point. Therefore, to maintain the equal regeneration point property, we shall assume that the essence of the regulatory process can be captured via the firm's opportunity cost of capital. Specifically, if r is the firm's opportunity cost of capital and s the allowed rate of return set by the regulatory commission, then for each dollar's worth of capital equipment C acquired by the firm, the firm is now able to earn $(s - r)C$. Thus, the net opportunity cost of capital equipment to the regulated firm is $rC - (s - r)C$ or $(2r - s)C$.

The impact of a lower effective cost of capital on the firm's behavior is twofold. First, in contradistinction to the cost-minimizing firm, the regulated firm will employ a higher K/H ratio at capacity since the horsepower variable has a large variable cost component while the line-pipe is virtually all capital cost. Second, since the opportunity cost of capital is effectively less for the regulated firm than for the cost-minimizing firm, the regulated firm will build larger pipeline loops so that the regeneration time is greater for it than for the cost-minimizing firm. Our empirical tests of the A–J hypothesis are based on these two observations.

3. Data Bases and Some Variable and Parameter Estimates

Most of the data used in this study are found in the Federal Power Commission (FPC) annual pipeline statistics, the FPC annual reports, *Moody's Public Utilities*, the National Petroleum Council (NPC) [1967] report on transportation capacities, and the O'Donnel [1973] cost study. These sources are sufficiently comprehensive to provide cross-sectional estimates for all but a few parameters.

The simulated K/H ratios in Table 2 are based on 1965 data sources. That year was chosen primarily because the NPC report published disaggregated line-pipe capacity data for 1965. Line-pipe capacity for other years is estimated from the more aggregated data given in the FPC statistics in conjunction with the NPC report.

The line-pipe capacity variable is measured in tons of main line steel. The NPC report and the FPC statistics provide a cross-sectional breakdown of pipeline mileage by outside diameters. Wall thicknesses are estimated by specifying an average industry steel technology, API Standard 5LX-46 with an operating pressure of 1000 psi.

The unit line-pipe capital cost is derived by summing the company's line-pipe-related capital expenditures in the 1965 accounts (found in the FPC statistics) and dividing the result by K.[14] This book value figure is employed in the depreciation expense component of the objective function.[15] In the remainder of the objective function, a 1965 constant-dollar unit capital cost is used. This figure is obtained by adjusting all line-pipe-related capital expenditures over the lifetime of the firm by a pipeline construction price index.[16] The unit horsepower capacity capital cost is estimated in exactly the same fashion although the assumption of a constant unit cost is apparently contradicted by the potential economies of scale in horsepower generation. Average cost per horsepower generated declines with the capacity of a compressor-prime mover unit up to some technological limit. In practice, there are severe limitations placed on the size of the compressor unit by the characteristics of the gas flow, the need for operational flexibility, and the dynamics of horsepower capacity utilization, so that in 1965 average capacity was only from 1000 to 2000 hp per unit.[17] Therefore, the assumption of a constant unit cost is not unreasonable.

The regeneration points are estimated from the maps in *Moody's Public Utilities* and the NPC report together with a year-by-year analysis of each company's history. Clearly, the larger multiloop companies give more regeneration point data than do the smaller companies which did not have such extensive growth or were built much later in time. Data on regeneration

---

[14] The assumption that line-pipe unit costs are constant is not unreasonable. The following 1960–1962 data and cost estimates give some indication of unit costs (on a per-ton basis) for 24-, 30-, and 36-in. pipelines constrained to a working pressure of approximately 950 psi:

Outside diameter (in.)	Wall thickness (in.)	Actual data ($)	Nordberg estimates ($)	Columbia gas estimates ($)
24	0.312	355	360	378
30	0.375	339	367	361
36	0.438		330	352

The Nordberg estimates are found in American Gas Association [1965, p. 8/95]. The actual cost data as well as the Columbia Gas estimates are from L. Rosenberg [1963, p. 215].

[15] See footnote 9 above. These depreciation rates are for tax purposes only.

[16] See O'Donnel [1973].

[17] See the NPC report. There are modest economies of scale in the size of the compressor stations. However, the cost of a reasonably sized station is proportional to the number and size of the compressor units and, therefore, to horsepower capacity.

points and K/H ratios were not collected prior to 1945 primarily because the FPC statistics begin in 1946. Also, the major expansion in demand for natural gas came after World War II, so that prewar expansion rates would not be typical of an environment with a growing demand.

The scale constant in the production function is estimated from the data and the functional form of the production function, that is, $A = (Q/H^{0.27}K^{0.9})$ where Q, H, and K take on their 1965 actual values.[18]

The opportunity cost of capital (r) is assumed to be the firm's weighted average cost of capital. The weighted average cost of capital is calculated for each company using the book value capitalization rates of debt, preferred, and equity capital as of 31 December 1965. The pretax cost of debt is determined from Moody's rating of the most recent (pre-1966) bonds issued by each pipeline company. The cost of preferred capital is taken to be the most recent (pre-1966) embedded preferred share dividend yield. The after-tax cost of equity capital is derived from the familiar dividend yield equation, where the growth rate is measured by the multiplicand of the retention rate and the return on (book value) equity capital, averaged over the period 1965–1970. In those cases where the shares of the subsidiary pipeline company did not trade on the open market, the cost of capital of the parent is used.

Breyer and MacAvoy [1974, pp. 31–32] tabulate allowed rates of return between 1961 and 1968 for about one-third of our sample. The differential between our estimated costs of capital (r) and the allowed rates of return for this subsample was between 1.6 and 2% in all cases, with an average differential of 1.7%. This differential is independent of the level of the estimated cost of capital. We therefore generalized this result to estimate the effective opportunity cost of capital of the regulated firm by subtracting 1.7% from r for each firm in our sample.

The depreciation rates (for tax purposes) for K and H are set at 3.2 and 3.9%, respectively, for all firms. These depreciation rates are commonly employed in FPC rate case proceedings.[19]

4. The Empirical Tests

4.1 The Data and Simulated Solutions

The actual times between regeneration points and the K/H ratios at these regeneration points are listed in Tables 1 and 2, respectively, for 28 "major"

---

[18] This is in the case of a single-loop pipeline. In the case of a multiloop pipeline, A has to be divided by the number of loops. See Callen [1978].

[19] See 13 FPC 53 (1954).

TABLE 1

Actual Years between Regeneration Points

Company	Expansion rates: years between regeneration points			Average expansion rates
1 Algonquin Gas Transmission	8	9	—	8.5
2 American Louisiana Pipeline	5	9	—	7.0
3 Atlantic Seaboard	7	10	—	8.5
4 Cities Service Gas	9	—	—	9.0
5 Colorado Interstate Gas	9	—	—	9.0
6 Consolidated Gas Supply	9	—	—	9.0
7 El Paso Natural Gas	5	7	12	8.0
8 Kentucky Gas Transmission	7	—	—	7.0
9 Manufacturers Light and Heat	9	10	—	9.5
10 Michigan Gas Storage	13	14	—	13.5
11 Michigan Wisconsin Pipe Line	9	9	—	9.0
12 Midwestern Gas Transmission	14	—	—	14.0
13 Mississippi River Transmission	10	13	—	11.5
14 Natural Gas Pipeline Co. of America	5	7	7	6.3
15 Northern Natural Gas	6	10	9	8.3
16 The Ohio Fuel Gas	10	11	—	10.5
17 Pacific Gas Transmission	9	—	—	9.0
18 Panhandle Eastern Pipe Line	12	12	—	12.0
19 South Texas Natural Gas Gathering	8	—	—	8.0
20 Southern Natural Gas	6	5	—	6.7
21 Tennessee Gas Transmission	5	5	10	6.7
22 Texas Eastern Transmission	6	5	8	6.3
23 Texas Gas Transmission	6	10	—	8.0
24 Transcontinental Gas Pipe Line	4	6	7	5.7
25 Transwestern Pipeline	14	—	—	14.0
26 Truckline Gas	6	9	9	8.0
27 United Fuel Gas	14	—	—	14.0
28 United Gas Pipe Line	11	—	—	11.0

interstate natural gas pipeline companies.[20] The corresponding simulated cost-minimizing (CM) K/H ratios for each of these firms [derived from Eq. (2)] are presented in the first column of Table 3. The second column gives a lower bound estimate (X_L) for the optimal expansion rate of the cost-minimizing pipeline system. This lower bound expansion rate is the optimal rate for a completely inflexible pipeline system where each loop is assumed

[20] Our sample is restricted to major pipeline companies as defined by the *FPC Statistics* 1965, p. VIII. The remaining interstate pipeline companies are either distribution companies or have small pipeline systems which cannot be described by a Cobb–Douglas production technology.

TABLE 2

Actual Line-Pipe-to-Horsepower Capacity Ratios at Regeneration Points

Company	K/H ratios at regeneration points				Average K/H ratios
1 Algonquin Gas Transmission	3.63	5.73	—	—	4.68
2 American Louisiana Pipeline	5.16	6.90	—	—	6.03
3 Atlantic Seaboard	4.44	5.54	—	—	4.99
4 Cities Service Gas	3.55	3.42	—	—	3.49
5 Colorado Interstate Gas	2.94	—	—	—	2.94
6 Consolidated Gas Supply	3.61	4.21	—	—	3.91
7 El Paso Natural Gas	3.06	2.75	2.93	2.81	2.89
8 Kentucky Gas Transmission	10.70	—	—	—	10.70
9 Manufacturers Light and Heat	6.14	7.11	6.79	—	6.68
10 Michigan Gas Storage	5.16	6.52	—	—	5.84
11 Michigan Wisconsin Pipe Line	2.89	3.40	—	—	3.15
12 Midwestern Gas Transmission	2.71	—	—	—	2.71
13 Mississippi River Transmission	2.26	2.12	2.91	—	2.43
14 Natural Gas Pipeline Co. of America	3.68	4.75	4.41	3.37	4.05
15 Northern Natural Gas	3.32	2.60	2.82	2.26	2.75
16 The Ohio Fuel Gas	3.11	4.11	4.06	—	3.76
17 Pacific Gas Transmission	1.55	—	—	—	1.55
18 Panhandle Eastern Pipe Line	2.86	2.96	2.53	—	2.78
19 South Texas Natural Gas Gathering	4.45	—	—	—	4.45
20 Southern Natural Gas	2.58	2.69	2.89	2.24	2.60
21 Tennessee Gas Transmission	2.80	3.25	3.74	3.16	3.24
22 Texas Eastern Transmission	2.57	2.88	2.03	2.13	2.40
23 Texas Gas Transmission	3.38	3.24	3.46	—	3.36
24 Transcontinental Gas Pipe Line	2.73	3.54	3.62	—	3.30
25 Transwestern Pipeline	2.87	—	—	—	2.87
26 Trunkline Gas	3.85	3.39	3.76	—	3.67
27 United Fuel Gas	1.30	—	—	—	1.30
28 United Gas Pipe Line	6.87	6.83	—	—	6.85

to operate at full capacity right from when the line-pipe is first put into the ground.[21] The third column provides an upperbound estimate (X_U) for the optimal expansion rate of the cost-minimizing pipeline system. This upper bound [derived from Eq. (7)] assumes that horsepower capacity can be varied continuously until the capacity of the loop is reached. The remaining three columns of Table 3 list the simulated K/H ratios, lower-bound, and upper-bound expansion rate estimates for the regulated (A–J) pipeline system.

[21] In this case, $Z(X) = BX^{1/1.17}/r$, a simple power function. Manne [1961] has shown that when $Z(X)$ is a power function then the optimal $\hat{X}$ satisfies the equation $(e^{-r\hat{X}} - 1) = r\hat{X}/a$ where a in our case equals $1/1.17$. Expanding $e^{-r\hat{X}}$ to a quadratic yields the simple formula $\hat{X} = 0.34/r$.

TABLE 3

Simulated Line-Pipe-to-Horsepower Capacity Ratios and Expansion
Rates for the Cost-Minimizing (CM) and Regulatory (A–J) Models

Company	CM			A–J		
	K/H	X_L	X_U	K/H	X_L	X_U
1	1.80	7.0	12.5	2.05	10.5	19.0
2	6.48	7.5	13.5	10.36	12.0	22.0
3	5.56	7.0	12.0	6.52	10.5	18.5
4	4.36	6.5	11.5	5.20	9.5	17.0
5	4.89	5.5	10.0	5.39	8.0	14.0
6	6.92	7.0	12.5	8.98	10.5	19.0
7	6.76	8.5	15.0	11.32	14.0	25.0
8	7.91	7.0	12.0	9.01	10.5	18.5
9	5.79	7.0	12.0	7.14	10.5	18.5
10	7.60	8.0	14.0	10.78	13.0	23.0
11	6.44	7.5	13.5	10.82	12.0	22.0
12	7.99	7.0	12.0	11.44	10.5	18.5
13	4.44	7.5	13.0	6.18	11.5	21.0
14	5.64	6.5	11.0	6.94	9.5	17.0
15	6.18	7.5	13.5	8.81	12.0	22.0
16	5.63	7.0	12.0	7.19	10.5	18.5
17	6.00	8.0	14.0	9.08	13.0	23.0
18	5.73	7.0	12.0	7.38	10.5	18.5
19	4.79	5.5	10.0	5.99	8.0	14.0
20	2.66	5.0	9.0	2.98	7.0	13.0
21	4.90	7.0	12.0	6.46	10.5	18.5
22	4.38	7.0	12.5	6.49	10.5	19.0
23	4.54	7.0	13.0	6.24	11.0	19.5
24	4.39	7.0	12.5	6.30	10.5	19.0
25	5.38	7.5	13.0	7.18	11.5	21.0
26	6.08	7.0	12.0	8.00	10.5	18.5
27	6.74	7.0	12.0	8.78	10.5	18.5
28	2.78	7.5	13.0	2.82	11.5	21.0

4.2 Comparing the Actual and Simulated Expansion Rates

The actual expansion rates are compared to the lower- and upper-bound
expansion rates for the cost-minimizing and regulatory models in Table 4.
Each of the columns in Table 4 evaluates the best predictive model for the
corresponding column in Table 1. If the actual expansion rate falls below
the cost-minimizing upper bound, but not within the regulatory (A–J)
bounds, then the CM model is judged to be the best predictor.[22] If the

[22] In some cases the actual rates are less than the lower bounds of the CM model, implying
that the CM model is, in some sense, an inadequate predictor of the actual. However, the CM
model is certainly a better predictor in these cases than the A–J model and is listed as such.

　　　　　　　　　　　　　　Varouj A. Aivazian and Jeffrey L. Callen

TABLE 4

The Best Predictive Model of Expansion Rates

Company	Best predictive model		
1 Algonquin Gas Transmission	CM	CM	—
2 American Louisiana Pipeline	CM	CM	—
3 Atlantic Seaboard	CM	CM	—
4 Cities Service Gas	CM	—	—
5 Colorado Interstate Gas	Both	—	—
6 Consolidated Gas Supply	CM	—	—
7 El Paso Natural Gas	CM	CM	CM
8 Kentucky Gas Transmission	CM	—	—
9 Manufacturers Light and Heat	CM	CM	—
10 Michigan Gas Storage	Both	Both	—
11 Michigan Wisconsin Pipe Line	CM	CM	—
12 Midwestern Gas Transmission	A–J	—	—
13 Mississippi River Transmission	CM	Both	—
14 Natural Gas Pipeline Co. of America	CM	CM	CM
15 Northern Natural Gas	CM	CM	CM
16 The Ohio Fuel Gas	CM	Both	—
17 Pacific Gas Transmission	CM	—	—
18 Panhandle Eastern Pipe Line	Both	Both	—
19 South Texas Natural Gas Gathering	Both	—	—
20 Southern Natural Gas	CM	CM	—
21 Tennessee Gas Transmission	CM	CM	CM
22 Texas Eastern Transmission	CM	CM	CM
23 Texas Gas Transmission	CM	CM	—
24 Transcontinental Gas Pipe Line	CM	CM	CM
25 Transwestern Pipeline	A–J	—	—
26 Truckline Gas	CM	CM	CM
27 United Fuel Gas	A–J	—	—
28 United Gas Pipe Line	CM	—	—

actual expansion rate falls within the regulatory bounds only, then the A–J model is considered to be the best predictor. If the actual falls within the CM and A–J bounds, then both models predict equally well. Of the 53 data points on actual expansion rates, 42 were predicted by the cost-minimizing model unambiguously and only three by the regulatory model. Both models predicted equally well in the remaining eight cases. Overall, the cost-minimizing model is an overwhelmingly superior predictor of expansion rates.[23]

[23] It should be pointed out, however, that while the CM model predicts much better than the A–J model, even the CM model had an overall average prediction error of 83%. If we eliminate United Fuel Gas and Pacific Gas Transmission, which have very large prediction errors, the overall average prediction error falls to 62%.

4.3 Comparing the Actual and Simulated (K/H) Ratios

The relative ability of the two models in predicting the actual K/H ratio is determined from the absolute prediction error criterion

$$\left| \frac{(K/H)_S - (K/H)_A}{(K/H)_A} \right|, \qquad (8)$$

where A and S stand for the actual and simulated solutions, respectively. Prediction errors were calculated for all 68 data points and then averaged for each firm. The average prediction errors for the cost-minimizing and regulatory models are presented in the first two columns of Table 5. The

TABLE 5

Average Absolute Prediction Errors and the Best Predictor of K/H Ratios

Company	Average absolute prediction errors CM	A–J	Best predictive model
1 Algonquin Gas Transmission	0.60	0.54	A–J
2 American Louisiana Pipeline	0.13	0.76	CM
3 Atlantic Seaboard	0.13	0.59	CM
4 Cities Service Gas	0.25	0.49	CM
5 Colorado Interstate Gas	0.66	0.83	CM
6 Consolidated Gas Supply	0.78	1.31	CM
7 El Paso Natural Gas	1.35	2.93	CM
8 Kentucky Gas Transmission	0.26	0.19	A–J
9 Manufacturers Light and Heat	0.13	0.07	A–J
10 Michigan Gas Storage	0.32	0.87	CM
11 Michigan Wisconsin Pipe Line	1.06	2.46	CM
12 Midwestern Gas Transmission	1.95	3.22	CM
13 Mississippi River Transmission	0.86	1.59	CM
14 Natural Gas Pipeline Co. of America	0.42	0.75	CM
15 Northern Natural Gas	1.29	2.27	CM
16 The Ohio Fuel Gas	0.52	0.94	CM
17 Pacific Gas Transmission	2.87	4.86	CM
18 Panhandle Eastern Pipe Line	1.07	1.66	CM
19 South Texas Natural Gas Gathering	0.08	0.35	CM
20 Southern Natural Gas	0.08	0.16	CM
21 Tennessee Gas Transmission	0.53	1.02	CM
22 Texas Eastern Transmission	0.86	1.76	CM
23 Texas Gas Transmission	0.35	0.86	CM
24 Transcontinental Gas Pipe Line	0.35	0.94	CM
25 Transwestern Pipeline	0.87	1.50	CM
26 Trunkline Gas	0.66	1.19	CM
27 United Fuel Gas	4.18	5.75	CM
28 United Gas Pipe Line	0.60	0.59	A–J

third column gives the model with the smallest absolute prediction error. Again, as in the case of expansion rates, the cost-minimizing model is clearly the best overall predictor, predicting better than the regulatory model for 24 of the 28 firms.

5. **Comparing Our Results with a Static Test
of the Averch–Johnson Hypothesis**

Since the methodological approach in this paper is substantially different from the typical static tests of the A–J hypothesis, it may be of some interest to compare them. A meaningful comparison is available from the earlier Callen study, which uses the same data base that we do. Callen [1978] simulated the long-run cost-minimizing, the profit-maximizing, and the constrained profit and revenue-maximizing solutions for each pipeline company in our sample. The constrained solutions refer to a static long-run regulatory constraint—patterned after the Atlantic Seaboard cost allocation formula—which was appended to specific objective functions, either profit maximization or revenue maximization. Callen found that while the unconstrained models predicted best on the input side, output was predicted far better by the constrained models. Comparing the input- and output-prediction errors, it was seen that the constrained revenue-maximizing model predicted best, followed closely by the constrained profit-maximizing model. The unconstrained profit-maximizing model was a poor overall predictor. Therefore, in marked contrast to our study, Callen concluded that rate of return regulation had a substantial impact on the firm's operating behavior.

The question naturally arises: Can these conflicting results be reconciled? One approach may be to argue that regulation had little if any impact during the period of rapidly growing demand which characterized the industry in the postwar years until the early 1960s. During a growth period the utility's rate base may be growing so quickly that the regulatory constraint is nonbinding. Therefore, there may be no incentive to distort factor proportions. On the other hand, during the relatively stable 1965 period analyzed by Callen, a period of excess capacity and relatively poor growth for natural gas pipelines, utility executives may have found it in their interest and in the interest of their shareholders to try to increase earnings by engaging in such activities, i.e., varying factor proportions.

However appealing or unappealing this reconciliation may be, it presupposes that the long-run static model can yield meaningful results in what is inherently a dynamic system. The very fact that pipeline systems are looped over time makes it difficult to estimate some long-run capital inputs. In the Callen study, it was assumed that the firm optimizes its long-run operating variables by treating the number of loops as a parameter. Unless one is willing to assume that each loop size is determined by the technological limit for pipelines, the looping decision is endogenous to the firm and cannot realistically be treated as a parameter. In addition, we have emphasized in this paper, and it is obvious from the data, that horsepower capacity adjusts over time to the capacity of the loop. Can such an inherently dynamic attribute of the horsepower variable be captured in a static long-run model? While there is, of course, no definitive answer to this question, it should make one wary of any reconciliation of the conflicting results. Instead, we would argue that a dynamic model is much better suited for testing the A–J hypothesis and that the current results are more reliable than static-model results.

6.   The Implications for Total Factor Productivity

The principal implication of our study for the measurement of total factor productivity in regulated industries is that, to the extent that one can abstract from regulatory-induced technological change in natural-gas pipeline design, regulation per se has little impact on the relationship between the growth in output and factor proportions. Therefore, the regulatory process need not be explicitly considered in devising a total factor productivity index, at least for the pipeline industry. On the other hand, our analysis does indicate one major problem that could arise in measuring total factor productivity in regulated industries. Regulated industries are characterized by indivisibilities in production and substantial economies of scale. As we have tried to emphasize, as Chenery did before us, these characteristics will lead to excess capacity except at regeneration points. If factor productivity is measured in an excess capacity period, the measurement will be biased downwards. If anything, the bias will be aggravated by technological change, whether or not such change is induced by the regulatory environment. Much of the evidence to date (e.g., Hughes [1971]) suggests that technological change in regulated industries primarily leads to further scale economies. The caveat seems clear. Indexes of total factor productivity should measure the effects of technological change and not capacity adjustment effects.

ACKNOWLEDGMENTS

We wish to acknowledge the helpful comments of Knox Lovell, Tom Cowing, and an anonymous referee.

7

Comparative Measures of Total Factor Productivity in the Regulated Sector: The Electric Utility Industry

Thomas G. Cowing

Department of Economics
State University of New York
   at Binghamton
Binghamton, New York

Jeffrey Small

Department of Economics
University of Wisconsin—Madison
Madison, Wisconsin

Rodney E. Stevenson

Graduate School of Business
University of Wisconsin—Madison
Madison, Wisconsin

Total factor productivity (TFP) is a measure of the growth in output that cannot be explained by growth in inputs and, as such, has been called a measure of the "unexplained residual." Conceptually, this residual can be thought of as an attempt to measure the degree of technological advancement. In practice, however, the residual may also reflect errors in appropriately accounting for the growth in output resulting from any given increase in inputs. These errors may be due to such factors as the use of inexact methods for aggregating outputs and inputs, and the failure to properly adjust for scale economies, changes in plant utilization, and any side constraints which affect the firm's input choices.

The purpose of this paper is to identify various TFP adjustments that may be required to account properly for the growth in output and productivity in the case of regulated industries. Several alternative TFP measures and

161

adjustments are specified and empirically evaluated. These measures fall into two general classes. The first set includes the traditional exact-index-number measures of productivity. The second approach is based upon an estimated base-period cost function, and compares actual deviations in any given comparison period to the associated predicted deviations. These alternative measures differ with respect to specification and whether or not the effects of differences in scale economies and capacity utilization are taken into account. In addition, we consider the appropriate specification of TFP measures for firms subject to effective rate-of-return regulation. The alternative TFP measures are derived in Section 1. The empirical results, including a comparative evaluation of the various measures, are reported in Section 2.

1.   Total Factor Productivity Measurement

1.1   Alternative TFP Measures

Productivity measures are intended to identify changes in the level of production that cannot be explained by changes in usage of the associated inputs and the characteristics of the original production process. Early productivity studies were often based on partial factor measures, i.e., the input index was limited either to one or to a small number of inputs. However, increases in such measures may simply reflect the substitution of one input for another, rather than purely technological advancement. Thus, the use of total factor productivity measures in which changes in output are related to changes in *all* inputs yields a more accurate measure of productivity advancement.

Much of the TFP analysis was pioneered by Kendrick [1961] and Denison [1962], and has been further refined by Jorgenson and Griliches [1967] and Hulten [1973, 1978]. The dominant approach to TFP measurement has been the exact-index-number approach in which TFP is measured by the ratio of the growth rate of output to the average growth rate of the inputs:

$$\text{TFP}_{0,t} = \frac{Q^t/Q^0}{Z^t/Z^0},\tag{1}$$

where Q and Z are the values of the aggregate output and input measures, respectively, and 0 and t are time period designations.

Since the typical production process may have several inputs and outputs, it is necessary to specify a method of aggregation. Early approaches to TFP measurement used a Laspeyres weighting system for the construction of aggregate input and output measures in which base-period prices were used as aggregation weights. Thus, the Laspeyres input index can be specified as

$$\frac{Z^t}{Z^0} = \sum_i P_i^0 X_i^t \Big/ \sum_i P_i^0 X_i^0, \qquad (2)$$

where the P_is and X_is are input prices and quantities, respectively. By rearranging terms in (2), the input growth index can be rewritten

$$\frac{Z^t}{Z^0} = \sum_i w_i X_i^t / X_i^0, \qquad (3)$$

where the appropriate weights, the w_is, are the base-period cost shares, i.e., $w_i = P_i^0 X_i^0 / \sum_i P_i^0 X_i^0$. A similar aggregation procedure using revenue shares would yield the Laspeyres output index Q^t/Q^0 in the case of multiple outputs.

The base-period prices are usually allowed to remain constant over time, giving the Laspeyres index a certain computational simplicity. Maintaining constant prices also has an intuitive appeal since all variations in the resulting TFP index must necessarily stem from variations in both physical input and output quantities. However, as Diewert [1976] has demonstrated, Laspeyres indexes are inexact except under conditions of perfect input (or output) substitutibility.

An alternative approach for measuring the relative growth rates of outputs and inputs is the Divisia index, which is based upon the underlying production function $Q = f(X)$. Intertemporal movements along the production frontier, as opposed to an intertemporal shifting of the frontier, can be represented by

$$\frac{\dot{Q}}{Q} = \sum_i f_i \frac{\dot{X}_i}{f(X)}, \qquad (4)$$

where a dot represents a time derivative and f_i is the marginal product of the ith input. Under conditions of constant returns to scale and cost minimization, the traditional assumptions of most TFP studies, Eq. (4) can be rewritten

$$\frac{\dot{Q}}{Q} = \sum_i w_i \frac{\dot{X}_i}{X_i}, \qquad (5)$$

where w_i is the cost share of the ith input. Using this continuous result, an output index reflecting the change in output arising from an intertemporal change in inputs, i.e., a movement along the frontier, is given by the line integral,

$$\left(\frac{Q^t}{Q}\right)' = \exp\left[\int_t \sum_i w_i^t \left(\frac{\dot{X}^t}{X_i^t}\right)\right]. \qquad (6)$$

The left-hand side of (6) is the familiar Divisia aggregate input index. Since the TFP measure is intended to represent shifts of a production function, as opposed to movements along a given production function, the TFP index can be represented by

$$\text{TFP}^{\text{D}}_{0,t} = \frac{Q^t/Q^0}{(Q^t/Q^0)'},$$ (7)

where Q^t/Q^0 is a Divisia output index and the denominator is given by (6), i.e., a Divisia input index.

As a measure of technological progress, the Divisia index is preferable to the Laspeyres index since the former is less restrictive. Also, as Diewert [1976] has shown, the Divisia index is exact for the case of transcendental logarithmic aggregation functions.

The expression in Eq. (6), however, is computationally difficult to evaluate. A convenient approximation to (6) is given by the commonly used Törnqvist approximation,

$$\ln \frac{Z^t}{Z^0} = \sum_i \overline{w}_i \ln\left(\frac{X^t_i}{X^0_i}\right),$$ (8)

where $\overline{w}_i = \frac{1}{2}(w^t_i + w^0_i)$.

An alternative approach to the measurement of firm productivity can also be based upon the cost function dual of the production function.[1] Casting the problem in cost function terms, we define TFP as the variation in (minimum) costs *not* accounted for by variations in output, input prices, and any other state of nature or exogenous variables. Assuming given input prices p and output Q, the cost function for a cost-minimizing firm can be written, in general,

$$C = C(Q, p, Y),$$ (9)

where C is (minimum) total cost and Y represents a set of additional relevant exogenous variables. A TFP index based upon the cost function can be written

$$\text{TFP}^{\text{C}}_{0,t} = C^t_{\text{p}}(Q^t, p^t, Y^t)/C^t_{\text{a}},$$ (10)

where C^t_{a} is actual costs in period t and C^t_{p} are the costs in time period t predicted from the estimated parameters of the base-period cost function and the values of the independent variables in time period t.

---

[1] Caves and Christensen [1980a] have suggested an exact-index-number approach based on the production-dual cost function. Our approach to measurement, however, is somewhat different from theirs. As Denny, Fuss, and Waverman have shown elsewhere in this volume, shifts in production and cost curves will not be identical. The ratio of a production function and related cost-function shift will be equal to the scale economies of the unit of observation under consideration.

1.2 Accounting for Capacity Utilization, Returns to Scale, and Regulatory Constraints

The traditional TFP measures have been constructed for application to firms or industries operating in a competitive environment. A straightforward application of these procedures to the regulated utilities, therefore, may yield biased TFP measures. Three factors require special attention: capacity-utilization adjustments, return-to-scale adjustments, and TFP specification for a firm facing effective rate-of-return regulation. We first discuss adjusting the Laspeyres- and Divisia-based TFP indexes, and then consider the empirical cost-function method.

Capacity utilization represents the relationship between the average rate of plant usage and maximum capacity. Since utilities are extremely capital intensive, relatively small differences in capacity-utilization rates can result in substantial differences in required capital inputs. One simple adjustment that can be made is to multiply the capital stock measure by the capacity utilization rate, giving a measure of utilized capital.[2]

Adjusting for returns-to-scale differences poses a somewhat more difficult problem. In general, failure to adjust for increasing (decreasing) returns to scale yields an overstatement (understatement) of TFP growth. Let us first consider the respecification of the Laspeyres TFP index. The output index can be partitioned into two components: the growth in output arising from an increase in inputs and the growth in output arising from the impact of technological advancement. Under constant returns to scale, the output index can be partitioned as

$$Q^t/Q^0 = \lambda(1 + g), \qquad (11)$$

where λ is the growth rate of inputs (assuming an equal growth rate for each input) and g is the unexplained residual growth rate. However, if returns to scale are constant but not unitary, the ratio of explained output to base-period output will be λ^r where r is the returns-to-scale parameter. Thus, the output index under more general assumptions as to the scale conditions can be specified as

$$Q^t/Q^0 = \lambda^r(1 + g) \qquad (12)$$

so that the Laspeyres TFP index becomes

$$\text{TFP}^L_{0,t} = \frac{\lambda^r(1 + g)}{\lambda} = \lambda^{r-1}(1 + g). \qquad (13)$$

[2] This approach implicitly assumes a production function of the form $Q = f(X_1, \ldots, X_n, Cu \cdot X_k)$. As Mel Fuss has pointed out, for a production function of the form $Q = f(X, Cu)$ and a cost function dual $C = g(p, Q, Cu)$, the Divisia index could be adjusted by letting

$$W_i = p_i X_i / \eta_{Cu} \sum_i p_i X_i, \quad \text{where} \quad \eta_{Cu} = \partial \ln C / \partial \ln Cu.$$

Therefore, in order to purge variations in the TFP measure arising from the realization of economies or diseconomies of scale, we can specify a scale-corrected TFP measure as

$$\text{TFP}_{0,t}^{L}\big|_{\text{corrected}} = \lambda^{r-1}\text{TFP}_{0,t}^{L}\big|_{\text{uncorrected}}, \tag{14}$$

where the uncorrected measure is given by (1).

With regard to the Divisia index, an alternative approach can be used to properly account for scale conditions. We note that

$$\sum_i f_i X_i = Q \sum_i f_i \frac{X_i}{Q}. \tag{15}$$

The summation term in the right-hand side of Eq. (15) is simply the sum of the input elasticities, that is, the measure of scale elasticity. Thus, we can restate the production function, $Q = f(X)$, as

$$Q = f(X) = \gamma(X) \sum_i f_i X_i, \tag{16}$$

where $\gamma(X)$ is the inverse of the returns-to-scale elasticity for the input set X. Substituting Eq. (16) into Eq. (4) yields

$$\frac{\dot{Q}}{Q} = \sum_i \frac{f_i \dot{X}_i}{\sum_j [\gamma(X) f_j X_j]}. \tag{17}$$

Assuming cost minimization, Eq. (17) can be rewritten

$$\frac{\dot{Q}}{Q} = \sum_i W_i \frac{\dot{X}_i}{X_i}, \tag{18}$$

where $W_i = p_i X_i / \gamma(X) \sum_j p_j X_j$. The construction of the scale-adjusted Divisia TFP index would then follow as per Eqs. (5)–(7).

So far, we have suggested how the Laspeyres- and Divisia-indexed TFP measures can be adjusted to account for capacity utilization and scale effects. Averch and Johnson [1962] have suggested that firms subject to a regulatory constraint may choose an input mix other than that adopted by an unregulated cost-minimizing firm. In the discussion that follows, we indicate how the Divisia TFP index can be corrected to adjust for Averch–Johnson (A–J) or rate-of-return constraint effects.

We assume that the regulated firm seeks to minimize costs under the regulatory constraint that revenues equal operating costs plus an allowed profit. The Lagrangian equation for this minimization is

$$L = \sum_i p_i X_i - \mu[Pf(X) - \sum_{i \neq k} p_i X_i - S X_k], \tag{19}$$

where $Pf(X)$ is the revenue of the firm, X_k is the capital input, S is the allowed rate of return, and μ is the Lagrangian multiplier. As with A–J, we assume $S > p_k$. The first-order conditions, with respect to the inputs, are given by

$$\left.\frac{\partial L}{\partial X_i}\right|_{i \neq k} = p_i - \mu(Pf_i - p_i) = 0, \qquad \frac{\partial L}{\partial X_k} = p_k - \mu(Pf_k - S) = 0. \quad (20)$$

Solving for the value of the marginal products, we have

$$Pf_i = \frac{1 - \mu}{\mu} p_i, \qquad Pf_k = \frac{p_k - \mu S}{\mu}, \qquad i \neq k. \quad (21)$$

To obtain a corrected specification for the Divisia TFP measure, we substitute these marginal productivity conditions, (21), into Eq. (17), yielding

$$\frac{\dot{Q}}{Q} = \sum_i W_i' \frac{\dot{X}_i}{X_i}, \quad (22a)$$

where

$$W_i' = p_i X_i / \gamma(X) \left[\sum_{i \neq k} p_i X_i + \frac{p_k - \mu S}{1 - \mu} X_k \right] \qquad i \neq k,$$

$$W_k' = \frac{p_k - \mu S}{1 - \mu} X_k / \gamma(X) \left[\sum_{i \neq k} p_i X_i + \frac{p_k - \mu S}{1 - \mu} X_k \right]. \quad (22b)$$

The construction of the corrected Divisia-based TFP index would then follow as per Eqs. (5)–(7).

With the empirical cost-function approach to TFP measurement, i.e., Eq. (10), the issues of capacity utilization, returns to scale, and regulatory constraints can be handled directly through the appropriate specification of the cost function. By using an appropriate flexible form of the generalized cost function, e.g., translog, cost variations due to increasing or decreasing returns to scale can be separated from variations due to technological progress. Furthermore, by including the appropriate variables in the generalized cost function, capacity utilization and rate of return regulation effects can be controlled for. The generalized cost function for a firm minimizing costs subject to the regulatory constraint and accounting for variations in capacity utilization would be

$$C = g(Q, p, S, \text{CU}), \quad (23)$$

where CU is the level of capacity utilization. The translog specification of this generalized cost function is given by

$$\ln C = \beta_0 + \sum_i \beta_i \ln p_i + \frac{1}{2} \sum_i \sum_j \beta_{ij} \ln p_i \ln p_j$$

$$+ \gamma_1 \ln S + \frac{1}{2} \gamma_2 (\ln S)^2 + \sum_i \gamma_{0i} \ln S \ln p_i$$

$$+ \delta_1 \ln Q + \frac{1}{2} \delta_2 (\ln Q)^2 + \sum_i \delta_{0i} \ln Q \ln p_i$$

$$+ \phi_1 \ln CU + \frac{1}{2} \phi_2 (\ln CU)^2 + \sum_i \phi_{0i} \ln CU \ln p_i$$

$$+ \rho_1 \ln S \ln Q + \rho_2 \ln S \ln CU + \rho_3 \ln Q \ln CU, \qquad (24)$$

where we assume $\beta_{ij} = \beta_{ji}$. If rate-of-return regulation is not constraining [i.e., if $\mu = 0$ from Eq. (19)], then

$$\gamma_1 = \gamma_2 = \gamma_{0i} = \rho_1 = \rho_2 = 0, \qquad (25)$$

and the linear homogeneity price constraints can be applied, i.e.,

$$\sum_i \beta_i = 1,$$

$$\sum_i \beta_{ij} = \sum_j \beta_{ij} = \sum_i \sum_j \beta_{ij} = 0, \qquad (26)$$

$$\sum_i \delta_{0i} = \sum_i \phi_{0i} = 0.$$

By estimating Eq. (24) for a base period, with conditions (25) and (26) imposed where warranted, costs may be simulated in the period of comparison by utilizing the data set (p^t, Q^t, S^t, CU^t) applied to the base-period equation parameters.[3] Such a simulation would properly account for variations in scale elasticity, capacity utilization, and regulatory tightness, and would yield accurate estimates of TFP growth using Eq. (10).

2. Empirical Results

The alternative TFP measures derived for this study are empirically evaluated on two bases: the divergence of average TFP levels for a given sample of firms, and the divergence of firm TFP order rankings for firms

---

[3] To obtain more efficient estimates of the cost-function parameters, the cost equation is estimated (iterative Zellner) jointly with $N - 1$ of the N factor cost-share equations. The factor cost share of the ith input is defined as $p_i X_i / \sum_i p_i X_i = \partial \ln C / \partial \ln p_i = s_i$.

in the sample set. In order to assess the magnitude of the potential biases associated with the various TFP measures, it is necessary to construct the indexes for a set of comparable firms. We have constructed the following TFP measures for a set of 81 electric utility firms for the period 1964–1975:

(i) Laspeyres TFP—unadjusted;
(ii) Laspeyres TFP—adjusted for capacity utilization;
(iii) Laspeyres TFP—adjusted for returns to scale;
(iv) Laspeyres TFP—adjusted for returns to scale and capacity utilization;
(v) Divisia TFP—unadjusted;
(vi) Divisia TFP—adjusted for capacity utilization;
(vii) Divisia TFP—adjusted for returns to scale;
(viii) Divisia TFP—adjusted for returns to scale and capacity utilization;
(ix) Cost function based TFP, adjusted for returns to scale and capacity utilization.

2.1 Data

Our sample comprises the generation activity of 81 electric utilities, with yearly observations for the period 1964–1975. Most of the data for this study are derived from various issues of the Federal Power Commission's (FPC) *Statistics of Privately Owned Electric Utilities in the United States,* the FPC's *Performance Profiles: 1963–70,* and the National Association of Regulatory Utility Commissioner's (NARUC) *The Measurement of Electric Utility Efficiency.* Fuel expenditures and associated average fuel prices are obtained directly from the FPC and NARUC data sources. Labor expenditures are calculated as the sum of salaries, wages, and employee pensions and benefits. Average yearly wage rates are estimated as the labor expenditures divided by the sum of the number of regular full-time employees plus one-half of the number of part-time and temporary employees. Capital expenditures are calculated as the product of the deflated capital stock and the capital service price. The deflated capital stock for an electric utility was computed as the sum of the deflated yearly net additions to "plant in service," correcting for mergers. The method used to compute a "price constant" capital stock for a utility is as follows:

$$CS_i = CS_{i-1} + \frac{NI_i}{HW_i}, \qquad i = 1951, \ldots, 1975, \qquad (27)$$

where CS_i is the adjusted capital stock for year i, NI_i the net investment for year i, and HW_i the Handy–Whitman index for year i (adjusted to reflect a 1967 base of 1.0). The base-period capital stock CS_{1950} is derived, employing a triangularized weighted average of the Handy–Whitman index, as

$$CS_{1950} = K \bigg/ \sum_{j}^{20} \left(j \bigg/ \sum_{j}^{20} j \right) HW_j, \qquad (28)$$

where j is the jth year from 1931 to 1950 and K the book value of plant in service in 1950. To take account of acquisitions of plant and equipment through merger, all mergers among class A and B electric utilities were identified for the period 1950–1975, and an adjusted capital stock measure was computed for each company which was acquired over the period of its corporate existence. The adjusted capital stock for any company, in year 1972 for example, was computed as the adjusted capital stock for that company net of acquisitions plus the adjusted capital stock of those class A and B companies that were acquired during the period 1950–1972. Capital stock for generation plant was estimated as the ratio of the book values of generation plant and total plant in service times the deflated capital stock measure.

The imputed capital service price for a given utility was estimated for the ith year as

$$p_{Ki} = (OR_i + DE_i)HW_i, \qquad (29)$$

where OR is the utility's cost of capital, and DE represents the depreciation rate.[4]

Output was measured as kilowatt-hours of net generation. Capacity utilization was measured by output/[total kilowatts of installed capacity × 8760 hours].

2.2   Unadjusted Measures and Adjustments for Capacity Utilization and Returns to Scale

Year-by-year Divisia- and Laspeyres-based TFP indexes were constructed for each of the 81 electric utilities for each of the years 1964–1975. Cost-function-based TFP indexes comparing the 1964 and 1975 periods were constructed for the same sample. In all cases, a single output—kilowatt-hours of net generation—was used as the measure of generation activity and inputs were classified as fuel, capital, and labor.

The average Divisia- and Laspeyres-based TFP indexes for the 81 utilities are presented in Table 1. The indexes presented are the average across the 81 firms of each firm's average year-by-year TFP index value. The first column

---

[4] The firm's financial cost of capital is estimated as the sum of the long-term debt interest rate, the preferred stock dividend rate, and the required return on equity capital, where each factor is weighted by its respective capital structure proportion. The required return on equity capital is computed from a simple DCF model.

TABLE 1

Sample Means and Standard Deviations for Divisia-
and Laspeyres-Based Total Factor Productivity Measures[a]

	Unadjusted (1)	Adjusted for capacity utilization (2)	Adjusted for returns to scale (3)	Adjusted for capacity utilization and returns to scale (4)
Divisia TFP	1.0169 (0.0138)	1.0200 (0.0121)	1.0135 (0.0134)	1.0168 (0.0123)
Laspeyres TFP	1.0111 (0.0140)	1.0151 (0.0109)	1.0079 (0.0129)	1.0122 (0.0101)

[a] Standard deviation in parentheses below mean.

TABLE 2

Rank Correlations of Laspeyres and Divisia TFP Measures

A. Correlations across measures—Laspeyres versus Divisia

Type of measure	Rank correlation coefficient
Unadjusted	0.827
Adjusted for capacity utilization	0.879
Adjusted for returns to scale	0.781
Adjusted for capacity utilization and returns to scale	0.855

B. Correlations across adjustments

	Rank correlation coefficient	
Type of adjustments	Divisia TFP	Laspeyres TFP
Unadjusted, adjusted for capacity utilization	0.723	0.661
Unadjusted, adjusted for returns to scale	0.958	0.975
Unadjusted, adjusted for capacity utilization and returns to scale	0.621	0.559

of Table 1 represents the unadjusted index. Column (2) represents the TFP indexes adjusted for capacity utilization. Column (3) contains the TFP indexes adjusted for returns to scale. Finally, column (4) contains the TFP measures that have been adjusted for both returns to scale and capacity utilization.[5] As indicated in the table, the "average" TFP growth rate for the "average" electric utility does not vary noticeably either across measures, Divisia vs. Laspeyres, or across adjustments. Thus with regard to the industry averages, little appears to be gained by using more refined exact-index-number TFP measures.

Although the effects of refinement on the firm level TFP averages appear insignificant, the effects on an individual firm's TFP measures may be much more pronounced. One way of evaluating individual firm impacts is to look at the effect of using various measures and adjustments on the rank–order standing of the individual utilities. The ordinal ranking information may be summarized through serial correlation and the use of two-way quartile analysis.[6] Table 2 shows the simple rank–order correlations for comparisons across measures, Divisia vs. Laspeyres, and across adjustments. As indicated in the table, correlations across measures, for a given type of adjustment, are moderately high, ranging from 0.78 to 0.88. A very high correlation exists between the unadjusted measure and the measure adjusted for returns to scale (0.96 and 0.98), while the correlation of the unadjusted measure and the measure adjusted jointly for capacity utilization and returns to scale is not as high (0.62 and 0.56). The correlation between the unadjusted and adjusted for capacity utilization measures lies between the other two sets of values (0.72 and 0.66).

The comparisons across measures and adjustments by quartile cell are reported in Table 3. This table reflects the extent to which agreement exists between quartile rankings under two different procedures. The chi-square statistics reported at the bottom of the table indicate whether the distribution frequency of rankings across cells is significantly different from a uniform distribution across the cells. High chi-square values imply strong

---

[5] Scale elasticities were estimated as the inverse of the firm by firm measures of scale economies. A measure of the firm specific cost-output elasticity was developed for each of the years 1964–1975. For each year, a cross-sectional translog cost function with arguments in factor prices, output, and capacity utilization was jointly estimated (using Zellner efficient estimation procedures) with a system of input cost share equations. Scale elasticity values for each firm were then derived by constructing $\partial \ln C / \partial \ln Q$ from the cost-function parameter estimates and the firm-specific values of factor prices, output, and capacity utilization. The scale elasticity measures were then incorporated into the TFP index as outlined earlier.

[6] Rank-order TFP comparisons of firms are likely to be more instructive for firms of significantly different rank than for firms of adjacent rank. Consequently, we use comparisons of quartile rankings to augment our tests of rank-order divergence among measures.

TABLE 3

Quartile Rankings Across Measures

Laspeyres TFP—unadjusted	A. Divisia TFP—unadjusted[a] 1	2	3	4		B. Divisia TFP—adjusted for capacity utilization[b] 1	2	3	4
1	16	4	0	1	Laspeyres TFP—adjusted for capacity utilization 1	16	4	0	1
2	5	10	4	1	2	5	11	4	0
3	0	6	9	5	3	0	5	11	4
4	0	0	7	13	4	0	0	5	15

Laspeyres TFP—adjusted for returns to scale	C. Divisia TFP—adjusted for returns to scale[c] 1	2	3	4		D. Divisia TFP—adjusted for capacity utilization and returns to scale[d] 1	2	3	4
1	16	2	2	1	Laspeyres TFP—adjusted for capacity utilization and returns to scale 1	16	4	1	0
2	5	11	4	0	2	4	12	3	1
3	0	7	7	6	3	1	4	7	8
4	0	0	7	13	4	0	0	9	11

Laspeyres TFP—adjusted for capacity utilization	E. Laspeyres TFP—unadjusted[e] 1	2	3	4		F. Laspeyres TFP—unadjusted[f] 1	2	3	4
1	12	6	3	0	Laspeyres TFP—adjusted for returns to scale 1	19	2	0	0
2	5	7	5	3	2	2	17	1	0
3	4	4	5	7	3	0	1	16	3
4	0	0	7	13	4	0	0	3	17

Laspeyres TFP—adjusted for capacity utilization and returns to scale	G. Laspeyres TFP—unadjusted[g] 1	2	3	4		H. Divisia TFP—unadjusted[h] 1	2	3	4
1	11	5	4	1	Divisia TFP—adjusted for capacity utilization 1	12	8	1	0
2	6	6	4	5	2	9	2	6	3
3	4	6	4	6	3	0	6	10	4
4	0	3	8	9	4	0	4	3	13

Divisia TFP—adjusted for capacity utilization	I. Divisia TFP—unadjusted[i] 1	2	3	4		J. Divisia TFP—unadjusted[j] 1	2	3	4
1	18	3	0	0	Divisia TFP—adjusted for capacity utilization and returns to scale 1	9	8	3	1
2	3	14	3	0	2	10	4	4	2
3	0	3	16	1	3	2	3	10	5
4	0	0	1	19	4	0	5	3	12

[a] $\chi^2 = 72.74$. [b] $\chi^2 = 87.38$. [c] $\chi^2 = 73.66$. [d] $\chi^2 = 72.85$. [e] $\chi^2 = 43.31$.
[f] $\chi^2 = 162.89$. [g] $\chi^2 = 22.82$. [h] $\chi^2 = 54.55$. [i] $\chi^2 = 151.69$. [j] $\chi^2 = 39.10$.

quartile ranking agreements between the two measures. As indicated in the table, agreement appears strongest for comparisons of the unadjusted measure and the measures adjusted solely for returns to scale.

For the comparative measure, rank–order quartile cell frequencies, a strong agreement exists with respect to the extremes (lowest and highest) of the quartile rankings. Visual inspection of the two-way frequency tables indicates that in virtually all cases, quartile ranking agreement is most likely to occur in the highest and lowest quartiles.

Our comparative analysis of Divisia- and Laspeyres-based TFP measures, with and without adjustments, shows very high levels of agreement for group averages and reasonably high levels of correspondence on the ordinal rankings of individual firms. The Divisia, and to a lesser extent the Laspeyres, measures are intended to be exact-index-number measures of shifts of the production frontier, and can be specified without knowledge of the parameters of the underlying production function. Some have suggested that better measures of TFP growth would be those that compare actual output in period t with the projected level of output that would have existed in that period had the base-period production function still been operative. Projected output would be derived by applying base-period production function coefficients to the actual input levels for period t. In this study we perform a similar analysis by using the cost-function dual of the production function. As noted in footnote 1, the cost-function and production-function shifts are not necessarily identical, the production-function shift due to technological advancement being equal to the cost-function shift multiplied by the scale elasticity.

To derive the cost-function-based measure, a translog cost function and the associated input cost shares were jointly estimated for a 1964 base period.[7] The base-period equation was then used to project the level of costs that would have existed in a later year if there had been no technological advancement.[8] The cost-function-based TFP measures were derived using both 1964 and 1975 comparison periods. Both capacity utilization and scale economies are controlled for in the cost function. The average value of the TFP index is 1.1427, which, on a comparable basis to the Divisia and Laspeyres measures, would become 1.0122. The comparable average Divisia and Laspeyres TFP values, adjusted for capacity utilization and returns to scale, are 1.0168 and 1.0122, respectively.

The rank-order correspondence of the Divisia and cost function TFP measures are shown in Tables 4 and 5. As indicated in the tables, there is virtually no correspondence in rank orderings between the cost function,

---

[7] The cost function is estimated under the assumption of unconstrained cost minimization.

[8] The projected cost level is adjusted proportionately to reflect the base period estimated error (i.e., $\ln C_i^0 - \ln \hat{C}_i^0$).

TABLE 4

Rank-Order Correlation

Correlation of cost function TFP, adjusted for capacity utilization and returns to scale, with	
Divisia TFP—unadjusted	0.097
Divisia TFP—adjusted for capacity utilization	0.480
Divisia TFP—adjusted for returns to scale	0.111
Divisia TFP—adjusted for capacity utilization and returns to scale	0.508

TABLE 5

Quartile Rankings

		A. Divisia TFP—unadjusted[a]						B. Divisia TFP—adjusted for capacity utilization[b]			
		1	2	3	4			1	2	3	4
Cost function	1	5	8	3	5	Cost function	1	12	4	4	1
TFP	2	5	4	7	4	TFP	2	2	5	4	2
	3	7	4	4	5		3	7	7	3	3
	4	4	4	6	6		4	0	4	2	14

		C. Divisia TFP—adjusted for returns to scale[c]						D. Divisia TFP—adjusted for capacity utilization and returns to scale[d]			
		1	2	3	4			1	2	3	4
Cost function	1	5	7	4	5	Cost function	1	12	4	4	1
TFP	2	6	4	6	4	TFP	2	4	4	9	3
	3	6	6	3	5		3	5	9	3	3
	4	4	3	7	6		4	0	3	4	13

[a] $\chi^2 = 5.61$.　　[b] $\chi^2 = 49.72$.　　[c] $\chi^2 = 4.90$.　　[d] $\chi^2 = 40.52$.

adjusted for capacity utilization and returns to scale, and the unadjusted Divisia TFP index. However, correspondence does increase when the Divisia TFP index is adjusted for scale and capacity utilization.

While the rank correlation between the cost function and Divisia TFP indexes is reasonably high, 0.51, it is not as high as might have been expected. If the estimated cost function represents the true base-period production relationship, then one might interpret the results as suggesting caution in the use of Divisia TFP indexes for measuring an individual firm's productivity growth. Several additional factors need to be considered, however, before such a conclusion can be reached. First, as noted in footnote 2, the capacity-utilization adjustment factor is not treated in a dual manner in the Divisia and cost-function measures. Second, the empirical cost function estimated was not a frontier cost function in the Aigner *et al.* [1977] sense. Third, the translog formulation provides only an approximation to the true underlying cost function. As Caves and Christensen [1978b] have shown, the quality of the translog approximation varies over the parameter domain of the true function. Finally, these measures do not incorporate adjustments for regulatory tightness.

2.3 Accounting for Regulatory Tightness

As indicated in Eq. (22) the Divisia TFP index can be adjusted in a straightforward manner to reflect varying levels of regulatory tightness. This adjustment, however, requires the determination of firm-specific values of the

TABLE 6

Divisia TFP Indexes Adjusted for A–J Effect

1. SAVANNAH ELECTRIC

Values of δ^b	Values of μ^a		
	0.1	0.5	0.9
0.99	1.0163	1.0162	1.0150
0.90	1.0162	1.0149	—
0.83	1.0160	1.0132	—

2. KANSAS CITY POWER AND LIGHT

Values of δ	Values of μ		
	0.1	0.5	0.9
0.99	0.9915	0.9915	0.9911
0.90	0.9915	0.9911	—
0.83	0.9914	0.9906	—

3. POTOMAC EDISON COMPANY

Values of δ	Values of μ		
	0.1	0.5	0.9
0.99	1.0231	1.0231	1.0230
0.90	1.0231	1.0230	—
0.83	1.0231	1.0231	—

[a] μ is the hypothetical value of the Lagrangian regulatory constraint coefficient.

[b] δ is the hypothetical ratio of the financial cost of capital to the allowed rate of return.

Lagrangian constraint μ and the allowed rate of return. While we do not attempt to estimate the regulatory effect directly in this paper, we do undertake a suggestive numerical analysis to determine the extent to which an adjustment for regulatory tightness would alter the value of the TFP index.[9]

Table 6 presents the effects on the Divisia TFP measure of allowing for rate-of-return regulatory effects. The TFP values for three utilities, adjusted for capacity utilization and returns to scale, are further adjusted under various assumptions as to the level of "regulatory tightness" and the difference between the allowed rate of return and the financial cost of capital. Under the traditional A–J assumptions, the value of the Lagrangian constraint is greater than zero and less than the ratio of the financial cost of capital and the allowed return, assuming effective regulation, so that only those cases for which μ is strictly less than δ are shown.

As indicated in the table, the effects of the regulatory adjustment are quite small, at least over the ranges of S and μ considered.

3.   Conclusions

The purpose of this paper was to set forth alternative measures of total factor productivity and to indicate how the various measures could be modified to account for capacity utilization, returns to scale, and effective rate-of-return regulation. The various measures were quantified with data from a sample of 81 electric utilities. While the group averages of the various measures, with and without adjustments, do not vary significantly, rank orders may vary significantly with TFP measure employed and the adjustments made to those measures. Such variation seems to be most pronounced where adjustments for capacity utilization were made. Returns-to-scale adjustments did not significantly alter ordinal rankings. And regulatory tightness adjustments appear to have only a minor impact on the value of TFP measures, at least for the case of the Divisia index.

ACKNOWLEDGMENTS

This research was funded by a grant from the National Science Foundation. We should like to thank Mel Fuss for helpful comments on an earlier draft.

[9] See Cowing [1978] for an econometric model that permits firm-specific values of the Lagrangian multiplier μ to be estimated.

8

The Measurement and Interpretation of Total Factor Productivity in Regulated Industries, with an Application to Canadian Telecommunications

Michael Denny

Melvyn Fuss

Leonard Waverman

Department of Political Economy
Institute for Policy Analysis
University of Toronto
Toronto, Ontario, Canada

1. Introduction

The conventional approach to growth accounting uses total factor productivity indexes to measure the residual growth in outputs not accounted for by the growth in factor inputs. The rate of growth of total factor productivity is conventionally defined as the rate of growth of aggregate output minus the rate of growth of aggregate input.

The interpretation of this residual has proceeded in at least two distinct directions. For example, Denison [1962, 1967] and Star [1974] have stressed the diversity of the factors that might be captured in the residual total factor productivity measure.[1] Kendrick [1961, 1973] might also be grouped with those who view productivity as a broad measure that captures the influence of many effects on output per unit of input. The other methodological approach has stressed the relationship of productivity to technical progress that causes a shift in the production function (Solow [1957], Jorgenson and Griliches [1967], and Hulten [1975, 1978]). Using an explicit production function in conjunction with certain technical and market assumptions, the equivalence of technical progress and total factor productivity may be demonstrated.[2]

In this paper, we encompass both approaches by developing in detail a methodology that permits the researcher to use the production-function framework explicitly, and still decompose total factor productivity growth into a number of causes.[3]

The key to our decomposition of total factor productivity growth is the realization that the computational method employed in moving from a postulated production process to an index constructed from observable prices and quantities imposes a number of assumptions. These assumptions include constant returns to scale and perfect competition in input and output markets. When these assumptions are not satisfied, conventional indexes of total factor productivity growth include not only the effect of technical change (which shifts the production function) but also the effects of non-constant returns to scale and market imperfections. The separation of these effects is what we call the decomposition of total factor productivity growth.

For regulated industries, the assumptions of constant returns to scale and perfect competition are likely to be particularly inappropriate. The high capital intensity of production of many regulated industries increases the probability of increasing-returns-to-scale phenomena. Monopolistic elements and cross-subsidization practices imply existence of non-marginal cost pricing of outputs. Effective rate-of-return regulation leads to imperfections in factor markets, since cost-minimizing or profit-maximizing regulated firms will not equate the marginal rates of substitution between capital and variable factors to the ratios of their market prices.

---

[1] These factors include scale, substitution, product mix, imperfect competition, research and development, human capital, and managerial efficiency, for example.

[2] The necessary assumptions are constant returns to scale in production and perfect competition in input and output markets. Kendrick [1973, pp. 1-31] has a useful nontechnical discussion of this relationship.

[3] The idea that total factor productivity growth as conventionally measured can be decomposed using an estimated production structure appears to have originated with Griliches [1963, 1964, 1967], who estimated the contributions of measurement errors, market imperfections, and scale economies to productivity growth in U.S. agriculture and manufacturing. Surprisingly, his methodology, which is conceptually similar to that developed in this paper, has not been widely used in productivity analysis.

Given the above possibilities for violation of the standard assumptions, the total factor productivity index will not measure technical change alone, and a decomposition of the index is desirable. In Section 4 of this paper, we derive the formulas necessary to effect this decomposition. One result of special interest emerges that has not been previously noted in the regulation literature. For firms that are subject to effective rate-of-return regulation, there exists a productivity measurement analog to the Averch–Johnson overcapitalization effect. For example, we show that in inflationary periods when the prices of variable (expensed) factors of production and the allowed rate of return are increasing, measured total factor productivity growth using conventional indexes always overstates technical change, even if corrections are made for nonconstant returns to scale and all other market imperfections.

In order to decompose the total factor productivity index, structural information about the production process is needed. This information can be obtained by estimating the firm's cost function.[4] As we demonstrate in Section 4, elements of the cost function that are of particular importance for measuring the relationship between total factor productivity and technical change correctly are cost elasticities (with respect to outputs) and the value of the Lagrangian multiplier in the rate of return model. Estimates of the required parameters of the cost function for Bell Canada are taken from Denny et al. [1979]. The cost-function model estimated in that paper is summarized in Section 5.

Section 2 contains a description of the basic data set used in this paper—production and cost data for Bell Canada for the period 1952–1976. In Section 3 we present estimates of productivity growth using a discrete approximation to the Divisia index of total factor productivity. Decomposition of this productivity index for Bell Canada is accomplished in Section 6. Concluding remarks in Section 7 complete the paper.

2.   Bell Canada and Canadian Telecommunications

Bell Canada is the largest telephone company in Canada. It provides telecommunications services primarily in the populous provinces of Ontario and Quebec. A private company, Bell Canada earned profits of $233 million on sales of $2133 million in 1977. At the beginning of our sample period, 1952, 2 million phones in the Bell Canada network were used to place approximately 3 billion calls. By 1977, 12 billion calls were placed, using

---

[4] Parametric representation of the cost function is necessary to identify, as well as to estimate, the separate effects due to scale economies and technical change. For further detail on this identification problem see Diamond et al. [1978].

8.5 million phones. In 1952, the network was run by about 30,000 employees using a capital stock of $626 million (constant dollars). By 1976, 48,000 employees and a capital stock of $4 billion (constant dollars) were servicing the Bell Canada system. A wide variety of telephone and telecommunications services are provided within Bell Canada's geographic region. Bell is linked with other Canadian companies through the Trans-Canada Telephone System and internationally through Teleglobe to offer toll services throughout Canada and the rest of the world.

All Canadian telephone companies are subject to some form of regulation by the governments of Canada. For example, in Manitoba, Saskatchewan, and Alberta, telephone services are provided by public enterprises regulated by a variety of direct government controls. Bell Canada is a private company with a federal charter, and is subject to regulation by the federal government through the Canadian Radio–Television and Telecommunications Commission (CRTC).

Regulation of Bell Canada since 1965 has taken the form of a constraint on the permitted upper levels of the rates of return on total capital and equity capital. In addition, the rate structure is regulated in a less explicit manner in order to produce rates that are "just and reasonable." One important effect of rate structure regulation is to yield rates for basic local residential service that are constrained to be below the profit-maximizing rates.

During the last 25 years, many specific technical innovations have been introduced that have led to productivity improvements. Perhaps the most significant one is direct distance dialing (DDD). Introduced in the late 1950s, DDD is now available throughout most of the urban areas of Bell's territory, permitting Bell to reduce substantially the number of telephone operators that it employs. Before DDD could be implemented, additional switching equipment was required in order to monitor usage. In 1952, step-by-step switching was predominant. By 1965, most of the older, pre-step-by-step switches had been eliminated and the quantity of Number 5 Crossbar switches had grown rapidly. Since 1965, step-by-step switching has remained stagnant in absolute terms. Expansion of facilities has been accompanied by increases in Number 5 Crossbar and, since 1972, by rapid growth in electronic switching. In Sections 5 and 6, we use several indicators of the rate of adoption of innovations in DDD and switching in estimating the characteristics of the production process and the technical change component of the growth in total factor productivity.

2.1 The Growth of Outputs and Inputs

In order to characterize the growth of Bell Canada over the period 1952–1976, the rates of growth of total revenue, aggregate real output, total costs, and aggregate real input have been calculated for several subperiods (Table 1). (Revenue shares were used to weight the individual outputs, whereas cost shares were used for the inputs.)

Total revenues grew at average rates that exceed 7.8% a year in all subperiods. Revenue growth slipped over the first 15 years but climbed sharply during the past 10 years. Aggregate real output growth was somewhat more stable but still rapid. The very rapid growth in the middle 1950s has never been equalled, primarily because this was a period of very rapid growth in the number of main telephones and new subscribers. Until the 1970s, aggregate output had grown almost as quickly as total revenue, indicating that modest price increases characterized this period.

Total costs grew more rapidly than total revenue in four of the five subperiods portrayed in Table 1. Costs here are calculated to *include* a user cost of capital and consequently, they are not equivalent to any cost figures calculated by the company. A detailed description of the variables used is included in the Appendix. In general, costs increased very rapidly in the first period and during the last decade. After the first period there was a dramatic decline in the growth of aggregate real input. From an average rate of increase of 8.5% a year in 1952–1957, the growth rate fell to below 5% for the following 20 years. Within this latter period, Bell was able to reduce the rate of growth of inputs by a further 25% in the past decade.

Since output growth showed no tendency to decline over the past 20 years, we can infer that the sharp decline in the growth of inputs implies impressive productivity growth. Productivity growth will be analyzed in detail in Sections 3 and 4. In this section we consider how each output and input has contributed to these aggregate patterns.

Table 2 displays the average annual rates of growth of real output for six aggregate outputs. Local service (column one) is the largest output that Bell produces. Throughout most of the quarter century, constant dollar

TABLE 1

Average Annual Percentage Rates of Growth of Outputs and Inputs, Bell Canada, 1952–1976

	Revenue (current dollars)	Output (constant dollars)	Cost (current dollars)	Input (constant dollars)
1952–1957	9.9	9.7	10.5	8.5
1958–1962	8.8	7.8	7.3	4.8
1963–1966	7.8	8.0	8.0	4.9
1967–1970	9.4	8.5	10.5	3.8
1971–1976	11.7	8.3	13.4	3.9

TABLE 2

Average Annual Percentage Rates of Growth of Real Outputs, Bell Canada, 1952–1976

	Local	Bell toll	Trans toll	U.S. toll	Other toll	Miscellaneous
1952–1957	9.23	8.23	22.60	14.98	30.47	7.85
1958–1962	7.34	7.68	12.43	6.55	16.72	7.62
1963–1966	6.83	7.85	12.06	16.54	19.96	1.42
1967–1970	7.03	9.29	12.25	11.78	14.97	6.82
1971–1976	7.31	8.58	15.60	14.03	12.78	−7.22

local service output grew at roughly 7% per year. The only period of more rapid growth was the mid-1950s. It must be remembered that local services include 75 or 80 separately priced services. Some of the most rapidly growing items are auxiliary equipment services for which separate data are not available.

The next three aggregate outputs comprise message toll outputs. A substantial difference exists in their growth rates. Intra-Bell message toll grew much more slowly than the two longer distance toll categories. Intra-Bell toll is the largest of the message toll outputs but the other two types are rapidly catching up.

The final toll category is "other toll," a mix of WATS and private line services. It is in this area that many of the specialized data transmission services are included. Although other toll did not grow at significantly higher rates than the non-Bell message toll, it is expected that future growth may be high in this area. The last aggregate output is a mixture of miscellaneous revenues that was approximately 5% of total revenue in 1967. The negative rate of growth during 1971–1976 is due to the formation of Teledirect, a separate corporation to handle directory advertising.

Aggregate output grew at an average rate of over 8% a year for the past 15 years. The very rapid growth in longer distance message toll and other toll only managed to raise the aggregate output growth about 1% above the growth rate for local service outputs. The continued importance of the large local service output is evident in these figures.

In this paper inputs into the production process are assumed to be the three aggregate inputs: labor, capital, and materials. The rates of growth of these inputs, shown in Table 3, had very distinct and different patterns.

All three inputs experienced very fast rates of growth from 1952 to 1957. However, in the four later periods the individual patterns diverged. Labor input actually declined from 1958 to 1962 at an annual average rate of 2% a year. This decline was due primarily to the introduction of direct distance

TABLE 3

Average Annual Percentage Rates of Growth of Real Inputs:
Labor, Capital, and Materials

	Labor	Capital	Materials
1952–1957	5.05	11.74	9.71
1958–1962	−2.00	10.02	6.04
1963–1966	2.37	6.69	4.50
1967–1970	0.13	5.71	4.72
1971–1976	2.53	4.40	4.33

dialing. Labor inputs grew modestly during 1963–1966 and 1971–1976. From 1967 to 1970, labor growth was practically zero.[5]

In real terms, the growth of the capital stock slowed continuously. From 1952 to 1962, growth was at a rate above 10% a year. After that time the growth rate declined steadily, falling below 5% in the period 1971–1976. Material inputs also grew at slower rates through time.

Overall, it may be said that in the past 15 years inputs have grown much more slowly than in the first decade. The exception for labor is due to a major technological change, the introduction and diffusion of DDD.

2.2 Difficulties Associated with the Measurement of Output

Bell Canada sells an enormous variety of outputs and the diversity in products has increased during the past 25 years. The best *available* output measures are those produced by Bell Canada—constant dollar revenues. These are the measures we have used in our analysis of productivity and they are discussed in the Data Appendix. In this section, we wish to introduce an alternative output measure that illustrates some of the difficulties of accurately measuring outputs when there are a large number of products with diverse characteristics. It should be noted that the alternative measure of aggregate output discussed here is an underestimate of Bell's actual output, and must be interpreted as an example.

---

[5] The reasons for the slow growth of labor during 1967–1970 are not as easily determined as the reasons for negative growth during 1958–1962. However, the empirical analysis in later sections of the paper indicates the following causes all played a role. First, direct distance dialing and modern switching facilities, both labor-saving innovations, continued to be diffused through the telephone system during this period. Second, capital and materials deepening occurred in response to changes in relative factor prices. Third, the apparent nonhomotheticity of the production function (biased toward labor-saving techniques at higher output levels) became more important during this period. Finally, there is a residual cause of input reduction per unit of output during 1967–1970, which is unexplained by the econometric model (see Table 11).

The largest share of Bell's revenue comes from local and toll message services. In these areas, the telephone network produces telephone calls both locally and throughout wider geographical areas. Suppose we measure output by the number of calls for each of these services. Local service is currently sold at a flat rate per month based on the number of phones that can be reached in the local exchanges. Substantial local service revenue is derived from auxiliary services charged on a recurring or non-recurring basis. Our alternative local service output quantity is the number of calls. If one makes a local call on a red Contempra touchtone extension phone with a long cord one may be making an expensive phone call under current pricing schedules, but it is still a local call. The price of local service output is the implicit price, given the output quantity (number of calls) and the total local service revenue. Our alternative estimate of local service output is similar to an output measure unadjusted for quality change. Output growth is understated, while the rate of increase in price is overstated. It might be considered an indicator of the minimum rate of growth of local service output.

For toll message output, the current Bell pricing schedules charge by time, distance, time of day, day of week, and type of call, at least. Using the number of toll calls understates output predominantly because the distance factor is not included and there has been a significant relative shift of toll calls into the larger distance bands. The price of toll message output is the implicit price, given total toll revenue. This is another indicator of the minimum increase in output in these services.

Although it is beyond the scope of this paper to determine a preferred output measure, the following important issues are involved in correctly measuring output. If the prices of many services do not equal their marginal costs then output aggregation using prices will be incorrect. Cross-subsidies will be present in these cases. Further, monopoly rents are being generated and redistributed among services by this process. In this paper we can only measure the quantitative differences for aggregate service categories (see Section 6). We believe that some of the major cross-subsidies occur within the local service constant dollar output measure, but do not have data available which would allow us to measure these effects.

If our alternative call measure of local service output is substituted for the standard measure, local output growth is reduced by about 2% a year. For toll calls, the switch to number of calls reduces the rate of growth of output by a larger amount. A crude guide to the magnitudes that might be involved in changing output definitions can be seen from Table 4. The value of seven indicators in 1976 (1952 = 1.00) are shown. Constant dollar local service revenue (line 2) is much larger than local calls (line 1) or any

TABLE 4

Alternative Output Indicators, 1976[a]

1. Local calls, number	3.85
2. Local service revenue, constant dollars	5.81
3. Telephones, number	4.03
4. Residential main stations, number	3.35
5. Business main stations, number	3.63
6. Toll calls, number	6.19
7. Message toll revenue, constant dollars	10.17

[a] Indexes 1952 = 1.00.

of the three measures of the number of telephones (items 3–5). Similarly, the constant dollar toll revenue indicator is 64% larger in 1976 than the indicator of the number of calls.

In the next section, we present a total factor productivity index based on substituting the number of local and message toll calls for their respective constant dollar output measures, and compare the resulting index with the one based on the constant dollar measures. It will be seen that the rate of total factor productivity growth is reduced to almost a third when constant dollar revenues are replaced by numbers of calls.

3. The Measurement of Total Factor Productivity for Bell Canada

3.1 The Conventional Divisia Index of Total Factor Productivity

From a conceptual point of view, one of the most defensible methods of aggregation for use in productivity analysis is Divisia aggregation. This has become well established through the research of Jorgenson and Griliches [1967], Richter [1966], Hulten [1973], and Diewert [1976], among others.

The conventionally measured Divisia index of total factor productivity is obtained in the following way. First we define total factor productivity (TFP) as the ratio of aggregate output (Q) to aggregate input (F). Aggregate output (input) is an index of disaggregated outputs (inputs). The Divisia indexes for aggregate output (Q) and input (F) are defined in terms of proportional rates of growth ($\dot{Q}$ and $\dot{F}$) as

$$\dot{Q} = \sum_j \frac{P_j Q_j}{R} \dot{Q}_j, \tag{1}$$

where P_j is the price of output j, Q_j the quantity of output j, $\dot{Q}_j$ the proportional rate of growth of output j, $R = \sum_j P_j Q_j$ the total revenue, and

$$\dot{F} = \sum_i \frac{w_i X_i}{C} \dot{X}_i, \tag{2}$$

where w_i is the price of input i, X_i the quantity of input i, $\dot{X}_i$ the proportionate rate of growth of input i, and $C = \sum_i w_i X_i$ the total cost.

Since TFP $= Q/F$, the proportionate rate of growth of total factor productivity (TĠP) is defined by

$$\dot{\text{TFP}} = \dot{Q} - \dot{F}. \tag{3}$$

The formulas (1)–(3) are in terms of instantaneous changes. For data obtainable at yearly intervals, the most commonly used discrete approximation to the continuous formulas (1) and (2) is given by the Törnqvist approximations:

$$\Delta \log Q = \log\left(\frac{Q_t}{Q_{t-1}}\right) = \frac{1}{2}\sum_j (r_{jt} + r_{j,t-1})\log\left(\frac{Q_{jt}}{Q_{j,t-1}}\right), \tag{4}$$

where Q_{jt} is the quantity of output Q_j produced in period t, $r_{jt} = P_{jt}Q_{jt}/\sum_j P_{jt}Q_{jt}$ the revenue share of output Q_j in total revenue during period t, and

$$\Delta \log F = \log\left(\frac{F_t}{F_{t-1}}\right) = \frac{1}{2}\sum_i (s_{it} + s_{i,t-1})\log\left(\frac{X_{it}}{X_{i,t-1}}\right), \tag{5}$$

where X_{it} is the quantity of input X_i used in period t and $s_{it} = w_i X_i / \sum_i w_i X_i$ the cost share of input X_i in the total cost during period t.

Finally, the corresponding discrete approximation to (3) is provided by

$$\Delta\text{TFP} = \Delta \log Q - \Delta \log F. \tag{6}$$

Choosing the index to equal 100.0 in a particular year and accumulating the measure in accordance with (6) provides estimates of what we call the *conventional* index of total factor productivity. As we demonstrate in Section 4, when linked to the theory of production this conventional index implies constant returns to scale, marginal cost pricing, and an absence of a rate-of-return constraint, as well as cost-minimizing behavior. The index requires careful interpretation when the above assumptions are incorrect. This interpretation is also developed in Section 4. However, before proceeding to an analysis of productivity indexes in terms of the theory of production, it is useful to describe the performance of Bell Canada for the 1952–1976 period as measured by the conventional Divisia index of total factor productivity.

3.2 Bell Canada Performance Measured by Conventional Divisia Index

The productivity index was calculated using seven outputs, seven labor inputs, a capital input index, and a materials input index. The data are explained in an appendix on the Bell Canada data. The index from 1952 to 1976, with 1967 = 100.0 is shown in Table 5. This index grew at an average annual rate of 3.35% per year, which is a very rapid growth in productivity. For comparison, in Canadian manufacturing a comparable index grew at only 1% per year (May and Denny [1979]). Bell Canada's performance was far above the manufacturing sector's performance.

While average productivity growth was rapid, there was substantial variation within the period. In Table 6, column one, the average growth

TABLE 5

Total Factor Productivity for Bell Canada, 1952–1976

	Index (1967 = 100)	Rate of change (%)
1952	66.9	—
	68.4	2.23
	68.7	0.46
1955	68.7	0.05
	68.9	0.33
	71.2	3.19
	71.6	0.54
	73.8	3.03
1960	75.8	2.75
	78.7	3.76
	82.8	4.97
	83.5	0.84
	86.4	3.48
1965	89.6	3.61
	93.7	4.45
	100.0	6.54
	104.7	4.64
	108.5	3.53
1970	112.8	3.91
	112.6	−0.23
	118.6	5.20
	125.4	5.62
	132.9	5.81
1975	144.0	8.01
1976	147.4	2.34
Average: 1952–1976	—	3.35

TABLE 6

Accounting for the Growth of Aggregate Output

Period	TFP Average annual growth (%)	$\dot{Q}$ Average annual growth (%)	Relative importance of alternative contributors to the growth of output (%)			
			TFP	$\dot{L}$	$s_K(K/L)$	$s_M(M/L)$
1952–1957	1.3	9.7	13.4	51.0	27.4	8.2
1958–1962	3.0	7.8	37.9	−27.9	72.9	17.1
1963–1966	3.1	8.0	37.0	29.9	28.7	4.4
1967–1970	4.7	8.5	55.3	1.2	36.2	7.3
1971–1976	4.5	8.3	48.4	28.7	15.1	7.8

of total factor productivity is shown for several subperiods. Productivity grew at a much faster rate after 1958. Until 1970, the rate of growth was increasing during each subperiod. A leveling off in the growth rate of productivity occurred during the 1970s.

To understand the importance of total factor productivity in accounting for the growth of output we can make use of the following relationship[6]

$$\dot{Q} = \text{TFP} + \dot{L} + s_K K/L + s_M M/L. \qquad (7)$$

The second column of Table 6 shows the rate of growth of output $\dot{Q}$. The remaining columns show the relative importance of growth in total factor productivity, labor, capital intensity, and materials intensity in the growth of output. These columns add (across) to 100% and are the individual terms in (7) converted to percentages.

From 1952 to 1957, output growth was very high but total factor productivity was low and contributed only 13% of the growth in output. Over half of the output growth was accounted for by the growth in labor. Increased capital and materials per unit of labor accounted for the remaining 36% of output growth.

The period from 1958 to 1962 is perhaps the most interesting. Output grew more slowly in this period but total factor productivity accelerated and grew at double the rate of the earlier period. Although output grew rapidly, labor input actually fell at an average rate of over 2% a year. As a consequence, productivity growth became much more important, accounting for almost 40% of the output growth during this period. Since labor was declining, the intensities with which capital and materials were combined with labor substantially increased.

[6] For a derivation of this formula, see Solow [1957].

For the next two subperiods, 1963–1966 and 1967–1970, output grew at 8.0 and 8.5% respectively, and productivity accounted for about 37 and 55% of growth. The major difference between the subperiods was the return to steady labor growth in the first period and almost zero labor growth in the second period.

After 1970, both output and total factor productivity grew slightly more slowly than during the 1967–1970 period. The growth in labor increased and was at a rate comparable to the 1963–1966 period. The relative importance of productivity growth remained high, but slipped somewhat from the very high level of the 1967–1970 period.

TABLE 7

Alternative Total Factor Productivity for Bell Canada,
1952–1976

	Index (1967 = 100)	Rate of change (%)
1952	92.2	—
	91.4	−0.89
	88.4	−3.33
1955	88.1	−0.40
	87.8	−0.28
	86.8	−1.13
	87.1	0.30
	88.1	1.15
1960	88.6	0.62
	90.1	1.64
	93.2	3.36
	93.2	0.00
	95.2	2.08
1965	95.6	0.48
	96.7	1.15
	100.0	3.32
	103.5	3.47
	105.6	2.02
1970	108.4	2.62
	107.7	−0.70
	113.9	5.57
	117.1	2.82
	125.5	6.90
1975	126.1	0.51
1976	128.4	1.77
Average: 1952–1976	—	1.38

3.3   Total Factor Productivity of Bell Canada Using Alternative Output Measures

We complete the measurement of total factor productivity section by demonstrating the sensitivity of TFP growth to alternative output measures. Table 7 presents the measurement of TFP using the concept of messages as output discussed in Section 2. The result is striking—total factor productivity growth declines from 3.35% per annum to 1.38% per annum. This estimate is likely to be a lower bound since only messages are considered to be output in local and message toll services. However, we believe that constant dollar output measures overstate actual output growth, so that 3.35% is likely to be an upper bound.

4.   Total Factor Productivity and the Theory of Production

4.1   The Case of a Single Output

In this section we develop the links between the measurement of productivity and the theory of production that permit us to adjust the conventional Divisia index for the market imperfections usually encountered in regulated industries. We begin with the case of a single output (Q) produced by inputs X_i, $i = 1, \ldots, n$. The production possibilities are described by the production function

$$Q = f(X_1, \ldots, X_n, t). \tag{8}$$

Define $\dot{A} = (\partial f/\partial t)(1/f)$, the proportional shift in the production function with time. The shifting of the production function through time is called technical change, and it is technical change that we wish to relate to the productivity index. If we totally differentiate the production function with respect to time, we obtain

$$\frac{dQ}{dt} = \sum_i \frac{\partial f}{\partial X_i} \frac{\partial X_i}{\partial t} + \frac{\partial f}{\partial t}. \tag{9}$$

Dividing (9) by Q and rearranging results in

$$\dot{Q} = \sum_i \frac{\partial f}{\partial X_i} \frac{X_i}{Q} \dot{X}_i + \dot{A}. \tag{10}$$

Assume that the firm minimizes the cost of producing Q. Then the first-order conditions for cost minimization imply $\partial f/\partial X_i = w_i/(\partial C/\partial Q)$ where $\partial C/\partial Q$ is the marginal cost of production. Substituting for $\partial f/\partial X_i$ in (10), we obtain

$$\dot{Q} = \sum_i \frac{w_i X_i}{\partial C/\partial Q \cdot Q} \dot{X}_i + \dot{A}. \tag{11}$$

Define the elasticity of cost with respect to output (ε_{CQ}) as

$$\varepsilon_{CQ} = \frac{\partial C}{\partial Q} \frac{Q}{C}. \tag{12}$$

Substituting (12) into (11) we obtain an expression for the proportionate rate of growth of output

$$\dot{Q} = \sum_i \varepsilon_{CQ}^{-1} \frac{w_i X_i}{C} \dot{X}_i + \dot{A}. \tag{13}$$

For the case of a single output, $\dot{Q}$ is identical to the proportionate rate of growth of output in the measurement of total factor productivity. The index of aggregate inputs F is defined by the growth equation [see Eq. (2)]

$$\dot{F} = \sum_i \frac{w_i X_i}{C} \dot{X}_i. \tag{14}$$

Substituting (14) into (13), we obtain

$$\dot{A} = \dot{Q} - \varepsilon_{CQ}^{-1} \dot{F}. \tag{15}$$

We now proceed to compare the measure of technical change $\dot{A}$ with our total factor productivity measure $\dot{\text{TFP}} = \dot{Q} - \dot{F}$. A rearrangement of (15) yields

$$\dot{A} = \dot{\text{TFP}} + (1 - \varepsilon_{CQ}^{-1})\dot{F} \tag{16}$$

or

$$\dot{\text{TFP}} = \dot{A} + (\varepsilon_{CQ}^{-1} - 1)\dot{F}. \tag{17}$$

In order to interpret Eq. (17) we begin by noting that the inverse of the elasticity of cost with respect to output is the scale elasticity. Therefore, if production is subject to constant returns to scale $\varepsilon_{CQ} = 1$ and

$$\dot{A} = \dot{\text{TFP}}. \tag{18}$$

In this case the total factor productivity growth rate is identically equal to the rate of technical change. We now can see the effect of a departure from one of the assumptions used to construct the total factor productivity index in Section 3—the constant-returns-to-scale assumption. Without constant returns to scale, total factor productivity will not identically measure shifts in the technology. In telephone companies such as Bell Canada, it is believed that increasing returns to scale may be present. With increasing returns to scale ($\varepsilon_{CQ}^{-1} - 1$) is positive; hence estimates of total factor productivity growth will overestimate shifts in the technology alone. If increases in inputs lead to scale effects on output, it is the scale effects that are being measured by the second term in (17). The standard measure of total factor productivity is not erroneous. Rather, it includes the static efficiency effects of scale as well as the dynamic efficiency effects of technical progress, although it cannot distinguish between these two effects.

If we wish to measure the separate efficiency effects of scale and technical progress, we require more information than standard productivity analysis uses. From Eq. (17) it is obvious that to separate the scale effects from the technical change effects we require an estimate of the cost elasticity ε_{CQ}.

It is useful at this time to analyze shifts in the technology in terms of the cost function rather than the production function. This change in emphasis will allow us to deal with the multiple-output case more easily. It will also allow us to analyze the effects on the relationship between total factor productivity and technical change of departures from the market assumptions of marginal cost pricing and no effective rate-of-return regulation.

Under the assumption of cost-minimizing behavior, the theory of duality between cost and production implies that for any production function of the form (8), there exists a cost function that provides an equivalent description of the technology. Suppose we represent the cost function by the equation

$$C = g(w_1, \ldots, w_n, Q, t). \tag{19}$$

Totally differentiating the cost function with respect to time we obtain

$$\frac{dC}{dt} = \sum_i \frac{\partial g}{\partial w_i} \frac{\partial w_i}{\partial t} + \frac{\partial g}{\partial Q} \frac{\partial Q}{\partial t} + \frac{\partial g}{\partial t}. \tag{20}$$

Rearranging Eq. (20) by dividing through by C and setting $\partial g/\partial w_i = X_i$ (from Shephard's lemma) yields

$$\frac{1}{C} \frac{dC}{dt} = \sum_i \frac{w_i X_i}{C} \dot{w}_i + \frac{\partial g}{\partial Q} \frac{Q}{C} \dot{Q} + \frac{1}{C} \frac{\partial g}{\partial t}. \tag{21}$$

Define $\dot{B} \equiv (1/C) \, \partial g/\partial t$, the proportionate shift in the cost function. Then Eq. (21), after rearrangement, becomes

$$\dot{B} = \dot{C} - \sum_i \frac{w_i X_i}{C} \dot{w}_i - \varepsilon_{CQ} \dot{Q}, \tag{22}$$

where $\varepsilon_{CQ} = (Q/C) \, \partial C/\partial Q = (Q/C) \, \partial g/\partial Q =$ the cost elasticity, as before.

The proportionate shift in the cost function ($\dot{B}$) equals the change in costs minus the change in aggregate inputs minus the scale effect ($\varepsilon_{CQ}\dot{Q}$).

It is useful to relate $\dot{B}$ to the proportionate shift in the production function ($\dot{A}$) and the rate of growth of total factor productivity (TFP). Totally differentiating $C = \sum_i w_i X_i$ with respect to time and rearranging yields the equation

$$\sum_i \frac{w_i X_i}{C}\dot{w}_i = \dot{C} - \sum_i \frac{w_i X_i}{C}\dot{X}_i. \qquad (23)$$

Substituting this equation into (22) we obtain

$$-\dot{B} = \varepsilon_{CQ}\dot{Q} - \sum_i \frac{w_i X_i}{C}\dot{X}_i \qquad (24)$$

or

$$-\dot{B} = \varepsilon_{CQ}\dot{Q} - \dot{F}. \qquad (25)$$

Multiplying (15) by ε_{CQ} puts that equation in the form

$$\varepsilon_{CQ}\dot{A} = \varepsilon_{CQ}\dot{Q} - \dot{F}. \qquad (26)$$

A comparison of (25) and (26) shows that[7]

$$-\dot{B} = \varepsilon_{CQ}\dot{A}. \qquad (27)$$

Shifts in the cost function are not identical to shifts in the production function unless the production structure exhibits constant returns to scale ($\varepsilon_{CQ} = 1$).

Using (25) and the definition TFP $= \dot{Q} - \dot{F}$ we obtain the relationship between shifts in the cost function and the growth in total factor productivity

$$-\dot{B} = \text{TFP} + (\varepsilon_{CQ} - 1)\dot{Q} \qquad (28)$$

or

$$\text{TFP} = -\dot{B} + (1 - \varepsilon_{CQ})\dot{Q}. \qquad (28a)$$

If constant returns to scale exist then once again $\varepsilon_{CQ} = 1$ and $-\dot{B} = \text{TFP}$. This is the case where changes in total factor productivity measure the shifts in both the production and cost functions since TFP $= \dot{A} = -\dot{B}$.

The point of the above analysis is to demonstrate that when scale effects are present, conventional total factor productivity estimates measure neither shifts in the production function nor the cost function. However, when

[7] An alternative derivation of this formula can be found in Ohta [1974].

the cost elasticity is known, scale effects and intertemporal shifts can be separated.

4.2 The Multiple Output Case

Telecommunication firms such as Bell Canada produce a number of different services. In this section we extend the analysis of the previous section to the multiple output case. If a producer is minimizing the cost of producing m outputs using n inputs, the cost function may be written

$$C = g(w_1, \ldots, w_n, Q_1, \ldots, Q_m, t). \tag{29}$$

Totally differentiating this function with respect to time and rearranging we obtain [analogously to (24)]

$$-\dot{B} = \sum_j \varepsilon_{CQ_j} \dot{Q}_j - \sum_i \frac{w_i X_i}{C} \dot{X}_i, \tag{30}$$

where $\varepsilon_{CQ_j} = (\partial C/\partial Q_j)Q_j/C$ is the cost elasticity of the jth output. Equation (30) may be rewritten as

$$-\dot{B} = \sum_j \varepsilon_{CQ_j} \dot{Q}_j - \dot{F} \tag{31}$$

since the last term in (30) is $\dot{F}$, the index of aggregate inputs. Given information on the growth in outputs and the cost elasticities, we can use (31) to calculate shifts in the cost function due to technological change.[8]

We now proceed to link shifts in the cost function $(-\dot{B})$ to the measure of total factor productivity growth (TFP). Aggregate output growth in the productivity index is defined by the equation

$$\dot{Q}^P = \sum_j \frac{P_j Q_j}{R} \dot{Q}_j, \tag{32}$$

where $R \equiv \sum_j P_j Q_j$ (total revenue) and P_j is the price of output j.

Define aggregate output growth using cost elasticities, rather than revenue shares, as weights as

$$\dot{Q}^C = \sum_j [\varepsilon_{CQ} / \sum_j \varepsilon_{CQ_j}] \dot{Q}_j = [\sum_j \varepsilon_{CQ_j}]^{-1} [\sum_j \varepsilon_{CQ_j} \dot{Q}_j]. \tag{32a}$$

To see the relationship between $\dot{Q}^P$ and $\dot{Q}^C$, suppose the firm engages in marginal cost pricing. Then

$$\varepsilon_{CQ_j} = \frac{Q_j}{C} \frac{\partial C}{\partial Q_j} = \frac{P_j Q_j}{C} \tag{32b}$$

---

[8] For an example of this approach see Caves and Christensen [1978a].

and

$$\sum_j \varepsilon_{CQ_j} = \sum_j P_j Q_j / C. \tag{32c}$$

Therefore

$$\dot{Q}^C = \sum_j [P_j Q_j / \sum P_j Q_j] \dot{Q}_j = \dot{Q}^P. \tag{32d}$$

Hence under marginal cost pricing $\dot{Q}^P = \dot{Q}^C$. In addition, it can be shown that $\dot{Q}^P = \dot{Q}^C$ as long as $P_j = \theta \, \partial C / \partial Q_j$ for any constant θ. Prices that are characterized by uniform markups over marginal costs for all outputs will also lead to $\dot{Q}^P - \dot{Q}^C = 0$. However this is clearly an unusual limiting case.

What is the importance of $\dot{Q}^P - \dot{Q}^C$ for the interpretation of TḞP? Using (32a), we can rewrite (31) as

$$-\dot{B} = (\sum \varepsilon_{CQ_j}) \dot{Q}^C - \dot{F}$$

$$= (\sum \varepsilon_{CQ_j} - 1) \dot{Q}^C + (\dot{Q}^C - \dot{Q}^P) + (\dot{Q}^P - \dot{F}). \tag{32e}$$

Recalling that TḞP $= \dot{Q}^P - \dot{F}$, Eq. (32e) can be rearranged to yield

$$\text{TḞP} = [-\dot{B}] + [(1 - \sum \varepsilon_{CQ_j}) \dot{Q}^C] + [(\dot{Q}^P - \dot{Q}^C)]. \tag{32f}$$

From Eq. (32f) it can be seen that $\dot{Q}^P - \dot{Q}^C$ is one of the components of a decomposed TḞP. We interpret it as the effect on TḞP of departures from marginal cost pricing. Note that departures from marginal cost pricing may have no effect on TḞP. This is the case when $P_j = \theta \, \partial C / \partial Q_j$ for $\theta \neq 1$. Hence the term $\dot{Q}^P - \dot{Q}^C$ has no implications for the inefficiency of resource allocation resulting from nonmarginal cost pricing policies. It simply measures the contribution (if any) of departures from marginal cost pricing to conventionally measured total factor productivity growth.

Equation (32f) provides a decomposition of the total factor productivity growth rate (TḞP) into the contributions due to: (i) a shift in the cost function (technical change) $-\dot{B}$; (ii) a movement along the cost function (scale economies) $(1 - \sum \varepsilon_{CQ_j}) \dot{Q}^C$; and (iii) nonmarginal cost pricing $\dot{Q}^P - \dot{Q}^C$.[9]

If producers sell at prices that equal marginal costs ($\dot{Q}^P = \dot{Q}^C$) and if there are no economies of scale ($\sum \varepsilon_{CQ_j} = 1$) then the second and third terms in (32f) equal zero. In this case TḞP correctly represents the effects of technical change as measured by shifts in the cost function. If economies of scale are

[9] If one wishes to eliminate problems of departures from marginal cost pricing from the outset, one could define a new total factor productivity growth rate $\text{TḞP}' = \dot{Q}^C - \dot{F} = -\dot{B} + (1 - \sum \varepsilon_{CQ_j}) \dot{Q}^C$. If one then assumes constant returns to scale, $\text{TḞP}' = \sum \varepsilon_{CQ_j} \dot{Q}_j - \dot{F} = -\dot{B}$, which implies total factor productivity growth measures the shift in the cost function. This formulation provides the analytical basis for the logic underlying Caves and Christensen's [1978a] association of their measure of total factor productivity with shifts in the cost function in the absence of scale economies.

present ($\sum \varepsilon_{CQ_j} < 1$), then $\dot{TFP}$ overstates ($-\dot{B}$) even if marginal cost pricing rules are used.[10]

In order to analyze departures from marginal cost pricing, an alternative decomposition of $\dot{TFP}$ is useful. Rearranging (31) and using (32) we obtain

$$-\dot{B} = \sum_j \left(\varepsilon_{CQ_j} - \frac{P_j Q_j}{R} \right) \dot{Q}_j + \dot{Q}^P - \dot{F} \tag{33}$$

or

$$-\dot{B} = \sum_j \left[\frac{MC_j Q_j}{C} - \frac{P_j Q_j}{R} \right] \dot{Q}_j + \dot{TFP}. \tag{34}$$

A rearrangement of (34) yields

$$-\dot{B} = \dot{TFP} + \sum_j \left[\frac{(MC_j - P_j)Q_j}{C} \right] \dot{Q}_j + \sum_j \left(\frac{P_j Q_j}{C} - \frac{P_j Q_j}{R} \right) \dot{Q}_j \tag{35}$$

or

$$\dot{TFP} = -\dot{B} + \sum_j \left[\frac{(P_j - MC_j)Q_j}{C} \right] \dot{Q}_j + \sum_j \left[(P_j Q_j)\left(\frac{1}{R} - \frac{1}{C} \right) \right] \dot{Q}_j. \tag{36}$$

Equation (36) provides a number of insights into the measurement of productivity for a regulated multiproduct firm such as Bell Canada. First, suppose there exist no economies of scale but due to imperfect competition $P_j > MC_j$. Then $R > C$ as well. Assuming all outputs are increasing ($\dot{Q}_j > 0$), then $\dot{TFP}$ overstates $-\dot{B}$ due to the second term in (36) and understates $-\dot{B}$ due to the third term. The net direction of the discrepancy is unknown. However, if $R = C$, perhaps due to diseconomies of scale and/or scope, then $\dot{TFP}$ overstates $-\dot{B}$. Now suppose the firm is engaging in cross-subsidization, so that some $P_j > MC_j$ and some $P_j < MC_j$, and that the firm earns a positive profit (in excess of the cost of capital) so that $R > C$. Then $\dot{TFP}$ understates $-\dot{B}$ from the third term. However, the second term has some components that lead to understatements and some which lead to overstatements. Finally, a particularly interesting case occurs when cross-subsidization is accompanied by a zero profit constraint ($R = C$) as would happen if the Ramsey-optimal pricing rule were chosen by the regulated firm. The discrepancy between $\dot{TFP}$ and $-\dot{B}$ now depends only on the

[10] The decomposition for the multiple-output case can also be analyzed from the point of view of shifts in the technology. Suppose the technology can be represented by the transformation function $F(Q_1, \ldots Q_m, X_1, \ldots X_n, t) = 0$. Following Hulten [1978] we can define the shift in the technology as $\dot{A} = -(\partial F/\partial t)/(\sum_j Q_j \, \partial F/\partial Q_j)$. Then it can be shown that the analog to (32f) is the equation $\dot{TFP} = \dot{A} + [((\sum \varepsilon_{CQ_j})^{-1} - 1) \cdot \sum s_i \dot{X}_i] + (\dot{Q}^P - \dot{Q}^C)$, where $(\sum \varepsilon_{CQ_j})^{-1}$ is the multiple-output scale elasticity. For further details, see Denny and Fuss [1979].

second term. Once again the direction of the discrepancy is unknown a priori. However, as with all the cases discussed above, the magnitude of the discrepancy can be computed once marginal costs are estimated. These marginal costs can be obtained from the estimated cost function.

4.3 Productivity Measurement and Rate of Return Regulation

In this section we explore the case where rate-of-return regulation is effective (i.e., the regulated firm expects to earn the allowed rate of return). We demonstrate that in this instance there is a discrepancy between measured total factor productivity growth and the shift in the cost (or production) function in excess of those discussed previously. In particular, if prices of expensed factors of production and the allowed rate of return are increasing over time (perhaps due to inflation), then estimates of technical change which ignore rate-of-return regulation *over-estimate* the true underlying technical change.

To demonstrate the above assertions, we use a model of rate-of-return regulation developed by Fuss and Waverman [1977]. Suppose a regulated firm such as Bell Canada minimizes the cost of producing a given output Q using inputs of labor (L), materials (M), and capital (K) subject to a constraint that limits the rate of return on capital to be less than or equal to s[11]. Assuming the firm expects to earn the allowed rate of return, there exists a "constrained" cost function dual to the production function of the form

$$C = C(w, m, r, s, Q, t),\qquad(37)$$

where w and m are the prices of labor and materials, respectively. A modified Shephard's lemma yields the following relationships (see Fuss and Waverman [1977]):

$$\frac{\partial C}{\partial w} = (1 - \lambda)L, \qquad \frac{\partial C}{\partial m} = (1 - \lambda)M$$

$$\frac{\partial C}{\partial r} = K, \qquad \frac{\partial C}{\partial s} = -\lambda K,\qquad(38)$$

where L, M, and K are the constrained cost-minimizing input levels and λ is the Lagrangian multiplier associated with the rate-of-return constraint.[12] Totally differentiating (37) with respect to time we obtain

$$\frac{dC(w, m, r, s, Q, t)}{dt} = \frac{\partial C}{\partial w}\frac{dw}{dt} + \frac{\partial C}{\partial m}\frac{dm}{dt} + \frac{\partial C}{\partial r}\frac{dr}{dt} + \frac{\partial C}{\partial s}\frac{ds}{dt} + \frac{\partial C}{\partial Q}\frac{dQ}{dt} + \frac{\partial C}{\partial t}.\qquad(39)$$

[11] In this section we first consider the case of a single output. The multiple-output case is completely analogous and easily derived and is also presented in this section.

[12] The Lagrangian multiplier can be bounded, since as Bailey [1973] has shown, $0 \leq \lambda \leq r/s$.

Using (38), (39) becomes

$$\frac{dC}{dt} = [(1 - \lambda)L]\frac{dw}{dt} + [(1 - \lambda)M]\frac{dm}{dt} + [K]\frac{dr}{dt} - [\lambda K]\frac{ds}{dt}$$

$$+ \frac{\partial C}{\partial Q}\frac{dQ}{dt} + \frac{\partial C}{\partial t} \tag{40}$$

or

$$\dot{C} = [(1 - \lambda)s_L]\dot{w} + [(1 - \lambda)s_M]\dot{m} + [s_K]\dot{r} - \left[\frac{\lambda s K}{C}\right]\dot{s} + \varepsilon_{CQ}\dot{Q} + \dot{B}. \tag{41}$$

Totally differentiating $C = wL + mM + rK$ with respect to time yields an alternative expression for $\dot{C}$ [see Eq. (23)]

$$\dot{C} = s_L \dot{L} + s_L \dot{w} + s_M \dot{M} + s_M \dot{m} + s_K \dot{K} + s_K \dot{r}. \tag{42}$$

Equating the right-hand sides of (41) and (42) and solving the resulting equation for $-\dot{B}$, we obtain

$$-\dot{B} = \{\varepsilon_{CQ}\dot{Q} - s_L \dot{L} - s_M \dot{M} - s_K \dot{K}\} - \left\{\lambda\left[s_L \dot{w} + s_M \dot{m} + \left(\frac{sK}{C}\right)\dot{s}\right]\right\} \tag{43}$$

or

$$-\dot{B} = \{\varepsilon_{CQ}\dot{Q} - \dot{F}\} - \left\{\lambda\left[s_L \dot{w} + s_M \dot{m} + \left(\frac{sK}{C}\right)\dot{s}\right]\right\}. \tag{44}$$

Equation (44) permits us to analyze the effect of rate-of-return regulation on productivity measurement. Suppose the technology exhibits constant returns to scale ($\varepsilon_{CQ} = 1$), and there is an absence of effective rate of return regulation ($\lambda = 0$). Then the term in the first set of brackets is TFP, the term in the second set is zero, and measured total factor productivity growth accurately represents technical change (the shift in the cost function). However, with effective rate-of-return regulation, TFP no longer measures technical change. In fact if $\dot{w}$, $\dot{m}$, and $\dot{s}$ are positive, then measured total factor productivity (even corrected for scale effects) *overestimates* actual technical change. Noting that TFP $= \dot{Q} - \dot{F}$, we can rewrite (44)

$$\text{TFP} = -\dot{B} + (1 - \varepsilon_{CQ})\dot{Q} + \lambda\left(s_L \dot{w} + s_M \dot{m} + \left(\frac{sK}{C}\right)\dot{s}\right). \tag{45}$$

The conventional total factor productivity growth index now measures three effects: (i) the shift effect; (ii) the scale effect; and (iii) the regulatory effect.

The decomposition corresponding to the multiple output case is easily derived. Comparing Eqs. (25) and (31) it is readily apparent that the multiple output analog to (44) is

$$-\dot{B} = \left\{\sum_j \varepsilon_{CQ_j}\dot{Q}_j - \dot{F}\right\} - \left\{\lambda\left[s_L\dot{w} + s_M\dot{m} + \left(\frac{sK}{C}\right)\dot{s}\right]\right\}. \tag{46}$$

Drawing on the development in Eqs. (32a)–(32f) we can obtain the multiple output analog of (45) as

$$T\dot{F}P = -\dot{B} + (1 - \sum_j \varepsilon_{CQ_j})\dot{Q}^C + (\dot{Q}^P - \dot{Q}^C) + \lambda\left(s_L\dot{w} + s_M\dot{m} + \left(\frac{sK}{C}\right)\dot{s}\right). \tag{47}$$

Equation (47) demonstrates that in the multiple output case the conventional total factor productivity index measures four effects: (i) the shift effect; (ii) the scale effect; (iii) the nonmarginal cost pricing effect; and (iv) the regulatory effect.

4.4   Summary

There are a number of reasons why a conventional total factor productivity measure will fail to represent accurately shifts in the cost or production function attributable to technical change. In this section we have provided a detailed analysis of the effects of (a) nonconstant returns to scale, (b) nonmarginal cost pricing, and (c) effective rate-of-return regulation. The linkages derived in this analysis will permit us to interpret the productivity performance of Bell Canada that we presented in Section 3.

5.   Estimation of the Cost Structure for Bell Canada

Conventional total factor productivity indexes can only provide evidence of the overall increase in aggregate output per unit of aggregate input. In Section 4 we showed how the theory of production and cost functions could be used to interpret productivity and to separate measures of productivity into a number of effects. In particular, knowledge of cost elasticities is important. These elasticities can be obtained from estimates of the cost structure. In this section we summarize the model used to obtain estimates of the cost elasticities for Bell Canada. A detailed description can be found in Denny et al. [1979].

A three-output cost function was estimated. The outputs chosen were (i) message toll (Q_1), (ii) other toll—private line services plus WATS (Q_2), and (iii) local service plus miscellaneous (Q_3). All outputs were constant-dollar revenue measures. The model estimated was the one developed by Fuss and Waverman [1977], in which the regulated telecommunications firm chooses the profit-maximizing levels of toll services (Q_1 and Q_2), but is constrained by the regulatory authorities to charge a price for local services below the profit-maximizing price. This constraint on the local service price is the only regulatory constraint assumed to be operative. In particular, the model was estimated assuming ineffective rate-of-return regulation.

The specification of the cost function chosen uses two technical change indicators in the estimation of the shift of the cost function. It is generally believed that during the sample period, the major technological innovation influencing the provision of toll services was the introduction of DDD facilities. In contrast, the introduction of modern switching facilities at central offices had its major impact on the provision of local services. The effect of these innovations is to reduce the cost of providing a given level of services, but the impact is essentially service specific. To capture the above reasoning in an econometric cost function, we assume that the cost function can be written in the "output-augmenting" form

$$C = C[P_L, P_K, P_M, Q_1 h_1(A), Q_2 h_2(A), Q_3 h_3(S)], \tag{48}$$

where P_L, P_K, P_M are prices of the services of labor, capital, and materials, respectively. A and S are technical change indicators: A is the percentage of telephones with access to direct distance dialing facilities, and S is the percentage of telephones connected to central offices with modern switching facilities. The h_i functions are augmentation functions such that for any given Q_1, Q_2, and Q_3, an increase in A and/or S will lead to a decline in costs, but an increase in A will have as its major impact a decline in the marginal cost of toll services and an increase in S will have its major impact on the marginal cost of local service. Define the "augmented" outputs by

$$Q_1^* = Q_1 h_1(A) = Q_1 e^{\lambda_1 A}, \tag{49}$$

$$Q_2^* = Q_2 h_2(A) = Q_2 e^{\lambda_2 A}, \tag{50}$$

$$Q_3^* = Q_3 h_3(S) = Q_3 e^{\lambda_3 S}. \tag{51}$$

Then the cost function (48) becomes

$$C = C[P_L, P_K, P_M, Q_1^*, Q_2^*, Q_3^*], \tag{52}$$

which can be approximated by the second-order translog cost function

$$\log C = \alpha_0 + \sum_i \alpha_i \log P_i + \sum_k \beta_k \log Q_k^* + \frac{1}{2} \sum_i \gamma_{ii} (\log P_i)^2$$

$$+ \sum_{i \neq j} \sum \gamma_{ij} \log P_i \log P_j + \frac{1}{2} \sum_k \delta_{kk} (\log Q_k^*)^2$$

$$+ \sum_{k \neq l} \sum \delta_{kl} (\log Q_k^* \log Q_l^*) + \sum_i \sum_k \rho_{ik} \log P_i \log Q_k^*, \tag{53}$$

where $i,j = L, K, M$; $k,l = 1, 2, 3$; and

$$\log Q_1^* = \log Q_1 + \lambda_1 A,$$
$$\log Q_2^* = \log Q_2 + \lambda_2 A,$$
$$\log Q_3^* = \log Q_3 + \lambda_3 S.$$

The cost-share equations can be obtained from Shephard's lemma as

$$S_i = \alpha_i + \sum_j \gamma_{ij} \log P_j + \sum_k \rho_{ik} \log Q_k^*, \qquad i = L, K, M, \qquad k = 1, 2, 3. \quad (54)$$

The fact that $\sum S_i = 1$ implies the constraints

$$\sum \alpha_i = 1, \qquad \sum_i \gamma_{ij} = 0, \qquad \sum_i \rho_{ik} = 0. \quad (55)$$

The second-order approximation property of the cost function implies the additional constraints

$$\gamma_{ij} = \gamma_{ji}, \qquad i \neq j; \qquad \delta_{kl} = \delta_{lk}, \qquad l \neq k. \quad (56)$$

Following Fuss and Waverman [1977], the profit-maximizing behavior with respect to toll services implies the two additional equations

$$\frac{P_1 Q_1}{C} = \left(\frac{1}{1 + 1/\varepsilon_1}\right)^{-1} [\beta_1 + \sum_l \delta_{1l} \log Q_l^* + \sum_i \rho_{i1} \log P_i], \quad (57)$$

$$\frac{P_2 Q_2}{C} = \left(\frac{1}{1 + 1/\varepsilon_2}\right)^{-1} [\beta_2 + \sum_l \delta_{2l} \log Q_l^* + \sum_i \rho_{i2} \log P_i], \quad (58)$$

where $i = L, K, M$ and $l = 1, 2, 3$; $\varepsilon_1 = -1.435$ and $\varepsilon_2 = -1.639$ are the own-price elasticities of demand for message toll and other toll services respectively, taken from Fuss and Waverman [1977].

The system of equations consisting of the cost function (53), two of the three cost-share equations (54), and the two revenue-"share" equations (57) and (58), were estimated as a simultaneous system. Cost–output elasticity estimates can be obtained once the parameters of the model are estimated; these elasticities are given by the equations

$$\varepsilon_{CQ_l} = \frac{\partial \log C}{\partial \log Q_l} = \beta_l + \sum_{k = 1, 2, 3} \delta_{lk} \log Q_k^*$$
$$+ \sum_{i = L, K, M} \rho_{il} \log P_i, \qquad l = 1, 2, 3. \quad (59)$$

Empirical estimates of the cost–output elasticities are presented in Table 8. For a detailed discussion of these elasticities within the context of the production structure, the reader is referred to Denny et al. [1979]. Also pre-

TABLE 8

Empirical Estimates of the Cost–Output Elasticities

Time	Cost–output elasticities ε_{CQ_j}			Cost–output elasticity weights $\varepsilon_{CQ_j}/(\sum \varepsilon_{CQ_j})$			Revenue share weights $P_jQ_j/(\sum P_jQ_j)$		
	Message toll	Other toll	Local and miscellaneous	Message toll	Other toll	Local and miscellaneous	Message toll	Other toll	Local and miscellaneous
1952	0.095	0.0056	0.979	0.088	0.005	0.907	0.307	0.009	0.684
1953	0.096	0.0049	0.943	0.092	0.005	0.904	0.303	0.015	0.686
1954	0.095	0.0039	0.911	0.094	0.004	0.903	0.301	0.014	0.686
1955	0.098	0.0057	0.866	0.101	0.006	0.893	0.309	0.018	0.673
1956	0.098	0.0086	0.825	0.105	0.009	0.886	0.311	0.024	0.666
1957	0.094	0.0098	0.793	0.105	0.011	0.884	0.306	0.026	0.668
1958	0.093	0.0116	0.771	0.106	0.013	0.880	0.298	0.029	0.673
1959	0.092	0.0130	0.747	0.108	0.015	0.876	0.297	0.029	0.675
1960	0.093	0.0150	0.726	0.111	0.018	0.870	0.294	0.032	0.675
1961	0.093	0.0158	0.703	0.115	0.020	0.866	0.289	0.035	0.676
1962	0.095	0.0171	0.668	0.121	0.022	0.857	0.292	0.039	0.668
1963	0.095	0.0188	0.648	0.125	0.025	0.850	0.289	0.044	0.666
1964	0.101	0.0241	0.619	0.135	0.033	0.832	0.295	0.058	0.648
1965	0.100	0.0254	0.592	0.140	0.035	0.825	0.303	0.061	0.637
1966	0.099	0.0261	0.564	0.144	0.038	0.818	0.304	0.063	0.633
1967	0.097	0.0266	0.537	0.148	0.040	0.812	0.309	0.065	0.625
1968	0.099	0.0288	0.513	0.155	0.045	0.800	0.309	0.072	0.618
1969	0.100	0.0310	0.483	0.162	0.051	0.787	0.319	0.078	0.603
1970	0.099	0.0305	0.459	0.168	0.052	0.780	0.333	0.080	0.587
1971	0.097	0.0295	0.444	0.170	0.052	0.778	0.325	0.080	0.595
1972	0.101	0.0317	0.419	0.184	0.057	0.759	0.334	0.086	0.581
1973	0.102	0.0346	0.390	0.194	0.066	0.740	0.349	0.093	0.558
1974	0.100	0.0360	0.364	0.201	0.072	0.727	0.358	0.094	0.548
1975	0.100	0.0366	0.334	0.212	0.078	0.710	0.363	0.098	0.539
1976	0.099	0.0367	0.313	0.220	0.082	0.698	0.360	0.105	0.535

sented in Table 8 are the cost–output elasticity weights and the revenue-share weights required to decompose TḞP in accordance with equation (32f).

6. The Contributions of Nonmarginal Cost Pricing, Scale Economies, and Technical Change to Total Factor Productivity Growth

In this section we attempt to determine for Bell Canada the relative importance of scale economies, nonmarginal cost pricing, and technical change in total factor productivity growth as conventionally measured. To allocate the relative contributions, we use the equation developed in Section 4[13]:

$$\text{TḞP} = -\dot{B} + (1 - \sum_j \varepsilon_{CQ_j})\dot{Q}^C + [\dot{Q}^P - \dot{Q}^C]. \tag{32f}$$

The required cost elasticities and cost elasticity weights are taken from Table 8. Table 9 presents the results of the allocation exercise. These results represent the decomposition of TḞP which appears in column 1 of Table 6.

The entries in Table 9 are calculated using the Törnqvist discrete approximations to the continuous variables $\dot{Q}^P$ and $\dot{Q}^C$. The approximation to the variable $\dot{Q}^P$ is calculated using (4), while the approximation to $\dot{Q}^C$ is obtained from the formula

$$\Delta \log Q^C = \frac{1}{2} \sum_j (c_{jt} + c_{j,t-1}) \log\left(\frac{Q_{jt}}{Q_{j,t-1}}\right), \tag{60}$$

where $c_{jt} = \varepsilon_{CQ_{jt}}/\sum_j \varepsilon_{CQ_{jt}}$. $(-\dot{B})$ is calculated residually, given the previous estimates of TḞP.

It can be seen from Table 9 that scale economies have become increasingly important over time. By contrast, the relative importance of nonmarginal cost pricing and technical change have fluctuated considerably. In particular, technical change appears to have become a very unimportant source of TFP growth during the 1970s. Over the complete 1952–1976 period, nonmarginal

---

[13] We have not included the effects of rate-of-return regulation in our decomposition calculation. At the present time we do not possess a series on the allowed rate of return that would permit us to estimate a rate of return model (such as that contained in Fuss and Waverman [1977]). We are in the process of constructing such a series, which will allow us to implement Eq. (47) in subsequent research. From (47) we know that if we ignore *effective* rate-of-return regulation, this action biases upward the sum of the contributions to TḞP of technical change, scale economies, and nonmarginal cost pricing when factor prices and the allowed rate of return are nondecreasing. The distribution of this bias is unknown, since, in general, estimates of cost elasticities will differ between a "rate-of-return regulation" restricted technology and an unrestricted technology.

TABLE 9

Sources of Conventionally Measured Total Factor Productivity Growth—Residual
Technical Change

| | | Percentage contributions to TḞP of | | |
| | | Efficiency gains due to | | |
Time period	TḞP (%)	Nonmarginal cost pricing $\dot{Q}^P - \dot{Q}^C$	Nonconstant returns to scale $(1 - \sum \varepsilon_{CQ_j})\dot{Q}^C$	Shifts of the cost function $-\dot{B}$
1952–1957	1.25	29.9	28.4	41.7
1958–1962	3.01	6.7	42.8	50.5
1963–1966	3.09	24.7	64.2	11.1
1967–1970	4.66	13.6	62.9	23.4
1971–1976	4.46	15.7	83.9	0.4
1952–1976	3.35	16.0	63.7	20.3

cost pricing and technical change each account for approximately one-fifth of conventionally measured TḞP, whereas increasing returns to scale account for about three-fifths.

The apparent unimportance of technical change in the growth process during the latter part of the sample is particularly surprising for telecommunications. There are a number of possible reasons for this counterintuitive result. First, the technical change indicators used in the estimation of the cost elasticities approach constancy during the 1970s as saturation levels are reached. Hence technical change that may have occurred during the 1970s is probably not adequately represented and may be attributed to scale economies. Second, as mentioned in Sections 2 and 3, constant-dollar revenue measures may mask intraservice nonmarginal cost pricing, which leads to an overstatement of the relative importance of scale economies, especially with respect to local service. Finally, we have been identifying shifts of the cost function with technical change. However, since the technology cannot be specified as homothetic with respect to outputs and technical change is not Hicks neutral (see Denny *et al.* [1979]), scale and technical change interact to create efficiency gains. For example, in the estimated cost function, technical change has the effect of increasing the returns to larger scale over what they would have been in the absence of technical change, since $\partial^2 \log C/\partial \log Q \, \partial \log A$ and $\partial^2 \log C/\partial \log Q \, \partial \log S$ are both negative. Some of the contribution of scale in Table 9 is in fact due to scale-augmenting technical change. It is included as an economies-of-scale contribution since larger scale is necessary to realize this additional cost savings from innovation.[14]

The estimates of efficiency gains due to technical change that appear in Table 9 are residually determined and hence suffer from two shortcomings. First, they include any errors resulting from the estimation of cost elasticities. Second, as with any residual, they represent a quantitative expression of our ignorance. However, we are able to carry our analyses a step further by using the cost function outlined in Section 5 to obtain a parametric representation of technical change. This representation allows us to quantify the sources of the rate of shift of the cost function, and thus further decompose the total factor productivity growth index.

Differentiating Eq. (53) partially with respect to time, we obtain

$$\frac{\partial \log C}{\partial t} = -\dot{B} = \frac{\partial \log C}{\partial \log A}\dot{A} + \frac{\partial \log C}{\partial \log S}\dot{S} \tag{61}$$

or

$$-\dot{B} = \varepsilon_{CA}\dot{A} + \varepsilon_{CS}\dot{S}, \tag{62}$$

where

$$\frac{\partial \log C}{\partial \log A} = A[\lambda_1 \varepsilon_{CQ_1} + \lambda_2 \varepsilon_{CQ_2}] \tag{63}$$

and

$$\frac{\partial \log C}{\partial \log S} = S[\lambda_3 \varepsilon_{CQ_3}]. \tag{64}$$

Given estimates of λ_j and ε_{CQ_j}, we can obtain a parametric estimate of $-\dot{B}$, say $-\dot{B}^P$, which will differ from the residually determined measure

---

[14] The definition of technical change used in this paper (the shift in the cost function) leads to a greater allocation of efficiency gains to scale than would the alternative definition (the shift in the transformation function) when there exists increasing returns to scale. This occurs because movements along the cost curve (greater output) not accompanied by measured input increases is allocated to scale by the former definition and to shift by the latter. Examples of such phenomena would be returns to increased use of capital, and the replacement of obsolete capital by equivalent constant-dollar higher-quality capital. The replacement phenomenon may have been important during the later years of our sample with respect to outside plant, and in our econometric model such technical change does not shift the cost function, nor is it embodied in augmented units of capital. In order to illustrate the effect of changing definitions of technical progress we have recomputed the allocation in Table 9 using the decomposition formula contained in footnote 10. The average contributions to TFP over the 1952–1976 period now become: departures from marginal cost pricing, 16.0%; nonconstant returns to scale, 57.6%; and shifts of the transformation function, 26.4%. For a more complete analysis of this issue of the dual versus primal representation of technical change, see Denny and Fuss [1979].

TABLE 10

A Comparison of Two Measures of Technical Change

Time period	Residually determined technical change $-\dot{B}^{R}$ (%)	Parametric technical change $-\dot{B}^{P}$ (%)
1952–1957	0.52	0.35
1958–1962	1.52	1.43
1963–1966	0.34	0.86
1967–1970	1.09	0.58
1971–1976	0.01	0.40

(denoted $-\dot{B}^{R}$). Table 10 presents a comparison of the two measures. The two measures differ because changes in the logarithm of cost predicted from the econometric cost function differ from actual changes due to the residual associated with estimation by regression. While the difference may appear large, it should be noted that we are estimating a very small quantity— approximately 1% of cost. In fact, the difference in the 1963–1966 period, which involves the largest residual from estimation (see Table 11), corresponds to a 0.17% average error in estimating the cost function.

Table 11 presents our complete accounting for the sources of total factor productivity growth using the parametric determination of technical change. It is based on the growth equation

$$\text{T}\dot{\text{F}}\text{P} = [\dot{Q}^{P} - \dot{Q}^{C}] + [(1 - \sum \varepsilon_{CQ_j})\dot{Q}^{C}] + [\varepsilon_{CA}\dot{A}] + [\varepsilon_{CS}\dot{S}] + R, \quad (65)$$

where R is the residual caused by the fact that all elasticities contained in (65) are based on estimated parameters.

In addition to the information contained in Table 9, Table 11 yields the estimated contributions to T$\dot{\text{F}}$P of the introduction and diffusion of direct distance dialing (DDD) and modern switching facilities. The life-cycle aspects of these innovations is readily apparent. The contribution of DDD and modern switching reach their peaks during the periods 1958–1962 and 1963–1966, respectively, and become progressively less important afterwards. Over the entire sample, the two innovations have appeared to contribute approximately equally to T$\dot{\text{F}}$P, with DDD more important in the earlier period and modern switching more important in the later period. The residual R can be viewed as an accounting discrepancy resulting from the need to estimate cost elasticities and technical change effects. It is fairly substantial in individual subperiods, but averages out over the whole period as expected, since its source is regression error.

TABLE 11

Sources of Conventionally Measured Total Factor Productivity Growth—Parametric Technical Change

Time period	TFP (%)	Efficiency gains due to		Shift of the cost function associated with		Residual from estimation R
		Nonmarginal cost pricing $\dot{Q}^p - \dot{Q}^c$	Nonconstant returns to scale $(1 - \sum \varepsilon_{CQ_j})\dot{Q}^c$	Access to direct-distance dialing $\varepsilon_{CA}\dot{A}$	Connection to modern switching facilities $\varepsilon_{CS}\dot{S}$	
1952–1957	1.25	29.9	28.4	14.0	14.1	13.5
1958–1962	3.01	6.7	42.8	35.4	12.2	3.0
1963–1966	3.09	24.7	64.2	10.2	17.6	−16.7
1967–1970	4.66	13.6	62.9	2.5	10.0	11.0
1971–1976	4.46	15.7	83.9	0.5	8.4	−8.6
1952–1976	3.35	16.0	63.7	10.2	11.4	−1.3

Percentage contributions to TFP of:

A possible alternative approach to total factor productivity analysis is to measure only the efficiency gains directly from the estimated cost function.[15] This, of course, eliminates the possibility of productivity measurement without structural estimation. However, this procedure can easily be accomodated within our interpretative framework. Define

$$T\dot{F}P^* = \frac{d \log C^*}{dt} - \sum S_i^* \dot{w}_i - \dot{Q}^C, \tag{66}$$

where C^* is estimated total cost, S_i^* is the estimated cost share of the ith factor, and $\dot{w}_i$ is the rate of change of the price of the ith factor.

Totally differentiating $\log C^*$ with respect to t, we obtain [analogous to (21)]

$$\frac{d \log C^*}{dt} = \sum_i S_i^* \dot{w}_i + \sum_j \varepsilon_{CQ_j} \dot{Q}_j + \frac{\partial \log C^*}{\partial t}. \tag{67}$$

Combining (66) and (67) yields

$$T\dot{F}P^* = [(1 - \sum \varepsilon_{CQ_j})\dot{Q}^C] + (-\dot{B}^P), \tag{68}$$

where

$$\dot{B}^P = -\frac{\partial \log C^*}{\partial t}$$

or

$$T\dot{F}P^* = [(1 - \sum \varepsilon_{CQ_j})\dot{Q}^C] + [\varepsilon_{CA}]\dot{A} + [\varepsilon_{CS}\dot{S}]. \tag{69}$$

Finally, combining (69) and (65) we obtain the relationship between $T\dot{F}P^*$ and $T\dot{F}P$:

$$T\dot{F}P^* = T\dot{F}P - [\dot{Q}^P - \dot{Q}^C] - R. \tag{70}$$

Hence $T\dot{F}P^*$ represents only estimated efficiency gains—those associated with increasing returns to scale and technical change. In computing $T\dot{F}P^*$ the effects on total factor productivity growth of departures from marginal cost pricing and the unexplained estimation residual have been excluded.[16] Table 12 presents a comparison of $T\dot{F}P^*$ and $T\dot{F}P$. Parametric total factor productivity growth ($T\dot{F}P^*$) is uniformly lower than conventionally measured total factor productivity growth ($T\dot{F}P$), reflecting the positive contribution of the net sum of nonmarginal cost pricing and the estimation residual

---

[15] For an example of this approach, see Berndt and Khaled [1979].

[16] If the effects of rate-of-return regulation had been included in the decomposition of $T\dot{F}P$, they would have also been excluded from $T\dot{F}P^*$ since no efficiency gains are associated with the contribution of rate-of-return regulation to measured total factor productivity growth.

TABLE 12

A Comparison of Two Measures of Total Factor
Productivity Growth

Time period	Residually determined total factor productivity growth TḞP (%)	Parametric total factor productivity growth TḞP* (%)
1952–1957	1.25	0.71
1958–1962	3.01	2.72
1963–1966	3.09	2.85
1967–1970	4.66	3.51
1971–1976	4.46	4.14
1952–1976	3.35	2.81

to TḞP. Unlike TḞP, TḞP* does not level off in the 1970s, but continues to increase.

Table 13 presents the quantitative decomposition of TḞP* consistent with Eq. (69). The characteristics of the decomposition are similar to those previously observed for TḞP. Scale economies dominate TḞP*, as well as TḞP, particularly in the latter portion of the sample.

TABLE 13

Sources of Efficiency-Related Parametric Total Factor Productivity Growth (TFP*)

		Percentage contributions to TḞP* of		
			Shift of the cost function associated with	
Time period	TḞP* (%)	Nonconstant returns to scale	Access to direct-distance dialing	Connection to modern switching facilities
1952–1957	0.71	50.3	24.8	24.9
1958–1962	2.72	47.3	39.2	13.5
1963–1966	2.85	69.8	11.1	19.1
1967–1970	3.51	83.5	3.3	13.2
1971–1976	4.14	90.4	0.5	9.1
1952–1976	2.81	74.6	12.0	13.4

7. Conclusions

In this paper we have presented a method of interpreting the growth of total factor productivity in regulated industries as conventionally measured and applied our methodology to Canadian telecommunications. We have shown that the productivity index can be decomposed into the effects due to (i) departures from marginal cost pricing, (ii) nonconstant returns to scale, (iii) technical change, and (iv) effective rate-of-return regulation.

The decomposition framework was applied to data drawn from Bell Canada production accounts, 1952–1976, assuming ineffective rate-of-return regulation. Total factor productivity as conventionally measured was found to grow at 3.35% per annum. Scale economies contributed about three-fifths of the growth, whereas nonmarginal cost pricing and technical change contributed about one-fifth each. However, interpretation of these results as indicating a dominance of scale economies must be tempered by the recognition of substantial difficulties encountered in measuring outputs and portraying technical change.

A parametric approach to technical change using technical change indicators was also presented. Diffusion of direct distance dialing facilities and modern switching facilities contributed about equally to productivity growth during the 1952–1976 period, with direct distance dialing more important at the beginning of the period and modern switching more important at the end.

Finally, the basic methodology presented in this paper is applicable to industries outside the regulated sector. Whenever market imperfections imply that conventionally measured total factor productivity growth does not represent technical change alone, the decomposition procedure that we have proposed can be used as an aid in interpreting this measure of efficiency gains.

Data Appendix: Bell Canada Data

A.1   Revisions to the Materials Series

Table III of the Bell Canada [1978] *Memorandum on Productivity and Bell Canada Productivity* shows current- and constant-dollar quantities for materials and for indirect taxes. Fuss and Waverman [1977] aggregated the constant-dollar quantities of materials and taxes to form a new constant-dollar materials series. To avoid the incorrect treatment of nonincome taxes, we have eliminated these components from the materials series. Consequently, our new materials series is simply the current- and constant-dollar series labeled "cost of materials, services, rent, and supplies" in Table III.

The information on indirect taxes in the *Memorandum* does not permit one to allocate the indirect taxes to the pertinent outputs and inputs. Data in the *Bell Canada Annual Charts* will permit such an allocation. On pp. 313–314, there is a complete breakdown of the taxes other than income. The allocation of these taxes was roughly determined. Labor expenses were increased by the indirect taxes in columns 3–5 of p. 313 and columns 1 and 2 of p. 314. The net revenue from production was decreased by the Ontario gross receipts tax in column 7 of p. 314. The remainder of the indirect taxes were allocated to capital.

These changes increase the prices of capital and labor, and reduce the price of aggregate output. The constant-dollar quantities of these variables are not changed. For materials, both the price and the quantity are changed.

TABLE A1

Revenues and Costs for Bell Canada, 1952–1976

	Total revenue[a] unadjusted (millions of dollars)	Total revenue (millions of dollars)	Total cost[b] (millions of dollars)
1952	184.842	182.335	171.828
1953	202.358	199.538	186.955
1954	219.889	216.934	205.207
1955	245.325	242.046	230.417
1956	274.565	270.858	262.387
1957	303.929	299.276	292.931
1958	329.975	324.687	321.702
1959	377.904	371.698	347.910
1960	406.578	399.712	371.491
1961	435.271	427.066	391.480
1962	472.981	463.891	420.953
1963	505.139	495.430	454.427
1964	544.837	534.078	480.096
1965	595.827	584.218	521.012
1966	648.093	635.274	580.757
1967	705.599	691.256	635.852
1968	761.810	746.095	696.533
1969	846.234	829.234	796.883
1970	942.887	924.766	884.179
1971	1023.09	1002.45	999.744
1972	1129.48	1109.05	1124.25
1973	1279.71	1247.96	1274.41
1974	1446.38	1411.28	1499.21
1975	1674.88	1634.03	1728.48
1976	1912.68	1865.88	1978.68

[a] See text for description of the adjustment for indirect taxes.
[b] Includes capital services evaluated at the user cost of capital.

Uncollectibles are subtracted from total revenue. This does not lower the output but does lower the price. Theoretically, this would be correct if all bad debts were anticipated. Since the magnitude of the change in the price level is very small, no significant errors are likely to arise from this change.

In Table A.1, total revenues (column 2) and total costs (column 3) are shown for Bell Canada after the adjustment for indirect taxes formerly included in materials. The first column shows the unadjusted total revenue figures as an example of the magnitude of the change relative to column 2.

A.2 Basic Output and Input Data

The major source of information on inputs and outputs is the *Memorandum on Productivity and Bell Canada Productivity.* Data in this memoran-

TABLE A2

Output Price Indexes, 1952–1976[a]

	LOCAL	INTRA	TRANS	USO	Other toll	Miscellaneous
1952	92.40	106.05	109.19	94.46	97.61	69.78
1953	93.30	106.05	112.26	94.46	100.14	69.82
1954	93.30	106.05	114.10	94.46	101.67	69.74
1955	93.30	106.05	114.10	94.46	101.67	73.20
1956	93.30	106.05	114.10	93.83	101.67	75.13
1957	93.30	106.05	114.10	91.45	101.67	77.93
1958	93.90	107.26	114.10	91.45	101.67	80.32
1959	100.00	113.31	113.64	91.45	101.67	86.03
1960	100.00	113.31	112.69	100.44	101.67	88.89
1961	100.00	111.81	109.56	102.34	101.67	89.25
1962	100.00	104.32	105.92	102.34	101.79	90.77
1963	100.00	104.32	104.10	102.34	101.92	97.50
1964	100.00	104.32	103.14	102.34	101.80	98.14
1965	100.00	104.32	102.18	102.34	101.39	98.79
1966	100.00	100.72	100.36	102.34	100.06	99.42
1967	100.00	100.00	100.00	100.00	100.00	100.00
1968	100.00	98.78	99.90	100.00	99.90	101.54
1969	100.30	99.22	99.65	100.47	101.66	105.99
1970	101.60	110.93	99.65	100.63	101.60	106.86
1971	105.60	113.41	99.65	100.63	104.00	111.49
1972	108.60	115.79	99.62	100.63	104.57	122.53
1973	111.60	119.25	99.45	100.63	107.36	133.33
1974	114.00	121.35	99.45	100.63	110.68	152.68
1975	119.60	124.16	105.40	106.78	115.84	169.29
1976	127.00	130.13	113.74	114.16	124.46	187.03

[a] 1967 = 100. Column headings are defined in the Appendix.

dum have been updated and revised to 1976 in Bell Canada's response to the National Anti-Poverty Organization's request for information before the CRTC. Unless otherwise noted, all data on inputs and outputs are taken from these sources.

Output prices and constant dollar quantities for six outputs are shown in Tables A.2 and A.3. The output quantities are not affected by our revision of materials. For convenience the output price indexes are given *in unrevised form*. This is because other researchers may wish to alter our procedure. The price indexes that we used differ by only a single scalar in each year. In order to obtain our price indexes, multiply the individual indexes in Table A.2 by the ratio of total revenue (Table A.1, column 2) to unadjusted total revenue (Table A.1, column 1).

The outputs are constant-dollar local-service revenue (LOCAL), toll message revenue within Bell Canada (INTRA), toll message revenue within

TABLE A3

Output Quantities, Constant 1967 Dollars 1952–1976[a]

	LOCAL	INTRA	TRANS	USO	Other toll	Miscellaneous
1952	126.40	45.20	2.10	6.10	1.70	14.90
1953	137.00	48.30	2.40	6.90	2.30	16.90
1954	148.00	51.70	2.60	7.90	2.90	19.50
1955	162.90	57.50	4.80	8.80	4.30	19.40
1956	181.70	64.00	5.70	10.40	6.30	19.30
1957	200.60	68.20	6.50	12.90	7.80	22.20
1958	216.60	70.10	7.50	14.20	9.30	25.40
1959	233.60	75.40	8.70	16.30	10.50	27.20
1960	250.90	78.80	9.50	17.30	12.50	28.80
1961	269.50	84.90	10.60	16.50	14.70	30.70
1962	289.60	100.10	12.10	17.90	18.00	32.50
1963	308.70	104.40	13.40	19.90	21.60	32.00
1964	325.00	112.50	14.80	24.30	30.20	32.20
1965	350.80	125.30	16.40	28.70	34.90	33.20
1966	380.70	137.00	19.60	34.70	40.00	34.40
1967	410.00	152.80	22.10	39.00	45.10	36.60
1968	437.60	164.70	25.30	42.70	54.10	38.90
1969	471.40	187.20	29.30	49.60	63.40	41.70
1970	504.30	198.70	32.00	55.60	72.80	45.20
1971	538.00	203.70	35.00	59.80	77.30	43.50
1972	579.80	220.90	42.60	71.30	90.90	28.40
1973	625.50	246.90	51.60	89.80	108.00	22.20
1974	679.40	277.20	64.30	104.20	119.70	22.40
1975	734.30	308.90	76.90	120.80	138.20	25.40
1976	779.70	332.40	81.60	129.00	156.70	29.30

[a] Column headings are defined in the Appendix.

Canada and outside of Bell Canada (TRANS), toll message revenue on calls to U.S. and overseas (USO), other nonmessage toll, and miscellaneous. The last category is a combination of directory advertising, rents, and other residual revenue sources. The sharp discontinuity in this series is created by the formation in 1971 of a separate corporation to handle directory advertising. We have made minor adjustments to this series in 1971–1972 to smooth the break.

The annual observations on the prices and quantities of capital, labor and material inputs are given in Table A.4. The quantity of capital is the constant-dollar net stock shown in Table 7, column 3, of the Bell response to the NAPO inquiry (*NAPO*). The labor quantity is the weighted man-hours (in

TABLE A4

Prices and Quantities of Inputs, 1952–1976

	Capital[a]	Labor[b]	Materials[a]
	Quantities (millions)		
1952	626.60	44.90	38.70
1953	690.40	46.10	41.60
1954	764.90	48.20	46.50
1955	871.30	51.90	53.30
1956	989.90	55.70	62.40
1957	1127.10	57.80	62.90
1958	1280.00	57.60	69.20
1959	1429.50	56.50	72.90
1960	1579.10	54.60	76.10
1961	1721.90	52.40	79.40
1962	1860.10	52.30	85.10
1963	2004.00	53.50	89.70
1964	2150.40	54.40	89.80
1965	2283.60	55.80	98.00
1966	2431.20	57.50	101.90
1967	2585.60	56.60	98.70
1968	2734.00	55.50	103.90
1969	2886.00	56.60	123.80
1970	3054.80	57.80	123.10
1971	3190.40	58.10	146.50
1972	3334.90	57.50	147.60
1973	3493.00	60.40	149.90
1974	3653.50	63.90	151.70
1975	3808.90	64.10	149.10
1976	3978.90	67.30	159.60

(*Continued*)

TABLE A4 (*Continued*)

	Capital[a]	Labor[b]	Materials[a]
		Prices	
1952	0.107104	1.69303	0.741602
1953	0.104903	1.81627	0.740384
1954	0.103069	1.89562	0.752688
1955	0.100474	1.97639	0.756097
1956	0.101772	2.02233	0.785256
1957	0.106881	2.11185	0.801272
1958	0.107180	2.22591	0.813584
1959	0.108826	2.33527	0.828532
1960	0.108809	2.48666	0.839685
1961	0.108405	2.63202	0.842569
1962	0.110074	2.74387	0.854289
1963	0.112139	2.83471	0.869565
1964	0.112478	2.90667	0.891982
1965	0.115471	2.99505	0.920408
1966	0.122637	3.21050	0.961727
1967	0.131990	3.46077	1.00000
1968	0.139274	3.75600	1.03272
1969	0.150062	4.07077	1.07754
1970	0.158857	4.50004	1.12754
1971	0.169790	4.94917	1.16382
1972	0.185697	5.64473	1.22222
1973	0.203335	6.02574	1.33422
1974	0.231050	6.61295	1.53263
1975	0.259583	7.57487	1.70490
1976	0.281448	8.33328	1.86717

[a] Materials is a constant 1967 dollar quantity with a price index 1967 = 1.00. Capital is a constant 1967 dollar quantity with an unnormalized service price.

[b] Labor is a weighted man-hours quantity and a dollar per man-hour price.

millions) from Table 6 of the same source. Materials in constant dollars is from Table 3, column 2, of the same source.

The price of capital services is the same as that used by Fuss and Waverman [1977]. It is the sum of an expected real rate of interest of 6% plus the rate of economic depreciation, all multiplied by the Bell Canada telephone plant price index. The depreciation rate is defined as the ratio of constant dollar economic depreciation (*NAPO*, Table 4, column 3) to the stock of capital (*NAPO*, Table 7, column 3). The telephone plant price index is given in *NAPO*, Table 8, column 2.

The price of labor is the implicit price derived by dividing the quantity of labor into the total employee expense (*Bell Chart Book*, p. 317, column 1). The price of materials is the implicit price calculated by dividing current-dollar materials (*NAPO*, Table 3, column 1) by constant materials (*NAPO*, Table 3, column 2).

ACKNOWLEDGMENTS

Financial support by the Canadian Department of Communications is gratefully acknowledged. However, all opinions expressed in this paper are those of the authors alone, and do not necessarily represent the views of the above-named agency. We also wish to thank Carol Everson and Charles Hulten for helpful comments.

9

The Structure of Production, Technological Change, and the Rate of Growth of Total Factor Productivity in the U.S. Bell System

M. Ishaq Nadiri

Mark A. Schankerman
Department of Economics
New York University
  and National Bureau of Economic Research
New York, New York

1. Introduction

The objectives of this study are threefold. The first is to analyze empirically the production structure of the Bell System at the aggregate level. Particular attention is focused on the pattern of substitution among the factor inputs and the degree to which the aggregate production function is characterized by economies of scale. In this connection, we explore the role of research and development in the Bell System as an input to the production process, and its interaction with the traditional inputs. Second, we examine the impact of technological change on the production structure of the Bell System. The issues here include not only the rate of such technical change, but also the extent to which it alters the optimal level and mix of inputs, that is, the factor bias of technical change. The third objective is to explore

219

the interrelationship between scale economies internal to the Bell System and external technical change in determining the rate of growth of total factor productivity (TFP). Specifically, we propose and illustrate a methodology for decomposing the measured growth of TFP into a part related to scale economies and a part induced by technical change.

The recent introduction of competitive elements in the telecommunications sector has revived interest in the structure of production in the Bell System, particularly in the degree of returns to scale. Whether a policy that is likely to fragment the market is a wise course of action depends, in part, on the magnitude of the scale economies. The available empirical work suggests the presence of scale economies in the Bell System (Vinod [1972], Sudit [1973], AT&T [1976]), but estimates of the scale elasticity are not very precise. Furthermore, recent developments in the theory of duality between cost and production functions have not been exploited in estimating the production structure of the Bell System. This is especially unfortunate since the available time-series data are quite limited and the statistical precision of the results can be enhanced by using duality theory.

Important issues are also raised by the rate and bias of technical change, and especially by the interaction of technical change and scale economies in determining the growth of TFP. Strong productivity growth in the communications industry is particularly important since communications services are used by every sector in the economy. Thus, the repercussions of a significant change in the growth of TFP in the Bell System would be widely felt. If economies of scale are present in the Bell System and if they are a significant determinant of TFP growth, then a policy that sacrifices these economies may have dynamic implications well beyond the boundaries of the communications sector.

We address these issues by first estimating an aggregate translog cost function for the Bell System, using annual data for the period 1947–1976. The implied estimate of the scale economies is then used to explore the sources of the growth in TFP. The paper is organized into seven sections. In Section 2 we provide a brief overview of duality theory and then present the formulation of the model. In Section 3 we describe the estimation and hypothesis testing procedures. The data are described in Section 4. In Section 5 we present and discuss the empirical results. In Section 6 we propose a method for decomposing the growth of TFP into a scale-related component and a component due to technical change. Using the empirical estimates from Section 5, we present some preliminary calculations on the sources of aggregate TFP growth in the Bell System during the postwar period. Brief concluding remarks follow.

2. Modeling the Structure of Production

In order to estimate the underlying technology, one can examine either the production function or the associated cost function. Recent work in duality theory has established that, under rather weak regularity conditions, there is a unique correspondence between the production and cost function and that all of the information about the underlying technology is contained in both functions (Shephard [1970]). The choice between them is a matter of statistical convenience and analytical purpose.

We have chosen to use the cost function for three reasons. First, the cost function expresses (minimal) total cost in terms of factor prices and the level of output, while the production function expresses output in terms of factor inputs. Factor prices are treated as exogenous in both cost and production functions. The main statistical issue is whether the level of output on which input decisions are based should be considered exogenous (cost function) or endogenous (production function).

In most regulated industries, including communications, the regulator fixes the output price and requires that the firm satisfy the corresponding demand. The level of output could then be treated as exogenous. Actually, it is only recently that federal and state regulatory authorities have concerned themselves with the details of the rate structure in communications. Attention had been confined primarily to ensuring that there be neither a revenue deficit nor surplus, leaving the regulated firm relatively (though not entirely) free to determine the rate structure. Under these circumstances the levels of the different outputs, and hence the aggregate level of output, would be endogenous. This endogeneity could be troublesome in a study of the production structure that disaggregated outputs (for such a treatment see Fuss and Waverman [1977]), but it is less problematic in an aggregate study like the present one. We therefore assume that the level of output is exogenously determined.

The second reason for using the cost function is that it yields direct estimates of the various Allen–Uzawa elasticities of substitution. These parameters are the key to describing the pattern and degree of substitutability and complementarity among the factors of production. In the production-function context, estimation of the elasticities of substitution requires that the matrix of production function coefficients be inverted. This exaggerates the estimation errors and reduces the statistical precision of the computed elasticities of substitution (Binswanger [1974a]).

The third advantage of the cost-function approach is that duality theory can be exploited without imposing any restriction on the returns to scale in the underlying technology. For example, according to Shephard's lemma, the derivative of the cost function with respect to a factor price yields the derived demand for the input. This implies a set of cost-share equations whose parameters are a subset of those in the cost function itself. Joint estimation of the cost function and share equations increases the degrees of freedom in the empirical work and enhances the statistical precision of the estimates. The cost shares are constrained by definition to add to unity, but this does not impose any restriction on the underlying technology concerning the degree of returns to scale. On the other hand, the use of the production function (instead of the cost function), together with the first-order conditions for profit maximization, implies a set of value-share equations. If the value shares are constrained to add to unity and if they are estimated jointly with the production function, constant returns to scale is implicitly assumed.

We have chosen the transcendental logarithmic (translog) specification of the cost function for our empirical work. The translog can be viewed as a second-order logarithmic approximation to an arbitrary twice-differentiable transformation surface (Christensen *et al.* [1973]). Since in its general form the translog imposes no prior restrictions on the production structure, it allows the testing of various restrictions—such as homotheticity, homogeneity, unitary elasticities of substitution—and the assessment of the sensitivity of parameters of interest to those restrictions.

Assuming that the firm minimizes total costs of production, we can represent the general form of the aggregate cost function as

$$C = f(\mathbf{P}, Q, T), \tag{1}$$

where C, $\mathbf{P}$, and Q are total costs, a vector of factor prices, and the level of output, respectively, and T is an index of the level of technology produced external to the firm. The translog approximation to the general form (1) can be written

$$\log C = \alpha_0 + \alpha_q \log Q + \sum_i \alpha_i \log P_i$$

$$+ \tfrac{1}{2}\gamma_{qq}(\log Q)^2 + \frac{1}{2}\sum_i \sum_j \gamma_{ij} \log P_i \log P_j$$

$$+ \sum_i \gamma_{iq} \log P_i \log Q + \sum_i \theta_i \log P_i \log T$$

$$+ \theta_q \log Q \log T + \beta_t \log T + \tfrac{1}{2}\beta_{tt}(\log T)^2, \tag{2}$$

where $i, j = 1, \ldots, N$ index the N different inputs and all the variables are defined around some expansion point.[1] In this paper an index of time is used as an indicator of the level of technology.[2] Therefore, in this paper the term "technical change" refers to time-related shifts of the cost function.

A set of cost-share equations associated with the translog cost function is implied by duality theory. According to Shephard's lemma, the derived demand for an input, X_i, is obtained by partially differentiating the cost function with respect to the factor (service) price of the input (see Shephard [1970]):

$$\frac{\partial C(\cdot)}{\partial P_i} = X_i.$$

Partially differentiating the translog function (2) and using Shephard's lemma, we obtain a set of cost-share equations

$$S_i = \alpha_i + \frac{1}{2}\sum_j \gamma_{ij} \log P_j + \gamma_{iq} \log Q + \theta_i \log T, \quad \text{for} \quad i = 1, \ldots, N, \quad (3)$$

where $S_i = P_i X_i / C$ is the share of costs accounted for by factor i. Note that the coefficients in the share equations are a subset of those in the cost function.

There are several parametric restrictions on the translog cost function. First, the cost function must be linearly homogeneous in factor prices at all values of factor prices, output, and the level of technology. This implies

$$\sum_i \alpha_i = 1 \quad \text{and} \quad \sum_j \gamma_{ij} = \sum_i \gamma_{iq} = \sum_i \theta_i = 0. \quad (4)$$

Note that the same restrictions are imposed by the constraint $\sum_i S_i = 1$, which also implies that only $N - 1$ of the N share equations in (3) are linearly independent. Second, since the translog is viewed as a quadratic (logarithmic) approximation, the cross partial derivatives of the cost function must be equal. This implies the symmetry condition

$$\gamma_{ij} = \gamma_{ji}. \quad (5)$$

---

[1] This means that the variables are normalized around some point, for example, the sample mean. The normalization affects the interpretation of the coefficients and the time path of any parameter derived from the translog by differentiation, such as the scale elasticity. For more on these and related points, see Denny and Fuss [1977].

[2] This implies that the logarithm of time enters the cost function specification in (2) and imposes a rate of technical change which varies over time in a particular way. An alternative is to assume a constant rate of technical change and use a simple time trend. We made the choice on empirical grounds.

The Allen–Uzawa partial elasticity of substitution between two factors i and j, σ_{ij}, and the output-compensated own- and cross-price elasticities of factor demand, ε_{ii} and ε_{ij}, can be computed directly from the translog cost function in the following manner (Binswanger [1974a]):

$$\sigma_{ij} = \gamma_{ij}/S_i S_j + 1 \qquad \text{for} \quad i \neq j, \tag{6a}$$

$$\varepsilon_{ii} = \gamma_{ii}/S_i + S_i - 1, \tag{6b}$$

$$\varepsilon_{ij} = \gamma_{ij}/S_i + S_j \qquad \text{for} \quad i \neq j. \tag{6c}$$

Note that the equality $\sigma_{ij} = \sigma_{ji}$, which is required by production theory, is guaranteed by the translog symmetry condition $\gamma_{ij} = \gamma_{ji}$. The special case of a unitary elasticity of substitution between factors i and j holds if $\gamma_{ij} = 0$. Also note that

$$\varepsilon_{ij} = S_j \sigma_{ij}. \tag{7}$$

The formulation of the cost function in (2) allows both for neutral and biased technical change. Neutral technical change acts as a pure shift of the cost function and leaves the factor shares unchanged; it is represented by the parameters β_t and β_{tt}. Biased technical change represents shifts in the level of technology that alter the equilibrium factor shares, holding factor prices constant, and is described by the parameters θ_i. Technical change is said to be ith-factor saving (i-using) if the cost share of the ith factor is lowered (raised) and is represented by $\theta_i < 0 \, (\theta_i > 0)$.

Hanoch [1975] has shown that economies of scale must be evaluated along the expansion path, whereas returns to scale are conventionally defined along an arbitrary input-mix ray. Returns to scale and economies of scale will differ unless the production function is homothetic. Since the scale elasticity (evaluated around a given point) is identical to the reciprocal of the elasticity of costs with respect to output (Hanoch [1975]), we can use the latter as a measure of economies of scale. It is evaluated along the expansion point automatically by the assumption of cost minimization. The general form of the scale elasticity from the translog (2) can be written

$$\text{SE} = (\alpha_q + \gamma_{qq} \log Q + \sum \gamma_{iq} \log P_i + \theta_q \log T)^{-1}, \tag{8}$$

which will vary with relative factor prices and the levels of output and technology.

The cost function is homothetic if it can be written as a separable function of factor prices and output (Shephard [1970]; Denny and Fuss [1977]). This implies that the optimal factor combination is independent of the scale of output, so that the expansion path is linear. It is clear from the share equations (3) that homotheticity requires

$$\gamma_{iq} = 0, \qquad i = 1, ..., N. \tag{9}$$

In view of the translog constraints in (4), homotheticity imposes an additional $N - 1$ independent parameter restrictions.

The cost function is homogeneous in output if the elasticity of costs with respect to output is a constant. From (8) homogeneity imposes the restrictions

$$\gamma_{qq} = \theta_q = 0 \qquad \text{and} \qquad \gamma_{iq} = 0, \qquad i = 1, ..., N. \tag{10}$$

There are $N + 1$ independent restrictions in (10), but $N - 1$ of them are identical to the homotheticity constraints in (9). Therefore, homogeneity imposes two additional restrictions that should be tested formally as a hypothesis conditional on the acceptance of homotheticity.

The cost function exhibits unitary partial elasticities of substitution among all inputs if the following restrictions hold:

$$\gamma_{ij} = 0, \qquad i, j = 1, \ldots, N. \tag{11}$$

In view of (4) and (5), there are $N(N - 1)/2$ independent restrictions imposed in (11). If the parameter restrictions in (10) and (11) hold jointly, then the cost function reflects a homogeneous technology with unitary partial elasticities of substitution, that is, a Cobb–Douglas technology.

The neutrality of technical change can be tested by imposing the restrictions

$$\theta_i = 0, \qquad i = 1, \ldots, N. \tag{12}$$

In view of (4), there are $N - 1$ independent parameter contraints in (12).

The various parameter restrictions described in this section will be tested formally in Section 5. The estimation and testing procedures are described next.

3. Estimation and Testing Procedures

In this paper we limit the formal testing procedure to five models. All models are estimated after imposing the translog symmetry condition and the constraints for linear homogeneity in factor prices. The models include an unconstrained translog cost function, a model with strict neutrality of technical change, homothetic cost structure, a cost structure with homogeneity imposed, and a Cobb–Douglas form that imposes both homogeneity and unitary elasticities of substitution. Two versions of each of the five models are estimated. The first is a four-factor model (4FM) that incorporates four productive inputs—labor, capital, intermediate materials, and research and development. Research and development is treated as a capital asset analogous to traditional capital, with an associated stock and service flow. We discuss its formulation in more detail later. The second version is a narrower three-factor model (3FM) which incorporates the traditional inputs but ignores research and development. The 3FM is explored not so much as an alternative to the 4FM, but because it is of some interest to know the way in which neglecting research and development affects the implied description of the underlying technology, such as economies of scale and elasticities of substitution. The formal relationship between the 3FM and the 4FM is discussed later.

We estimate a system of equations consisting of the cost function and $N-1$ of the cost-share equations. As indicated earlier, exploiting duality theory and estimating the cost-share equations jointly with the cost function increases the statistical degrees of freedom, since the cost-share parameters are a subset of the cost-function parameters. The limited time series (1947–1976) and the multicollinearity in the data make this procedure imperative. Including the cost function itself in the multivariate regression system is important because certain coefficients needed to evaluate the scale elasticity (α_q and γ_{qq}) do not appear in the share equations. We follow the literature in specifying additive disturbances in each share equation and the cost function; the former represent errors in optimizing behavior (for example, Christensen and Greene [1976]). The disturbances are specified to have a joint normal distribution (as required for formal testing), but contemporaneous correlation across equations is allowed. The system can be estimated by Zellner's [1962] seemingly unrelated regression technique, which is a generalized least-squares technique. Typically the parameter estimates are not invariant to the choice of which share equation to delete. An extension of a result by Barten [1969], however, shows that a maximum-likelihood procedure guarantees such invariance. Kmenta and Gilbert [1968] have shown that iteration on the Zellner method until the residual covariance matrix converges yields maximum-likelihood estimates. In fact, it is computationally equivalent to maximum likelihood and therefore ensures invariance of the parameter estimates to the choice of the share equation that is deleted.[3]

---

[3] We want to note two econometric problems, even though nothing is done about them in this paper. First, the conventional approach (which we adopt) argues that since the share equations are obtained by differentiating the cost function, the error in the cost function does not appear. Disturbances are then added to the share equations to represent "errors in optimization" (Berndt and Christensen [1973]; Christensen and Greene [1976]). This rationale assumes

We employ the iterative Zellner method. Since we obtain maximum-likelihood estimates of the parameters, the various parameter restrictions are tested with the likelihood ratio test. We compute

$$\lambda = \Omega(R) - \Omega(U),$$

where $\Omega(R)$ and $\Omega(U)$ are the log likelihood values under the restricted and unconstrained versions, respectively. Then -2λ is distributed asymptotically as a chi-squared variate with degrees of freedom equal to the number of independent restrictions being tested.

4. Description of Data[4]

The required data include measures of aggregate output, and the quantities and prices of labor, capital, intermediate materials, and research and development. Unless otherwise indicated, the data pertain to the American Telephone and Telegraph Company, which includes the operating telephone companies and Long Lines but excludes Western Electric and the Bell Laboratories.

The measure of aggregate output is the sum of adjusted operating revenues for four service categories—local service, intrastate toll, interstate toll, and a miscellaneous category. Adjusted operating revenues are computed as total operating revenues minus property and other nonincome taxes. The adjusted operating revenues for each category are deflated by a category specific, chain-linked Paasche price index (normalized in 1967).

The quantity of labor input is the quality-adjusted man-hours actually worked (excluding vacations, holidays, sick leave, and labor attributable to construction, which is included in the measure of plant and equipment). The man-hours worked are cross-classified into four nonmanagement and two management occupational categories, divided, respectively, into four and three categories by years of service. The quality adjustment involves

---

that the firm is optimizing by choosing the factor shares rather than the quantity of the input. However, errors in optimization could refer to the firm not being on the derived demand for the input—the error may be in $\partial C/\partial P$, not in $(\partial C/\partial P)P/C$. In that case, the cost function errors will appear in the share equations in a nonadditive way (for a related discussion, see Mundlak [1964]). Second, no account has been taken of the fact that the shares are bounded by zero and one. This means the disturbances cannot be normally distributed, and any estimates based on that assumption will be inefficient. In addition, we are not aware of any demonstration that Barten's invariance theorem holds when the errors follow some nonnormal (truncated) distribution.

[4] The raw data used in this paper were provided by the Bell System. These data are proprietary and inquiries regarding them should be addressed to Peter B. Linhart, Director of Regulatory Research, AT&T.

weighting the man-hours in each of the 22 categories by the ratio of the average hourly wage for that category in the base year (1967) to the average wage for all groups.[5] An implicit price index for labor services is obtained by dividing the total employee compensation charged to expense (including all fringes and social security taxes) by the quantity of labor input.

The stock of capital is defined as the sum of tangible plant (including land), cash, net accounts receivable, and inventories of materials and supplies. Tangible plant, which constitutes the bulk of capital stock (more than 95%), is broken down into 23 separate accounts. For each plant account of a particular vintage, the historical depreciation reserve is determined from plant mortality tables. The vintage depreciation reserve for the plant account is subtracted from the gross book value of that vintage to obtain the net surviving plant for that vintage and account. The Bell System Telephone Plant (Laspeyres) Indexes are applied to the net surviving plant of each vintage and account and the results summed to obtain the constant 1967 dollar value of net plant. Net capital stock is obtained by adding to net plant the deflated value of net accounts receivable, inventories, and cash.

We construct the service price of capital, c_k, for each year as follows:

$$c_k = P_I \frac{[1 - uz - w + w \cdot u \cdot z]}{1 - u} (r + \delta) + \tau,$$

where P_I is the investment goods deflator, u is the corporate income tax rate, w and z are the effective rate of investment tax credit and the present value of depreciation allowances, τ is the indirect tax rate, r is the realized after-tax rate of return, and δ is the depreciation rate. These parameters are constructed from Bell System data whenever possible.[6]

---

[5] Since the compensation weights are fixed to 1967 wages, one component of labor quality, namely, changing relative wages, is excluded. The data for this adjustment are not available.

[6] The investment goods deflator is computed as the ratio of the current cost to constant cost value of net plant; the underlying deflater is the Bell Telephone Plant Index. The corporate income tax rate is the ratio of federal, state, and local income taxes plus the investment tax credit to net property compensation. Property compensation is computed as the value of output minus employee compensation, materials and supplies, property and other nonincome taxes, and depreciation expense, in current dollars. The indirect tax rate is the ratio of property and other nonincome taxes to the value of net plant. The realized rate of return is computed as the ratio of the value of output minus all taxes, materials and supplies, employee compensation, and depreciation expense, to the value of net plant. The depreciation rate is given by the depreciation expense in 1967 dollars divided by the 1967 value of net plant.

The investment tax credit applies only to durable equipment. Since the service price of capital computed in this paper is applied to the entire capital stock, the rate of investment tax credit must correspond to the aggregated capital stock. We compute the effective rate on durable equipment as the ratio of the investment tax credit claimed by AT&T to the sum of investment in central office and station equipment. The rate used in the service price of capital is this effec-

The stock of research and development, R, is constructed as a geometrically weighted sum of deflated, nonmilitary research-and-development expenditures by the Bell System, lagged four years:

$$R_t = \sum_i (1 - \delta)^i R\&D_{t-4-1},$$

where δ is the geometric rate of obsolescence, taken as $\delta = 0.15$. The cumulation begins in 1925. The four-year lag is taken to reflect the gestation period during which research and development has no effect on output.[7] Nominal research-and-development expenditures are deflated by the price index for research and development proposed by Milton [1972] and updated by Battelle [1976]. The service price of research capital is computed as $c_r = P_r(r + \delta)$, where P_r is the Milton price index. This is analogous to the service price of traditional capital; the tax parameters are absent because R&D expenditures are treated as an operating expense rather than as a capital asset for tax purposes.

The intermediate input consists of six categories of materials, rents, and supplies (MR&S). The available nominal expenditures on MR&S are adjusted for the following reason. Bell System R&D is performed by the Bell Laboratories and is funded both by AT&T and Western Electric. The AT&T portion of R&D is included in the available measure of MR&S (though not in the capital and labor variables), so the research input is double-counted. We therefore adjust nominal expenditures on MR&S by subtracting the AT&T-funded portion of annual R&D expenditures. For the price series on the intermediate input, we use the Laspeyres price index of intermediate materials and supplies from the *Survey of Current Business* [1978], normalized in 1967.

Total costs are defined in the four-factor model as the sum of four elements: nominal expenditures on labor, adjusted current expenditures on MR&S, the product of the service price of capital and the constant dollar value of the net stock of capital, and the service price of research times the deflated value of the stock of research. Note that the last term is not the same as annual R&D expenditures, which are analogous to gross investment in

---

tive rate times the ratio of investment in central office and station equipment to total gross investment.

The present value of depreciation allowance is taken as a weighted average of the separate values for producers' durables and structures. These values are taken from Christensen and Jorgenson [1969, Table 8]. The weights reflect the fraction of total gross investment accounted for by producers' durables and structures in 1976, constructed from the 23 separate plant accounts.

[7] We experimented with different rates of obsolescence and gestation periods, but the empirical results are similar to those reported in this paper.

the stock of R&D. In the three-factor model, total costs are limited to the first three elements (labor, capital, and materials).

5. Empirical Results

In this section we present the empirical results for the three- and four-factor models and discuss the formal tests of parametric restrictions. To conserve space, Table 1 presents only the parameter estimates for the unconstrained version of the 3FM and 4FM.[8]

Before turning to Table 1, we note that the models fit the data quite well, both for the cost function and the share equations. In the 4FM (3FM) the R^2s are: 0.99 (0.99) for the cost function; 0.86 (0.83) for the labor share; 0.82 (0.81) for the capital share; and 0.85 for the materials share equation in the 4FM.[9] This is encouraging since translog models often yield relatively poor fits for the cost-share equations (Denny and Fuss [1977]. Moreover, the share-equation fits are not due predominantly to the time variable. Variations in factor prices and output account for between 60 and 70% of the total variance in the labor and capital shares in the 3FM and 4FM, and for 85% of the variance in the materials share in the 4FM. The levels (rather than shares) of input use predicted by the fitted share equations correlate very closely with the actual input levels, the correlation coefficients all being above 0.95.

The parameter estimates in Table 1 indicate that the 3FM and 4FM yield generally similar results for common parameters. All except one of the interaction terms between factor prices (γ_{mr} in the 4FM) are statistically significant, which suggests that the partial elasticities of substitution are

---

[8] Two points should be noted. First, in the empirical work we constrain $\theta_q = 0$. We experimented with leaving θ_q free, but because of collinearity, the empirical results proved to be nonrobust and generally inferior. Second, in order for the translog to be an adequate representation of the underlying technology, the estimated cost function must be monotonically increasing and concave in factor prices over the range of observation. Monotonicity is satisfied if the fitted cost shares are positive. Concavity is ensured if the bordered Hessian of the cost function is negative definite. The 3FM estimates in Table 1 satisfy monotonicity and concavity at all observations. The 4FM estimates satisfy monotonicity at all sample points; concavity is violated in a few of the early years. The occasional failure of concavity in the 4FM does not preclude obtaining good parameter estimates, nor does it necessarily undermine the assumption of cost minimization. This is especially true since the abberations occur at the beginning of the sample period, far from the expansion point (sample means). See Wales [1977].

[9] There is strong evidence of serial correlation in the residuals of the regressions in Table 1. We tried imposing a first-order serial correlation scheme in accordance with the requirements of a singular system of equations (Berndt and Savin, 1975), but this did not remove the autocorrelation. As a result, the true significance levels of the hypothesis tests somewhat exceed the nominal ones.

TABLE 1

Translog Cost-Function Parameters for the Unconstrained Three- and Four-Factor Models[a]

	3FM	4FM		3FM	4FM
α_0	−0.014	−0.038[b]	γ_{km}	−0.033[b]	−0.031[b]
	(0.016)	(0.015)		(0.011)	(0.010)
α_q	0.565[b]	0.472[b]	γ_{kr}		−0.003[b]
	(0.070)	(0.065)			(0.001)
α_l	0.426[b]	0.420[b]	γ_{mr}		0.001
	(0.003)	(0.003)			(0.002)
α_k	0.430[b]	0.424[b]	γ_{lq}	0.006	−0.006
	(0.003)	(0.003)		(0.019)	(0.018)
α_m	0.144[b]	0.142[b]	γ_{kq}	0.009	0.018
	(0.001)	(0.001)		(0.017)	(0.016)
α_r		0.015[b]	γ_{mq}	−0.015	−0.018[b]
		(0.0001)		(0.010)	(0.009)
γ_{qq}	−0.163[b]	−0.085	γ_{rq}		0.006[b]
	(0.053)	(0.050)			(0.001)
γ_{ll}	0.014	0.029	θ_l	−0.051[b]	−0.044[b]
	(0.025)	(0.023)		(0.010)	(0.009)
γ_{kk}	0.114[b]	0.128[b]	θ_k	0.050[b]	0.047[b]
	(0.019)	(0.018)		(0.009)	(0.009)
γ_{mm}	−0.035	−0.044[b]	θ_m	0.001	0.001
	(0.020)	(0.019)		(0.003)	(0.003)
γ_{rr}		0.011[b]	θ_r		−0.003[b]
		(0.001)			(0.0003)
γ_{lk}	−0.082[b]	−0.094[b]	β_t	−0.012	0.100
	(0.018)	(0.017)		(0.082)	(0.076)
γ_{lm}	0.068[b]	0.074[b]	β_{tt}	0.005	0.048
	(0.019)	(0.018)		(0.032)	(0.029)
γ_{lr}		−0.009[b]			
		(0.002)			

[a] Estimated standard errors are in parentheses. The parameter estimates may only approximately satisfy the restrictions in Eqs. (4) because of rounding error. The subscripts q, k, l, m, and r refer to output, capital, labor, intermediate input, and research, respectively.
[b] Statistical significance at the 0.05 level.

not unitary. The cost shares have been affected by technical change. The pattern of the biased technical change coefficients suggests that technical change is capital-using, labor- and research-saving, and essentially neutral with respect to materials. Surprisingly, there is no evidence of a neutral time drift of the cost function. In the 3FM the point estimates of β_t and β_{tt} indicate a downward neutral drift (at a decelerating rate), while the 4FM estimates reveal an implausible upward shift in the cost function. However, neither the 3FM nor 4FM estimates are statistically significant. Finally, the 3FM estimates of the factor-price output interaction terms, γ_{iq}, do not provide evidence of nonhomotheticity in the production structure, but the 4FM estimates point to statistically significant nonhomotheticity involving materials and research.

These impressions are confirmed by the formal tests of parametric restrictions in Table 2. The hypothesis that there is only neutral technical change is decisively rejected in both the 3FM and 4FM. In the 3FM we cannot reject the hypothesis that the production structure is homothetic, but in the full 4FM the hypothesis is strongly rejected. Similarly, homogeneity is rejected in the 4FM but not in the 3FM. Homogeneity is a special case of homotheticity, and it is apparent from Table 2 that homogeneity is rejected in the 4FM chiefly because homotheticity is so strongly rejected.

TABLE 2

Test Statistics for Parametric Restrictions on Three- and Four-Factor Models

	Neutrality	Homotheticity	Homogeneity	Homogeneity and unitary elasticities of substitution
Number of restrictions	2	2	3	5
Critical χ^2 (5%) in 3FM	5.99	5.99	7.82	11.07
Computed χ^2, 3FM	21.6	1.8	6.6	52.2
Number of restrictions	3	3	4	7
Critical χ^2 (5%) in 4FM	7.82	7.82	9.49	14.07
Computed χ^2, 4FM	52.4	17.2	21.4	124.8

TABLE 3

Partial Elasticities of Substitution for the Unconstrained Four-Factor Model[a]

Traditional inputs		Research input	
σ_{lk}	0.48[b]	σ_{lr}	−0.45
	(0.10)		(0.28)
σ_{lm}	2.32[b]	σ_{kr}	0.52[b]
	(0.31)		(0.14)
σ_{km}	0.46[b]	σ_{mr}	1.67[b]
	(0.15)		(0.70)

[a] The elasticities of substitution are evaluated using 1965 cost shares but they are similar for other years. Numbers in parentheses are estimated standard errors.

[b] Statistical significance at the 0.05 level.

The joint hypothesis of homogeneity and unitary elasticities of substitution, that is, the Cobb–Douglas form, is easily rejected and it is clear that the main reason for the rejection is that the elasticities of substitution are non-unitary.

A concise description of the production structure is provided by the Allen–Uzawa elasticities of substitution and the elasticities of factor demand. Tables 3 and 4 present the results from the 4FM; the 3FM yields virtually identical results for the traditional inputs that are common to both models. Turning to Table 3, note that all three traditional inputs are substitutes (σ_{lk}, σ_{lm}, $\sigma_{km} > 0$), with labor and materials the closest substitutes. All three elasticities of substitution are significantly different both from zero and from unity. Therefore, both the fixed-coefficient (Leontief) and Cobb–Douglas models would misrepresent the substitution possibilities among the traditional inputs. The estimates also indicate that research is substitutable with capital and materials. Complementarity between labor and research is obtained, but the estimated elasticity of substitution is not statistically different from zero.

Each element in Table 4 is the elasticity of demand for the input in the row after a price change of the input in the column. All the own-price elasticities of factor demand (along the main diagonal) have the correct sign and are statistically different from zero. The demand for materials is essentially unitary elastic, followed by labor with an elasticity of -0.55, and finally capital and research. Note that the capital assets in the model, traditional capital and research, have essentially the same price elasticities of demand, -0.26 and -0.31 (with no statistically significant difference). The

TABLE 4

Own- and Cross-Price Elasticities of Factor Demand for the Unconstrained Four-Factor Model[a]

	Labor	Capital	Materials	Research
Labor	-0.55^b	0.20^b	0.34^b	-0.009^b
	(0.06)	(0.05)	(0.05)	(0.004)
Capital	0.17^b	-0.26^b	0.08^b	0.008^b
	(0.04)	(0.04)	(0.02)	(0.002)
Materials	0.87^b	0.24^b	-1.12^b	0.026^b
	(0.12)	(0.07)	(0.13)	(0.011)
Research	-0.20	0.23^b	0.25^b	-0.31^b
	(0.11)	(0.06)	(0.10)	(0.03)

[a] The elasticities of demand are evaluated using 1965 cost shares but they are similar for other years. Numbers in parentheses are estimated standard errors.
[b] Statistical significance at the 0.05 level.

cross-price elasticities (off-diagonal terms) contain the same information as the elasticities of substitution in Table 3, but cross-price elasticities are not symmetric since they depend on the input shares [Eq. (7)]. If one is interested in a policy to affect the quantity of a specific input used in the production process by subsidizing factor prices, cross-price elasticities indicate which factor prices it would be most effective to alter and in what direction they should be changed.

The empirical results for the unconstrained 3FM and 4FM in Table 1 point to substantial economies of scale in the Bell System at the aggregate level. At the expansion point (given by the sample mean, since we use mean-scaled data), the elasticity of costs with respect to output is equal to α_q. The point estimates (standard error) of the cost elasticity in the 3FM and 4FM are 0.57 (0.07) and 0.47 (0.07), respectively. The implied point estimates of the scale elasticity (α_q^{-1}) in the 3FM is 1.75 with a 95% confidence interval (1.50, 2.12). The 4FM yields a point estimate of 2.12 with a confidence interval (1.75, 2.69). Two points should be noted. First, neither confidence interval contains unity. The hypothesis that there are no economies of scale can be rejected by a wide margin. Second, while the point estimate of the scale elasticity is larger in the 4FM, the confidence intervals overlap. There is no statistically significant difference between the two point estimates.

Two additional results are worth noting. First, previous empirical studies of the Bell System production structure have been based on value added rather than on gross output, using double deflation to construct value added (e.g., Vinod [1972], Sudit [1973], Mantell [1974]). The existence of a double-deflated value-added function requires that materials be strongly separable in the production process (May and Denny [1979]). In the 3FM (4FM) strong separability requires that $\sigma_{lm} = \sigma_{km} (=\sigma_{mr}) = 1$ and that there be no interaction between materials and either output or technology. In terms of the parameters in Table 1, the constraints are $\gamma_{lm} = \gamma_{km}(=\gamma_{mr}) = \gamma_{mq} = \theta_m = 0$. Using a likelihood ratio test of these restrictions, we obtain a computed chi-squared value for the 3FM (4FM) of 52.4 (55.0), compared to a critical value of 9.49 (11.07). The strong separability of materials is easily rejected in both the 3FM and 4FM. Therefore, the use of double-deflated value added is not supported by the data.

The second result involves the formal relationship between the 3FM and 4FM. The 3FM focuses exclusively on the traditional inputs (capital, labor, and materials), ignoring the price of research in the cost function and defining costs to include only payments to traditional inputs. The traditional likelihood ratio test (i.e., the significance of the research price terms) does not apply to a comparison of the 3FM and 4FM, because the dependent variable is different in the two models. The key to the proper test is to recognize that the 3FM is simply a cost function defined over a subset of inputs (i.e., only the traditional inputs). That is, let $C = f(\mathbf{P}, P_r, Q, T)$ represent the four-factor cost function, where $\mathbf{P}$ is a vector of prices of traditional inputs, P_r is the price of research, and other symbols were defined earlier. If we can write this cost function as $C = f[g(\mathbf{P}, Q, T), P_r]$, the subaggregate $g(\mathbf{P}, Q, T)$ represents a value-added cost function defined over the traditional inputs, which is exactly the 3FM. The existence of the subaggregate $g(\mathbf{P}, Q, T)$ requires the weak separability of research in the 4FM. This is equivalent to imposing the nonlinear constraints (Denny and Fuss [1977])

$$\alpha_i \gamma_{jr} = \alpha_j \gamma_{ir}, \qquad i, j = l, k, m, q, t.$$

These ten constraints reduce to four independent restrictions:

$$\alpha_l \gamma_{ir} = \alpha_i \gamma_{lr}, \qquad i = k, m, q, t.$$

Testing these constraints against the unconstrained version yields a computed chi-squared value of 45.8, compared to the critical value of 9.49. The weak separability of research in the cost function is not supported by the data. Therefore, the 3FM is not an empirically valid special case (subaggregate) of the 4FM.

6. Sources of Total Factor Productivity Growth

In this section we propose a method of decomposing the measured growth in total factor productivity (TFP) into a part related to economies of scale and a part attributable to technical change. TFP is basically a measure of output per unit of total factor input. Total factor input is a weighted average of inputs, where the weights depend on the underlying production function. If there are increasing returns to scale, part of the growth in TFP will reflect the change in the scale of operations, while the remainder can be ascribed to a shift in the production frontier itself. If there were constant returns to scale, the change in TFP would be identical to the technological shift (assuming other factors are exhaustive and accurately measured).

This is easier to visualize in terms of the long-run average-cost curve. Suppose we observe over time that the average cost of production (in real terms) has fallen. With constant returns to scale, the average cost does not depend on the level of output, so that the average cost curve is horizontal. It follows that the observed decline in average cost must be due solely to shifts of the average-cost curve downward over time, which we shall label the direct contribution of technical change. If there are economies of scale, however, average cost declines with increases in the level of output. Then the observed reductions in average cost over time will be due partly to movements along a given downward-sloping average-cost curve, and partly to downward shifts in the curve. However, since technical change raises the output produced with the existing level of inputs and thereby shifts the derived demands for inputs, part of the growth in total factor input is indirectly induced by technical change (Hulten [1979]). In the presence of increasing returns, this raises the level of TFP. This indirect contribution of technical change illustrates one level of interaction between scale economies and technical change, which should be taken into account if a proper attribution of the growth in TFP is to be made. In this section we explore these concepts more fully and suggest a way of measuring them.

6.1 Preliminary Decomposition

We begin by decomposing TFP growth into the direct contribution of technical change and a gross scale effect. The rate of growth of TFP is defined as

$$\dot{\text{TFP}} = \dot{Q} - \dot{F}, \tag{13}$$

where Q is output, F is total factor input, and a dot represents a rate of growth (rather than a time derivative). At the aggregate level there is only one output (by assumption), so that $\dot{Q}$ is defined unambiguously. For measuring $\dot{F}$, the Divisia index has become increasingly popular. The Divisia index is a weighted sum of rates of growth, where the weights are the components' shares in total value. Hulten [1973] demonstrates that the Divisia index conserves all the information contained in the components and that no other index can do better. It is well known that the Divisia index is a line integral and that its value may therefore not be path independent. The index will be path independent if and only if the aggregate over which it is defined actually exists (Hulten [1973]). Path independence is therefore an essential element of any acceptable Divisia index.

The conventional Divisia index of $\dot{F}$ is the cost-share weighted average of rates of growth of inputs:

$$\dot{F} = \sum_i \left(\frac{P_i X_i}{C}\right) \dot{X}_i; \qquad \sum P_i X_i = C, \tag{14}$$

where P_i and X_i are the ith factor's price and quantity, and C is total cost. Hulten [1973] has shown that (14) is path independent if and only if F is linearly homogeneous, i.e., if the production function exhibits constant returns to scale. To preserve path independence when F is not linearly homogeneous, we must use the "quasi-Divisia" index (Hulten [1973]):

$$\dot{F} = \sum \left(\frac{P_i X_i}{PQ}\right) \dot{X}_i, \tag{15}$$

where PQ is the value of output. This is a weighted sum (not average) of the rates of growth of the factor inputs where the weights are value (not cost) shares. The path-independent Divisia index of TFP becomes

$$\text{T\.FP} = \dot{Q} - \sum_i \left(\frac{P_i X_i}{PQ}\right) \dot{X}_i. \tag{16}$$

The next step is to relate this measure of T\.FP to technical change without regard for the input inducement effect. Consider the production function defined over inputs X and the level of technology, T (which need not be identified as time),

$$Q = F(X, T).$$

Differentiating with respect to time and dividing by Q,[10]

$$\dot{Q} = \sum_i \left(\frac{\partial F}{\partial X_i} \frac{X_i}{Q}\right) \dot{X}_i + \dot{T}. \tag{17}$$

Assuming cost minimization,[11]

$$\frac{\partial F}{\partial X_i} = \frac{P_i}{\partial C/\partial Q}, \tag{18}$$

so (17) becomes

$$\dot{Q} = \sum \left(\frac{P_i X_i}{Q(\partial C/\partial Q)}\right) \dot{X}_i + \dot{T} = \frac{P}{\partial C/\partial Q} \sum \left(\frac{P_i X_i}{PQ}\right) \dot{X}_i + \dot{T} \tag{19}$$

Substituting (19) into the Divisia index (16),

$$\text{T\.FP} = \dot{T} - \left(1 - \frac{P}{\partial C/\partial Q}\right) \dot{F}. \tag{20}$$

Define the cost elasticity as $\eta = (\partial C/\partial Q)Q/C$ and substitute in (20) to obtain

$$\text{T\.FP} = \dot{T} + [k\eta^{-1} - 1]\dot{F}, \tag{21}$$

where $k \equiv PQ/C = P/AC$ is the ratio of output price to average cost.

Equation (21) gives the relationship between measured growth in TFP

---

[10] The result in (17) does not assume that technical change is Hicks neutral. If it is Hicks neutral, then $\dot{T}$ will be independent of the levels of inputs X. Otherwise, $\dot{T}$ will depend on X. In that case, part of what is normally interpreted as neutral technical change will be factor-biased technical change (related to X). On this point see Mundlak and Razin [1969].

[11] If there are increasing returns, marginal productivity pricing would overexhaust the value of output. By assuming cost minimization in (18), we are in effect scaling down the marginal payment to all factors proportionally. This excludes the case where one factor input is a residual claimant on the value of output.

and the (not necessarily neutral) shift of the production function.[12] The two will differ unless there are constant returns to scale ($\eta = 1$) and the output price is set to earn zero profits ($k = 1$). It should be noted that regulation does not ensure that $k = 1$, since the accounting definition of costs may differ from the economic one, and, of course, because the allowed rate of return may differ from the real cost of capital. As a practical matter, however, k may be close to unity, in which case $k\eta^{-1} \simeq \eta^{-1}$ is the scale elasticity. We assume $k = 1$ in the rest of the analysis, that is, that there is average-cost pricing. This behavioral assumption is the obvious one to make in a one-output regulated context.

Equation (21) decomposes TFP growth into a pure shift of the production function that is unrelated to factor input decisions and a gross scale effect from increasing the level of factor use. However, the pure shift does not properly identify the full contribution of technical change to TFP growth. Part of the growth in factor input is due to technical change, which alters the marginal productivity of inputs and disturbs the preexisting equilibrium use of inputs (that is, shifts the derived demands for factors).[13] If (and only if) there are economies of scale, this input inducement effect makes an indirect contribution to TFP growth. The next task is to formulate this inducement effect and to reassign it from the gross scale effect to the contribution of technical change.

6.2   Input Inducement Effect

Suppose there is an initial equilibrium that is disturbed by a shift in the level of technology. All else is kept constant, including factor prices, which are considered exogenous. At the old level of inputs, the shift in technology lowers the average cost curve and hence raises the equilibrium level of output, depending on the elasticity of product demand. Since the derived demand for a factor depends inter alia on the level of output, the old levels of inputs will no longer be optimal. Some input expansion will be called for as long as inputs are not regressive. On the other hand, the shift in the technology level also lowers the input requirement per unit of output, that is, it shifts isoquants toward the origin. This lowers the total factor input required to produce a given level of output. We seek an expression for the net growth

---

[12] Fuss et al. (Chapter 8 in this volume) derive an equation identical to (21) except that k does not appear. Their analysis is based on the conventional Divisia index of $\dot{F}$—see (14) above—and hence is not path independent. While the path-independent form (16) is preferable from a theoretical point of view, the practical difference between Fuss's and our equation may be small. In fact, we later assume $k = 1$.

[13] See Hulten [1975, 1979] for a discussion of induced accumulation with constant returns to scale. In that context, the distinction is between the direct and indirect contribution of technical change to the growth in output. With constant returns, additional input accumulation cannot affect the level of TFP.

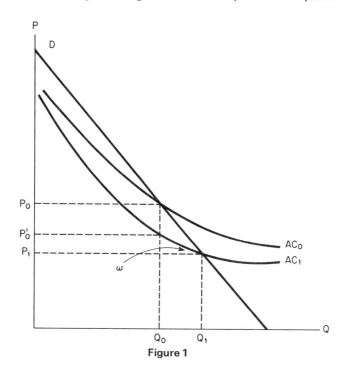

Figure 1

in total factor input induced in this way. We approach the problem in two steps. First, the equilibrium shift in the level of output is determined. This is then translated into a shift in total factor input, with consideration for the inward shift of the isoquants that technical change causes.

In Fig. 1 the initial equilibrium is fixed by the intersection of the old average-cost curve and the demand schedule (AC_0 and D), at output level Q_0 and price P_0. We can normalize the initial values of all variables (that is, work with index numbers), so that $P_0 \equiv Q_0 \equiv T_0 \equiv 1$, where T is the level of technology. Then the shift in the average cost at the initial level of output, from P_0 to P_0', is exactly $-\dot{T}$. The remaining decline in price (average cost) from P_0' to P_1 is approximately equal to $\dot{Q} \tan \omega$, where $\tan \omega$ is the slope of the AC_1 curve in the neighborhood of the new equilibrium. It can be shown that $\tan \omega = \eta - 1$, where η is the cost elasticity defined earlier.[14] Com-

---

[14] Note that

$$\tan \omega = \frac{\partial (C/Q)}{\partial Q} = \frac{\partial C/\partial Q - C/Q}{Q}.$$

Dividing the numerator and denominator by C/Q, recalling the definition of η and the normalization of all variables, yields $\tan \omega = \eta - 1$.

bining these results, we can write

$$\dot{P} = -\dot{T} + (\eta - 1)\dot{Q}. \qquad (22)$$

But

$$\dot{Q} = -e\dot{P}, \qquad (23)$$

where e is the elasticity of product demand, defined to be positive. Solving (22) and (23), we obtain the expression for the expansion of equilibrium output induced by technical change:

$$\dot{Q} = \psi \dot{T} \quad \text{where} \quad \psi = \frac{e}{1 - e(1 - \eta)}. \qquad (24)$$

Next, we use this expression to analyze the induced growth in total factor input. The growth in the use of any specific input, say $\dot{X}_i$, induced by $\dot{T}$ consists of two parts: (1) the extra X_i required by cost minimization to produce the additional output given by (24), *minus* (2) the amount of X_i saved due to the fact that input requirement per unit of output has declined. Using (24), the first component equals $\eta_i \psi \dot{T}$ where η_i is the elasticity of input use of factor i with respect to output.

To analyze the second component, consider Fig. 2. The initial isoquant is given by I with the old factor mix at point A. Technical change shifts the old isoquant toward the origin; it still refers to the same level of output. Suppose technical change is biased, so that it also twists the isoquant, say to I' (neutrality is a special case). With fixed factor prices, the new equilibrium is at point B. It is useful for our purpose to decompose the movement

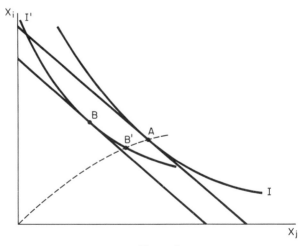

Figure 2

from A to B into two parts: (1) a (locally) "neutral" movement from A to B', where B' is constrained to be on the new isoquant but along the old expansion path (indicated by the dashed line); and (2) a factor bias measured as the movement from B' to B. Consider the "neutral" movement. If the input use were unchanged, the level of output would rise by $\dot{T}$. Therefore, input use must decline enough to reduce the level of output by the same amount, that is, by $-\dot{T}$, since output is held constant in Fig. 2. Moving inward along the old expansion path, it follows that the (locally) "neutral" reduction in X_i is equal to $-\eta_i\dot{T}$.

Gathering these results together, we can write the induced expansion of X_i as

$$\dot{X}_i = \eta_i\psi\,\dot{T} - [\eta_i\dot{T} + \text{bias}_i] = \eta_i(\psi - 1)\,\dot{T} - \text{bias}_i, \tag{25}$$

where bias$_i$ refers to the movement from B' to B, measured in terms of changes in X_i. Then the growth in total factor input which is induced by technical change, $\dot{F}_T$, is obtained by aggregating over (25) with value share weights (s_i):

$$\dot{F}_T = \sum_i s_i\eta_i(\psi - 1)\,\dot{T} - \sum_i s_i\,\text{bias}_i. \tag{26}$$

It is easy to show that $\sum_i s_i\eta_i = \eta$.[15] The second term in (26) is the value-share weighted average of factor biases, which must vanish by definition along a given isoquant.[16] Therefore, the aggregate input inducement effect of technical change becomes

$$\dot{F}_T = \eta(\psi - 1)\,\dot{T}. \tag{27}$$

To bring out the intuition behind (27), consider the special case where the product demand is completely inelastic. Then, since the level of output is fixed, the shift of the cost curve cannot induce additional demand. The only effect of $\dot{T}$ is to shift isoquants toward the origin. If input use did not change, output would rise by $\dot{T}$. Therefore, total factor input must fall enough to lower output by $\dot{T}$. With economies of scale (working in reverse direction here), the requisite reduction in total factor input is less than $\dot{T}$. This is confirmed by (27), for $e = 0$ implies $\psi = 0$. Then $\dot{F}_T = -\eta\dot{T} < 0$, and $|\dot{F}_T| < \dot{T}$ if there are scale economies ($\eta < 1$).

In order to decompose TFP into the net scale effect and the full contribution of technical change, substitute (27) in (21):

$$\text{TFP} = \eta^{-1}(1 - \eta)\dot{F}' + (1 - \eta)(\psi - 1)\dot{T} + \dot{T}, \tag{28}$$

---

[15] This can be obtained by defining total costs using the optimal factor levels X^*, that is, $C^* = \sum P_i X_i^*$, and differentiating with respect to output.

[16] This can be shown by totally differentiating the production function $Q = F(X, T)$ and rearranging, using (18) and the fact that $dQ = dT = 0$ along a given isoquant.

where $\dot{F}' \equiv \dot{F} - \dot{F}_T$ is the growth in total factor input that is not induced by technical change. The first term on the right-hand side of (28) is the contribution made by that part of total factor input growth that is not induced by technical change. The second term is the indirect contribution of technical change; the last term is its direct contribution.

We can go one step further by decomposing the net scale effect in (28). There are two possible sets of factors other than technical change that could affect the growth in total factor input: changes in factor prices and exogenous shifts of the product demand. In fact, factor price changes and technical change may be recognized as constituting the supply-side determinants of the level of inputs, the rest being due to shifts in product demand. The next task is to decompose the first term in (28) into a factor price effect and an exogenous demand effect. We focus first on the factor price effect.

Consider a rise in real factor prices, other things held constant. This induces an upward shift in the average cost curve and hence some reduction in the equilibrium level of output, as depicted in Fig. 1 for the reverse case. If there are economies of scale, this entails some decline in the level of TFP. The argument is similar in structure to the development of (24), and reference to Fig. 1 may be helpful. Formally, let P_i denote the real factor price of input i, and normalize all variables in the initial equilibrium. Suppose real factor prices rise by $\dot{P}_i$. Then the average cost curve shifts upward at the old equilibrium by the share-weighted average of these price changes, $\sum_i s_i \dot{P}_i$. By the same argument that led to (22) and (23), the change in the equilibrium price of output is

$$\dot{P} = \sum_i s_i \dot{P}_i + (\eta - 1)\dot{Q}.$$

But $\dot{Q} = -e\dot{P}$, so the expansion of equilibrium output is

$$\dot{Q} = -\psi \sum_i s_i \dot{P}_i, \tag{29}$$

where ψ was defined earlier.

Factor price changes have two effects on the use of an input. The first is the pure output expansion effect due to the change in the equilibrium level of output induced by the shift of the cost curve. Second, factor price changes alter the optimal input mix. Using (29), the response of input i can be written

$$\dot{X}_i = -\eta_i \psi \sum_j s_j \dot{P}_j + \sum_j \varepsilon_{ij} \dot{P}_j, \tag{30}$$

where ε_{ij} is the output-compensated cross-price elasticity of demand for input i. The first term in (30) is the output expansion effect, while the second reflects changes in the optimal input mix. Aggregating (30), the impact of changing factor prices on total factor input, $\dot{F}_f$, is

$$\dot{F}_f = -\psi \sum_i S_i \eta_i \sum_j S_j \dot{P}_j + \sum_i \sum_j S_i \varepsilon_{ij} \dot{P}_j$$

$$= -\psi \eta \sum_j S_j \dot{P}_j \tag{31}$$

since $\sum_i S_i \eta_i = \eta$ (see footnote 15) and $\sum_i S_i \varepsilon_{ij} = 0$.[17] Equation (31) confirms that rising real factor prices ($\dot{P}_i > 0$) reduce the level of total factor input.

Finally, we note the identity

$$\dot{F} \equiv \dot{F}_T + \dot{F}_f + \dot{F}_d, \tag{32}$$

which says that factor input growth consists of parts induced by technical change, factor price changes, and exogenous shifts in demand. We have formulated $\dot{F}_T$ and $\dot{F}_f$. Given the actual growth, $\dot{F}_d$ can be computed from the identity.

Substituting (31) and (32) in (28), we obtain the final decomposition of the rate of growth of TFP:

$$\dot{\text{TFP}} = \eta^{-1}(1 - \eta)\dot{F}_d - (1 - \eta)\psi \sum_i s_i \dot{P}_i + (1 - \eta)(\psi - 1)\dot{T} + \dot{T}. \tag{33}$$

The decomposition requires two parameters, the cost elasticity and the price elasticity of product demand (on which ψ partly depends). Given these parameters, the computational procedure is: (1) retrieve $\dot{T}$ as a residual using (21) and setting $k = 1;$ (2) compute $\dot{F}_T$ and $\dot{F}_f$ from (27) and (31), respectively; and (3) then compute $\dot{F}_d$ as a residual using the identity (32). The rest is straightforward, following (33).

We provide an illustrative application of this methodology to TFP growth in the Bell System during the period 1947–1976 and for three subperiods, 1947–1957, 1958–1967, and 1968–1976. The terms $\dot{\text{TFP}}$ and $\sum_i s_i \dot{P}_i$ in (33) are constructed using discrete approximations to the Divisia index, namely, Törnqvist indexes. Real factor prices are taken as nominal factor prices deflated by the Consumer Price Index. For these calculations the cost elasticity is set at 0.55. Three values for the aggregate price elasticity of demand are used, -0.6, -0.8, and -1.0. These values are generally consistent with estimates reported in the econometric literature on telephone demand (Dobell et al. [1972], Davis et al. [1973]).

The results of the decomposition are presented in Tables 5–7. The direct effect of technical change ($\dot{T}$, which is independent of e) accounts for about

---

[17] Note that since $\sum_i S_i \varepsilon_{ij} \equiv (P_j/C) \sum_i P_i \partial X_i/\partial P_j$, where C is total costs, it is sufficient to show that $\sum_i P_i \partial X_i/\partial P_j = 0$. From (18) we obtain $\sum_i P_i \partial X_i/\partial P_j = (\partial C/\partial Q) \sum_i (\partial F/\partial X_i) \times \partial X_i/\partial P_j = 0$, where the second equality holds because the level of output is held constant.

TABLE 5

Decomposition of TFP Growth, 1947–1976[a]

	Source (%)					
Period	Technical change Direct (a)	Technical change Indirect (b)	Factor prices (c)	Exogenous demand (d)	Net scale effect (e) = (c) + (d)	TFP (average annual rate)
1947–1957	13.7	−1.1	−21.4	108.8	87.5	0.0350
1958–1967	23.8	−1.9	−9.6	87.7	78.1	0.0365
1968–1976	44.0	−3.6	−9.0	68.7	59.7	0.0496
1947–1976	30.6	−2.4	−11.7	83.5	72.8	0.0409

[a] $e = -0.6$. Columns (a) through (e) are computed from (33) in the text. Several years for which the measured TFP growth was negative were deleted; these include the Korean War period (1952–1953) and 1948–1949.

TABLE 6

Decomposition of TFP Growth, 1947–1976[a]

	Source (%)					
Period	Technical change Direct (a)	Technical change Indirect (b)	Factor prices (c)	Exogenous demand (d)	Net scale effect (e) = (c) + (d)	TFP (average annual rate)
1947–1957	13.7	1.3	−32.3	117.1	84.8	0.0350
1958–1967	23.8	2.2	−14.5	88.5	74.0	0.0365
1968–1976	44.0	4.2	−13.7	65.5	51.8	0.0496
1947–1976	30.6	2.9	−17.6	84.1	67.2	0.0409

[a] $e = -0.8$. Columns (a) through (e) are computed from (33) in the text. Several years for which the measured TFP growth was negative were deleted; these include the Korean War period (1952–1953) and 1948–1949.

a third (30.6%) of TFP growth over the entire period. There is a distinct trend over the subperiods, however, with the contribution rising from 13.7% during 1947–1957 to 44.0 during 1968–1976. The size and even the direction of the indirect contribution of technical change are sensitive to the elasticity of demand. The indirect contribution is negative when the elasticity of demand is quite low ($e = -0.6$). (See Table 5.) This is because the output expansion effect of technical change is highly restricted, so the reduction of input use due to the inward shift of the isoquants predominates. With

TABLE 7

Decomposition of TFP Growth, 1947–1976[a]

	Source (%)					
Period	Technical change Direct (a)	Technical change Indirect (b)	Factor prices (c)	Exogenous demand (d)	Net scale effect (e) = (c) + (d)	TFP (average annual rate)
1947–1957	13.7	4.3	−46.3	128.3	82.0	0.0350
1958–1967	23.8	7.7	−20.8	89.3	68.5	0.0365
1968–1976	44.0	14.1	−19.6	61.5	41.9	0.0496
1947–1976	30.6	9.8	−25.2	84.8	59.6	0.0409

[a] $e = -1.0$. Columns (a) through (e) are computed from (33) in the text. Several years for which the measured TFP growth was negative were deleted; these include the Korean War period (1952–1953) and 1948–1949.

$e = -0.8$ (Table 6), the indirect effect is positive and about 10% as large as the direct effect over the whole period $(2.9/30.6 = 0.10)$. With unitary elasticity of demand (Table 7), the indirect effect of technical change takes on quantitative significance. Over the whole period, it accounts for nearly 10% of TFP growth, and 14.1% during 1968–1976. Moreover, with $e = -1.0$, the indirect effect is almost a third as large as the direct effect.

As expected, the tables show that the rise in real factor prices over time has been a drag on TFP growth. The magnitude of the effect is sensitive to the demand elasticity; for the whole period it varies from 11.7% with $e = -0.6$ to 25.2% with $e = -1.0$. That is, the tables suggest that the rate of growth of TFP during 1947–1976 would have been from a half to a full percentage point higher $(0.12 \times 0.0409 \simeq 0.005; 0.25 \times 0.0409 \simeq 0.01)$ if the contractionary effect of factor prices had been absent.

Shifts in the demand curve appear to be a major source of TFP growth. The measured contribution of demand shifts does not vary much with the specific assumption about the elasticity of demand. During the first period the negative effect of factor prices swamps the contributions of technical change, so that the measured contribution of shifts in demand exceeds 100%. This is not impossible; it says that if the demand had remained stationary, TFP would have declined. The contribution of demand to TFP growth declines steadily over time, however, to about 65% during the last period.

The tables also present the net scale effect, which is the sum of the factor price and exogenous demand effects. Empirically, the net contribution of economies of scale varies inversely with the elasticity of demand. Over the entire period, scale economies account for between about 60 and 70% of the growth in TFP, but this is not constant over time. The relative contribution of scale economies to the growth in TFP declines steadily, regardless of the assumption on the elasticity of demand. Note that the (average) rate of growth of TFP steadily increased over that same time period. Scale economies still remain an important source of TFP growth, accounting for between 40 and 60% of the total during 1968–1976, but their relative importance has eroded over time.

7. Concluding Remarks

In this paper we explored the production structure and the sources of the growth of total factor productivity in the Bell System during the period 1947–1976. Four main empirical conclusions emerge:

1. The cost structure is well approximated by a translog cost function. Despite the limited availability of data, the empirical estimates we obtain are quite precise. This underscores the importance of exploiting duality theory. The evidence indicates that there is some scope for substitution among the three traditional inputs and research, but in most cases the elasticities of substitution are distinctly smaller than unity. The cost function is not homothetic; the optimal input mix is affected by the scale of operations.

2. The results suggest the presence of strong economies of scale at the aggregate level. Estimates of the scale elasticity (at the expansion point) are around 1.8 or higher, with the lower bound of the confidence interval falling around 1.5.

3. The evidence indicates that (time-related) technical change has exhibited a factor bias, being capital-using, labor- and research-saving, and neutral with respect to materials. The cost-minimizing mix of inputs is therefore related both to technical change and to scale. There is no statistically significant evidence of a neutral, downward drift of the cost curve.

4. The decomposition of the growth of TFP indicates that scale economies account for between 60 and 70% of such growth over the entire postwar period, but the relative importance of scale economies as a source of TFP growth has declined over time. This shift in relative influence does not reflect the exhaustion of scale economies. It is due to the fact that total factor input grew at a slower rate (relative to TFP) during the later periods. Since economies of scale affect the level of TFP through the growth of inputs, there was less room for economies of scale to exert an influence on TFP.

Several lines of research warrant further investigation. The first is to relax the assumption that the firm is cost minimizing at every moment of time, expecially with respect to traditional capital and possibly research. This could be done either by explicitly introducing adjustment lags, or by formulating a short-run cost-minimization model and deriving the implied envelope curve from it. Second, some attempt should be made to disaggregate the production structure of the Bell System and estimate a multioutput cost function. This would help to identify the sources of the economies of scale, test for jointness of production, and provide a more detailed view of the sources of total factor productivity growth. Finally, it would be useful to focus more directly on the production of the level of technology itself. Specifically, the roles of internal R&D and of external R&D in related fields could be assessed. This would also enable measurement of the separate contributions of internal and external R&D to the growth in total factor productivity.

ACKNOWLEDGMENTS

We received helpful comments and suggestions from participants in a seminar at the Bell Laboratories, especially William Taylor, and from several referees. Any remaining errors are ours. S. Puglia, I. Yew, and D. Cardona provided competent research assistance.

10

Productivity Measurement and Environmental Regulation: An Engineering–Econometric Analysis

Raymond J. Kopp
Resources for the Future
Washington, D.C.

V. Kerry Smith
Department of Economics
University of North Carolina
Chapel Hill, North Carolina

1. Introduction

The purpose of this paper is to examine the implications of regulations of the emissions of atmospheric and waterborne residuals for the measurement of productivity change. While the analysis focuses on single factor productivity measurement at the micro level, our findings also have direct implications for the construction of aggregate measures of the impacts of many forms of social regulation on productivity change. Indeed, this relationship between the micro level analysis and these aggregate measures in part motivated our inquiry.[1]

[1] There are a number of other reasons for considering the problems associated with extending productivity measurement to take explicit account of these regulations. Indeed, Nadiri's [1970] review of the theory and measurement of factor productivity noted, in commenting on the Jorgenson–Griliches–Denison [1972] exchange over the sources of an unaccounted for residual in productivity growth, that

Unfortunately, the specific results are too sensitive to changes in the types of data and methods of estimation to provide concrete quantitative figures about the contributions of various factors to the growth of output. It will be most useful if Denison's and Jorgenson–

249

According to conventional measurement techniques, the United States has enjoyed over a quarter of a century of increasing productivity.[2] In the late 1960s there was some evidence of a slowdown in the growth of productivity, but it was not regarded as a source of concern. However, there appears to have been a halt in productivity growth in 1974 and with it has come widespread concern over its causes and potential implications. At the request of policy makers, at least four major evaluations of productivity measurement and its meaning are under way or near completion at this writing.[3] Equally important, Denison [1978a] recently estimated that real output per worker had a negative growth rate over the period 1973–1976. Specifically, he observed:

> The adjusted growth rate in national income per person employed fell from 2.7 percent a year in 1948–69 to −0.6 percent in 1973–76, a drop of 3.3 percentage points. ... A drop of 1.6 percentage points can be specifically allocated (Denison [1978a], p. 12).

A part of his allocation is to the diversion of factor inputs (i.e., labor and capital) to meet the requirements of social regulations.[4] His estimates suggest that these factors, in total, retarded the real output per person employed by only 0.4 percentage points. This estimate of the impact of social regulations is not especially disquieting, even when it is supplemented with Denison's [1972] breakdown of the impact of these regulations, which showed that their effects have increased over time. Nonetheless, there seems to be a nagging anxiety that these estimates understate the full impact of

---

Griliches's approach is extended to more disaggregate levels. *It would be necessary to take account of additional environmental variables (presently excluded) such as air and water, and government services such as law and subsidies which definitely contribute to the productivity growth of an industry.*" (Nadiri [1970, p. 1169], emphasis added.)

[2] See Jorgenson and Griliches [1972] for a discussion of some of the measures of productivity in the context of an evaluation of Denison's [1962] early work, and, more recently, Diewert [1976].

[3] The four studies include: the Committee for Economic Development's study of technology policy, the Business Roundtable Study, the President's Domestic Policy Review on Industrial Innovation, and the National Academy of Science's review of productivity measures conducted under the auspices of the Assembly for Behavioral and Social Science of the National Research Council.

Related activities include work by the Office of Technology Assessment, Congressional Research Service, and Directorate for Science, Technology and Industry of the OECD.

[4] Actually, Denison includes a subset of all social regulations in his calculations. These include pollution-abatement and health and safety regulations. He also includes the resources estimated to be required for crime prevention. The complete set is described as representing changes in the legal and human environment in which business operates that might affect productivity. See Denison [1978a] for more details.

social regulations. Indeed, many analysts suspect, without the quantitative evidence to substantiate the suspicion, that a more complete analysis of the impacts of regulations would attribute to them a larger share of the unexplained negative residual in Denison's calculations.[5]

In order to initiate the process of unraveling the productivity–environmental-regulations nexus, it is essential to begin at the firm level. Productivity statistics are, after all, simply convenient indicators of the firm's performance in using the resources at its disposal. To understand how particular regulations would affect these indexes we need to consider how they alter the firm's behavior. More specifically, if we assume the firm seeks to minimize the cost of production of a given set of outputs, then regulations that affect this process will also alter the observed patterns of change in single and total factor productivity statistics. We shall demonstrate these links in what follows by showing how single factor productivity statistics can be observed to change in response to the "parameters" of the firm's cost minimization decisions. Moreover, the nature of these adjustments will directly affect what are appropriate methods for allocating any observed pattern of productivity changes to its presumed "sources."

Unfortunately, actual data on micro level production processes are not sufficiently complete to permit an empirical analysis of the importance of these issues with information based on existing firms' behavior.[6] As a consequence, in this study we have used for our data the cost-minimizing solutions to large-scale, linear-programming, process-analysis models. Such solutions, christened *pseudo-data* by Lawrence Klein, have been used in a number of different applications in the recent literature.[7] Our analyses are related to the solutions from three process-analysis models developed by Russell and Vaughan [1976] for steelmaking plants of different technologies. One of the important advantages of these models for our purposes is the explicit accounting they provide for materials and heat balances in the production activities. In addition, the three different technologies generate quite diverse levels of atmospheric and waterborne residuals and therefore

---

[5] Suggestions for a regulatory budget to control additions to existing regulations and the propagation of new regulations are, in part, a reflection of this. Also, arguments have been developed suggesting that the effects of regulations may not be additive (see Miki and Humphrey [1979]).

[6] Recent publications of the Department of Energy report estimates of the atmospheric emissions of particulates, sulfur dioxide, and nitrogen oxides as well as the temperature changes in waste water for electric power plants. However, these data do not permit full control over the behavioral actions at the plant level so that there are potential problems in interpreting the results.

[7] The first applications of pseudo data were undertaken by Griffin [1977a, 1978a, 1978b, 1979]. More recently, applications have been directed toward using the pseudo-data to test the properties of neoclassical production models (see Kopp and Smith [1979]).

provide some perspective on the implications of our arguments for production activities with varying propensities to generate by-product effluents.

In the next section we develop formally the implications of the micro relationship between the regulation of effluent discharges and single factor productivity for conventional practices for measuring productivity indexes. In Section 3 we outline the strategy we have selected to examine the potential empirical importance of these issues. In Section 4 we describe the Russell–Vaughan models and the nature of our data. In Section 5 we summarize our findings, and in the last section consider their implications for the measurement of productivity at micro and at aggregate levels.

2. Productivity Measurement and Environmental Regulations

The analysis of productivity statistics in the past literature has remained broadly consistent with micro models of firm behavior. Indeed, the dual interpretation of productivity statistics in terms of either output and input levels or their respective prices reflects this consistency. Of course, it should be acknowledged that the rationale for direct parallels between the movements in productivity indexes and the predictions of a comparative static model of the firm's behavior declines with the level of aggregation of the data. Nonetheless, to understand the impacts of environmental regulations on productivity, the analysis must begin with the effects of these restrictions on the firm's resource allocation decisions. Consider the case of a cost-minimizing firm (or plant). The firm's optimal input selections can be fully described by Eq. (1), a neoclassical cost function expressing total costs C as a function of output (in the single output case) Q, and input prices $(P_i, i = 1, 2, \ldots, n)$:

$$C = g(Q, P_1, P_2, \ldots, P_n). \qquad (1)$$

We can derive a relationship between single factor productivity measures and the unit cost function for this firm using duality theory.[8] That is, given that the unit cost function is (2), then $\partial \bar{C}/\partial P_i$ will be the inverse of the ith factor's average productivity as given in (3):

$$\bar{C} = C/Q = f(Q, P_1, P_2, \ldots, P_n), \qquad (2)$$

$$\frac{\partial \bar{C}}{\partial P_i} = \frac{X_i^*}{Q} = h_i(Q, P_1, P_2, \ldots, P_n), \qquad (3)$$

where X_i^* is the optimal level of ith factor input. It should be noted that (3)

---

[8] For a discussion of duality theory, see Shephard [1970] and McFadden [1978].

suggests that the movements in single factor productivity will be dependent upon output and all input prices. This observation is important because most analyses of productivity statistics have focused on their changes over time. Moreover, evaluations of the impacts of regulations have attempted to link such changes to the introduction (and/or changes in the stringency) of one or more regulations. This practice implies that an understanding of the processes through which a firm *adjusts* to a given set of regulations will be necessary before it is possible to interpret the resulting changes in factor productivities. Indeed, in the single output case we can directly link these adjustment functions [i.e., the $h_i(\cdot)$s] to total factor productivity by showing that the change in the latter is the weighted sum of the changes in the single factor productivity indexes as given by

$$\frac{\dot{G}}{G} = \frac{\dot{Q}}{Q} - \sum_{i=1}^{n} \theta_i \frac{\dot{X}_i}{X_i} = \sum_{i=1}^{n} \theta_i \frac{Q/\dot{X}_i}{Q/X_i}, \tag{4}$$

where θ_i is the share of total costs accounted for by the ith factor ($\sum_{i=1}^{n} \theta_i = 1$), G is the total factor productivity, and the overdot indicates the time derivative. Thus any measure of the efficiency costs of social regulation, as reductions in the rate of growth of total factor productivity, will also require full understanding of these adjustments.

Since all models of production activities must be consistent with the first law of thermodynamics (i.e. mass balance conditions), we can expect that constraints on the emission of residuals from these production processes will also be reflected in neoclassical cost functions [i.e., in Eq. (1)]. Of course, if the disposal of these residuals is not constrained (or priced), their production levels will not be reflected in behavioral functions such as (1). Thus, a dual interpretation of productivity measures is an especially useful means of gauging the effects of environmental regulations. In the absence of regulations we expect no relationship between effluents and single or total factor productivity measures.[9] This framework is also useful in examining the implications of the practices used to assign any reductions in productivity to environmental regulations.

More specifically, past empirical analyses have tended to treat the firm's adjustment to a given set of environmental regulations in a rather special way. Nearly all estimates of the impacts of regulations have assumed that it is possible to reflect fully these effects as additive increments to each micro unit's total costs of producing a given level of output.[10] This framework

[9] Of course, at an aggregate level we might wish to include environmental quality as an output in the composite output measure. If this were the objective, we would have a problem different from the one addressed here.

[10] For a discussion of the estimates of environmental cost, see Denison [1978a].

presupposes that regulatory costs are separable from the total costs of producing output, as illustrated by

$$C^* = g(Q, P_2, P_3, \ldots, P_n) + \psi(E, P_1, P_2, P_3, Q), \tag{5}$$

where E is the level of effluent restriction imposed on the firm.

This specification provides an example of the logic involved and implies that the increment to total costs associated with meeting environmental regulations can be associated with specific factor inputs, such as the treatment equipment needed to remove effluents from water used in the production process. At first this assumption may not seem crucial to the measurement of either the level or the changes in productivity indexes. However, further analysis indicates that such a conclusion would be misleading. Assume the unit cost corresponding to (5) is given as

$$\bar{C}^* = f(Q, P_2, P_3, \ldots P_n) + \bar{\psi}(E, P_1, P_2, P_3, Q). \tag{6}$$

In this example the input requirements ratios (i.e., inverses of single factor productivities) can be shown to have two distinct functions that depict the adjustment patterns in input usage in response to price changes. These functions depend upon whether the input is used in production activities or treatment activities, or in both. They are given, for our example, in (7a) and (7b) and in (7c):

$$\frac{\partial \bar{C}^*}{\partial P_i} = \frac{X_i^*}{Q} = \frac{\partial f}{\partial P_i}, \qquad i = 4, \ldots, n, \tag{7a}$$

$$\frac{\partial \bar{C}^*}{\partial P_1} = \frac{X_1^*}{Q} = \frac{\partial \bar{\Psi}}{\partial P_1}, \tag{7b}$$

$$\frac{\partial \bar{C}^*}{\partial P_k} = \frac{X_k^*}{Q} = \frac{\partial f}{\partial P_k} + \frac{\partial \bar{\Psi}}{\partial P_k}, \qquad k = 2, 3. \tag{7c}$$

In order to relate this argument to the evaluation of the effects of regulation on productivity change, it is necessary to consider elasticity measures of the adjustment of single factor productivity ratios to factor price changes. Following Berndt [1978] it can be shown that the response of a single factor productivity ratio to a change in one of the factor prices, measured as an average productivity elasticity, equals the negative of the price elasticity, as in

$$\frac{\partial \ln(Q/X_i)}{\partial \ln P_j} = -\frac{\partial \ln(X_i/Q)}{\partial \ln P_j} = -\frac{\partial \ln X_i}{\partial \ln P_j}, \tag{8}$$

where Q and P_k, $k \neq j$, are held constant. Thus, for our purposes, the form of the measured single factor adjustment elasticities depends upon whether the factors are considered important to the incremental costs of meeting environmental standards. For factors included in the incremental environmental cost function, the measured adjustment elasticities will be a weighted function of the responses from each of the two cost relationships, as given by

$$\alpha_{ij} = W_1 \varepsilon_{ij} + W_2 \beta_{ij} \qquad \text{for all} \quad i \text{ and } j, \tag{9}$$

where

$$\alpha_{ij} = \frac{\partial \ln(Q/X_i)}{\partial \ln P_j},$$

$$\varepsilon_{ij} = -\frac{\partial^2 f}{\partial P_j \partial P_i} \cdot \frac{P_j}{\partial f/\partial P_i},$$

$$\beta_{ij} = -\frac{\partial^2 \bar{\psi}}{\partial P_j \partial P_i} \cdot \frac{P_j}{\partial \bar{\psi}/\partial P_i},$$

$$W_1 = \frac{P_i \cdot \partial f/\partial P_i}{P_i \cdot X_i},$$

$$W_2 = \frac{P_i \cdot \partial \bar{\psi}/\partial P_i}{P_i \cdot X_i}.$$

A question that arises in response to this development is whether these analytical issues are of practical importance. To answer it, we must consider two dimensions of the question. First, how are the incremental costs of environmental regulations estimated and to what extent does the procedure recognize the differences in potential roles for inputs in production and treatment activities? And, second, do actual production activities suggest that inputs other than those used in the incremental cost calculations are important in meeting environmental regulations?

The first question can be answered directly with the most influential evaluation of the impact of environmental regulations to date, by Denison [1978a]. His analysis assumes that the only inputs involved in treatment are labor and capital, and further, that it is possible to estimate their contributions to treatment as distinct from their productive activities. The second question cannot be answered for all industries but is the subject of the empirical analysis of the remainder of this paper. That is, we propose to use the solutions of the process analysis models developed for ironmaking and steelmaking plants to detect whether our single factor elasticities for inputs other than labor and capital are affected by regulations limiting the disposal of atmospheric and waterborne residuals.

The specific form of α_{ij} will depend on whether the factors are exclusively associated with productive activities ($\alpha_{ij} = \varepsilon_{ij}$), or treatment activities ($\alpha_{ij} = \beta_{ij}$) or both [as in Eq. (9)].

These differences in the factor adjustment elasticities have direct implications for the measurement of the *sources* of change in both single and total factor productivity statistics. Consider first the case of a single factor productivity index. Using the dual representation of the adjustment function for productivity statistics [i.e. equations like (3)], the rate of change in that index can be decomposed into components due to factor price change, output change, and environmental regulation change, as in

$$\frac{Q/\dot{X}_i}{Q/X_i} = -\sum_{j=1}^{n} \frac{\partial X_i}{\partial P_j} \frac{P_j}{X_i}\left(\frac{\dot{P}_j}{P_j}\right) + \frac{\partial X_i}{\partial Q} \frac{Q}{X_i}\left(\frac{\dot{Q}}{Q}\right) - \frac{\partial X_i}{\partial E} \frac{E}{X_i}\left(\frac{\dot{E}}{E}\right). \tag{10}$$

The elasticities weighting each of the rates of factor price change in the first set of terms on the right-hand side of Eq. (10) are the same adjustment elasticities discussed above. Our point is that environmental regulations (and many other regulations) have more subtle influences than Denison's method assumes. Thus, assume that regulations change at one discrete point and not continuously over time; then Denison's method assumes it is possible to identify specific factor inputs that will *only* be associated with meeting the regulations (e.g., our input X_1)—that is, they make no contribution to production otherwise. Under this framework, measuring the effects of these regulations on productivity change requires determining which of the n factors are of this type and estimating their contribution to the first set of terms on the right-hand side of Eq. (4). By contrast, our model permits factors to serve two roles—contributing to production and controlling effluent emissions (e.g., X_2 and X_3 in our example). For instance, labor is often required in both activities. Unless the types of labor involved are different, we may not be able to sort out the firm's acquisition decisions for labor into the separate components implied by Denison's approach. Equally important, many primary treatment processes are associated with the recovery of by-products and therefore serve double roles, simultaneously enhancing production and assisting in meeting an environmental regulation.

Thus a recognition of the potential roles for factor inputs in production and treatment activities is essential for partitioning the adjustment elasticities (i.e., the α_{ij}s) so as to measure the effects of regulations on the growth of productivity. This argument can be extended directly to the case of total factor productivity measures by using the relationship between the two indexes given in Eq. (4).

3.   An Outline of the Methodology

Our objective is to evaluate whether, in practice, environmental regulations affect the adjustment elasticities of a variety of inputs in addition to labor and pollution-related capital equipment. As we noted at the outset, this would be especially difficult to evaluate with the data that are available. Accordingly, we have chosen to address it using the solutions from cost-minimizing linear programing models that were specifically designed to estimate residuals generation processes.[11] Aside from the ability to control the character of the data used in our empirical analysis, these data have additional advantages: (1) materials and heat balances are incorporated in the process analysis models so as to measure the residuals generated at each stage in the production process; (2) residuals treatment activities are modeled as they would exist in actual production processes throughout the various processing stages rather than in an end-of-the-pipe fashion as with many simpler process analysis models (see Smith and Vaughan [1979]); and (3) the behavioral objectives of the hypothetical micro unit are known and correspond to cost minimization—the basis of our analytical derivation in the preceding section.

As with other types of models, such as econometric models of firms or industries, process analysis models also vary in their ability to depict actual outcomes. The Russell–Vaughan models selected for use in our applications would likely rank among the best representations of these production processes, considering both their estimates of costs and residuals discharges. At least two independent sets of information support this judgment. The first of these arises from Russell and Vaughan's own comparisons with actual data. After quite detailed comparisons of their benchmark solutions with information from the Council on Economic Priorities subsample of steel plants, a Delaware region steel mill, and the Cost of Clean Water estimates of discharges together with cost information from the American Iron and Steel Institute, they concluded the model does mimic real world behavior rather well.[12]

A second independent comparison is available in the Council on Wage

---

[11] See Bower [1975] for a more complete discussion of the advantages of these models.

[12] More specifically, they say

> . . . the model does rather well at mimicking the world when allowance is made for our assumptions. The estimated and observed atmospheric discharges match well for all furnaces. Our water-course discharge estimates on balance appear high relative to observed discharges. This is primarily attributable to the tremendous range of operating, by-product recovery, and treatment possibilities available on the water side since the choice among

and Price Stability's report, *Prices and Costs in the United States Steel Industry* [1977]. This report compares the cost-minimizing solutions of the Russell–Vaughan model with confidential cost data for the six largest firms made available to the Council for the period 1972–1977, adjusted to a standard volume basis. Analysis of the two indexes suggests that the Russell–Vaughan model tracks the industry cost movements well.[13]

With this background on the validation of the models used for our analysis, we can now turn to our primary objective: appraising the effects of environmental regulations on the adjustment elasticities in a controlled setting. Denison's analysis implicitly maintains that the only way to meet environmental restrictions on the discharge of effluents is with the use of pollution-abatement equipment and labor. Even a casual review of the materials balance, process-analysis models constructed as part of Resources for the Future's industry studies program suggests that this conception of the firm's reaction is misleading (see Bower [1975]; Russell [1973]; and Russell and Vaughan [1976]). These engineering models identify many avenues for reducing the residuals generated in production through changes in the composition of the raw materials used in the production activities. For example, low-sulfur, low-ash coal can be used in place of coal with a higher content of both potential residuals. In many cases, a neoclassical model fails to identify these potential substitutions because the level of input aggregation does not permit the identification of inputs by their attributes.[14] However, it should also be acknowledged that the scope for such substitution is constrained as the limitations on discharges become more stringent. Progressive increases in the severity of the restrictions will require the use of treatment equipment in addition to those materials with lower effluent potential. Thus, while one can identify the potential for substitution among different types of materials from the technology matrix of a given process-analysis model, this description alone will not offer a measure of the importance of other inputs in meeting discharge restrictions of varying degrees of stringency. If such intramaterial substitutions account for a rather small share of the task associated with meeting a given set of discharge restrictions, then the Denison assumptions may yield reasonable first approximations.

It is difficult to appraise the quantitative significance of these technical

---

these is very sensitive to assumptions about base cost and price conditions and base operating equipment. (Russell–Vaughan [1976], p. 209.)

Further detail on the nature of the comparisons is available in chapter 9 of Russell and Vaughan [1976].

[13] A further evaluation of the model relative to other process analysis models is available in Smith and Vaughan [1979].

[14] For an interesting discussion of the problems associated with developing a materials aggregate, see Lau [1979b].

possibilities on the basis of the technology matrix alone. Therefore we have used the process-analysis models as a source of data in the form of cost-minimizing solutions to measure the responsiveness of the adjustment elasticities to alternative types of environmental discharge restrictions. These estimated elasticities are derived from a neoclassical cost function that is used to summarize the responses of the steel models.[15] Although, these estimated cost functions are approximations to the "true" underlying piecewise-linear cost surface, it should be noted that this approach is consistent with the origins of neoclassical production models. Indeed, Marsden *et al.* [1974] have observed that neoclassical production models are best interpreted, on theoretical grounds, as compact approximations of more complex underlying sets of engineering activities.[16]

We have selected a flexible functional form, the translog cost function, to summarize the responses of each of the three process-analysis models. This specification has a number of advantages. Griffin's [1978b] recent comparisons of the translog function with generalized Leontief and generalized square-root quadratic specifications suggest that it offered the best approximation for piecewise-linear cost surfaces such as the ones we are estimating here. His criteria were based on the mean absolute errors derived in comparing the estimated arc and point price elasticities of factor demand, over the widest price range.[17] The specification of a flexible functional form, such as the translog, has the further advantage of permitting estimates of the price elasticity of demand and, therefore, estimates of our adjustment elasticities [by Eq. (8)] for each solution.[18]

[15] This is basically the approach that Griffin's analyses [1977a,b, 1978a,b] have taken. Lau [1978] has criticized this approach, arguing that there are a number of alternative approaches (other than regression-based methods) for approximating a piecewise-linear cost surface. In our case the analysis focuses on summarizing the responses in terms of the factor demand relationships rather than the levels of costs. Thus, it is not clear that Lau's criteria would be appropriate for this case.

[16] For example, Marsden *et al.* [1974] note that the primitives involved in the analysis shift from economic properties of the production functions to their consistency with engineering relationships: "The validity of the final production functional forms rests on the accuracy of the engineering relationships used rather than on the preciseness of the economic properties assumed" (p. 127).

[17] Griffin [1978b] observed that ". . . for actual pseudo data drawn from the iron and steel model, the differences among functional forms in the implied price elasticities were substantial. These results indicated that the translog function offered the lowest approximation error for the price elasticities drawn over larger price ranges" (p. 11). The iron and steel model referred to was the Russell–Vaughan [1976] model. However, Griffin employed the model using all three steelmaking furnaces as alternative types of capital rather than as distinct plants as in our applications.

[18] The specific relationship for the Allen [1938] elasticity of substitution is given as $\sigma_{ij} = (\gamma_{ij} + k_i k_j)/k_i k_j$, where γ_{ij} is the second-order term for P_i, P_j in translog cost function and k_i the cost share for ith factor input. The price elasticity of factor demand corresponding to σ_{ij} is $\varepsilon_{ij} = k_i \sigma_{ij}$.

The specific details of our test involve three steps. For each of the process-analysis models described in Section 4, we estimate a translog cost function, using the appropriate number of cost share equations. The estimator used is a restricted variant of Zellner's [1962] seemingly unrelated regressions estimator.[19] The restrictions are necessary to ensure linear homogeneity in factor prices, as a result of cost minimization, and symmetry. With these estimated parameters it is possible to estimate the average productivity elasticities for each sample point and quantity–price pair. These estimates then provide the inputs to the last stage of the analysis in which we test— using further regression analysis—whether the levels of discharge constraints implicit in our samples influence these elasticities for all factor input combinations.

In particular, the last stage consists of testing a set of exclusion restrictions for a set of qualitative variables in models of the form given by[20]

$$\alpha_{ij} = \gamma_0 + \sum_{k=1}^{N} \gamma_k \ln P_k + \sum_{s=1}^{S} a_s A_s + \sum_{r=1}^{R} b_r W_r, \qquad (11)$$

where A_s is the qualitative variable for the sth level of restriction on atmospheric residual and W_r the qualitative variable for the rth level of restriction on waterborne residuals. These results provide a direct means of evaluating whether discharge restrictions affect the adjustment of single factor productivity indexes. Moreover, by estimating these equations for all factor pairs we can isolate those inputs most directly impacted.

4. The Process-Analysis Models and Sample Composition

The Russell–Vaughan [1976] models provide a way to represent individually each of three different steelmaking activities—the basic oxygen (BOF), open hearth (OH), and electric are (ARC) furnaces. These models identify 480–541 structural activities (or columns), depending on the steelmaking technology. While a complete description of the models is beyond

[19] Most applications of the translog estimator use the iterative Zellner estimator, rather than the one-step seemingly unrelated regressions. As we note in the next section, the size of our system (nine factor inputs) and associated computer costs prevented its use in our case. In earlier analysis we have tested for the sensitivity of our findings to this selection and there was no appreciable change in our estimates (see Kopp and Smith [1979] for further details).

[20] The adjustment elasticities are calculated for each observation as $\alpha_{ijt} = -k_{jt}\sigma_{ijt}$, where k_{jt} is the cost share for jth factor for observation t and σ_{ijt} the Allen partial elasticity of substitution between factors i and j evaluated for observation t, as defined in note 18. The values of the adjustment elasticities were calculated using the actual cost shares. However, the translog cost function implies that each cost share will be a linear-in-logarithms function of factor prices as $k_{it} = \theta_i + \sum_{k=1}^{n} \gamma_{ik} \ln P_{kt}$. Thus it is reasonable to specify Eq. (11) as an approximate means of standardizing for the effects of factor prices.

the scope of this paper, in order to understand our empirical results and their implications some key features of each type of plant's technology must be reviewed. Figure 1 outlines the processing stages in converting the inputs to each of these plants into finished steel products. The essential feature distinguishing the technologies associated with the plants is the source of heat. The BOF and OH furnaces correspond to hot metal technologies for

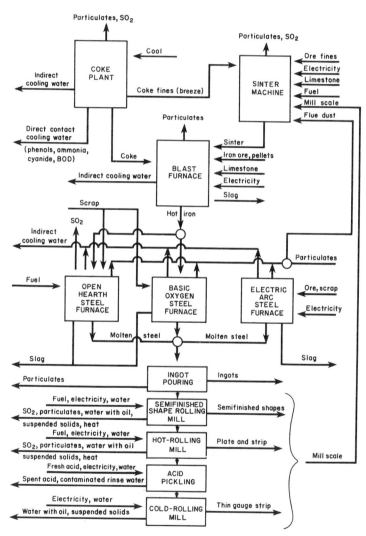

Figure 1 Schematic Overview of Russell-Vaughan model. (From C. S. Russell and W. J. Vaughan, "Steel Production: Processes, Products and Residuals," p. 22. Baltimore, Maryland: Johns Hopkins Univ. Press, 1976.)

producing molten steel. As a result, these furnaces indirectly process iron ore by manufacturing a reductant, coke (in the process activities designated as *coking* in Fig. 1), smelting a type (or mix of types) of this ore with the coke and fluxes to produce molten iron (in the process activities designated as the *blast furnace*), and then further refining the output by oxidizing the unnecessary silicon, manganese, phosphorus, and carbon in either the BOF or OH steelmaking furnaces. The molten steel derived from this sequence of activities then undergoes a similar set of finishing activities to produce ingots, semifinished shapes, plate, and strip, and thin-gauge strip steel products.

One of the most important distinctions among these technologies arises with the source of heat in the final refining stage for molten iron (i.e., in the steelmaking furnace). In the case of the BOF furnace, the molten iron and oxidation reactions are the primary sources of refining heat. These sources impose physical limits on the range of refining temperatures that can be realized within this type of furnace. These limits, in turn, constrain the proportions of cold metal (scrap) to hot metal that can be accommodated in the production of molten steel of any particular alloy content. By contrast, the OH furnace has the option of using auxiliary heat in this refining stage and consequently it can realize a wider range of refining temperatures. This wider temperature span permits the use of a large range of cold to hot metal combinations. Accordingly, we can expect two effects in our summaries of these technologies. First, differences in the source of heat and attendant prospects for materials substitution will result in quite different interrelationships between the inputs' productivity responses (i.e., the α_{ij}s). For example, we would expect differences in the relations between scrap and iron ore and between coal and other fuels with these two technologies. Second, and more important to our objective, we can expect that the two technologies will have quite different responses to restrictions of their discharge of residuals. This conclusion follows directly from the attributes of the two furnaces once it is recognized that the coking and blast furnace activities generate a substantial volume of residuals. In the OH technology we can reduce the total emissions by lowering the proportion of hot to cold metal in the production of the same set of finished steel shapes. Such an action will reduce coking and blast furnace activities without the need for treatment equipment. By contrast, the narrow range of refining temperatures with the BOF furnace limits the scope for such action and, hence, ceteris paribus, increases its reliance on the use of treatment equipment to meet a given discharge reduction standard.

The ARC furnace is the most inflexible technology in its hot to cold metal practices. This technology is designed primarily for direct reduction of molten steel from scrap. The source of heat for this furnace is an electric arc. While all three models include steam-generating electric-power production activities in their plants, the ARC furnace requires the greatest use of these activities. However, this technology is the cleanest of the three since it does not, for the most part, require coking, sintering, and blast furnace activities.

We have classified the residuals accounted for in the models according to whether they are emitted into the atmosphere or the watercourses. Eight types of residuals are separately recorded by the models including biochemical oxygen demand (BOD), oils, phenols, ammonia, suspended solids, heat, SO_2, and particulates. The physical properties of the production activities imply, however, that control over one or two kinds of waterborne residuals will lead to control over the other waterborne effluents.[21] To gauge the propensity of each furnace to generate residuals, we report in Table 1 the percentage reductions in the discharges of each type of residual from a base solution of each model (at the 1973 input price levels, given output levels, and no residuals discharge restrictions) that each of three constraint levels would imply. These constraints were defined to be increments of the minimum technically feasible emission levels of the worst performer of the three plants, so that each type of plant would face the same constraints and all would be capable of being attained. They are defined by[22]

$$C_{Lj} = TM_j + 0.70(D_{BOFj} - TM_j), \qquad (11a)$$
$$C_{Mj} = TM_j + 0.30(D_{BOFj} - TM_j), \qquad (11b)$$
$$C_{Hj} = TM_j, \qquad (11c)$$

[21] A more detailed analysis of the differences in the effects of controls on different residuals is available in Russell and Vaughan [1976].

[22] The minimum technically feasible discharge levels for each residual are given in the following table:

	Minimum technically feasible (TM)	
Water		
BO	444	lb/day
Oils	338	lb/day
Phenols	14	lb/day
Ammonia	41	lb/day
Suspended solids	694	lb/day
Heat	98	10^6 BTU/day
Air		
SO_2	11,500	lb/day
Particulates	1151	lb/day

TABLE 1

Percentage Reductions in Discharges from the Unconstrained Base Case
by Steelmaking Furnace

Residual emissions	Basic oxygen furnace (BOF)			Open hearth (OH)			Electric arc (ARC)		
	Low	Medium	High	Low	Medium	High	Low	Medium	High
Water									
BOD	29.0	67.6	96.6	21.9	64.4	96.3	NL[a]	46.1	94.4
Oils	28.7	66.9	95.5	27.3	66.2	95.4	22.2	63.9	95.1
Phenols	29.2	67.7	99.1	9.1	58.5	98.9	NL	NL	36.4
Ammonia	29.7	69.2	98.1	9.7	60.5	98.5	NL	NL	26.8
Suspended solids	28.3	65.9	94.1	27.0	65.2	93.9	22.9	62.9	93.5
Heat	25.1	67.4	99.2	24.1	67.0	99.2	36.9	72.6	99.0
Air									
SO_2	13.6	31.7	45.2	44.0	55.7	64.5	50.8	61.0	68.8
Particulates	28.9	67.5	96.5	1.2	54.9	95.1	NL	NL	56.3

[a] NL indicates the constraint was not limiting to the model.

where C_{kj} is the constraint at level k [k = L (low), M (medium), H (high)] for discharge into the atmosphere (A) or watercourse (W), j = A, W; TM_j the minimum technically feasible levels for discharge of each type (j = A, W), and $D_{BOF,j}$ the discharge level of the BOF plant to source j. The intermediate constraint level corresponds approximately to the 1977 BPTCA (best practicable technology currently available) and the high constraint to the 1983 BATEA (best available technology economically achievable).

The results in the table clearly indicate that the BOF plant generates the highest levels of both atmospheric and waterborne residuals. The OH plant is somewhat less "dirty," and the ARC is the "cleanest" of the three technologies. Of course, this information alone is not sufficient to determine the character of the response of the α_{ij}s to the level of environmental regulation.

The econometric analysis reported in the next section is based on samples of cost-minimizing solutions from each of these models. Nine inputs are defined for each of the plants: coal, natural gas, fuel oil, scrap, iron ore, labor, maintenance, pollution abatement capital, and all other operating inputs.[23] It should be noted that we have treated plant and equipment (not

[23] The exact composition of the "all other operating inputs" category depends on the steelmaking furnace. In the case of BOF and OH plants it includes limestone, oxygen, lime, fluorspar, water, and sulfuric acid. With the ARC plant is includes oxygen, lime, fluorspar, electrode, and water.

associated with effluent treatment) as a fixed factor with the capacity of each plant held at 2000 short tons of finished steel products per day. This level is approximately comparable to a small United States plant.[24] The output level and mix in terms of finished shapes is held constant for all solutions for the three types of plants. The linear technology of a LP model requires constant returns to scale. Thus, given our analysis of Section 2, the output effects will be of no direct interest in the movements of the average productivity elasticities.

The data sample for each furnace is composed of two types of solutions with approximately half of the observations coming from each: (a) unconstrained cost-minimizing solutions in response to alternative specifications of factor prices; and (b) constrained cost-minimizing solutions in response to variations in the levels of the discharge restrictions at various factor price levels. Our experimental design permits each factor's price to vary individually from the 1973 base level to high and low values based on two considerations: (1) the observed monthly variation in a comparable wholesale price index from 1967 to 1975; and (2) the potential for bias in the estimated cost function due to the nondifferentiability of the production surface (see Griffin [1978a,b] and footnote 26 for more details). These limits are different multiples of the base prices for several of the factors such that solutions for all factors at the high and low values were also included. The variations lead to 21 solutions for each furnace as a result of factor price changes. As we noted, constraints on the discharge of atmospheric and waterborne residuals were each varied as a unit over the low, medium, and high levels of restrictions defined above for each of three price levels (base, low, and high) for all of the factors. Thus, these parameterizations lead to 18 solutions and a total sample of 39 observations for each plant.[25]

One final consideration should be noted before proceeding to the empirical results. It relates to the measurement of the prices for each input. One way to increase the detail in a process-analysis model like those developed by Russell and Vaughan is to classify inputs and their associated outputs

[24] In 1977 the median annual raw steelmaking capacity of integrated U.S. steel plants was 2.30×10^6 tons per year per plant. The lower bound of the second quartile for the capacity distribution of these plants was 1.40×10^6 tons per year per plant. See the Institute for Iron and Steel, *Commentary* **6**, Nos. 1 and 2 (January/February 1977), for additional information.

[25] Each factor price was varied individually over low and high values holding the remaining factors at the base prices. In addition, solutions with all prices at the base, low, and high values were considered, yielding $2 \times 9 + 3 = 21$ observations due to price variation.

The observations due to discharge restrictions were generated by varying air and water restrictions individually over low, medium, and high levels while all factor prices were held at base, low, and high levels. This procedure yields $3 \times 2 \times 3$ or 18 observations.

Thus, the full sample, including both sources of variation, contains 39 solutions for each steelmaking plant.

according to their attributes. For our application, this feature is a distinct advantage since the models identify separate types of coal, iron ore, scrap, fuel oil, etc., according to their individual sulfur or iron content (or combinations of such attributes). However, in such a framework one might reasonably ask whether there are problems in developing price measures for each of the general classes of inputs defined from these more detailed classifications. In our case this issue does not arise since the price of each constituent element within each input class was varied in the same proportion[26] and, therefore, the Hicks [1939] composite commodity theorem can be applied.

5. Results

Our analysis of the importance of factor inputs other than labor and pollution-abatement capital in the firm's response to limits on its discharges of industrial effluents requires that Eq. (11) be estimated for all pairs of inputs with each of the samples corresponding to the three steelmaking technologies.[27] Furthermore, these models are used to test whether

---

[26] The input prices were varied as multiples of the 1973 levels with the low and high levels determined by the following multipliers:

Input	Low	High
Natural gas	0.27	1.73
Coal	0.27	1.73
Fuel oil	0.27	1.73
Iron ore	0.67	1.33
Scrap	0.22	1.78
Labor	0.59	1.41
All other operating	0.50	1.50
Maintenance	0.59	1.41
Pollution abatement capital	0.50	1.50

[27] We report in Tables A.1–A.3 in the Appendix a subset of estimated Allen [1938] partial elasticities of substitution calculated at the mean cost shares for each furnace. Our selection is based on the criterion that the estimated elasticity must be at least twice its asymptotic standard error. The remaining estimates are regarded as noninformative.

Several qualifications should be noted with respect to these estimated elasticities of substitution and the selection procedure. First, the samples used in estimating them exclude the observations with discharge constraints to avoid reflecting their influence on the perceived technology. Second, there are problems with both the evaluation of the asymptotic standard errors for these elasticities (with a translog cost function) and with using conventional inference in these cases. The problem arises because the elasticity is a nonlinear combination of random variables and we do not know how good this approximation is as an estimate of the scale parameter in the estimator's distribution. Further, we do not know that the ratio of estimated coefficient to

the qualitative or dummy variables included to reflect the impact of discharge restrictions would be perceived as exerting a significant effect on the adjustment elasticities for each pair of inputs.[28] Clearly, this procedure involves a substantial volume of statistical results. In order to highlight the central features of our analysis, we have summarized in Table 2 the results of our exclusion tests for these qualitative variables by adjustment elasticity and type of steelmaking furnace. Before discussing these findings, it is important to recognize that the adjustment elasticities (i.e., the α_{ij}s) are not symmetrical.[29] They are derived from the price elasticities of factor demand (as we demonstrated in Section 2). Thus, in principle, our evaluations of the sensitivity of these elasticities to the discharge constraints may well depend on which factor's price is changing. Accordingly, we have performed the tests using both elasticities for each pair. Table 2 reports those cases in which the estimated models for at least one of these elasticities lead to a conclusion that the exclusion restrictions on the qualitative variables must be rejected.[30]

---

asymptotic standard error follows an asymptotic t ratio. Hazilla's [1978] recent sampling experiments suggest that it may have slightly thicker tails and that the properties depend upon whether the translog is an approximation to the true form or is the true specification. Clearly, these issues are beyond the scope of this paper, but they should be recognized in interpreting the estimated features of the technology. For further discussion of these details in relation to the application of pseudo-data, see Kopp and Smith [1979]. More general evaluations of the translog functional form are available in Guilkey and Lovell [1979] and Hazilla [1978].

[28] Tables A.4–A.6 in the Appendix report the estimated equations for those average productivity elasticities rejecting the exclusion restrictions on the qualitative variables associated with the discharge restrictions. We report only the α_{ij}s and not the equations for the opposite variable's price change. These are available on request from the authors.

These equations correspond to the statistics reported in the first, third, and fifth columns of Table 2.

All equations were estimated with OLS. As a result, one might suggest that an Aitken estimator could have been used. The rationale for this suggestion follows from the asymptotic expression for the standard error for the estimated α_{ij}s, since it will vary as the cost share of the ith factor changes. Given the considerations discussed in footnote 27 and the nonstochastic nature of the pseudo-data, we felt this refinement was not warranted.

[29] The estimated average productivity elasticities for the case of cost minimization can be derived from the Allen partial elasticities of substitution (see footnote 20 for more details).

[30] The test used is a simple F test for the exclusion restrictions associated with the qualitative variables (see Kmenta [1971], pp. 370–371). We should acknowledge that, given the nonstochastic character of the pseudo-data, it is applied as a gauge of the magnitude of the impact of the discharge restrictions on the adjustments in factor productivity implied by the model.

In order to provide an inferential interpretation of the test results one would need to identify precisely the source of stochastic elements in the model. The only possible source is the approximation errors associated with fitting a piecewise-linear cost surface with a smooth translog function. There is little reason a priori for these errors to be consistent with classical assumptions; therefore we prefer the interpretation of the test results as a gauge of the impact of the discharge restrictions on each model's adjustment patterns.

TABLE 2

Test Results for Exclusion of Discharge Constraint Variables from Average Productivity Elasticity Equations[a]

| | Furnace | | | | | |
| | BOF | | OH | | ARC | |
Factor inputs[b]	α_{ij}	α_{ji}	α_{ij}	α_{ji}	α_{ij}	α_{ji}
Maintenance–PA capital	47.505	—	48.556	4.261	77.718	19.478
Maintenance–coal	16.410	5.104	—	—	—	—
Maintenance–fuel oil	—	—	—	—	5.514	—
Maintenance–labor	10.290	9.785	—	—	—	—
Maintenance–all other operations	6.178	—	—	—	—	—
PA capital–PA capital	—	—	4.266	4.266	19.480	19.480
PA capital–coal	—	7.725	4.255	11.080	19.478	4.788
PA capital–fuel oil	—	—	—	—	19.478	3.947
PA capital–iron ore	—	30.061	4.251	20.666	19.480	4.570
PA capital–scrap	—	—	4.235	—	19.464	5.630
PA capital–labor	—	30.488	4.244	46.462	19.478	62.849
PA capital–all other operations	—	28.500	4.260	13.566	19.480	17.780
Coal–iron ore	—	10.333	—	—	—	—
Coal–scrap	12.660	4.002	—	—	—	—
Coal–labor	6.688	22.497	—	—	—	—
Coal–all other operations	7.689	16.198	—	—	—	—
Fuel oil–scrap	—	—	—	—	—	4.220
Fuel oil–labor	—	—	—	—	—	4.923
Iron ore–scrap	5.345	—	—	—	—	—
Iron ore–labor	5.398	—	—	—	—	—
Labor–labor	5.721	5.721	—	—	—	—
Labor–all other operations	17.893	10.840	5.979	—	—	—

[a] The statistics reported in this table are the F ratios for the test of the exclusion restrictions on the qualitative variables for discharge restrictions by severity and medium (atmospheric or waterborne) of the constraint. They are reported for those cases in which the null hypothesis can be rejected at the 99% significance level. Otherwise, a dash is indicated in the table.

[b] PA = pollution abatement.

Several general observations can be made with respect to the findings in this table. First, our results indicate that the α_{ij}s for pollution-abatement capital and labor are among the inputs most consistently affected by the discharge constraints across all three technologies. This observation is reinforced once it is recognized that the maintenance input typically includes a substantial measure of indirect labor and would likely be included in the labor measures used for conventional analyses of the productivity impact of environmental regulations.[31]

It should also be noted, however, that these are *not* the only inputs affected by the discharge restrictions. Our results suggest that the specific factors involved will depend upon the technology under study and which factor's price is changed. With two of the three plant types, the OH and ARC furnaces, this latter influence does not seem to be important. The results of the exclusion tests are quite consistent regardless of which factor's price (in a given α_{ij}) is varied. By contrast, the results with the BOF furnace are quite sensitive to which price is varied. In order to interpret these responses, we must consider them relative to the engineering properties of each technology.

The first element in this review relates to the composition of pollution-abatement capital. It includes, by definition, both treatment equipment and that capital equipment used for recovering by-products, since it is often impossible to separate these two activities. Thus, for example, the coking process yields gas and liquid residuals that can, after certain treatment activities, substitute for other sources of auxiliary heat in an OH furnace or be used to generate electricity. The recovery of these by-products will depend upon factor prices. Low fuel oil or natural gas prices would, in this example, limit the prospects for substitution of by-products for purchased fuels. At the same time, the treatment of residuals reduces the level of effluent discharges. Thus, to analyze the response of the adjustment elasticities for particular factor pairs to discharge constraints, we must recognize that some forms of treatment may generate a usable by-product and that these activities would be undertaken for certain factor price levels regardless of whether the discharge restrictions were present. Equally important, the presence of discharge restrictions may reduce the shadow price of obtaining these by-products.[32]

A further dimension of these comparisons relates to the role of cold metal in the steelmaking practices of each furnace. Both the OH and ARC furnaces can accommodate a large proportion of scrap, whereas the BOF cannot. As a result, this prospect for substitution offers a means of meeting discharge restrictions independent of the use of treatment equipment. Where the technology permits individual inputs other than pollution-abatement capital to reduce emissions, the presence of discharge constraints may affect the responsiveness measured in the adjustment elasticities. The furnaces most

[31] A comparison of the treatment of indirect labor in process analysis models supports this conclusion. For more details, see Russell and Vaughan [1976].

[32] The point here is simply that the shadow price of the discharge constraint will be affected by these by-product uses—making it less costly for the plant to meet the restrictions than it would be for those effluents where by-product recovery was not possible.

consistent with this pattern are the OH and ARC, in varying degrees. The arc furnace is, of course, an exclusively cold metal technology. Here the impacts for all inputs, except iron ore and scrap, are through their effects on electric generation. In the case of scrap, we should note that scrap comes in different forms to the model (with different effluent generation propensities), and thus the substitution prospects between it and pollution capital will depend on the presence of discharge constraints.

With the BOF technology the analysis is somewhat more complex and the seemingly inconsistent results, depending on which factor's price is changed, offer clues as to why this is the case. The heavy reliance on hot metal in its steelmaking practice implies that the proportions of coal or iron ore cannot be changed greatly relative to pollution-abatement capital as one of their prices changes. Moreover, the presence or absence of discharge constraints cannot alter these patterns greatly. This kind of furnace can change the coal or iron ore used to those with lower effluent potential, but such an action would imply that all of the constituent elements contributing to the production of hot metal would need to change in order to proceed with such substitution in response to discharge constraints. It would seem that this conclusion is precisely what is indicated by the reversal in test results between α_{ij} and α_{ji} with pollution-abatement capital relative to coal, fuel, oil, iron ore, scrap, and all other operating inputs. Basically, we find a significant impact for the variables taking account of the level of the discharge constraints because all their usage patterns can change in response to a change in the price of pollution-abatement capital.

Overall, these results confirm our initial suggestions. The regulation of effluent discharges affects the adjustments of single factor productivity measures in other ways than simply through changes in labor and pollution-abatement capital. Moreover, the nature of these effects can vary rather substantially with the features of the underlying technology. A review of the estimated equations for the adjustment elasticities in Tables A.4–A.6 in the Appendix suggests that the discharge variables exert a quantitatively significant impact on the level of most of the factor elasticities presented. Thus, practices that measure the change in productivity due to environmental regulations by associating it with one or more factors alone, such as pollution-abatement capital, may seriously understate the effects of these measures on resource allocation decisions and therefore on productivity measures. Equation (10) provides the link between these estimates and the change in single factor productivity measures. Clearly, by using associations comparable to that identified in Eq. (4), we can expect an equally, if not more important (depending upon the magnitude of the respective θ_is) impact on total factor productivity measures.

6. Implications

This analysis has questioned the conventional practice of measuring the impacts of environmental regulations on productivity growth. We have argued that any effort to devise measures capable of associating changes in either single or total factor productivity indexes with one or more environmental regulations must begin with an understanding of how these regulations affect the micro behavior of the firms that must respond to them. In order to substantiate our arguments we developed an analytical relationship between the determinants of the rate of change in any given factor's productivity index and changes in the "parameters" to a firm seeking to allocate resources so as to minimize the costs of producing a given output. Among these parameters are factor prices, output levels, and environmental restrictions.

To understand the productivity consequences of a given set of such regulations, we must appreciate how they are met. The conventional practice assumes it is through the use of such specific inputs as pollution-abatement equipment. Thus, we can estimate the productivity impacts of a given set of regulations by determining the impacts of these specific inputs. Unfortunately, actual production processes are not this simple. Meeting environmental regulations can involve a wide array of subtle changes greatly more involved than simply providing some means of "catching the effluent before it enters a given receptacle medium." These changes involve the switching to different types of raw materials inputs, reallocating the use of labor, and similar changes, each of which is often difficult to isolate. Nonetheless, they are consequences of regulations and will be reflected in the patterns of change of both single and total factor productivity measures. Therefore, in attempting to assign some portion of observed changes in factor productivities to meet regulations we must explicitly model and measure the adjustment processes.

This paper has developed a simple analytical model for these arguments. We have used the optimal solutions from a set of process analysis models for ironmaking and steelmaking plants to evaluate their quantitative importance. For these technologies, simple assignment of the adjustments to a specific factor (or factors) would not be correct. Our estimates indicate that the quantitative impacts of discharge restrictions on the measured factor adjustment elasticities are substantial and extend over a large number of inputs. Thus, estimates seeking to associate a portion of the productivity change to one or two specific factors, as in Denison's analysis, would be biased.

Since our objective was to appraise the methodologies in use and since our example is based on a single set of production processes, we cannot infer from it the magnitude of the biases in measures of the impact of regulation at an aggregate level. Indeed, there are good reasons for questioning the possibility of developing any measures of the effects of environmental regulations on productivity changes at such aggregate levels.

The generation of industrial residuals is a process that must be understood in terms of the physical transformations inherent in each class of production activities. Accordingly, we can expect the responses to restrictions on effluent discharges arising from each type of production process to differ. General rules intended to be applied at aggregate accounting levels that include composites across distinct types of physical production activities would therefore seem either elusive or nonexistent.

Thus, our analysis suggests that measures of the productivity consequences of environmental regulations at the very least must be first carried out at the industry level, where there is some homogeneity in the nature of the physical transformations taking place. In general, they will also require a more detailed accounting of raw material inputs in production activities than has previously been available. Productivity analyses in the past have often attempted to work in value-added terms. These practices can only further obscure the adjustments required to meet environmental regulations.

ACKNOWLEDGMENTS

Thanks are due Thomas Cowing, Robert Crandall, and Bernard Tenenbaum for most constructive comments on an earlier draft of this paper and to Mary Kokoski for her fine research assistance. Initial support for this research was provided by the Directorate of Applied Research of the National Science Foundation.

Technical Appendix

TABLE A1

Informative Allen Partial Elasticities of Substitution: BOF Furnace, Unconstrained Residual Discharges, Nine-Factor Benchmark Case[a]

Inputs	Maintenance	Capital	Coal	Gas	Oil	Ore	Scrap	Labor	Other
Maintenance	-0.3030	—	—	—	—	0.2149	—	—	—
Capital		-205.71	-2.3151	—	—	4.9354	6.7345	-3.2972	6.6085
Coal			-2.2626	305.5	—	0.7679	1.1381	-0.2865	0.2620
Gas				-31173.0	19.1371				
Oil					-415.84				
Ore						-1.1098	0.9112	0.3346	
Scrap							-17.248		
Labor								-0.3758	
Other									

[a] Informative estimates are those estimates in which the ratio of the estimated Allen elasticity of substitution to its respective asymptotic standard error exceeds 2. For a discussion of the rationale for this screening criterion, see Kopp and Smith [1979].

TABLE A2

Informative Allen Partial Elasticities of Substitution OH Furnace, Unconstrained Residual Discharges, Nine-Factor Case[a]

Inputs	Maintenance	Capital	Coal	Gas	Oil	Ore	Scrap	Labor	Other
Maintenance	-0.2681		—	—	—	0.2166	—	—	—
Capital	-379.26	—	-3.9804	-82.856	-34.484	7.6487	—	-4.8003	14.7329
Coal			-3.321	6.7856	7.9171	0.4426	1.8918	-0.1887	—
Gas				-259.94	—	—	—	—	—
Oil					-85.586	—	—	—	—
Ore						-2.0378	2.8356	0.2397	—
Scrap							-12.559	0.4425	—
Labor								-0.3505	—
Other									0.3117

[a] Informative estimates are those estimates in which the ratio of the estimated Allen elasticity of substitution to its respective asymptotic standard error exceeds 2. For a discussion of the rationale for this screening criterion, see Kopp and Smith [1979].

TABLE A3

Informative Allen Partial Elasticities of Substitution: ARC Furnace, Unconstrained Residual Discharges, Nine-Factor Benchmark Case[a]

Inputs	Maintenance	Capital	Coal	Gas	Oil	Ore	Scrap	Labor	Other
Maintenance	−0.4264	—	—	—	—	—	0.0527	—	—
Capital		−1134.4	—	—	—	—	—	—	11.9182
Coal			−14.4	—	—	—	—	—	—
Gas				−39.608	28.925	—	—	—	—
Oil					−22.284	—	—	—	—
Ore						−10.033	—	—	—
Scrap							—	0.2851	0.6244
Labor								−0.6739	—
Other									—

[a] Informative estimates are those estimates in which the ratio of the estimated Allen elasticity of substitution to its respective asymptotic standard error exceeds 2. For a discussion of the rationale for this screening criterion, see Kopp and Smith [1979].

TABLE A4

Estimated Determinants of Average Productivity Elasticities: BOF Furnace[a]

	Elasticities				
Independent variables	Maintenance/ PA capital	Maintenance/ coal	Maintenance/ labor	Maintenance/ other	Coal/ scrap
Intercept	−0.0135	0.0214	0.0437	−0.0008	−0.0667
	(−12.2145)	(3.9773)	(7.3345)	(−0.2830)	(−26.9628)
Maintenance	−0.0044	−0.0691	−0.1113	−0.0547	0.0038
	(−2.3390)	(−7.5923)	(−11.0377)	(−11.0415)	(0.8968)
PA capital	0.0021	0.0005	0.0054	−0.0012	−0.0008
	(1.4070)	(0.0727)	(0.67936)	(−0.3068)	(−0.2365)
Coal	0.0033	−0.0576	0.0597	0.0235	0.0147
	(3.9914)	(−14.2235)	(13.3064)	(10.6696)	(7.8612)
Gas	0.0001	−0.0069	0.0005	−0.0007	−0.0001
	(0.0753)	(−1.6989)	(0.1039)	(−0.3098)	(−0.0381)
Oil	0.0002	−0.0126	0.0047	0.0024	0.0013
	(0.2828)	(−3.1063)	(1.0470)	(1.0765)	(0.6994)
Ore	−0.0051	0.0462	0.0810	0.0543	−0.0075
	(−2.1319)	(4.0155)	(6.3460)	(8.6738)	(−1.4115)
Scrap	−0.0011	0.0056	0.0080	0.0051	−0.0155
	(−1.5375)	(1.5951)	(2.0383)	(2.6754)	(−9.5449)
Labor	0.0070	0.0603	−0.1014	0.0403	0.0021
	(3.7563)	(6.6271)	(−10.0584)	(8.1425)	(0.5007)
Other	−0.0033	0.0241	0.0431	−0.0734	0.0014
	(−2.1985)	(3.3524)	(5.4070)	(−18.7339)	(0.4249)
WATER 1	0.0108	−0.0328	−0.0246	−0.0112	0.0131
	(13.7347)	(−8.5607)	(−5.7782)	(−5.3572)	(7.4327)
WATER 2	0.0086	−0.0393	−0.0287	−0.0115	0.0145
	(8.3738)	(−7.8436)	(−5.1597)	(−4.2029)	(6.2884)
WATER 3	0.0038	−0.0399	−0.0298	−0.0097	0.0146
	(3.6415)	(−7.9484)	(−5.3512)	(−3.5679)	(6.3292)
AIR 1	0.0059	−0.0115	−0.0206	−0.0067	0.0070
	(7.4137)	(−3.0082)	(−4.8433)	(−3.2122)	(3.9770)
AIR 2	0.0064	−0.0145	−0.0192	−0.0064	0.0076
	(6.1686)	(−2.8815)	(−3.4585)	(−2.3669)	(3.2867)
AIR 3	0.0057	−0.0108	−0.0145	−0.0051	0.0070
	(5.4870)	(−2.1494)	(−2.6118)	(−1.8713)	(3.0346)
R^2 =	0.9404	0.9797	0.9718	0.9673	0.9022

[a] Figures in parentheses are t ratios.

		Elasticities			
Coal/ labor	Coal/ other	Ore/ scrap	Ore/ labor	Labor/ labor	Labor/ other
0.2012	0.0269	−0.0278	−0.0381	−0.0132	0.0072
(6.7941)	(2.6896)	(−10.0390)	(−9.5126)	(−0.8536)	(2.3326)
0.1321	0.0533	0.0126	0.0820	−0.1401	0.0497
(2.6354)	(3.1416)	(2.6907)	(12.0839)	(−5.3364)	(9.4722)
0.0211	0.0038	0.0006	0.0027	−0.0180	−0.0008
(0.5322)	(0.2813)	(0.1740)	(0.4989)	(−0.8680)	(−0.2044)
−0.2418	−0.0867	−0.0017	0.0371	−0.0795	0.0262
(−10.8369)	(−11.4894)	(−0.8385)	(12.2970)	(−6.8034)	(11.2117)
−0.0088	−0.0042	−0.0005	−0.0011	−0.0046	−0.0012
(−0.3922)	(−0.5572)	(−0.2266)	(−0.3747)	(−0.3924)	(−0.5162)
−0.0022	−0.0078	0.0003	0.0023	−0.0080	0.0011
(−0.9978)	(−1.0365)	(0.1289)	(0.7586)	(−0.6868)	(0.4607)
0.1124	0.0594	−0.0134	−0.0471	−0.1120	0.0513
(1.7726)	(2.7690)	(−2.2664)	(−5.4836)	(−3.3739)	(7.7306)
0.0106	0.0054	−0.0147	0.0052	−0.0144	0.0050
(0.5468)	(0.8240)	(−8.1237)	(1.9778)	(−1.4185)	(2.4550)
−0.0603	0.0490	0.0104	−0.1216	0.4783	−0.0629
(−1.2034)	(2.8900)	(2.2137)	(−17.9292)	(18.2207)	(−11.9898)
0.0581	−0.0711	0.0061	0.0389	−0.0645	−0.0735
(1.4658)	(−5.3034)	(1.6559)	(7.2568)	(−3.1044)	(−17.7190)
−0.1232	−0.0461	0.0083	−0.0150	0.0574	−0.0217
(−5.8267)	(−6.4453)	(4.2114)	(−5.2453)	(5.1885)	(−9.7991)
−0.1356	−0.0489	0.0094	−0.0126	0.0647	−0.0214
(−4.9044)	(−5.2270)	(3.6518)	(−3.3697)	(4.4667)	(−7.4050)
−0.1317	−0.0451	0.0099	−0.0094	0.0613	−0.0178
(−4.7656)	(−4.8193)	(3.8272)	(−2.5217)	(4.2351)	(−6.1552)
−0.0442	−0.0141	0.0068	−0.0005	0.0246	−0.0081
(−2.0913)	(−1.9733)	(3.4484)	(−0.1706)	(2.2198)	(−3.6706)
−0.0429	−0.0139	0.0071	−0.0012	0.0290	−0.0084
(−1.5522)	(−1.4873)	(2.7642)	(−0.3104)	(2.0062)	(−2.8950)
−0.0286	−0.0094	0.0067	−0.0020	0.0225	−0.0065
(−1.0335)	(−1.0002)	(2.6032)	(−0.5419)	(1.5575)	(−2.2621)
0.9471	0.9660	0.9011	0.9831	0.9543	0.9702

TABLE A5

Estimated Determinants of Average Productivity Elasticities: OH Furnace[a]

Independent variables	Elasticities							
	Maintenance/ PA capital	PA Capital/ PA capital	PA Capital/ coal	PA Capital/ ore	PA Capital/ scrap	PA Capital/ labor	PA Capital/ other	Labor/ other
Intercept	0.0714	−0.8868	−2.7342	7.1707	−1.9892	−2.6594	5.6594	0.0096
	(6.2819)	(−0.6629)	(−1.4579)	(1.3562)	(−1.4443)	(−1.5165)	(1.3813)	(−4.0605)
Maintenance	0.3446	−1.1240	−1.5535	4.4758	−1.1099	−1.4195	3.4636	0.0409
	(17.9160)	(−0.4962)	(−0.4892)	(0.4999)	(−0.4760)	(−0.4780)	(0.4993)	(10.2512)
PA capital	−0.0076	1.9580	2.7410	−7.7468	2.0312	2.5634	−6.0008	−0.0035
	(−0.5012)	(1.0928)	(1.0913)	(−1.0940)	(1.1012)	(1.0914)	(−1.0936)	(−1.1069)
Coal	−0.0380	2.0528	2.8229	−8.0979	2.0933	2.7222	−6.2761	0.0180
	(−4.4391)	(2.0363)	(1.9974)	(−2.0323)	(2.0159)	(2.0599)	(−2.0328)	(10.1336)
Gas	−0.0084	1.8758	2.6233	−7.4123	1.9341	2.4580	−5.7440	−0.0008
	(−0.9792)	(1.8607)	(1.8562)	(−1.8603)	(1.8635)	(1.8600)	(−1.8604)	(−0.4273)
Oil	−0.0134	1.8827	2.6267	−7.4373	1.9421	2.4683	−5.7640	−0.0008
	(−1.5684)	(1.8676)	(1.8586)	(−1.8665)	(1.8712)	(1.8678)	(−1.8669)	(−0.4340)

Ore	-0.0846 (-3.4774)	-8.2855 (-2.8916)	-11.5894 (-2.8851)	32.6623 (2.8841)	-8.5823 (-2.9094)	-10.8139 (-2.8790)	25.3885 (2.8931)	0.0337 (6.6800)
Scrap	-0.0266 (-3.5724)	-1.5102 (-1.7238)	-2.1214 (-1.7272)	5.9442 (1.7166)	-1.5639 (-1.7340)	-1.9685 (-1.7141)	4.6325 (1.7265)	0.0102 (6.6237)
Labor	-0.0884 (-4.5977)	4.6977 (2.9739)	6.6114 (2.0820)	-18.5068 (-2.0671)	4.8263 (2.0696)	5.9995 (-2.0205)	-14.7185 (-2.0714)	-0.0433 (-10.8559)
Other	-0.0403 (-2.6488)	-5.1550 (-2.8772)	-7.2235 (-2.8758)	20.3763 (2.8774)	-5.2782 (-2.8615)	-6.7413 (-2.8703)	15.7185 (2.8646)	-0.0602 (-19.0601)
WATER 1	-0.0127 (-1.5696)	2.8466 (2.9808)	3.9693 (2.9648)	-11.2068 (-2.9690)	2.9135 (2.9634)	3.7092 (2.9629)	-8.6969 (-2.9735)	-0.0091 (-5.4149)
WATER 2	-0.0029 (-0.2758)	0.2471 (0.1978)	0.3222 (0.1840)	-0.9326 (-0.1889)	0.2440 (0.1897)	0.3024 (0.1847)	-0.7358 (-0.1924)	-0.0083 (-3.7627)
WATER 3	0.0007 (0.0630)	0.0481 (0.0385)	0.0506 (0.0289)	-0.1625 (-0.0329)	0.0447 (0.0348)	0.0495 (0.0303)	-0.1380 (-0.0361)	-0.0050 (-2.2735)
AIR 1	0.0061 (0.7492)	2.5592 (2.6798)	3.5865 (2.6788)	-10.0906 (-2.6733)	2.6268 (2.6718)	3.3454 (2.2495)	-7.8398 (-2.6805)	-0.0028 (-1.6876)
AIR 2	0.0127 (1.1955)	2.8185 (2.2565)	3.9451 (2.2530)	-11.1101 (-2.2505)	2.8965 (2.2525)	3.6831 (2.2495)	-8.6323 (-2.2566)	-0.0033 (-1.5038)
AIR 3	0.0112 (1.0586)	0.6287 (0.5033)	0.8744 (0.4994)	-2.4566 (-0.4976)	0.6433 (0.5003)	0.8129 (0.4965)	-1.9231 (-0.5027)	-0.0031 (-1.4170)
$R^2 =$	0.9510	0.7584	0.7564	0.7579	0.7577	0.7580	0.7581	0.9698

[a] Figures in parentheses are t ratios.

TABLE A6

Estimated Determinants of Average Productivity Elasticities: ARC Furnace[a]

Independent variables	Maintenance/ PA capital	Maintenance/ oil	Elasticities PA Capital/ PA capital	PA Capital/ coal	PA Capital/ oil	PA Capital/ ore	PA Capital/ scrap	PA Capital/ labor	PA Capital/ other
Intercept	-0.0102 (-13.2749)	0.0249 (2.5471)	-270.7381 (-4.1746)	246.7880 (4.1891)	146.5498 (4.1892)	444.8604 (4.1894)	-984.8015 (-4.1911)	-779.4791 (-4.1907)	1202.5162 (4.1894)
Maintenance	-0.0011 (-0.8407)	-0.0269 (-1.6223)	27.1732 (0.2475)	-24.6706 (-0.2473)	-14.6451 (-0.2472)	-44.4759 (-0.2474)	98.4858 (0.2475)	79.9696 (0.2476)	-120.2305 (-0.2474)
PA capital	0.0022 (2.1164)	0.0051 (0.3864)	241.6858 (2.7825)	-219.5208 (-2.7823)	-130.3623 (-2.7825)	-395.6970 (-2.7824)	875.5769 (2.7823)	710.9532 (2.7826)	-1069.6682 (-2.7825)
Coal	0.0001 (0.1919)	0.0042 (0.5636)	-20.7035 (-0.4236)	18.7889 (0.4232)	11.1701 (0.4237)	33.9015 (0.4237)	-75.0156 (-0.4236)	-60.8974 (-0.4236)	91.6368 (0.4236)
Gas	0.0001 (0.2262)	-0.0297 (-4.0336)	-16.9249 (-0.3463)	15.3757 (0.3463)	9.0975 (0.3451)	27.7153 (0.3464)	-61.3212 (-0.3463)	-49.7800 (-0.3463)	74.9147 (0.3463)
Oil	0.0001 (0.2340)	-0.0039 (-0.5340)	-16.0568 (-0.3285)	14.5872 (0.3286)	8.6549 (0.3283)	26.2940 (0.3286)	-58.1749 (-0.3285)	-47.2257 (-0.3285)	71.0728 (0.3286)

Ore	0.0007 (0.4143)	0.0096 (0.4604)	−29.2616 (−0.2107)	26.5873 (0.2107)	15.7879 (0.2107)	47.8915 (0.2106)	−106.0471 (−0.2107)	−86.0689 (−0.2106)	129.5253 (0.2107)
Scrap	0.0004 (0.7001)	0.0168 (2.6187)	40.8706 (0.9623)	−37.1362 (−0.9626)	−22.0378 (−0.9619)	−66.9297 (−0.9624)	147.9739 (0.9616)	120.2650 (0.9626)	−180.8738 (−0.9622)
Labor	0.0007 (0.5182)	0.0189 (1.1412)	9.3473 (0.0851)	−8.4807 (−0.0850)	−5.0326 (−0.0850)	−15.2918 (−0.0851)	33.8824 (0.0852)	27.3785 (0.0848)	−41.3425 (−0.0851)
Other	−0.0023 (−2.2764)	0.0138 (1.0564)	−210.6171 (−2.4248)	191.3111 (2.4247)	113.6131 (2.4250)	344.8435 (2.4248)	−763.0263 (−2.4246)	−619.5330 (−2.4248)	932.0717 (2.4246)
WATER 1	−0.0102 (18.5663)	0.0024 (0.3451)	275.2214 (5.9447)	−249.9827 (−5.9442)	−148.4491 (−5.9445)	−450.6004 (−5.9443)	997.0755 (5.9442)	809.5723 (5.9445)	−1218.0736 (−5.9445)
WATER 2	0.0081 (11.2552)	0.0011 (0.1258)	0.1397 (0.0023)	−0.1199 (−0.0022)	−0.0711 (−0.0022)	−0.2161 (−0.0022)	0.4725 (0.0022)	0.3848 (0.0022)	−0.5895 (−0.0022)
WATER 3	0.0037 (5.2160)	0.0005 (0.0528)	0.0258 (0.0004)	−0.0202 (−0.0004)	−0.0120 (−0.0004)	−0.0364 (−0.0004)	0.0780 (0.0004)	0.0638 (0.0004)	−0.1007 (−0.0004)
AIR 1	0.0014 (2.6042)	−0.0282 (−4.0467)	275.0131 (5.9402)	−249.8011 (−5.9399)	−148.3704 (−5.9413)	−450.2726 (−5.9400)	996.3547 (5.9399)	808.9884 (5.9403)	−1217.1809 (−5.9402)
AIR 2	0.0018 (2.4801)	−0.0088 (−0.9633)	306.0787 (5.0547)	−278.0141 (−5.0544)	−165.1081 (−5.0550)	−501.1321 (−5.0545)	1108.8921 (5.0544)	900.3720 (5.0548)	−1354.6690 (−5.0547)
AIR 3	0.0018 (2.4807)	−0.0047 (−0.5183)	306.1511 (5.0559)	−278.0798 (−5.0556)	−165.1430 (−5.0561)	−501.2505 (−5.0557)	1109.1543 (5.0566)	900.5849 (5.0560)	−1354.9892 (−5.0559)
$R^2 =$	0.9566	0.7226	0.8557	0.8557	0.8557	0.8557	0.8556	0.8557	0.8557

[a] Figures in parentheses are t ratios.

11

Regulation, Technological Change, and Productivity in Commercial Banking[1]

Charles F. Haywood

College of Business and Economics
University of Kentucky
Lexington, Kentucky

Government regulation, in some degree, has been a feature of commercial banking in the United States since the Continental Congress and the Commonwealth of Pennsylvania chartered the Bank of North America in 1780. Within the past decade, new forms of regulation have caused increasing concern within commercial banking about the "cost burden" of regulation. Representatives of trade and professional organizations serving commercial banks have recently established an interassociation task force to collect information on the costs of regulation. The three federal agencies that regulate commercial banks—the Comptroller of the Currency, the Board of Governors of the Federal Reserve System, and the Federal Deposit Insurance Corporation—now have units within their respective organizations to analyze regulatory policies and practices with a view to reducing

[1] This paper is drawn in part from the author's study "Regulation, Structure, and Technological Change in the Consumer Financial Services Industry" prepared for Abt Associates, Inc., with the financial support of the National Science Foundation RANN (NSF-C76-18548), *The Costs and Benefits of Public Regulation of Consumer Financial Services* (Cambridge: Abt Associates, Inc., 1979). The author's participation in that study was cost-shared by the American Bankers Association.

the burden of regulation. Similar efforts are being encouraged at the state level by the Conference of State Bank Supervisors. Scholarly interest in the measurement of productivity in commercial banking, one of the major economic sectors closely regulated by government, would be a timely development.

This paper takes as its purpose the encouragement of research into the measurement of productivity in regulated financial intermediaries. Because of the author's background and experience, the paper's focus is on commercial banks, but the discussion could be readily extended to include such other types of financial institutions as mutual savings banks, savings and loan associations, credit unions, and finance companies.

The approach of the paper is that of a commentary—"a series of illustrative or explanatory notes." The first two "notes" or sections provide background information on commercial banking and the regulatory regime under which it operates. In the third section the discussion of regulation is extended in a description of the nature of the "compliance burden" imposed by new legislation during the past decade. The problem of measurement of productivity in commercial banking is addressed in the fourth section, including some partial and fragmentary data on changes in productivity. The only aspect of productivity in commercial banking that has been given extensive study is economies of scale; the findings are briefly summarized in the fifth section. The next two sections report on work I have previously published dealing with the effect of regulation on technology and technological change in commercial banking. The paper ends with a brief summary.

Unhappily, the notes making up this commentary fall far short of providing an integrated approach to the subject at hand. The reason is that inquiry into the factors affecting productivity in commercial banks and other financial intermediaries is an undeveloped area of research. That is why encouragement of research has been taken as the purpose of this paper.

1. Some Background Information

Approximately 14,500 commercial banks provide deposit and loan services to businesses, consumers, and governmental entities in the United States. Some 2300 of these banks are affiliated with 350 or so multibank holding companies, so that the number of separate banking organizations is about 12,500. There is great diversity in the size of banking organizations, currently ranging from less than $1 million to almost $100 billion in assets. Most commercial banks are relatively small enterprises. Between 50 and 60% of the commercial banks have fewer than 30 employees. Only about 10% have more than 125 employees. The 100 largest banking organizations, all with assets in excess of $1 billion, account for 45% of the total domestic deposits in commercial banks.

Under long-standing federal policy, the branching of commercial banks is governed by state laws. Also, since 1956 bank holding companies have been barred from acquiring banks in more than one state unless permitted by the state in which the acquisition is made. The effect on branching and holding companies has been to limit interstate operation of multioffice banking organizations to a small number of "grandfathered" situations, and interstate expansion of multioffice banking has been effectively prohibited. Of course, it is not necessary to have offices in another state in order to conduct business there. Many banks have extensive interstate operations, aided in some instances by representatives, loan-production offices, and Edge Act corporations (dealing with customers significantly engaged in foreign commerce). The variegated forms of organization and operations as well as size differences in commercial banking organizations greatly complicate the task of describing, much less estimating, input–output relationships.

Elsewhere I have suggested that it is useful to think of the production process of commercial banking as having two stages [Haywood, 1977]. The inputs to the first stage are land, labor, capital, and management. The outputs of this stage are a set of depository and payment services and a "throughput" in the form of excess reserves, the material from which loans and investments are derived. In the second stage, the "throughput" is treated with additional doses of labor, capital, and management to yield a set of loan-related services and the earning assets of the bank. The conventional approach to the production problem in commercial banking, as reflected in leading texts and other relevant literature, was—and mainly continues to be—to treat it as a problem in funds management or portfolio allocation. As the role of real resources is thus neglected, it is not surprising that the conventional approach has given little or no attention to productivity analysis.

Since the mid-1960s, when I began lecturing to bankers on the economics of managing real as well as financial resources, their receptivity to such exhortations has intensified as they have sought to cope with declining trends in earnings margins and capital positions. As shown in Table 1, the ratio of net current operating earnings to gross revenues, which I have characterized as the "pretax earnings margin," was 21.85% in 1969. That is, out of every $100 of gross revenue, $21.85 fell through to the bottom line before adjustments for nonrecurring items of income and expense and before payment of income taxes. The margin decreased in each of the next seven years, falling to 12.29% by 1976. A slight improvement, to 12.80%, was registered in 1977. It is expected that data for 1978, when available, will

TABLE 1

Pretax Earnings Margin,[a]
Commercial Banks, 1969–1977

Year	Percent
1969	21.85
1970	20.53
1971	18.46
1972	18.02
1973	16.42
1974	13.57
1975	13.49
1976	12.29
1977	12.80

[a] Net operating income before taxes and securities gains as a percentage of total operating revenue.
Source: Federal Deposit Insurance Corporation. *Annual Report*, various years.

show some further improvement, as many banks individually reported relatively significant increases in net earnings in 1978 and early 1979. However, decline in the pretax earnings margin has been a persistent trend since the late 1950s. Changes in reporting requirements and accounting treatment in 1969 preclude comparison of the data in Table 1 with reported data for years prior to 1969. Under the old method of reporting, the pretax earnings margin declined by about one-third between 1957 and 1968. The relative decrease from 1969 to 1977 for the data in Table 1 was about 40%.

Table 2 shows the pretax and after-tax earnings margins as percentages of total assets. The decline in the pretax earnings margin is less pronounced when this measure of profitability is used, the decrease being from 1.30% in 1969 to 0.93% in 1977. Two developments are implied: (1) Commercial banks have been working their assets harder, by reducing the ratio of non-earning cash to total assets and by increasing the ratio of loans and investments to total assets. (2) Income from noninterest sources—service charges, trust department fees, direct leasing, and similar sources—rose at a slightly faster rate than growth in total assets. However, fee income has not contributed as much to improvement in bank earnings as many banks had hoped.

The after-tax earnings margin held up fairly well through 1973, but dropped from 0.85% in that year to 0.71% in 1977. To bolster their after-tax earnings margins in the face of decline in the pretax margin, commercial banks have shifted the composition of their investment portfolios toward state and local government obligations, which are exempt from federal

TABLE 2

Pretax and After-Tax Earnings
as Percentages of Total Assets,
Commercial Banks, 1969–1977 [a]

	Percent	
Year	Pretax	After-tax
1969	1.30	0.84
1970	1.31	0.89
1971	1.11	0.87
1972	1.07	0.83
1973	1.12	0.85
1974	1.06	0.81
1975	0.97	0.78
1976	0.88	0.70
1977	0.93	0.71

[a] Source: Federal Deposit Insurance Corporation, *Annual Report*, various years.

income tax, and away from U.S. Government debt and corporate bonds. The decline in the after-tax earnings margin in 1974–1977 reflects a combination of factors, including higher funds costs in 1974, larger provisions for loan losses in 1975 and 1976, and a decrease in yields on tax-exempts and other securities in 1977.

Commercial banking is financially a highly leveraged business. Total equity accounted for only 7% of total resources in 1977. In 1969 it was 7.5%, having been close to 10% in the late 1950s. Erosion of equity positions has been a source of concern to the bank regulatory agencies as well as to bank directors and management. The downward trend in earnings margins has not been favorable to the sale of new stock issues nor to adequate building of equity positions through retained earnings, which for many years have accounted for more than 80% of the growth in bank capital.

Operating with much-reduced earnings margins and thin capital positions, commercial banks have become increasingly sensitive to changes in regulation that impinge adversely on costs and productivity. There is a great need for, but also a dearth of, meaningful assessments of the benefits and costs of regulatory changes.

2. The Regulatory Regime

The regulatory regime under which commercial banks operate has been characterized by Arthur Burns, then Federal Reserve Chairman, as a "jurisdictional tangle that boggles the mind." Commercial banks are regulated by the federal government and by the states. At the federal level, three agencies—the Comptroller of the Currency, the Board of Governors of the Federal Reserve System, and the Federal Deposit Insurance Corporation—have regulatory purviews that overlap in various ways and are distinctive in other ways. In addition, the Treasury Department, the Justice Department, Department of Labor, Securities and Exchange Commission, and Federal Trade Commission have certain specialized responsibilities in the regulation of commercial banks and bank holding companies. Any attempt at succinct description necessarily involves a highly selective approach. The following discussion, therefore, focuses on those aspects of banking regulation that seem most relevant to inquiry into the effects of regulation on technology. Our approach is influenced by studies of other regulated industries indicating that the specific effects of regulation on technology appear to depend upon the regulatory techniques employed as well as the intentions of the regulatory agencies. The discussion draws heavily from a recent paper of ours, funded in part by the National Science Foundation [Haywood, 1979].

The regulation of commercial banking organizations encompasses a number of types of regulatory activity:

1. control of entry through chartering, branch approval, and other licensing procedures;

2. authorization or proscription of specific financial practices, activities or services through legislation and administrative rule making;

3. periodic examination for compliance with laws, rules, and standards of sound financial management;

4. maintenance of selected price ceilings—deposit interest ceilings and loan rate ("usury") ceilings;

5. scrutiny of mergers and acquisitions for adverse competitive and financial implications;

6. protection of consumers as borrowers and investors through disclosure requirements and other restrictions on sharp or abusive practices.

The regulations are directed to three general purposes involving protection of the public: (i) against instability in financial markets and the failure of banking institutions; (ii) against undue concentration of market power; and (iii) against sharp or unfair dealing.

For many years, mainly from the early 1930s to the early 1960s, banking regulation was concerned almost entirely with the first of these three purposes—prevention of market instability and institutional failure. Such policy was established in federal legislation in the period 1933–1935, which also set a pattern for extensive changes in state laws.

Emerging concern with undue concentration of economic power was reflected in the Federal Reserve's long, drawn-out attempt to break up the old Transamerica Corporation in the late 1940s and early 1950s. However, federal policy did not become well established until after the passage of the Bank Holding Company Act (1956) and the Bank Merger Act (1960), the Supreme Court decisions in the Philadelphia (1963) and Lexington (1964) cases, the 1966 amendments of the Bank Holding Company Act and Bank Merger Act, and the 1970 amendment of the Bank Holding Company Act.

Federal concern with protection of consumers as investors dates, of course, from the Securities Exchange Acts of 1933 and 1934. It may be that by making the issuance and marketing of corporate securities more costly, these acts contributed to the subsequent growth of commercial banks, but the acts were not aimed especially at such institutions. Indeed, commercial banks, but not bank holding companies, were exempted from the direct purview of the Securities and Exchange Commission, and the federal bank regulatory agencies were charged with responsibility for regulation of banks in the issuance of securities. The passage of the Truth-in-Lending Act in 1968 marked the beginning of federal policy to protect consumers as borrowers and debtors. Subsequent legislation has greatly expanded the scope of federal policy, but state laws also continue to be important in the protection of consumers in loan and credit transactions.

Federal regulation of commercial banks has thus gone through a layering process: policy aimed at reducing instability and failure of commercial banks since 1933; policy aimed at preventing undue concentration since 1956; and policy aimed at consumer protection since 1968. The relative importance of these purposes continues to evolve.

Reflecting the basic concern with instability and failure, federal regulatory technique has been "structure oriented." Such orientation is obvious in policies governing entry, mergers, and acquisitions. Regulation of the types of assets that institutions can acquire and the types of liabilities they can issue can also be regarded as a regulatory technique affecting structure. Examination of institutions for soundness similarly has a structural orientation. The rationale for prohibition of interest on demand deposits and the regulation of interest rates on savings and time accounts is also structural.

In the free-market model based on Euro-American cultural values and externalities conducive to the mobilization of capital and a high degree of development of entrepreneurship, technology can be said to be the basic determinant of industry structure. In actual fact, however, regulatory intervention has constrained or biased the influence of technology on structure in various industries. In commercial banking in the United States, regulation has been the dominant influence on structure at least since the early 1930s.

This does not mean that technology has not affected structure, but in the absence of structurally oriented regulation, the structure of commercial banking would almost certainly be different from what it is today.

Has regulation, through its dominant influence on structure, exerted indirectly a significant effect on technology in commercial banking? To be sure, we should also ask whether restrictions on output mix—the types of assets, liabilities, and services permitted to commercial banks—have directly exerted significant effects on technology. Also, what have been the effects of the examination process and controls on certain prices? At the present time, impressions and fragmentary evidence provide the only basis for answers to these questions.

It is clear, however, that the structural orientation of regulation, especially restrictions on multioffice banking, has maintained a more proliferated banking structure than would have otherwise evolved over the past several decades. Local banking markets have often been characterized by some economists, as well as by Justice Department attorneys, as "oligopolistic," but the Chamberlin model of monopolistic competition is, I think, closer to the mark. Product differentiation is evident in bank marketing programs and locational strategies. Excess capacity and less-than-optimal levels of output, although not obvious to the naked eye, are readily apparent on close observation. Modest increases in output could be achieved by many banks at declining average cost, but such increases are constrained by expectations that market price would decline more rapidly than average cost. Though admittedly impressionistic, these observations, which come from many years of firsthand experience in and observation of commercial banks, tend to confirm the relevance of the Chamberlin model and imply that regulation has been conducive to some misallocation of resources in commercial banking, with adverse implications for productivity.

3. The New Regulatory Orientation

The new layer of banking regulation put in place since 1968 does not have the structural orientation that has been such an important part of the regulatory regime since the early 1930s. The new regulation is oriented to performance in that banks are required to conform to certain procedures in the conduct of their business. Thus, a "compliance" orientation has developed to a degree not previously found in banking regulation.

Contributing to this compliance orientation have been certain measures affecting businesses in general, such as regulations dealing with occupational safety and health, discrimination in employment, and environmental protection. Measures specifically affecting banking have dealt with truth in lending, real-estate settlement practices, discrimination in lending, bank security and protection, fair credit billing, credit-card distribution and liability limits, creditor remedies, insider transactions, and performance in serving local credit needs, including low- and moderate-income neighborhoods. To help meet their expanded responsibilities for enforcement, the federal bank regulatory agencies have instituted an additional type of bank examination, the "compliance examination." All insured commercial banks are now subject to two distinct and separate types of examinations: the traditional examination for safety and soundness and the compliance examination.

Compliance regulation directly affects the costs of doing business. Additional forms are required to effect certain types of transactions. Specific types of files and records must be maintained. In some instances, new procedures and new equipment need to be put in place. Mailings of various kinds of general and special notices, of an informational or advisory nature, are required. As the banking business involves the handling of large numbers of transactions at small cost per transaction, compliance requirements that increase the time and paperwork needed to execute a transaction can easily have a relatively large effect on per-item and total costs.

In addition to the ongoing costs directly associated with compliance activities, significant "startup" and "maintenance" costs may be incurred. New regulations and changes in regulations must be read and interpreted. New forms and procedures must be designed, or existing ones revised. Personnel must be trained and retrained. Training costs are compounded by employee turnover and by internal reassignments and promotions. Moreover, deficiencies in compliance actions, errors in forms, or mistakes in disclosure calculations may expose a bank to civil damage suits or to regulatory orders to effect restitution. Restitution is currently a hotly debated issue. Small errors in the calculation of annual percentage rates on consumer installment loans, revealed on compliance examinations, can result in relatively substantial administrative expenses to make and explain to customers numerous refunds that individually amount to only a few dollars. Also, there is some question whether the typical consumer borrower attaches much significance to differences in stated annual percentage rates in comparison to the dollar amount of interest charges set forth in the loan agreement.

Some of the larger banks have found it necessary to establish compliance departments, staffed by one or more attorneys and paralegal assistants. In a recent study sponsored by the National Science Foundation, Batko [1979] has reported on survey findings indicating that "commercial and savings banks with less than $100 million in assets were somewhat less compliant . . .

than larger banks" in stating annual percentage rates as required under truth in lending regulations.[2] By way of explanation, Batko suggested that the larger banks may be more sensitive to public and regulatory scrutiny and tend to have better-trained personnel. We would add that the larger banks are often able to afford specialized compliance personnel because costs can be spread over large volumes of transactions and perhaps passed along to borrowers more readily.

The current level of complaints from commercial banks and other types of consumer financial institutions indicates that the burden of compliance weighs heavily on small organizations. Included in this group are 12,000–13,000 commercial banks with assets less than $100 million or thereabouts. These banks seldom have the staff to keep up with changes in and additions to the growing volume of regulations, to interpret correctly the language of regulations, to revise forms and procedures promptly, and to train and retrain personnel.

The traditional orientation of regulation toward soundness and stability served to strengthen and protect the smaller financial institutions. This was clear in the closer regulation of commercial banks and the structuring of federal deposit insurance following the banking crisis of 1933. It also became clear in the regulation of savings and loan associations in the 1950s and credit unions in the 1960s. If the new regulatory orientation is relatively more burdensome for small institutions than large ones, as it appears to be, new sources of economies of scale may be in the making. Compliance regulation, by directly impinging on technology, could thus come to have an indirect effect on banking structure.

Assuming that the rapid expansion of compliance regulation since 1968 is the government's response to market failure, it would be meaningful to inquire whether the costs of compliance are outweighed by the social benefits attained through correction of market deficiencies. Such analyses are exceedingly difficult to accomplish, but the subject merits a great deal more attention in the financial services sector than it has thus far received. Congressional actions in the area of compliance regulation have been grounded somewhat more in a perception of changing social values than in measurements of market failure. Testimony in support of some of the compliance measures is almost entirely anecdotal, yet from it sweeping generalizations have been made. Compliance regulation has therefore been directed to requiring that financial institutions demonstrate and document that they are doing the "right" things in the "right" ways, and little or no change in the quality of performance in the market may be involved.

[2] Batko [1979].

My purpose in this paper, however, is not to argue a case for or against compliance regulation. Such regulation has come to exist, and it has brought a new orientation to banking regulation. Its effects on productivity have not been analyzed in any systematic way. This is an area in which research is much needed.

4.   Productivity Measurement in Banking

In a 1974 report on technological changes and manpower trends in banking, the Bureau of Labor Statistics (BLS) made the following observations[3]:

> Because of limitations in available data, a productivity index for banking is not published by the BLS. However, limited evidence indicates that productivity in banking rose during the decade of the 1960's. . . . Although an official annual series of total checks handled by all banks is not published, the rate of growth is estimated by the Federal Reserve Board to be about 6 to 7 per cent annually. Other measures of bank output which have been increasing in recent years include the number of deposit accounts and the volume of trust and loan department activities.
>
> During 1960–1973, total banking employment rose by 4.5 per cent annually, less than the rate of growth in several major measures of bank output over the period; this trend is expected to continue. It should be recognized that banks offer a growing range of new services to individuals and businesses which constitute an important but difficult-to-measure component of bank output.

Elsewhere the same report notes that "reductions in unit labor requirements in check processing operations are expected to be a major source of productivity gains."

Between 1972 and 1977 employment in commercial banking rose at an average annual rate of about 5% compared with the BLS estimate of 4.5% for 1960–1973. A cyclical pattern is quite evident with employment rising by 6.6% and 6.1% in 1973 and 1974, respectively, then slowing to a growth rate of 2.3% in 1976, and rebounding to 5.2% in 1977. At the end of 1977 approximately 1.32 million persons were employed in commercial banks.

Table 3 contains some numerical data on productivity in commercial banks. The data, except for item 1, are taken from various issues of *Functional*

---

[3] U.S. Department of Labor [1974], *Technological Change and Manpower Trends in Six Industries*, Bulletin 1817, pp. 41, 49.

TABLE 3

Selected Measures of Productivity: Sample of Commercial Banks, 1969, 1972, 1977

		Banks with deposits of	
	$50 million or less	$50 million to $200 million	More than $200 million
1. Average hourly earnings per production worker			
1969 $2.93 100			
1972 $3.42 117			
1977 $4.54 155			
2. Number of personnel per $1 million of available funds			
1969	1.83	1.69	1.57
1977	1.28	1.12	1.10
3. Daily deposits per teller			
1969	75	79	89
1972	92	90	98
1977	94	98	97
4. Daily checks cashed per teller			
1969	77	79	80
1972	100	95	105
1977	105	102	109
5. Daily home debits per processor			
1969	381	325	234
1972	394	396	438
1977	452	441	378
6. Number of accounts per processor			
1969	480	365	245
1972	496	445	445
1977	546	487	376
7. Cost per home debit (cents)			
1969	7.5	8.2	9.9
1972	7.6	7.3	9.0
1977	8.5	8.8	11.6
8. Cost per deposit (cents)			
1969	10.5	11.5	13.8
1972	13.3	15.1	18.4
1972	17.3	18.1	23.8
9. Cost per transit check (cents)			
1969	2.7	3.0	3.6
1972	3.3	4.1	5.0
1977	4.6	4.9	6.4
10. Cost per savings deposit (cents)			
1969	32.8	33.8	32.5
1972	25.0	27.0	30.0
1977	40.0	41.0	41.0

	Banks with deposits of		
	$50 million or less	$50 million to $200 million	More than $200 million
11. Cost per savings withdrawal (cents)			
1969	36.1	37.2	35.7
1972	49.0	53.0	58.0
1977	78.0	80.0	81.0
12. Number of real real estate loans serviced per worker			
1969	220	169	145
1972	172	174	186
1977	166	176	142
13. Number of installment loans serviced per worker			
1969	410	406	370
1972	389	363	336
1977	366	362	319
14. Installment loan volume per worker ($000)			
1969	439	387	351
1972	552	541	568
1977	761	791	774
15. Cost to make an installment loan			
1969	$19.98	$24.69	$26.63
1972	24.66	28.93	34.21
1977	40.98	41.70	49.10
16. Cost to collect an installment loan payment			
1969	$1.23	$1.44	$1.99
1972	2.00	2.16	2.55
1977	2.90	2.74	3.40
17. Number of commercial loans serviced per worker			
1969	255	143	71
1972	249	151	68
1977	218	142	65
18. Commercial loan volume per worker ($ mil)			
1969	1.25	1.48	1.88
1972	1.39	1.75	1.95
1977	1.72	2.09	2.31

Cost Analysis published annually as a cooperative effort of the 12 Federal Reserve Banks.[4] The number of participating member banks varies from year to year: 881 in 1969, 945 in 1972, and 846 in 1977. Comparability of data from year to year is affected by changes in the number of participating banks as well as by alterations in methodology. However, it is the only regularly published source of information on bank income and expenses allocated to functional areas. Despite the limitations affecting the data in Table 3, several observations appear to be reasonably well demonstrated. The decline in number of personnel per million dollars of available funds (item 2) mainly reflects inflation. Average sizes of checks and loans have increased, but personnel requirements are more closely related to the number of transactions than average dollar amount.

Teller efficiency (items 3 and 4) increased significantly between 1969 and 1972, but improvement since then has been relatively modest.

Items 4–6 are closely related in the production process. Home debits and account maintenance are relatively important in the total workload of check processing and permit the fullest application of machine processing of any production area. The small rise in unit costs for home debits is consistent with the fact that this area has been the focal point for application of electronic data processing technology in commercial banking. Machine processing has also been applied intensively to deposit tickets and transit checks (items 8 and 9). The large percentage increases in these unit costs are surprising and suggest declines in productivity.

Savings tickets (items 10 and 11) involve considerable manual work despite application of machine processing. The decline in unit costs on deposit tickets between 1969 and 1972 may reflect extensive introduction of machine processing. Many banks in the 1960s moved to apply electronic data processing to check handling and to installment loan accounting before extending it to savings and time deposits.

The decline in number of real-estate loans serviced per relevant worker in small banks may be a result of the increasing burden of regulation, but it may also be indicative of reorientation of lending policies to more profitable credit areas.

The next four items (13–16) show rather clearly that the administrative costs of handling consumer installment loans have risen substantially. However, the dollar volume of loans per relevant worker has also increased. It would appear that inflation, resulting in larger loan amounts per transaction, enabled banks to offset the higher administrative costs. Or it may be that volume growth in this area fostered a permissive attitude with respect

---

[4] *Functional Cost Analysis*, Data Furnished by Participating Banks in Twelve Federal Reserve Districts, 1969 Average Banks, 1972 Average Banks, and 1977 Average Banks.

to cost increases. That seems less likely than the first interpretation, but the cost data may reflect some additional loading of overhead on an area experiencing good growth.

The relative stability in number of commercial loans serviced per relevant worker (item 17) in banks of $50 million of deposits and larger is of interest, especially when compared with the decline in number of installment loans per worker. The decrease in the number of loans per worker in banks under $50 million may reflect the fact that small business loans in banks of this size are often handled in much the same way as installment loans. Also, there have been uncertainty and confusion about application of truth-in-lending procedures to such loans.

The data in Table 3 cast some doubt on the idea that gains in productivity have been substantial in commercial banking. At the very least, they suggest that the optimistic observations of the Bureau of Labor Statistics in 1974 may have been based too much on apparent gains in productivity in check processing.

Despite the extensive diffusion of computer technology in commercial banking, it remains a labor intensive industry. Its cost structure benefited, I think, in the 1960s and early 1970s from high rates of entry into the labor force by young persons and women. Demographic trends are becoming less favorable in this regard. Further improvements in technology will be needed in the 1980s to offset rising personnel costs. Thus far, electronic-funds-transfer systems are still high-cost operations. Also, automatic teller machines appear to be generating a new type of transactions volume rather than reducing volume at teller windows. One of the more promising technological changes being innovated by a few banks is the truncation of check movement. Truncation means that checks are not returned to the drawer of the check but are microfilmed and destroyed by either the drawer's bank or the payee's bank. Among the banks innovating this change, use is concentrated in business accounts where computer reconciliation of accounts is also provided. However, share-draft accounts for individuals, innovated by several hundred credit unions in recent years, also involve truncation. About ten years ago, in a study projecting the growth of commercial banking through the 1970s, I predicted that commercial banks would not be under significant pressures in that decade to shift away from checks toward electronic transfer devices [Haywood and McGee, 1969]. I would not make the same prediction about the 1980s.

Although fragmentary, the data set forth in Table 3 and discussed above suggest that a more systematic approach to the measurement of productivity in banking is possible. Certainly it would be useful to have something more meaningful than the sort of casual empiricism found in the 1974 report of the Bureau of Labor Statistics. The Federal Reserve's Functional Cost

Analysis data, despite limitations, could well be the place to begin the development of one or more productivity series. One of the significant limitations of the Functional Cost Analysis is that it is not representative of the largest 150–200 commercial banks that account for more than 40% of total employment. A few large banks, notably Bank of America, have used types of "time and motion" analyses to determine staffing needs in branches and certain other units, but the proprietary nature of the data limits access. The willingness of large banks to cooperate in a program to develop productivity measures has probably improved in recent years, but an essential requirement for such cooperation would be that the data already be available within the organization.

5. Economies of Scale in Banking

Extensive study has been given to one aspect of productivity in commercial banking—the question of whether or not economies of scale are found in commercial banks. An excellent review of this literature up to 1972 has been provided by Benston [1972]. More recent contributions of note include articles by Kalish and Gilbert [1973] and by Longbrake and Haslem [1975]. Also, the early work of Greenbaum [1967] continues to be of fundamental interest.

Study of economies of scale in commercial banking is affected by a number of measurement problems, the most basic problem being the quantification of output. It is not merely that commercial banks produce services rather than tangible goods. The mix of services is virtually unique for each bank, and certain services are joint products. Moreover, the mix of services produced by each bank is affected by conditions of joint demand.[5] Attempts to derive measures of composite output have encountered difficulties in the assignment of weights to cost and income variables. A good deal of arbitrary treatment has necessarily been involved. The work of Kalish and Gilbert and of Longbrake and Haslem is of interest because of their use of disaggregated measures of output. Their results do not have the elegance of single-equation estimates but are appealingly realistic.

The conclusion that has emerged from the extensive study and controversy since the early 1960s is that commercial banking is affected by economies of scale. However, study of large banking organizations has not been sufficient to confirm the persistence of scale economies in organizations with financial resources in excess of several hundred million dollars. An inherent part of the growth process of individual commercial banks is the adding on of new

---

[5] The terms "joint product" and "joint demand" are used here as defined by Marshall [1949], pp. 381–393.

types of services and activities. For banks with assets in excess of several hundred million dollars, output mix varies significantly not only from bank to bank but also over time. In certain lines of activity, including some reflected in the partial productivity measures in Table 3, diseconomies of scale are encountered. However, other lines of activity, which can be successfully entered only after a certain size has been reached, provide new profit opportunities. Comparisons between small and large banks are complicated by important differences in types of activities.

Although the last word on the subject of economies of scale in banking has not been written, I do not regard it as an especially promising field for further inquiry. Much of the impetus for study of economies of scale in banking came from legislation and court decisions in the early 1960s extending the full reach of the antitrust laws to bank mergers and bank holding company acquisitions. The results of such study have had no perceptible effect on regulation, perhaps because the analyses were too complicated and the conclusions too dependent on particular circumstances to provide a basis for broad public policy. In any event, economies of scale, even when demonstrable in specific situations, are given little or no weight by the federal bank regulatory agencies and the Justice Department in their reviews of bank merger and acquisition applications.

In the early 1960s there was speculation that the application of computer technology to commercial banking operations would confer significant economies of scale on large and medium-size banks. Various predictions were made to the effect that 3000–4000 small banks would cease to be economic operations as larger computer-based competitors drove down costs and cut prices on banking services. Such predictions have obviously not come to pass. One reason is that advancements in computer technology and design have made it possible for a number of small banks to have their own computers. More important, the correspondent banking system, through which large banks sell services to small banks, facilitated a relatively rapid diffusion of computer-based services throughout commercial banking. The role of correspondent banking has generally been overlooked in studies of economies of scale. The operation of this system tends to obscure the incidence of economies of scale. The large banks compete vigorously in selling services to smaller banks, and payment has traditionally been made in the form of deposit balances rather than fees.

6. Diffusion of Innovations

Factors affecting innovation in commercial banking have received some attention over the past decade. Discussion of the rather limited literature through 1975 can be found in *Financial Innovation* (Silber [1975]). More recently, interest has been stimulated by the development of electronic-funds-transfer systems (EFTS).[6] An early effort by Greenbaum and Haywood [1971] emphasized the role of regulation in influencing technological change in commercial banking. We relied on theoretical analysis and verbal interpretation of observed events and apparent trends. I have recently extended this work by applying quantitative techniques to data on the diffusion of computer technology in commercial banking [Haywood, 1979].

Data on the diffusion of computer technology were obtained from triennial surveys conducted since 1966 by the Operations and Automation Division of the American Bankers Association. These surveys produced detailed information on industry practices and procedures but were not designed to generate the types of information most suitable for regression analysis. The data suffer, of course, from nonresponse error, especially among small banks. More important, the information items that can be treated as independent variables are quite limited in number, and all of the dependent variables relevant to our inquiry are enumerations of yes–no responses.

Preliminary findings using regression analysis indicated that bank size was, by far, the dominant variable explaining diffusion of computer technology. Affiliation with a bank holding company and location in a state permitting multioffice banking via branching or holding companies were also identified as favorable to the diffusion of such computer-based activities as credit cards and automated customer services. Unfortunately, the data did not permit differentiation between one-bank and multibank holding companies.

Because of the enumerative character of the dependent variables and the apparent interaction among bank size, holding-company affiliation, and state laws governing multioffice banking, the data were analyzed through the use of two-, three-, and four-way contingency, or cross-classification, tables. Table 4, taken from the numerous tables in our 1979 paper, illustrates the use of the technique. In every cross-classification that was analyzed the test statistic exceeded tabulated values of chi-square at levels of critical probability of 0.5% or below.

Strong interaction between bank size and incidence of computer technology was evident in all cases. Holding-company affiliation also showed substantial interaction. Interaction with state laws governing multioffice banking was found to be statistically significant but less substantial than with bank size or holding company affiliation. These observations, as explained in our paper, are based on inspection of disaggregated test statistics.

---

[6] See, for example, Mandell [1977], Mason [1977], and National Commission on Electronic Funds Transfer [1978].

TABLE 4

Incidence of Credit Cards among Commercial Banks, by Bank Size, State Multioffice Categories, and Holding-Company Status[a]

Bank size ($ millions)	State multioffice categories				
	SB1[b]	SB2[c]	SB3[d]	SB4[e]	SB5[f]
Credit card, yes; Holding company, no					
0–5	8–11[g]	4–12	3–7	3–9	2–8
5–10	11–15	13–17	2–10	4–12	3–11
10–25	21–28	34–31	22–18	21–23	8–20
25–50	18–18	16–20	9–12	21–14	12–12
50–100	16–25	41–28	22–16	26–20	28–18
100–500	10–22	6–24	11–14	25–18	21–15
500 & over	1–9	1–10	0–6	6–7	6–6
Credit card, yes; Holding company, yes					
0–5	0–3	1–4	0–2	0–3	1–2
5–10	0–5	2–5	1–3	0–4	1–3
10–25	2–9	2–10	1–6	3–7	1–6
25–50	2–6	6–6	0–4	1–5	2–4
50–100	8–8	16–9	8–5	20–7	6–6
100–500	17–7	21–8	20–5	21–6	28–5
500 & over	4–3	8–3	11–2	24–2	29–2
Credit card, no; Holding company, no					
0–5	47–13	36–15	11–9	6–11	8–9
5–10	51–19	53–21	21–12	16–15	5–13
10–25	61–35	58–39	38–23	41–28	26–24
25–50	32–22	34–24	18–14	20–18	20–15
50–100	29–31	29–35	11–20	12–25	18–22
100–500	14–27	9–30	11–18	11–22	14–19
500 & over	0–11	0–13	6–7	1–9	1–8
Credit card, no; Holding company, yes					
0–5	2–4	2–5	0–3	2–3	0–3
5–10	2–6	5–7	1–4	3–5	0–4
10–25	3–11	4–12	4–7	3–9	1–8
25–50	4–7	2–8	3–5	3–6	1–5
50–100	7–10	9–11	7–7	3–8	2–7
100–500	5–9	5–10	5–6	10–7	13–6
500 & over	2–4	4–4	1–2	2–3	8–3

[a] Actual and expected frequencies, sample data 1975. Test statistic = 1,633.1. Chi-square quantile = 177.3 at p = 0.999 and d.f. = 127.
[b] SB1—unit banking without multibank holding companies (mbhc's).
[c] SB2—unit banking with mbhc's.
[d] SB3—limited-area branching without mbhc's.
[e] SB4—limited-area branching with mbhc's.
[f] SB5—statewide branching.

TABLE 5

Incidence of Credit Cards, by Bank Size, State Multioffice Categories, and Holding-Company Status[a]

State multioffice categories	Holding-company affiliation and size of banks							
	Not affiliated with holding company				Affiliated with holding company			
	Under $50 mm		Over $50 mm		Under $50 mm		Over $50 mm	
	No card	Card	No card	Card	No card	Card	No card	Card
SB1	191	58	43	27	11	4	14	29
SB2–5	411	177	123	193	34	22	69	212
Coefficient of association	0.1729^b		0.4284^b		0.2804		0.1946	
Standard error	0.0848		0.1108		0.2971		0.1702	
SB1–2	372	125	81	75	24	15	32	74
SB3–5	230	110	85	145	21	11	51	167
Coefficient of association	0.1747^b		0.2964^b		−0.0880		0.1722	
Standard error	0.0753		0.0960		0.2465		0.1287	
SB1–3	460	161	109	108	32	17	45	113
SB4–5	142	74	57	112	13	9	38	128
Coefficient of association	0.1964^b		0.3296^b		0.1316		0.1458	
Standard error	0.0818		0.0944		0.2591		0.1296	
SB1–4	543	120	133	165	43	21	60	178
SB5	59	25	33	55	2	5	23	63
Coefficient of association	0.0456		0.0483		0.6732^b		−0.0399	
Standard error	0.1258		0.1243		0.2400		0.1426	

[a] Sample data 1975.
[b] Significant at critical probability of 0.05.

Quantitative measures of dependence are available for certain types of contingency tables but are not applicable or are difficult to compute and interpret for data as extensively cross-classified as in Table 4. The cross-classifications were therefore collapsed into sets of two-way classifications as shown in Table 5. Each two-way classification formed a "tetrad" for which Yule's coefficient of association was computed.[7] Of the 16 coefficients of association in Table 5, 7 are statistically significant at a critical probability of 5%. Six of the seven significant coefficients are found in columns relevant

[7] Kendall [1948], pp. 310–313.

to banks not affiliated with holding companies. It thus appears that the incidence of computer-based services (in this case, credit cards) among banks not affiliated with holding companies is significantly greater when these banks are located in states with more liberal regulation of multioffice banking than in states with less liberal statutes.

The lack of statistically significant coefficients in seven of the eight tetrads for banks affiliated with holding companies tends to confirm the observation that size and holding company affiliation dominate over state multioffice policies in explaining the incidence of computer technology. Also, the presence of only one statistically significant coefficient in the row comparing statewide branching states (SB-5) with all other states reflects the fact that the incidence of computer technology is almost as great in states permitting limited-area branching with multibank holding companies (SB-4) as in state-wide branching states.

Our study dealt with a regulatory variable—state multioffice policies—that did not impinge directly on the type of technological change being analyzed. More pronounced effects would be expected, of course, from regulatory policies impinging directly on the exploitation or diffusion of innovations. Current and proposed public policies affecting EFTS impinge directly on the deployment and conditions of use of EFTS. Research into the implications of these policies is needed.

Study of innovative activity in the financial services sector has barely scratched the surface of a large and complex subject. The usefulness of further probing is enhanced by an apparent trend in regulation towards measures that directly affect the internal operating procedures of commercial banks and other types of lending institutions.

7. Regulation and "Synthetic" Technology

In our 1971 article Greenbaum and I introduced a diagram, shown in Fig. 1, to depict the effect of regulation on the output mix of commercial banks. As noted above, our interest at that time was in explaining the effects of regulation on financial innovations. I have recently given further attention to the diagram and extended the analysis of its implications (Haywood [1979]), which seem sufficiently germane to the purpose of this paper to warrant review.

Figure 1 shows three production possibility frontiers, based on an assumption of fixed input quantities. The frontier characterized as "natural technology" (BCD) depicts the alternative combinations of outputs S_1 and S_2 attainable in the absence of regulation. The "synthetic technology" frontier (ACE) shows the alternative combinations that are or would be permitted

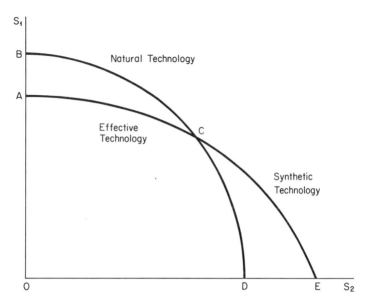

Figure 1   Production possibility frontiers.

by regulation. The intersection of these two frontiers results in a third production possibility frontier (ACD), characterized in Fig. 1 as "effective technology," i.e., those combinations of S_1 and S_2 that are both attainable and permitted under regulation.

In the absence of regulation, the "efficient" production possibility frontier would be BCD, characterized in Fig. 1 as the "natural technology." With regulation the "efficient" frontier is constrained to ACD, denoted as the "effective technology." As shown in Fig. 1, the "synthetic technology" frontier (ACE) has a segment (CE) lying outside the "efficient" frontier. This may appear to violate the rules for drawing production possibility frontiers, but CE is not a technical frontier. It is, so to speak, a regulatory frontier, depicting combinations of output that would be permitted if they were technologically attainable. The reason for its inclusion is that it depicts an area where technological change can occur without constraint by regulation.

The line segment BC in Fig. 1 identifies combinations of S_1 and S_2 that would be attainable in the absence of regulation and are potentially more efficient than the combinations of output defined by the AC segment of the effective technology frontier. For any specified output of S_2, the output of S_1 is lower on AC than on BC, except, of course, at the point of intersection of AC and BC.

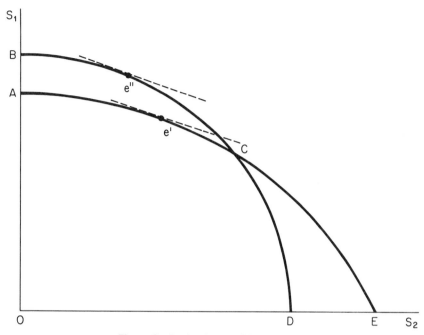

Figure 2 Production possibility frontiers.

To illustrate certain aspects of the effective technology diagram, Fig. 2 is drawn for a single firm with output capacity that is not large enough to affect the relative market values of S_1 and S_2. That is, a price line is introduced to define the optimum output combination. The output combination identified at e' is inferior for the firm to the combination identified at e'', because the market value of output at e'' is greater than at e'. The firm can be expected to try to move from e' in the direction of e'', but cannot do so in the absence of a change in regulation. If the industry in general is similarly affected, pressure for regulatory change that permits movement closer to e'' can be expected.

Innovations that seek to circumvent regulation can be viewed as an attempt to bend upward the AC segment of the effective technology frontier. Such innovations have sometimes been characterized as "socially wasteful." It might be more useful to term such changes in technology as "synthetic innovations," for their effect is to expand the synthetic technology frontier. Moreover, any change that moves AC closer to BC reduces the private cost of regulation to the firm and to consumers. If such reduction in costs is not fully offset by loss in the public benefits of regulation, the result is social gain rather than social waste.

It is possible, of course, that the relative market values of S_1 and S_2 would yield a price line in Fig. 2 tangent to a point on the CD segment of the effective technology frontier. There would then be incentive to expand the natural technology frontier toward the synthetic technology frontier, and the resulting efforts might be termed "natural innovations." Innovations of this type might not be directed to attaining any particular point on the synthetic technology frontier but rather be directed mainly to pushing outward the natural technology frontier.

The intersection of the natural and synthetic technology frontiers results in a "kink" in the effective technology frontier. Referring again to Fig. 1, it can be seen that the slope of the effective technology frontier changes discretely at C. This suggests that there is some range of relative market values for S_1 and S_2 over which the mix of output is either unchanged or changes by relatively small amounts. The implication is that large changes in prices may be needed to provide incentive for innovations in the presence of regulation.

Stability of relative prices for a period sufficient to permit changes in the effective technology through either synthetic or natural innovations would be conducive to the attainment of a "kink" solution. Therefore, the "kink solution" might be regarded as the normal solution, with periods of innovative activity being associated with large changes in the relative market values of S_1 and S_2. Swings in the relative market values of S_1 and S_2 would also help explain variations in industry pressures for changes in regulation. Such explanations are consistent with the observation that since the late 1950s innovative activity of the synthetic variety has increased during periods of stringent monetary policy, i.e., as the value of short-term claims has risen relative to the value of long-term claims. As fixed input quantities were assumed in the foregoing discussion of Figs. 1 and 2, changes in factor prices and supplies have not been noted as possible incentives for innovation. The argument could be extended to include such sources of incentive for technological change.

The possibility of a "corner solution" at B or D in Figs. 1 and 2 should be noted. Corner solutions become relevant if an institution can place itself under less restrictive regulation or escape regulation by specializing in either S_1 or S_2. A rationale for specialization of institutions can be elaborated by comparing corner solutions with alternatives along AC, at C, or along CD. The observed tendency of specialized institutions to depart at times from corner solutions can also be described within the framework of the effective technology frontier.

8. Summary

After a long period of structurally oriented regulation, commercial banking has come under a new form of regulation that impinges directly on costs. Emphasis has thus been given to the need for systematic study of the effects of regulation on technology and productivity in commercial banking. Except for studies of economies of scale, little attention has been given to the general area of productivity analysis in commercial banking. Concern with the effects of regulation on innovation prompted me to engage in some theoretical and empirical work resulting in limited conclusions about the direction of regulation's influence on innovation but not its relative importance. Much more research in this area remains to be done.

12

The Effect of Health Manpower Regulations on Productivity in Medical Practices

Kenneth R. Smith

College of Business
and Public Administration
University of Arizona
Tucson, Arizona

A. Mead Over, Jr.

Department of Economics
Williams College
Williamstown, Massachusetts

1. Introduction

The purpose of this paper is to investigate the effect of health manpower regulations on productivity in ambulatory medical care. As the production of ambulatory care is physician intensive and as the physician has been the expensive and scarce resource, at least under the traditional organization of medical practice, emphasis has been on the opportunities to increase physician productivity by the introduction of new methods of production. Prior to 1960, significant gains were the result of a shift from home visits to office visits, the latter requiring less physician time per unit of output, as well as the widespread use of new drugs that simplified the treatment of a number of common diseases. During the 1960s interest developed in the implications of introducing a substitute for the physician that would increase the potential productivity of the physician and reduce the costs of producing ambulatory care. There is considerable disagreement regarding the impact of these more recent changes on physician productivity.

309

The two greatest difficulties faced by economists in their attempts to estimate the production structure of medical care firms and to measure changes in productivity are the multiplicity of outputs and the lack of clear definitions for those outputs. To define the multiple outputs, we have found it useful to develop an explicit model of the operating procedures and processes of the medical care firm as it responds to the medical problems of patients.

Our methodology was developed in the context of an investigation of the possibilities for substituting new nonphysician practitioners for physicians in ambulatory practices (Smith *et al.* [1976]). In Section 2, this context is used to motivate our approach to the problem of identifying the outputs. In Section 3, we define some terms and notation to structure the problem more formally and we introduce an unobservable variable to represent output. In Section 4 we describe the data and the methodology by which the observed units (or "encounters") were subdivided into groups within which patients had "similar" complaints. In Section 5 we use data on the inputs of production to estimate the technical coefficients of the ambulatory care production process. In order to measure the potential productivity impact of using a new type of medical practitioner, we propose to represent the production problem by an activity analysis model, which we describe in Section 6. In Section 7, we examine the impact of regulatory constraints on measured productivity.

2. The Problem

Consider a medical practice that employs two classes of health care providers: physicians (MDs) and intermediate level health practitioners (HPs). Suppose that two patients, A and B, are separately treated by the practice. Each of these two interactions between a patient and the practice staff is closely observed and recorded. The data collected on each patient's "encounter" with the practice include:

(1) a list of all the elementary medical tasks performed on the patient;
(2) whether the staff member performing each task is an MD or an HP;
(3) the total number of minutes spent with the patients by each staff member.

In addition to these descriptors of the medical care process, characteristics of the individual patients are also recorded. These include

(1) the patient's complaint;
(2) the patient's age;

(3) the patient's sex;
(4) whether the visit is the first for this problem (i.e., the "status" of the encounter).

Suppose an economist wishes to use this information on the encounters of A and B with this practice to estimate the degree to which the services of an HP are substitutable for those of an MD. If he can assume that the encounters of A and B are both examples of the technologically efficient production of a unit of the same output, then he can consider the two observed input combinations to be points on the same unit isoquant. In this case he can proceed to estimate the substitutability of the HP for the MD by calculating the marginal rate of technical substitution along this isoquant.

However, suppose the economist examines the data collected on A and B more closely and discovers that 15 minutes of provider time are used to treat patient B, while only 5 minutes are used to treat patient A. On the basis of this evidence, the economist may question his assumption that one unit of the same output is efficiently produced on each encounter. Various interpretations are possible. Perhaps more of the same output was produced on encounter B than on encounter A. Perhaps encounters A and B are examples of two disparate outputs of quite distinct medical "character." Perhaps patient B received a more "intense" or "higher quality" version of the same output received by A. Perhaps encounter A is produced with more technical efficiency than B. Perhaps the providers serving the two patients differ idiosyncratically in their response to a specific complaint. A final possibility is that the apparent difference between encounters A and B is entirely due to a random component in the medical care production process.

If the difference between the two encounters is due primarily to a random element in the production process, it may be possible to obtain an unbiased estimate of the marginal rate of technical substitution between the two types of providers from these two observed data points. However, if the two encounters belong to two distinct production functions (corresponding for example, to distinct medical problems) or perhaps to two distinct isoquants of the same production function, then nothing can be learned from the two encounters about the substitution possibilities between the two inputs. Thus it is important to determine the source of the difference between the two encounters.

Assuming for convenience that only one output is produced during an encounter, the two remaining questions are: "What is the identity of that output?" and "How much of that output is produced?" One possible approach would be simply to ask a medical expert whether the same amount of the same output was produced on the two encounters. Unfortunately there is considerable disagreement among medical experts on such questions (Over [1978]). Another approach, which has often been taken in the absence of well-established conventions for defining and measuring output, is to use input measures as proxies for the unobserved output measure (Baron [1975]; Redisch [1974]; Feldstein [1977]). However, using input information to answer either of the two questions posed above invalidates an important feature of the further analysis that would be pursued once the output measure was obtained. For instance, it might be proposed that an encounter with a high ratio of MD-time input to HP-time input is a different kind of output than an encounter with a low MD/HP ratio. However, this convention would render difficult or impossible the analysis of substitution possibilities between the MD and the HP. Alternatively, we might try to use input information to infer the quantity of output produced by assuming that, because more input time was used to treat patient B than patient A, therefore more output was produced on encounter B. But this convention would make it impossible to distinguish between efficient and inefficient production of the same output. It is for these reasons that output measures should be definitionally independent of input measures.

In the present example, in addition to input information two other types of information are available to help identify and measure the output produced on each encounter. First, we have several "characteristics" of the patient on arrival at the practice. Second, we have the number and identity of individual tasks performed on the patient. Our approach is to confine ourselves to these two types of information in order to develop an output measure definitionally independent of input measures.

We begin by assuming that only one unit of output is produced on each encounter, so that the problem reduces to that of attaching a label to the output (and thus to the encounter). We further assume that the identity of the output produced on an encounter is related to the characteristics of the patient and to the tasks performed by the providers (but not to the identity of the providers or to the amount of time they spend with the patient for the reasons explained above). It then follows that it should be possible to infer that two encounters (such as A and B above) are examples of the same output if the characteristics of the patients treated *and* the number and identity of tasks performed are "sufficiently" similar between the two encounters.

Note that our approach would result in the classification of two encounters in the same output class if they have the same characteristics and tasks, despite the fact that they may have different diagnoses and/or different outcomes. We argue that diagnosis is not a useful grounds for classifying encounters into output classes because two patients with different characteristics may require quite different medical "workups" for the practice to render the same diagnosis while patients with "sufficiently" similar characteristics leading the practice to perform "sufficiently" similar tasks seem likely to be examples of the same production process despite different diagnoses. If outcome information were available on our patients, we might be able to use it to help us capture possible differences in the quality with which the same tasks are delivered to patients with the same characteristics. However, since outcome information is not available, we assume that all differences in quality are observable as differences in the tasks with which a practice responds to a patient with given characteristics.

3.   Output as an Unobservable Variable

The term "encounter" will be used to refer to a single continuous visit by a patient to an ambulatory medical care practice. The encounter is a convenient unit of analysis of ambulatory care. The production technology of ambulatory care can be characterized as the set of processes by which factor inputs (different types of health practitioners) can be combined to produce outputs during encounters.

Each encounter can be represented by a pair of vectors, (p, s), where p is the input vector and s is the output vector. An element of the input vector p_i represents the flow of the ith factor input into the production of this encounter. An element of the output vector s_j represents the quantity of the jth output produced during the associated encounter. It is assumed that each encounter represents the production of one unit of one particular output so that the vector s will have one element equal to one and all other elements equal to zero.

In recognition of the difficulty of measuring the output of an ambulatory medical care practice, the output vector s is defined to be unobservable. Since s is unobservable, it is necessary to infer its value from the values of observable variables that can be assumed to be structurally related to s, either as causes of s or as effects of s. The form of these structural relationships can be hypothesized on the basis of an examination of the production process.

The production process consists of a production decision regarding what output to produce during the encounter, paired with an allocation decision regarding who will produce the encounter. Closer examination reveals that the production decision itself actually consists of two steps, the classification step and the execution step. The classification step occurs on the arrival of the patient at the practice. In response to the patient's characteristics x, the practice classifies the patient into one of the S output categories. The most relevant element of the x vector is the patient's chief complaint while other elements of x (age, sex, and status) vary in importance depending on the chief complaint.

The execution step occurs after the practice has allocated its personnel to the production of the given encounter. The execution step is defined as the performance of a sequence of discrete, observable, elemental activities. These activities are called tasks. Examples of tasks include "inquire about current medication," "inspect ears," "obtain nose/throat culture," "prescribe medication," "remove cast." Since tasks are performed in order to execute a given unobservable output, the tasks should provide useful information on what that output is. Furthermore, we define the tasks to ensure their independence of which provider performs them and of how much provider time they consume. For example, this definitional independence would be violated if two separate tasks were defined for "MD inspects ears" and "HP inspects ears" or if "two-minute ear inspections" were a separate task from "one-minute ear inspections."

Let y be a vector whose T elements correspond to the T different ambulatory care tasks. An element of y, y_k, will equal 1 if the kth task is performed on a given encounter; otherwise $y_k = 0$. Figure 1 illustrates the ambulatory care production process, including the production and allocation decisions and the classification and execution steps. This schematic makes clear that the x vector of characteristics is assumed to *cause* the choice of output s, while the y vector of tasks is assumed to *be caused by s*. Despite this difference, both x and y are structurally related to the unobservable output vector. Since x and y are both independent of the inputs, they can be used together to infer the identity of the output produced on any encounter.

This paper develops and applies an approach to defining the outputs of an ambulatory care practice based on the descriptive model depicted in Fig. 1. The application uses data collected on 4895 encounters. After de-

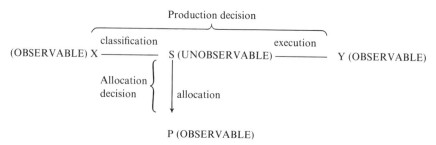

Figure 1   Diagram of production and allocation decisions.

scribing the data, we apply the numerical technique called hierarchical clustering analysis to partition the total sample of encounters into relatively homogeneous subsets.[1]

4. The Data and the Definition of Homogeneous Groups of Encounters

In order to identify the outputs of ambulatory medical care firms, it is necessary to obtain a data base that includes information on both the causes and indicators of the unobserved output. During the two-year period between the summers of 1972 and 1974, the Efficient Health Manpower Utilization project employed and trained a number of observers and then assigned them to observe and record in detail as many encounters as possible in a two-week period spent in each of 60 ambulatory care practices across the country. The selected practices represented, to as great an extent as possible, both excellence of care and a complete range of patterns of use of traditional assistants and newly emerging categories of health practitioners.

A total of 4895 encounters were observed and recorded. The observational methodology required the observer to code every task performed and the identity of the performer during each 30-second interval of the encounter. Codes existed for a total of 369 different tasks. This task list was developed by partitioning the universe of ambulatory care activity by purpose, body system, and procedure. The final level of detail was reviewed to ensure that the resulting tasks were observable with satisfactory accuracy and that they were medically significant. The task description of the encounter thus reveals the content and sequential logic of the medical response. It is this information that enters into an analytical effort to define the outputs of the medical care firm.

Our analysis focuses on the chief complaint as the primary determinant (cause) of the type of practice response and on the diagnostic tasks as a description (indicator) of that response.[2] We define the observable response to a chief complaint as the vector y of tasks performed during encounters in

---

[1] A certain amount of heterogeneity of task content remains within these subsets. In Over and Smith [1979] this variability in task content is explored within the context of a formal statistical model of the multiple-indicator–multiple-cause type. The purpose of this exploration is to determine whether the existence of an unobservable dichotomization of the encounters might explain this variation.

[2] Before we proceeded with the chief complaint analysis, the data were subdivided on the basis of the reason for visit. The three reasons of "acute," "chronic," and "health maintenance" are thought to imply differences in the medical content of the visit and the resultant tasks performed.

which the patient expressed a given chief complaint. Since on any single encounter, anomalous tasks might occur, we eliminate from the analysis any chief complaint that was observed fewer than six times. For the remaining chief complaints we construct an "average task vector," which contains an element for each diagnostic task. The ith element of the average task vector for a given chief complaint is simply the proportion of all patients expressing the chief complaint on which task i was performed. Thus, the elements of the average task vector are relative frequencies.

The technique of data analysis known as hierarchical clustering was then used to discover the appropriate partition of the sample of chief complaints. Given the dissimilarity (or distance) between all pairs of objects in a parent set, the hierarchical clustering algorithm produces a sequence of partitional clusterings in which each clustering in the sequence is indexed by an ordinal level. The first clustering is the trivial one which consists of n clusters, one object to a cluster. The next clustering is formed by joining the two closest of the n clusters into a single cluster, leaving $n - 1$ clusters. Subsequent steps always join the two most similar or closest clusters, thereby decreasing by one the number of clusters, until the nth clustering is formed by joining two clusters into one inclusive cluster containing all n objects.

Once all chief complaints are assigned average task vectors located in a T-dimensional task space, the Euclidian metric is used to measure the distance or dissimilarity between pairs of chief complaints. The problem of aggregating similar chief complaints can be viewed as the problem of finding "clouds" or "clusters" of chief complaints in task space that are identifiably distinct from one another. An independent test of the validity of the methodology is the degree to which within-cluster homogeneity is confirmable by subjective medical consideration of the complaints that are aggregated.

The measure of "closeness" proposed by Ward [1963] is used to generate the hierarchical clusterings considered here. It chooses two clusters to merge that produce the smallest increase in a measure of total dispersion within all the clusters in the clustering. Define W_c as the cross-product matrix of deviations of all vectors in cluster c from cluster c's centroid. The trace of W_c is equal to the sum of the squared Euclidian distances between all members of cluster c and c's centroid. Then

$$E = \sum_{c=1}^{C} \text{tr}(W_c)$$

is the total within-cluster error sum of squares, where C is the number of clusters. In moving from C to $(C - 1)$ clusters, Ward's method is based on minimizing E. The value of E can be interpreted as the "information loss" associated with a particular clustering.

Figure 2 presents the dendrogram from the clustering of 121 acute chief

TABLE 1

Acute Chief-Complaint Clusters and Acute Homogeneous Encounter Groupings

Subgroup	Number of encounters	National ambulatory medical care survey complaint code	Chief complaint
Major group I			
I.1	134	0010	Chills
		0050	Sick malaise
		0040	Fatigue
		0130	Pain
I.2	203	5400	Abdominal pain
		5550	Diarrhea
		5750	Nausea
I.3	59	5450	Abnormal appetite
		0620	Bad sleep
		9970	No complaint
		0070	Fluid imbalance
		3130	Flu
I.4	149	0560	Headache
		0690	Vertigo
I.5	99	3060	Breathlessness
		3220	Pain in chest
I.6	50	3070	Other respiratory disorders
		3080	Asthma
		3301	Bronchitis
		3303	Pneumonia
I.7	31	2000	Irregular pulse
		9852	Blood pressure check
		5801	Hepatitis
		2101	Anemia
Major group II			
II.1	501	0020	Fever
		3010	Nasal congestion
		3110	Cough
		3120	Cold
		3302	Nonspecific congestion
		3210	Congestion in chest
		3040	Sinus problems
II.2	374	2320	Swollen neck glands
		5200	Sore throat
		5270	Tonsil symptoms
II.3	47	0200	General symptoms infants and children
		3250	Voice disorders
		3140	Croup
		0300	General infections disorders

(*Continued*)

TABLE 1   (Continued)

Subgroup	Number of encounters	National ambulatory medical care survey complaint code	Chief complaint
II.4	276	7310	Hearing problem
		7360	Otitis
		7350	Ear ache
		7370	Plugged ear
Major Group III			
III.1	100	9104	Prescription renewal
		9106	Other injections
		9450	Find out test results
		9857	Postoperative visit
		9310	Medical counseling
III.2	286	1110	Warts
		1163	Suture removal
		9855	Wound progress check
		1161	Puncture wound
		1162	Laceration
		1165	Bite
III.3	345	9805	Fracture check
		9861	Cast removal
		2202	Phlebitis
		4000	Injury—lower extremities
		4050	Injury—upper extremities
III.4	232	1060	Infectious disease abscess skin
		1168	Burns
		1152	Cyst of skin
		1090	Mole
		1151	Growth of skin
		1122	Poison
		1130	Skin irritations
		1200	Other skin symptoms
		1164	Insect bites
		1167	Bruises
Major group IV			
IV.1	131	1040	Discoloration of skin
		1121	Diaper rash
		1120	Allergic skin reaction
		1131	Rash
IV.2	81	1150	Swelling
		4100	Injury of face/neck
		5100	Mouth symptoms
		5302	Lump in neck/throat

(*Continued*)

TABLE 1   (Continued)

Subgroup	Number of encounters	National ambulatory medical care survey complaint code	Chief complaint
IV.3	73	7040	Discharge from eye
		7050	Eye pain
		7100	Eyelid symptoms
		7200	Other eye symptoms
		7150	Foreign body in eye
		7160	Eye injury
Major group V			
V.1	228	0110	Weight loss
		5500	Gastrointestinal bleeding
		4150	Back pain
		8100	Nervousness
		5540	Constipation
		5900	Other digestive symptoms
		2140	Fainting
		4250	Other musculoskeletal symptoms
		4200	Atrophy of extremities
		7010	Other vision problems
V.2	127	4160	Pain in side
		6040	Painful urination
		6200	Other urinary tract symptoms
		6010	Frequency of urination
		5420	Abdominal swelling
		5470	Hernia
		6000	Urine abnormalities
V.3	52	5600	Symptoms of anus/rectal
		5610	Hemorrhoids
		6310	Pain of male genitalia
		6520	Menstrual cramps
		6800	Breast: lump or mass
		6810	Breast pain
V.4	84	0530	Menstrual disorders
		6570	Vaginal bleeding
		6700	Other female reproduction symptoms
		6550	I.U.D. check
		6600	Pelvic symptoms—female
		6630	Vulvan disorders
		6613	Vaginal infection
		9051	Suspected pregnancy

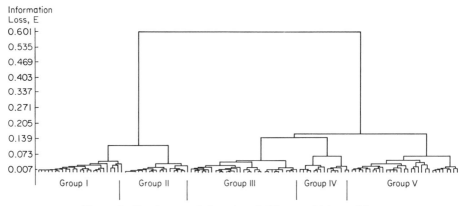

Figure 2   Dendrogram of clustering of 121 acute chief complaints.

complaints. From this analysis, five major groups and a total of 22 sub-groups are identified. These chief-complaint groupings are listed in Table 1.[3]

The next stage of the analysis was to use the chief-complaint clusters to partition the sample of encounters into subsets representing groups of patients who received a similar output from the medical care firm. These are called homogeneous encounter groups (HEGs). An HEG is defined as a set of encounters each of which has a chief complaint in the same chief-complaint cluster.

5.   The Technology of Ambulatory Care

Having identified the outputs of the medical care firm, we are now in a position to consider data on the inputs and to estimate the technical co-efficients that describe the ambulatory care production process. Our goal is to examine the degree of substitutability between an intermediate-level health practitioner and a physician.

A fundamental assumption of our analysis is that the task vector used in the previous section to define the outputs is independent of the production process used; otherwise, output would not be definitionally independent of the inputs. In a previous article (Over and Smith [1979]) we have subdivided one of our HEGs into two classes using a structural model of the relationship between patient's characteristics and the tasks performed on those patients. If the two classes had corresponded to distinctly different subsets of tasks

---

[3] The corresponding dendrograms and chief complaint groupings for encounters in the chronic and health maintenance categories are included in the Appendix.

performed, one might then look for a relationship between tasks and inputs. However, the two classes corresponded not to different tasks but to different probabilities of the same tasks. Patients with certain characteristics were more likely to receive all of the tasks included in the analysis. This "higher-intensity care" was delivered by both MDs and HPs. We interpret this result as support for our assumption that the tasks constituting the response to the patient are independent of which provider participates in the process.

5.1   The Health Practitioner as an Innovation in the Production of Ambulatory Care

Until the decade of the 1960s, a physician in general practice had little difficulty deciding how to staff his practice. Custom and common sense dictated that he hire an aide to help him with routine work, "who might be a secretary, nurse or general medical aide" (American Medical Association [1976], p. 3). A busy physician might hire two or even three aides. In general, and as we shall see shortly, these traditional aides (TA) did not substitute for the physician in the medical content part of the encounter.

Today the acceptance of the physician-aide paradigm is no longer as complete as it once was. In the middle 1960s the search began for an alternative. Training programs were initiated that were designed to create a new type of health practitioner who would be less costly to educate than a physician but more independent than an aide. The proliferation of training programs has been rapid; the proliferation of names for the products of these programs has been almost as rapid. We shall adopt the term "health practitioner" (HP) to signify a health care provider trained specifically to fill a slot intermediate between the physician and the traditional aide; that is, trained to substitute for the physician in the medical content part of the encounter.

Health practitioners can be divided into two main groups. The first group consists of graduates of training programs that require a nursing degree for admission. Sadler et al. ([1975], pp. 206–239) enumerate 256 programs with such a requirement. The graduates of these programs are effectively "upgraded" nurses, who have been specifically trained to accept more responsibility for patient care and treatment in an ambulatory setting than is traditional for the nursing role.

The second broad group contains those HPs who are graduates of programs not requiring a nursing degree for admission. These programs, of which there are approximately 50, produce graduates called, variously, physician's assistants, physician's associates, child health associates, Medex, and health assistants, differ in their admissions requirements as well as in the roles for which graduates are trained.

Our study of the ambulatory care production process collected data on inputs for the physician (MD) and traditional aide (TA), and for the general categories of health practitioners physician's assistants (PA), Medex (MDX), child health associate (CHA), and nurse practitioner (NP). For ease of exposition, we shall limit our analysis of the health practitioner to data on the Medex (MDX).

The various pressures that resulted in the implementation of HP training programs, combined with the fact that more than 7000 HPs trained by these programs are currently proving themselves on the job, have considerably weakened the physician-aide paradigm. However, several unanswered questions regarding the adoption of the HP include the following:

What are the acceptable roles for HPs?

What changes occur in an ambulatory care setting with the introduction of an HP?

What factors influence the costs of HP services?

What influences would the various reimbursement policies and practices have on the efficient use of qualified HPs?

5.2   Resource Combinations and Techniques

We assume that the resource allocation process used to produce a single unit of output of primary care during an encounter can begin in one of only three distinct ways. The practice can assign the physician (MD) to the production of the encounter without help. The practice can divide the encounter into two parts, assigning one part to be completed by the MD and the other by an intermediate-level health practitioner (HP). Or the practice can assign the encounter to an HP with instructions to follow an algorithm that may or may not result in referring the patient to the MD.[4] We call these three alternatives the "MD-only process," the "joint process," and the "delegation process."

Consider a medical practice staffed by one MD and one HP. Abstracting from the other resources of the firm, the time that the MD and HP use to produce a given encounter constitutes the resources expended in producing the unit of output associated with that encounter. The various resource expenditures that could result from the production of a unit of output can be represented as points in the first quadrant of the MD–HP plane, the two coordinates of a point being the time expenditures of the two providers. The three alternative production processes will result in four different types of observed resource combinations. These four typical combinations are

---

[4] The term algorithm signifies an explicit step-by-step procedure designed to solve a specific medical problem within a broad predefined category of problems. The instructions accompanying the assignment of an encounter to an HP are not usually defined that explicitly, however.

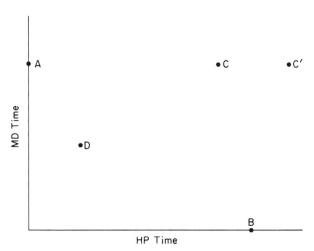

Figure 3   Hypothetical observed resource combinations for producing one unit of a given output.

displayed in the MD–HP plan in Fig. 3 as the points labeled *A*, *B*, *C*, and *D*. Point *A* on the MD axis is typical of the observed resource expenditure that is likely to result if the practice chooses to produce an encounter with the MD-only process. Since the MD never refers a patient to an HP (barring an emergency that would call the MD away in the middle of the encounter), the MD-only process will typically be terminated without the expenditure of any HP time.

Point *D* represents the typical resource expenditure likely to result from a decision to use the joint process. Assuming that the practice allocates tasks efficiently between the two providers, one would expect the MD to spend less time than on the MD-only process, but still produce the major part of the visit. In this context, where the MD assumes responsibility for the encounter, the tasks done by the HP are likely to be relatively uncomplicated and therefore be completed in a period not very much longer than would be required of the MD to perform the same tasks. Thus, a ray from the origin through point *D* is likely to have a slope greater than 1, while a line passing through points *A* and *D* will have a negative slope.

The third alternative, using the delegation process to produce the encounter, could result in one of the two typical resource expenditures represented by points *B* and *C* (or *C'*). If the HP is able to follow the algorithm through to its conclusion without referring the patient to the MD, then point *B* on the HP axis of Fig. 3 will typify the resulting resource expenditure; no MD time will be used. If the HP is obliged by one of the branch points of the algorithm to refer the patient to the MD, the resulting resource expenditure will lie above the HP axis at a point like C (or C'). The height of point C above the HP axis, representing the time required by the MD to finish the encounter, will be related to the severity and complexity of the medical problem. Since the HP will tend to refer the more complicated problems, point C may be as high as or higher than point A, and, depending on how early in the encounter the HP recognizes the need for referral, may involve less (C) or more (C') of the HP's time than when the visit is completed without referral.

Define a "technique" for producing one unit of a given medical care output as the expected value of the vector of resource requirements corresponding to one of the three alternative types of production processes. If the resource requirements of the MD-only process and the joint process are known with certainty, then points A and D represent two techniques for producing this output. A third technique corresponding to the delegation process can be defined as the expected value of the vector of resources required when an encounter is delegated to the HP. If the only two possible outcomes of the delegation decision are points B and C with coordinates (MD_B HP_B) and (MD_C HP_C), the coordinates of the technique corresponding to this decision are given by

$$E\begin{bmatrix} MD \\ HP \end{bmatrix} = r\begin{bmatrix} MD_C \\ HP_C \end{bmatrix} + (1 - r)\begin{bmatrix} MD_B \\ HP_B \end{bmatrix},$$

where r is the "referral parameter" defined as the probability that a given type of HP will be required to refer a patient in a given output category to the MD for completion of the visit. Call the coordinates of the point representing the delegation technique (MD_E HP_E).[5]

Figure 4 contains points A, B, C, and D from Fig. 3 with the addition of two possible locations for the delegation technique, E_r, corresponding to two possible values of the referral parameter r. The technology of producing a hypothetical output of primary care is thus composed of the three techniques represented by points A, D, and E_r. However, all three of these techniques will not necessarily be relevant to the decisions of the practice manager. The manager who optimizes an objective function subject to a resource constraint will only be interested in the "efficient" techniques for producing a given output. A technique is efficient if and only if no other

---

[5] This approach to the interpretation of type C resource combinations differs from that taken by Pondy *et al.* [1973, p. 342]. They reasoned that a rational practice would not choose to produce at points like C when points like A or D were available. When they observed points like C as well as A and D in their data for a single output category, they concluded that the output class must be insufficiently homogeneous and proceeded with that subset of their data that "appear[ed] to be reasonably free of such obvious instances of nonhomogeneity."

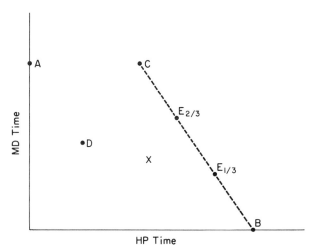

Figure 4   The effect of two hypothetical referral parameters on the location of the delegation technique E.

technique uses less of at least one resource and no more of any other resource for the production of the same amount of the same output. Given the hypothesized positions of points A, B, C, and D, the efficiency of the technique represented by point E_r clearly depends on the value of r. For example, if $r = \frac{2}{3}$ rather than $\frac{1}{3}$, the resulting referral technique, $E_{2/3}$ is dominated by the joint technique D. Even when no joint technique exists for a given output

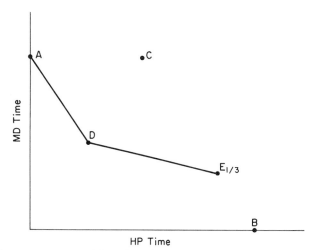

Figure 5   Isoquant constructed from hypothetical observed resource combinations and referal parameter.

class, if the MD time expended at point C is larger than at A and if the referral parameter is large enough, the delegation technique E_r can be inefficient.

Although to be efficient the practice must choose to produce any given encounter by one of the three techniques A, D, $E_{1/3}$, it is possible that a practice would choose to produce some encounters in this output class with one technique and some with another. As a result, the definition of the technology of producing this medical care output can be extended to include all points on the convex enclosure of the set of techniques. The convex enclosure for this example is illustrated in Fig. 5. Because any combination of resources on the curve $ADE_{1/3}$ can produce one unit of the given output, the curve is the one-unit isoquant corresponding to this output class.

5.3 Observed Resource Combinations and the Role of the Traditional Aide

Observed input times for encounters in the upper respiratory HEG are displayed in Fig. 6 of this section and Fig. 7 of the next section. These

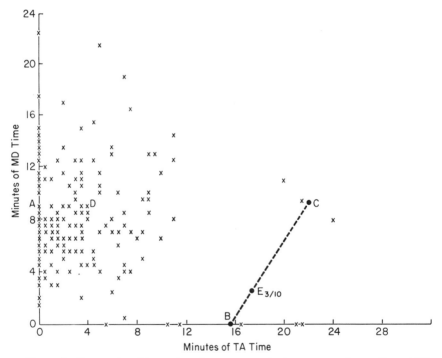

Figure 6 Scatter plot of input times for encounters in the upper respiratory illness HEG on which no HP time was expended.

illustrations are typical of the data in general. Ordinarily it would be misleading to display observations of a multiple-input production process in a series of two-dimensional projections as we do in these figures. However, two special features of the primary care production process for the upper respiratory HEG as well as for other output categories make the two-dimensional scatter plot a good vehicle for summarizing input data. First, none of the 501 encounters in this HEG were produced with more than one MD or TA and only six were produced with more than one HP. We exclude these six encounters from the scatter plots and from the ensuing analysis, leaving only encounters produced by three or fewer providers, no two of whom are of the same type on a given encounter. Second, there is evidence that the TA's involvement in an encounter does not significantly reduce the time required of the other providers. To reach this conclusion, we first apply the typology of A, B, C, and D encounters developed in the previous section to the scatter plot of MD and TA times in Fig. 6. Then, we show that encounters of type B and C occur very infrequently for the TA and that encounters of type D appear to represent inefficient techniques. Since we seek the set of efficient techniques for producing this HEG, we will argue in this section that the TA can be ignored for the purpose of examining the possibilities for substitution between the MD and an HP.[6]

In Section 5.2 we hypothesized the existence of three basic types of techniques for the production of primary care, which are based, in turn, on four basic resource combinations represented by points A, B, C (or C'), and D in Figs. 3–5. If all four points are fixed from one encounter to the next, observations of a large number of encounters in this hypothetical output class would result in only four different observed resource combinations.

In actual medical practice, of course, the points referred to as A, B, C, and D are not fixed, but rather are subject to random variation. Therefore, even if our typology of resource combinations holds exactly, observations on resources expended during real encounters will not be located at only four points in input space. At best the observations will be distributed in small groups or clusters around points representing the four types of observable resource combinations. As a result, we cannot distinguish the MD-only and joint techniques from the delegation technique on the basis of the deterministic nature of the first two and the stochastic nature of the last. In reality all the techniques are stochastic. The difference between the

---

[6] Clearly the TA plays a productive role in the nonmedical content part of practice activity. To understand why the MD uses a TA during the encounter when there is no saving in MD time, one must appeal to lack of knowledge, the desire of the TA to have some contact with patients during the encounter, or the desire of the MD to have assistance even where there is no saving. This use of the TA may be affected by considerations of status that are feasible given the laxity of economic constraints.

MD-only and joint techniques on the one hand and the delegation technique on the other is that the variation in ultimate resource expenditure may be greater for the latter than for the former two.

The implication of the fact that all techniques are stochastic is that the coordinates representing the MD-only and the joint techniques must be estimated by averaging observed input times, just as the coordinates of the delegation technique are. The problem is to identify correctly the observations that are manifestations of each technique type, prior to calculating the averages.[7]

This section examines a subset of the encounters in the upper respiratory HEG, which excludes all encounters during which an HP contributed to the production process. By excluding the HP from the analysis we can focus on the role of the traditional aide (TA). Then in the next section we take up the role of one type of HP, the Medex (MDX).

The quantities of MD and TA time expended on all encounters that were produced without an HP are represented by the points in Fig. 6. Points on the MD axis represent random drawings from the distribution of type A resource combinations. Points on the TA axis represent random drawings from the distribution of type B resource combinations. Points between the two axes represent random drawings from either a distribution of type C resource combinations or a distribution of type D resource combinations.

In Section 5.2 we discussed the characteristics of the type C and type D resource combinations. Whereas both types ultimately involve both the MD and the other provider, type C is the result of an initial practice decision to delegate, which subsequently leads to referral to the MD, while type D is the result of an initial practice decision to produce jointly. Because joint production typically involves the assignment of relatively routine predictable tasks to the non-MD, variations in the intensity or severity of the encounter are more likely to result in variation in the MD's time than in variation in the non-MD's time. Thus, the distribution of type D resource combinations is likely to lie near the MD axis. On the other hand, delegation and subsequent referral frequently require that the MD repeat the diagnostic tasks that produced the results causing the non-MD to refer. Thus type C resource combinations may involve large expenditures of the time of both providers

---

[7] T. Cowing has correctly pointed out that there is a problem in distinguishing empirically between D, or joint-process observations, and C, or delegation-process observations. The basic problem is that, although D involves "certain" referral while C involves "uncertain" referral, there is no observable information for distinguishing between certain and uncertain referrals. Essentially, we have another unobservable variable problem. Since we have not been able to identify structurally related observable variables that could be used to determine whether specific observations represent joint-process or delegation-process production, we have had to make somewhat arbitrary distinctions.

TABLE 2

Estimated Coordinates of Typical MD–TA Resource Combinations (Minutes)

	Point A ($n = 57$)	Point B ($n = 7$)	Point C ($n = 3$)	Point D ($n = 129$)
MD time	8.61 (0.54)[a]	0	9.17 (1.01)	8.09 (0.31)
TA time	0	15.36 (2.38)	22.00 (1.15)	3.88 (0.24)

[a] Standard errors of the estimated expected input times appear in parentheses beneath the estimates.

and produce points in the northeast portion of the first quadrant of input space.

On the basis of this characterization of the distinction between type C and type D resource combinations, we classify all but three of the 132 points between the axes in Fig. 6 as examples of attempted joint production. The three exceptional combinations, which appear to be examples of delegation followed by referral, are the right-most three points between the axes in Fig. 6.

The coordinates of the centroids of the four sets of observations representing the four types of resource combinations are estimates of the four expected resource combinations facing the practice. The points labeled A, B, C, and D locate these four centroids in Fig. 6. The estimated coordinates and their standard errors are presented in Table 2.

We defined the referral parameter in Section 5.2 as the probability that a delegated encounter would be referred to the MD for completion. The referral parameter can be estimated as the number of referred encounters divided by the total number of delegated encounters or $\frac{3}{10}$.[8] This estimate of the referral parameter is used to situate the point $E_{3/10}$ on the line connecting points B and C in Fig. 6. The point $E_{3/10}$ represents the estimated expected outcome of the practice decision to delegate the encounter to a TA.

The application of our typology of resource combinations to the observed MD–TA resource combinations in Fig. 6 reveals that the TA can play two different roles in the production processes for the outputs in this HEG. The predominant role, played by the TA in 129 of the 139 encounters in which the TA was involved, is participation in a joint production process that may require the performance of a small number of routine tasks at the beginning of the patient's visit. Another potential role of the TA appears

[8] One of the six visible Xs on the horizontal axis of Fig. 6 represents two encounters with the same coordinates.

to be represented by the ten encounters summarized by point $E_{3/10}$ in Fig. 6. On these encounters the TA appears to have been delegated independent responsibility for the patient. Further analysis would be required to determine whether these encounters were produced by a single TA at a single practice who had been explicitly trained for independent responsibility in this HEG or by several TAs at more than one practice. In any event the rarity of the independent role for the TA justifies the exclusion of this role from a description of the technology of ambulatory care.[9]

If the predominant role of the TA is the joint production of encounters with another provider, and if the TA substitutes for a significant amount of that provider's time in the course of fulfilling this role, then the analysis of the substitution possibilities between the MD and each of the HPs must control for TA involvement in the visit. Thus, it is important to determine the extent to which the TA can substitute for another provider's time when the TA is jointly involved in the encounter.

According to Table 2, if the practice chooses to produce an encounter in this HEG using the MD and the TA jointly, it can expect to save an estimated 0.52 minutes of the physician's time in exchange for the expenditure of 3.88 minutes of TA time.[10] To test the null hypothesis that this reduction in MD time is zero or negative against the alternative hypothesis that the choice of joint production achieves a positive savings of MD time, we first compute the standard error of the estimated difference between the population means from the standard errors given in Table 2:

$$\sqrt{(0.54)^2 + (0.31)^2} = 0.62.$$

The estimated difference between the population means is a linear combination of independently distributed random variables. Therefore, under the null hypothesis the test statistic:

$$(0.52 - 0)/0.62 = 0.84$$

is distributed approximately as a student's t with 184 degrees of freedom. Since a value of t as large as 0.84 could be obtained under the null hypothesis

---

[9] In a related paper, Davenport et al. [1975] have used the observational data to analyze empirically the "roles" of practitioners in terms of their task profiles and to determine the minimum number of such roles that adequately characterize the universe of practitioners observed in the study. Their results question the homogeneity of the roles played by providers with the same occupational or training titles.

[10] The implied rate of technical substitution is 7.6 minutes of TA time for 1 minute of MD time. The rate of technical substitution of Reinhardt's [1975, p. 163] production function evaluated at the sample mean is 4.04 hours of TA time for 1 hour of MD time. Although the approaches used to derive these two estimates of the rate of technical substitution are too different to permit comparison of the estimates, the fact that the estimates are of the same order of magnitude is of interest.

with a probability of 0.20, we fail to reject the null hypothesis at conventional confidence levels of 90 or 95%. We conclude, therefore, that involving the TA jointly with the MD in the production of the average encounter in this HEG results in no significant reduction in the amount of MD time required to produce the encounter.

On the basis of this finding, we shall ignore TA input in the analysis of the substitution possibilities between the MD and the HP in the following section. Since we have excluded the six encounters that involve more than one type of HP, we assume the remaining encounters can be represented without loss of significant information as points in a two-dimensional scatter plot with axes MD time and HP time.[11]

5.4   Observed Resource Combinations and the Technology Matrix

The input times required of the MD and the MDX for the production of each encounter in the upper respiratory HEW are plotted in Fig. 7. Points labeled *A* and *B* appear at coordinates that are calculated by averaging the

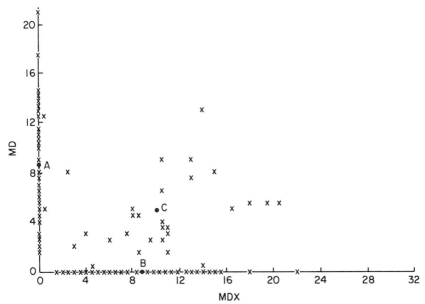

Figure 7   Scatter plot of input times for encounters in the upper respiratory HEG in which MD time and/or MDX time was expended.

[11] T. Cowing has suggested that a stronger test of the separability of the TA would be to repeat the above analysis holding HP time constant at several levels in addition to zero. Small sample size prevents our pursuing this suggestion.

TABLE 3

Estimates of Time Requirements for MD and MDX

Service number	Homogeneous encounter group	Number of encounters	a_i	b_i	c_i^{MD}	c_i^{MDX}	r_i
Acute services							
1	I.1	134	8.0	16.0	9.5	14.0	0.33
2	I.2	203	10.0	11.0	6.5	6.0	0.23
3	I.3	59	10.0	9.0	10.0	7.5	0.73
4	I.4	149	9.5	10.0	10.5	12.0	0.30
5	I.5	99	12.0	9.5	11.0	14.5	0.63
6	I.6	50	6.0	Not defined	—	—	
7	I.7	31	9.0	Not defined	—	—	
8	II.1	501	8.5	8.5	5.0	10.0	0.30
9	II.2	374	8.0	9.0	6.0	12.0	0.33
10	II.3	47	8.5	Not defined	—	—	
11	II.4	276	6.5	7.5	4.0	11.0	0.42
12	III.1	100	7.0	7.5	5.0	8.0	0.50
13	III.2	286	6.0	6.0	4.0	13.0	0.45
14	III.3	345	8.0	8.0	5.5	11.5	0.35
15	III.4	232	8.5	7.5	5.0	8.0	0.53
16	IV.1	131	8.5	8.0	6.5	11.5	0.56
17	IV.2	81	8.0	8.0	5.5	7.0	0.46
18	IV.3	73	6.5	7.0	6.0	7.5	0.44
19	V.1	228	10.0	10.5	8.0	11.0	0.52
20	V.2	127	9.0	9.0	6.0	8.0	0.35
21	V.3	52	10.5	Not defined	—	—	
22	V.4	84	10.0	Not defined	—	—	
Health maintenance							
23	IV.3	111	12.0	16.0	9.5	17.0	0.27
24	IV.2	171	16.5	26.5	16.0	21.0	0.47
25	IV.1	369	14.0	14.5	8.0	10.0	0.55
26	III.	123	5.5	5.5	8.5	3.0	0.34
27	II.2	147	5.0	8.0	6.5	4.5	0.50
28	II.1	74	8.5	Not defined	—	—	
Chronic							
29	I.2	152	8.0	8.0	7.5	9.0	0.37
30	I.3	134	8.5	Not defined	—	—	
31	II.1	81	8.5	10.5	7.0	8.0	0.65

input times of all observed MD-only and HP-only resource combinations, respectively. The observed resource combinations between the axes are averaged and graphed at a point labeled C. The decision to call that point C assumes that these combinations represent referrals rather than the use of a "joint process." In this example, the MDX refers 32 of 109, or 30%, of the encounters that were delegated to him.

Table 3 presents estimates of the time requirements for MD and MDX in producing encounters of each HEG using the MD-only process and the two possible outcomes using the delegation process—that is, with and without referral. The parameters in the column labeled a_i represent the number of minutes of MD time required to produce one encounter in the ith HEG with the MD-only technology; those in the column labeled b_i represent the number of minutes of MDX time required to produce one encounter in the ith HEG when it is not necessary for the MDX to refer to the MD; and those in the columns c_i^{MD} and c_i^{MDX} represent the number of minutes of MD time and MDX time, respectively, required to produce one encounter in the ith HEG when it is necessary for the MDX to refer the patient to the MD. The last column presents the referral rates for each HEG.

6.   An Activity Analysis Model

In order to examine the potential productivity impact of using a new health practitioner, we need some way of combining the empirical information contained in Table 3. We propose to represent the production problem of the ambulatory medical care practice by an activity analysis model.

A practice can be defined by a set of weights indicating the proportional demand for the various medical services (that is, the proportions in which encounters in the 31 HEGs must be produced). For a given scale of practice— the total number of encounters produced per period—the economic issues are (1) to identify the least costly or best staffing pattern and (2) to determine the corresponding choice of processes or techniques for producing the encounters of each type. Moreover, it must be recognized that to a large extent medical practice is organized around small physician-controlled firms. The indivisibility of labor inputs leads to a specification wherein medical workers are employed for normal work weeks.

The problem can be stated formally as an integer programming problem. So stated, the problem is amenable to computational solution. In order to concentrate on the productivity questions, we shall recast the problem in the form: maximize the total number of encounters produced given the technology and given specific amounts of available provider time. Let w_i be the proportion of total encounters produced by the practice S that are in the ith HEG. Then the requirement that this demand be met using one or more of several feasible techniques is expressed by the equation

$$w_i S - X_i - Y_i - Z_i = 0, \qquad i = 1, \ldots, 31,$$

where X_i is the number of encounters in the ith HEG produced by the MD-only technology, Y_i the number of encounters in the ith HEG produced by the MDX when it is not necessary to refer to the MD, and Z_i the number produced when it is necessary for the MDX to refer the patient to the MD.

The operation of any technique involves the use of MD and/or MDX time. The total time required of the MD and MDX can be written

$$\sum_i a_i X_i + \sum_i c_i^{MD} Z_i \qquad \text{and} \qquad \sum_i b_i Y_i + \sum_i c_i^{MDX} Z_i,$$

respectively, and each of these requirements must be less than the amount of time available by a full-time equivalent. Since the emphasis here is on the medical contact portion of practice activity, it is assumed that the available time of each person is 25 hours or 1500 minutes per week.

A final set of constraints reflects the rate at which the MDX must refer delegated encounters to the MD. In Section 5.2 we defined a "technique" as the expected vector of resource requirements corresponding to a given production process. The two alternative techniques associated with production of an encounter in the ith HEG are the MD-only technique and the delegation technique. The delegation technique is expected to consume a linear combination of the resource vectors illustrated by points B and C in Fig. 4. Since activities Y_i and Z_i correspond to points B and C, respectively, the referral constraint can be represented by requiring that activity Z_i be performed in fixed proportion to activity Y_i. If r_i represents the proportion of delegated encounters referred, then

$$Z_i \geq \frac{r_i}{1 - r_i} Y_i, \qquad i = 1, \ldots, 31.$$

The complete program can now be written

Maximize S subject to

    (i) $w_i S - X_i - Y_i - Z_i \leq 0, i = 1, \ldots, 31,$
    (ii) $\sum_i a_i X_i + \sum_i c_i^{MD} Z_i \leq 1500,$
    (iii) $\sum_i b_i Y_i + \sum_i c_i^{MDX} Z_i \leq 1500,$
    (iv) $r_i Y_i - (1 - r_i) Z_i \leq 0, i = 1, \ldots, 31.$

We begin by presenting the solution for the MD practicing without an MDX,

TABLE 4

Results for an MD Practicing With and Without an MDX[a]

| | Problem I | | Problem II | | Problem III | | Problem IV | |
| | Practice with MD and without MDX | | Practice with MD and MDX and no constraints on referral | | Practice with MD and MDX and constraints on referral | | Practice with MD and MDX and without MDX-only techniques | |
	TC_1	TC_2	TC_1	TC_2	TC_1	TC_2	TC_1	TC_2
Maximum scale of practice; encounters per week	168		339		287		215	
Practice revenue per week @ $11.25 per encounter	$1890		$3814		$3229		$2419	
Total cost (professional expenses) excluding cost of MDX	907		1831	1369	1549	1229	1161	1035
Net income before deducting cost of MDX	983		1983	2445	1679	2000	1258	1384
Cost of MDX	—		380	380	380	380	380	380
Net income of physician	983		1603	2065	1299	1620	878	1004

[a] $TC_1 = 5.4$ (output). $TC_2 = 454 + 2.7$ (output).

that is, without the existence of techniques Y_i and Z_i. The maximum scale in this case is 168 encounters per week. This is almost identical to the estimated average number of total visits per week of a general practice physician, which is reported to be 167.8.[12] Using data from the AMA's Periodic Survey of Physicians, such a practice would have gross income of \$89,845 and professional expenses of \$42,407 or 47% of gross income, leaving a net income of \$47,438.

Table 4 presents these results along with three alternative solutions in which the MD uses an MDX. In the first alternative there are no constraints on referral [that is, without constraints (iv)]. The second alternative solution is for the problem with referral constraints. The third alternative removes the Y_i technique, thereby requiring that when the MDX is used, the MD must also be involved in the encounter.

7. Economic Potential and Barriers to Change

Clearly, potential gains from using a health practitioner are substantial. When there are no constraints on referral the potential practice productivity increases from 168 to 339 encounters per week, or by approximately 100%. Even with constraints on referral, potential practice productivity increases from 168 to 287 encounters per week, or by about 70%.

In order to obtain some understanding of how this increased productivity affects the income of the physician it is necessary to make assumptions about the way revenues and costs depend on the scale of practice output. Based on aggregate data from the AMA Periodic Survey of Physicians, we assume an average revenue of \$11.25 per encounter. We present results for two alternative versions of the total cost function. In the first alternative we assume that total cost (professional expense, other than the cost of the MDX) is proportional to output. Using aggregate data we obtain an average cost of \$5.40 per encounter and the following total cost function:

$$TC_1 = 5.4 \, (\text{output}) + \text{cost of MDX.}$$

As a second alternative, we consider a linear cost function with a marginal cost equal to \$2.70 or one-half of average cost at the maximum scale of output for a practice with MD and without MDX. Thus, we use the following total cost function:

$$TC_2 = 454 + 2.7 \, (\text{output}) + \text{cost of MDX.}$$

We see in Table 4 that with an MDX and constraints on referral, the potential net income of the physician increases by \$316 per week with TC_1 and by \$637 per week with TC_2. This represents a potential incentive for the physician who uses an MDX.

However, a number of considerations have affected and are likely to continue to affect the extent to which this potential is realized. Whether or not the choices made by physicians are technically and economically efficient depends upon the physician's knowledge of the production function; the constraints—either perceived or actual—imposed on his behavior; and the economic losses associated with deviations from efficiency. In addition, the actual increase in physician productivity will depend on the amount of unmet demand.

Observed variability in delegation suggests that even physicians who have adopted new health practitioners are uncertain about their appropriate roles and the methods for achieving them. The essential issues of how to relate patients to practitioners and how to provide the physician with assurance that the management of patient care is appropriate have, for the most part, been neglected. Moreover, economic incentives that might help to overcome these uncertainties are particularly weak in the medical care sector. Competition, as an institutional mechanism that would discipline producers who failed to use scarce resources in an efficient manner, is limited by restrictions on entry, licensure, the inability of consumers to make informed rational decisions, and the dominant role of insurance, which results in a lack of financial responsibility by the consumer for his own care. As a result, there is no obvious reason to believe that all the benefits of improved productivity from employing health practitioners will be achieved.

Another major impediment to the use of health practitioners is the result of specific government policy. The Social Security Administration has ruled that under Title XVIII of the Medicare Act, a noninstitutional medical practice cannot be reimbursed for any services rendered solely by a helath practitioner (HP) even if these services were performed on the premises of the employing physician's practice. In order to be reimbursable, the participation of nonphysicians in the medical care process must be incidental to the physician's own activities. In Table 4, the last column illustrates the effect of this constraint. Having removed the Medex-only techniques from the set of technological alternatives, the potential productivity of the practice is 215 encounters per week. The increase in productivity from using an MDX is reduced from 70% to less than 30% above the level obtainable by an MD practicing without an MDX. Moreover, this constraint severely reduces and may actually eliminate the potential economic incentive of increased net income for the physician who uses the MDX. This reimbursement policy is in conflict with the government's support of health practitioner education;

by reducing economic attractiveness, the acceptance of this new technology is discouraged.

Finally, the level and composition of demand for the services of the practice place constraints on the economically efficient use of health manpower. The question of whether there will be sufficient demand for the additional patient visits will influence the physician's decision to hire a health practitioner as well as limit the actual increase in practice productivity. Figures 8a and b illustrate the relationship between revenue and costs on the one hand and the scale of practice on the other. Depending upon the

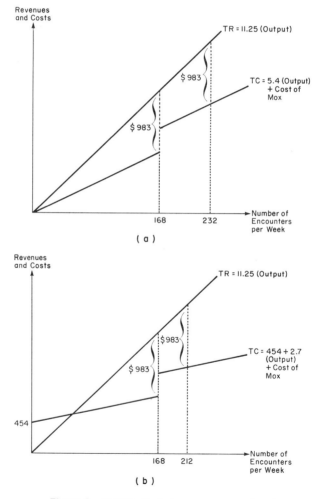

Figure 8   Relationship between revenue and cost.

assumed cost function, the scale of practice must be increased to 212 or 232 encounters per week before the physician reaches a net income equal to that which he could realize practicing alone.

8.   Conclusion

In this paper we have presented a methodology for studying the productivity of ambulatory medical practices and the impact on productivity of introducing a new nonphysician practitioner into the production process. Our conclusions are that (i) potential productivity may increase by as much as 100%, but (ii) regulations on the type of delegation allowed might severely limit the extent to which this potential is realized, and (iii) the practice must face enough unmet demand that production can be increased substantially if the adoption of this new provider is to be economically attractive.

Appendix: Dendograms and Chief-Complaint Groupings for Encounters in the Chronic and Health Maintenance Categories

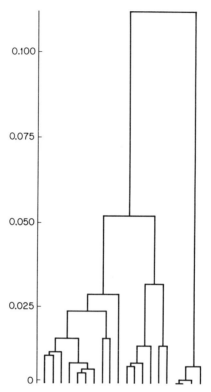

Figure A1   Dendrogram of clustering of 20 chronic chief complaints.

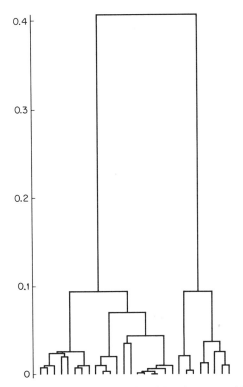

Figure A2 Dendrogram of clustering of 28 health maintenance chief complaints.

TABLE A1

Chronic Chief-Complaint Clusters and HEGs

Subgroup	Number of encounters	National ambulatory medical care survey complaint code	Chief complaint
Major group I			
I.1	86	0560	Headache
		9970	None
		9856	Heart check
		0620[a]	Disturbance of sleep
		(6200)[b]	(Urinary tract infect.)
		(9203)	(Blood test)
I.2	152	9852	Blood pressure check
I.3	134	9802	Diabetes check
		0690[a]	Vertigo, dizziness[a]
		(5400)	(Abdominal pain)
I.4	25	9808	Thyroid/goiter check
		4100[a]	Pain in face/neck[a]
Major group II			
II.1	81	4000	Pain/swelling in lower extremity
		9803	Chronic arthritis
		4050	Pain/swelling in upper extremity
		4150	Pain/swelling in back
II.2	14	9101	Allergy shots
II.3	16	9809	Colitis, ulcer check
Major group III			
III	49	1000	Acne
		1060	Infections
		1110	Warts
		1130	Skin irritations
		1131[a]	Rash[a]

[a] Chief complaints not included in the clustering depicted by the dendrogram in Fig. A.1. Nevertheless, encounters with these complaints were included in the corresponding HEG on the basis of other clustering results and prior information.

[b] Chief complaints enclosed in parentheses were not used to define the corresponding HEG despite the clustering results presented in Fig. A.1 because of evidence that encounters with these complaints more properly belong to the acute or health maintenance categories.

TABLE A2

Health Maintenance Chief-Complaint Clusters and HEGs

Subgroup	Number of encounters	National ambulatory medical care survey complaint code	Chief Complaint
Major group I	162	(0040)	(Fatigue)[a]
		(8100)	(Nervousness)
		(9501)	(Preoperation check-up)
		(1131)	(Rash)
		(4000)	(Pain/swelling)
		(5400)	(Abdominal pain)
		(9450)	(Get test results)
		(9104)	(Prescription renewal)
Major group II			
II.1	74	9040	Gynecological exam
		9052	Postnatal exam
		9300	Desire counseling
		9051	Suspect pregnancy
II.2	147	9050	Pregnancy exam
		(9400)	(Physician counselling)
Major group III	123	9101	Allergy shots
		9601	Ears pierced
		9103	Injections
		9106	Other injections
		9102	Immunizations
		9203	Blood test
Major group IV			
IV.1	369	(3120)	(Cold)
		9060	Well baby exam
		9061	Well child exam
IV.2	171	9000	General med exam
		(9852)	(Blood pressure check)
IV.3	111	9013	Social Security exam
		9014	High school exam
		9016	Preemployment exam

[a] Chief complaints enclosed in parentheses were not used to define HEGs. Encounters having only parenthesized complaints were excluded from the analysis. Reasons for excluding these complaints included small sample size, inappropriate classification as health maintenance, and the desire to maximize the homogeneity of the HEGs.

Part IV

POLICY IMPLICATIONS

13

Pollution Controls and Productivity Growth in Basic Industries

Robert W. Crandall
The Brookings Institution
Washington, D.C.

The decline in productivity growth that has occurred in the United States and other countries since 1973 has most observers puzzled. The disruptive changes in relative energy prices, changes in the demographic composition of the labor force, reduced rates of real investment, and reduced outlays for research and development have been advanced as partial explanations for the decline. For the United States, however, all of these factors combined are not sufficient to explain the sharp drop in productivity that has occurred in the nonfarm private sector. At least part of the explanation may lie in expensive new regulatory programs. Denison [1978a] argues that as much as 0.35 percentage points of the growth in output per unit input were sacrificed to environmental and employee health and safety regulation in 1975, the most recent year he analyzes. While this is a small fraction of the recent decline in productivity, it does not bode well for the future. Environmental policy is likely to reduce the potential flow of privately produced goods and services at an even more rapid rate in the next five to ten years.

In this paper, I shall argue that environmental policy has been designed in a manner that has deleterious effects upon economic growth beyond its direct effect of mandating resources for pollution control. In large part, this design may be purposive since the cause of environmental purity may be served by reduced economic growth. But this is not a stated goal of our

347

environmental legislation, nor does everyone accept it as a goal. Since there are still those who would argue that environmental purity should be achieved at the lowest possible social cost, it might be useful to examine the political forces that dictate the inefficiency of the current policy.

In the first section of this paper, I detail the political rationale for the current standards-setting policy. In the second section, I offer some limited evidence of the immediate manifestation of this policy for air-pollution control—systematically different costs of control per unit of pollution removal across major sources. In the third section, I examine differences in the growth of labor productivity in the 1970s across industries to determine if there is any basis for suspecting that environmental policy is contributing to the deceleration of productivity growth that has occurred since 1973. Finally, I offer some very tentative results for individual industries based upon labor productivity alone.

Before proceeding through this political–economic analysis, the reader should be warned that I am attempting to assess the effects of environmental policy upon *measured* output per unit input. Presumably, environmental policy contributes improvements to the "quality of life," which are largely unmeasured in conventional output statistics. In fact, given current measurement techniques, these increments to environmental quality are probably unmeasurable. This is not a major problem for the purposes of this paper since it is still useful to determine how much measured output we are sacrificing for environmental reasons. No judgment as to the appropriate degree of sacrifice is possible without a measure of the value of the environmental improvements generated, however, and none is attempted in this paper.

1. Politics and Technology in Pollution Control

The guiding principle behind the basic water and pollution control strategies underwritten by Congress in the past nine years has been that regulation should be "technology forcing."[1] In addition, controls should be imposed in such a manner as to minimize the potential political cost of workers being laid off because of new controls mandated by government. Predictably, these basic principles have been translated into the following regulatory approach:

1. Environmental standards for individual polluters are engineering standards rather than performance standards.

[1] For a comprehensive description of this and other features of environmental policy see Ruff [1978], pp. 251 ff.

2. New industrial plants are treated much more harshly than older facilities.

3. Rapidly growing industries are likely to have tighter standards than their less-dynamic counterparts.

4. Capital-intensive industries are likely to be saddled with the tightest regulations while labor-intensive industries escape with lighter burdens.

5. Firms subject to binding rate-of-return regulation are especially likely to be singled out for tight standards.

Each of these requirements is likely to create economic waste and to slow the rate of productivity growth.

1.1 Engineering Standards

There are a variety of reasons why environmental policy is effected through a set of engineering rather than performance standards. In the first place, monitoring techniques are in a rather primitive state of development. As a result, enforcement is much simpler if it can be presumed that the presence of a given piece of equipment connotes compliance than if continuous or intermittent monitoring of pollution is required. To argue that engineering standards are more efficient, however, requires that the absence of monitoring not reduce the performance of the capital-intensive equipment. Flue-gas scrubbers, wastewater treatment facilities, and even automobile catalytic converters require attention and maintenance. If lax enforcement allows owners of this equipment to neglect such maintenance, the savings in monitoring costs may be largely illusory.

Second, the goal of forcing technology is likely to lead to de facto engineering standards. A particular control technology can be certified as the "best available" until the next generation of control techniques emerges.

Third, standards that discriminate among polluters in the same area for political reasons are more easily justified if they are described as the "best available" technological choice. Different performance standards would be too visible an indication of political favoritism. These factors add up to a powerful set of political forces for opposing performance standards and (especially) pollution discharge fees or marketable rights.

Engineering standards are likely to embody a more capital-intensive technique of control than performance standards. To the extent that productivity growth is related to the embodiment of new technology in capital equipment, investment directed toward capital-intensive pollution control must have unduly harsh effects upon productivity, since the scarce capital resources could be better used to produce other goods and services. For instance, requiring that public utilities use stackgas scrubbers when they could burn low-sulfur coal with the same effect upon pollution is likely to divert savings from other productive uses, thereby reducing the growth in productivity.[2] Environmental policy would have to increase the aggregate savings rate to offset this negative effect upon productivity—an unlikely possibility.

1.2 New versus Old Facilities

For stationary sources of air and water pollution, the Environmental Protection Agency (EPA) is required by statute to distinguish between existing and new sources of pollution. Under the Federal Water Pollution Control Act of 1972, EPA had to specify effluent guidelines for all pollution sources based upon the best practicable and the best available technologies (BPT and BAT). In addition, it was to promulgate "best available demonstrated control technology" standards for new sources coming into production prior to 1983. In effect, new sources were subject to more rigorous standards than existing sources—in no small part because compliance with BPT did not occur for many existing plants and because BAT has effectively been delayed.

For air pollution, the legislative mandate is much clearer. New sources are generally required to use the best available control technology while existing sources are left to play the political game with state authorities who draft state implementation plans. Moreover, pristine and undeveloped regions in the country are to be protected to a greater degree than urbanized areas—despite the apparent intent of Congress to stress human health in designing clean-air policy. As a result, new plant construction may be severely impeded in these areas of "prevention of significant deterioration" (PSD), which are likely to be the best locations for new paper, cement, metals, or chemical facilities.

In effect, the stronger standards for new plants reduce the incentive for business to replace old plants and to embody new technology in new equipment. Since any new facility within an existing plant qualifies as a "source" under the Clean Air Act, there are disincentives even to replace outdated equipment at existing plants.[3]

---

[2] U.S. Environmental Protection Agency, *Standards of Performance for New Stationary Sources: Electric Utility Steam Generating Plants*, September 5, 1978. EPA promulgated scrubbing standards that required all new utility plants to install scrubbers regardless of the sulfur content of coal. This was a somewhat more efficient strategy than an earlier EPA proposal that was so onerous as to actually generate more pollution and substantially greater costs than the slightly "weaker" standard.

[3] This is not affected by the EPA "bubble" policy, which allows plants to achieve plant-wide standards. New sources are still defined as individual points of discharge within the plant and are subject to technology-based standards. See "Blowing Bubbles at EPA," *Regulation*, March–April, 1979.

1.3 The Bias against Rapidly Growing Industries

The setting of pollution standards is a political process. A serious political threat created by new environmental or occupational health regulations is unemployment, especially that arising from plant closings. If standards can be introduced into dynamic, growing industries, the prospects for reducing employment levels from those predating the standards are much reduced. Moreover, the higher costs created by regulation can be absorbed into product prices in these industries without actually reducing output levels and thereby placing existing plants in jeopardy. For this reason, among others, one would expect the chemicals industry to be the recipient of tight standards while copper smelters or steel firms receive much more lenient treatment.[4]

This growth-industry bias is shown in Table 1, derived from BEA data on pollution-control outlays. The major industries identified in the table accounted for more than 75% of all pollution-control capital outlays in 1973–1976. Of these, only petroleum refining and steel were growing more slowly than manufacturing in general prior to 1970. But one might argue that this distribution is not due to a bias against growing industries by environmental authorities. It could simply reflect the fact that these industries are the heaviest polluters. In fact, they are the most important polluters, but we shall see that the most rapidly growing among them—utilities and chemicals—generally are saddled with the highest control costs per ton of pollution removed. They have less political strength than steel mills, for example, because environmental controls are not likely to cause them to reduce employment.

1.4 The Capital-Intensity Bias

Not only rapidly growing industries are likely to fare less well in the standards-setting process, but highly capital-intensive industries are also likely to fare poorly, and for precisely the same reason. Labor-intensive industries can be expected to suffer greater adjustments in output and employment from the shock of major pollution-control outlays. Except for the relatively labor-intensive steel industry, most pollution-control expenditures

---

[4] EPA collects plant-closure data, attempting to ascertain the closures for which pollution costs were alleged to be a factor. These data show a very small number of jobs lost or threatened by pollution controls—only 0.2% of manufacturing employment—since 1971. By themselves they tell us very little about the political–economic strategy employed in environmental policy other than to demonstrate that old-plant standards have either been so generous or so poorly enforced as to cause little dislocation. An efficient strategy of pollution control, raising the price of using clean air or clean water from zero to its appropriate social cost, would probably generate much more dislocation. But if standards are set very leniently for industries such as copper smelting, few jobs will be lost and pollution will not be controlled at the lowest possible social cost.

TABLE 1

Relative Growth Rates of Pollution-Control Impacted Industries and All Industries,
1955–1970[a]

Industry	SIC code	Pollution-control capital expenditures, 1973–1976[b] (million $)	Annual growth in output[c] 1955–1970
Paper	26	1860	4.7
Chemicals	28	2357	7.4
Petroleum refining	291	3902	3.5
Steel	331	1321	0.8
Primary nonferrous metals	333	1986	4.3
Electric utilities	49 (part)	6716	7.6
Total		18,142	5.5[d]
Total, all industries		24,166	4.1

[a] Sources: U.S. Department of Commerce, Bureau of Economic Analysis (BEA), *Capital Expenditures by Business for Pollution Abatement*; Federal Reserve Board (FRB), *Industrial Production*.

[b] BEA data.

[c] FRB index.

[d] Average, weighted by pollution-capital expenditures.

are undertaken by capital-intensive firms. As Table 2 shows, most of the affected industries are more capital intensive than the average manufacturing industry. Again, this could reflect the fact that capital-intensive industries are the major polluters. More conclusive evidence would be the relative costs of pollution control at the margin for these industries.

1.5 The Regulated Industry

Finally, one can identify the ideal political target for the environmentalist—the firm that has been growing rapidly, is highly capital intensive, faces price-inelastic demand, and is subject to rate-of-return regulation. The electric utility industry is just such a target, and politicians have been quick to realize this. Labor is less likely to be displaced by very tight utility standards for air pollution because returns to capital can be maintained without even a transitional loss if the utility can persuade its state regulatory commission to act in a timely fashion. Technology-based standards can be imposed without the public understanding how much of its monthly utility bill is due to stringent environmental controls. The result is that nearly one-

TABLE 2

Nonlabor Share of Value Added in Pollution-Control-Affected Industries, 1976[a]

Industry	SIC code	Pollution-control capital expenditures 1976 (census data)	Nonlabor share in value added, 1976
Grain milling	204	33.9	0.718
Pulp mills	2611	96.3	0.683
Paper mills	2621	274.7	0.513
Paperboard mills	2631	89.9	0.609
Building paper mills	2661	2.2	0.438
Inorganic chemicals	281	178.0	0.669
Plastics materials	282	131.4	0.597
Industrial organic chemicals	286	412.5	0.749
Miscellaneous chemicals	289	34.6	0.632
Petroleum refining	2911	427.6	0.796
Hydraulic cement	3241	29.5	0.610
Steel	331	495.4	0.315
Primary nonferrous metals	333	234.3	0.592
Average (weighted by pollution control capital expenditures)		(Total: 2440.3)	0.602
Average, excluding steel		(Total: 1091.4)	0.675
All manufacturing		(Total: 2531.7)	0.502

[a] Source: U.S. Bureau of the Census, Current Industrial Reports, *Pollution Abatement Costs and Expenditures*, 1976; *Annual Survey of Manufactures*, 1976, *Industry Profiles*.

third of all environmental capital outlays now flow from utilities,[5] and the percentage is rising as the Congress writes ever more specific provisions to require that tight standards be forced upon utilities while copper smelters are to be given lenient compliance schedules.

2.   The Stringency of Air Pollution Standards across Industries

While I believe that it is still too early to discern the full effect of even the current environmental controls upon productivity, the basis for my concern that high-productivity growth industries are penalized in the standards-setting process deserves greater scrutiny. An obvious method for testing this

[5] Bureau of Economic Analysis, U.S. Department of Commerce estimate as published annually in the *Survey of Current Business*. See Rutledge *et al.* [1978].

political theory of setting standards would be to examine marginal control costs for various pollutants across industries. Unfortunately such data are not readily available, in large part because they are not very important in the regulatory process. However, limited information can be obtained for air pollution control costs, although it is for manufacturing industries only.

As a preliminary measure of the differences in control costs across industries, solely for air pollution, I use data on tons of pollution removed and control costs as reported to the Bureau of the Census by manufacturers. The pollutant data are divided into four categories: (i) total particulates (TP); (ii) sulfur oxides (SO); (iii) hydrocarbons (HC), carbon monoxide (CO), and oxides of nitrogen (NO); and (iv) emissions of hazardous materials and heavy metals.

Given the nature of pollution control, one would expect control costs, C_{ij}, to increase at an increasing rate with the amount of pollution removed, P_{ij}, at each point source:

$$C_{ij} = f(P_{ij}), \qquad f' > 0, \quad f'' > 0, \tag{1}$$

$$i = 1, \ldots, n \text{ sources}, \quad j = 1, \ldots, 4 \text{ pollutants}.$$

Unfortunately data are reported by industry only for given geographical breakdowns—states or SMSAs. Therefore, the cost of controlling the ith air pollutant in a given area is equal to

$$\sum_i C_{ij} = \sum_i f(P_{ij}). \tag{2}$$

Unless one knew something about the distribution of pollution across states or SMSAs, it would be very difficult to estimate Eq. (1). However, it is possible to use the state data to estimate the *average* cost of removal for an industry by writing the total pollution control costs for the kth industry as

$$\sum_i \sum_j C_{ijk} = \left[\frac{\sum_i \sum_j f_j(P_{ijk})}{\sum_i \sum_j P_{ijk}} \right] \sum_i \sum_j P_{ijk}, \tag{3}$$

$$i = 1, \ldots, n \text{ sources in the industry},$$
$$j = 1, \ldots, 4 \text{ pollutants}, \quad k = 1, \ldots, K \text{ industries}.$$

Estimates of (3) from the available cross-sectional data allow us only to infer the magnitudes of each of the $\sum_i f_j(P_{ijk})/\sum_i P_{ijk}$ for each of the industries.

For statistical estimation, the cost function is written

$$\sum_i \sum_j C_{ijk} = a_0 + a_1 \sum_i P_{i1k} + a_2 \sum_i P_{i2k} + a_3 \sum_i P_{i3k} + a_4 \sum_i P_{i4k} + u_k,$$

$$k = 1, \ldots, K, \tag{4}$$

where each of the a_j's is equal to $\sum_i f_j(P_{ijk})/\sum_i P_{ijk}$, the average cost of pollution removal across the states within each of the K industries for each of the four pollutants.

Data on pollution abatement by state are available only for two-digit manufacturing industries, and only four two-digit industries are worth considering in estimating Eq. (4): paper; chemicals; petroleum and coal products; and primary metals. Data for electric utilities are not available since they are not in the manufacturing sector. As Table 3 demonstrates, however, the four industries account for most of the pollution removal in manufacturing industries for the relevant pollutants. The data used are for 1975 because 1976 data are riddled with disclosure problems. The unit of observation is the state. The estimated coefficients from Eq. (4) are reported in Table 4, with t-statistics in parentheses below them.

Control costs vary across industries by more than 7:1 for particulates and by more than 9:1 for SO. As one might expect, hazardous emissions do not affect costs significantly, nor does the HC–NO–CO combination except in chemicals. Surprisingly, petroleum refining does not show a significant coefficient for HC–NO–CO, perhaps a reflection of the fact that the HC it captures is its principal product.

How can the results in Table 4 be translated into a measure of efficiency loss? We cannot deduce the shape of (1) from the regression coefficients in (4). To do this, we need to know something about how control costs increase as all sources in a given jurisdiction are forced to tighten controls over time.

TABLE 3

Pollutants Removed by Selected Two-Digit Manufacturing Industries, 1976[a]

| SIC code | Industry | Thousand tons | | | |
		TP	SO	HC–CO–NO	Hazardous emissions
26	Paper	4565.7	189.8	43.2	71.2
28	Chemicals	3490.9	603.6	1572.2	512.1
29	Petroleum and coal products	4525.3	3591.4	8717.6	15.3
33	Metals	8329.0	1974.4	971.4	279.9
	Total of four industries	20,910.9	6,359.2	11,704.4	878.5
	All manufacturing	42,724.9	6,652.1	11,835.4	1,111.5
	Share of above four industries in total	48.9%	95.6%	98.9%	79.0%

[a] Source: U.S. Bureau of the Census, *Pollution Abatement Costs and Expenditures*, 1976.

TABLE 4

Estimated Average Cost of Pollution Removal, 1975[a]

SIC code	Industry	Dollars per ton			
		TP	SO	HC–CO–NO	Hazardous emissions
26	Paper	12.03	69.44	—	—
		(2.59)	(1.05)		
28	Chemicals	13.42	245.19	25.97	—
		(2.36)	(4.69)	(4.24)	
29	Petroleum and coal products	6.10	87.21	—	—
		(4.10)	(12.22)		
33	Metals	46.53	26.66	—	—
		(21.35)	(4.41)		

[a] From Eq. (4); t statistics in parentheses.

TABLE 5

Pollutants Removed and Pollution Control Costs, All Manufacturing Industries, 1974 and 1976[a]

Year	Pollutants removed (Thousand tons)			
	TP	SO	HC–CO–NO	Hazardous emissions
1974	40,096.2	5362.7	10,953.0	1417.4
1976	42,724.9	6652.1	11,835.4	1111.5
Percent change	+6.6	+24.0	+8.1	−22.6

Year	Air pollution operating costs for all manufacturing industries (millions of dollars)	
	Costs	Costs deflated to 1974
1974	1172.1	1172.1
1976	1842.2	1597.6
Percent change	+57.2	+36.3

[a] Source: U.S. Bureau of the Census, *Pollution Abatement Costs and Expenditures*, 1974 and 1976.

Unfortunately, there are only four years of data. Looking at 1974 and 1976 in Table 5, we see that TP, SO, and HC–NO–CO emissions reductions increased by 6.6, 24.0, and 8.1%, respectively, for all U.S. manufacturing, while control costs increased by 36.3% in 1974 dollars. One possible functional form that is crudely consistent with these changes is:

$$C_{ij} = b_0 P_{ij}^2. \tag{5}$$

Of course, the inference depends importantly upon the *distribution* of the tightened controls across sources, but (5) is at least plausible as a first approximation. Assuming (5), we can obtain the cost of removing the same total SO and TP pollution from the four industries under the economically efficient rule that f'_{ij}, the marginal cost of pollution reduction for the ith source and the jth pollutant, be equated across states. The result is that 40% of the one billion dollars spent in 1976 on these two pollutants by four major industries might be saved by more efficient (and less political) control strategies, assuming that the form of (5) is a reasonable approximation of (1).[6]

The above results are rather crude and speculative. First, the data on pollution reduction may not be very reliable. For instance, the aggregate total of particulates removed in manufacturing seems very high compared to EPA data on current pollution loadings. Second, it is impossible to know what percentage reduction is being achieved in each state, and it is very likely that incremental and average control costs vary more with the percentage reduction than with the absolute quantity removed. Finally, insufficient time series data are available to estimate a "production function" for pollution removal.

Nevertheless, the data on SO removal do seem to support the political theory of pollution control. Chemical plants, refiners, and paper mills pay much more per ton for sulfur removal than do metal smelters, but it also appears that steel firms are paying more for particulate control than their more prosperous and dynamic brethren in the other three industries. Perhaps steel manufacture is one exception to our political rule—a fact reflected by its prominence in repeated government jawboning exercises.

Partial confirmation of these results may be found in EPA data on control costs for selected pollutants across industries. Some data are available for SO, NO, and HC, but not for particulates. These data are summarized in Table 6.

---

[6] If $C_{ij} = b_0 P_{ij}^2$, then $dC_{ij}/dP_{ij} = 2b_0 P_{ij}$. Since we know $\sum_i P_{ij}$ and have estimates of $\sum_i C_{ij}/\sum_i P_{ij}$, we can solve for b_0. The lowest-cost equilibrium requires adjusting the $\sum_i P_{ij}$ across industries until all $2b_0 \sum_i P_{ij}$ are equated. For particulates, for instance, the paper, coal, and refining industries would have to reduce their discharges by 5.93 million tons per year while primary metals increased theirs by 5.3 millions tons. As a result, the incremental costs across industries would be equated at $26.80 per net ton removed.

TABLE 6

Estimated Control Costs for Selected Air Pollutants

	(Dollars per ton removed)			
	Sulfur oxides[a]		Hydrocarbons[b]	
	(1978$)			
Source	Existing sources	New sources	Prospectively under RACT (1978$)	
Electric utilities	228	619–833	Gasoline storage	200
Copper smelters	65	121	Gasoline service stations	−110–375
Refineries	110	538	Automobile assembly painting	205–2910
H₂SO₄ plants	62	—	Can coating	100–215
			Chemicals	−275–220
			Marine terminals	4000

1976 Estimate of incremental control costs for available technology (1976$)[c]

Nitrogen oxides		Hydrocarbons	
Source	Cost	Source	Cost
Industrial boilers	150	Refining	13
Utility boilers	200–225	Industrial refining	100
Stationary IC engines	340–1700	Miscellaneous chemicals	200
1981 auto standards	450	Gasoline distribution	270
		Coke ovens	435
		1981 auto standards	470

[a] Source: EPA.

[b] Source: EPA, *Cost and Economic Impact Assessment for Alternative Levels of NAAQS for Ozone.*

[c] Source: EPA, *Air Quality, Noise and Health*; Report of Interagency Task Force on Motor Vehicle Goals Beyond 1980.

Perhaps the best available data are for SO because of the controversy created by the stack-gas scrubber and the abortive proposal for a sulfur tax. EPA data show that existing SO and nonferrous smelter sources have control costs that are less than 60% of the costs of SO removal for petroleum refineries and roughly 25% of those for utilities. This is quite in keeping with the theory advanced in Section 1 and the results shown in Table 4.

For NO and HC emissions, the data are more speculative. As the standards have been reappraised for automobiles, various government agencies have analyzed the alternative costs of removing NO, HC, or CO from stationary sources. What they have generally found is that tightening stationary source standards would be much more cost effective than pursuing the 1981 automobile standards for HC and NO, but Congress has obviously been unmoved by this analysis. A range of hypothesized control costs for tightened stationary and automobile standards is reproduced as the "1976 Estimate" of prospective control costs in Table 6.

Finally, EPA is now required to set stringent "reasonably available control technology" (RACT) standards for nonattainment areas. While the agency has not yet done so, a staff report has identified the possible range of control costs across sources, some of which are reproduced in Table 6. In reviewing this evidence, the staff stated:

> While cost effectiveness serves a useful purpose as one factor in comparing control measures, it cannot serve as the only decision-making tool. Cost effectiveness in itself does not give any indication of the economic feasibility of alternatives since it does not take into account the baseline economic or financial conditions of the industry.[7]

Thus "economic feasibility" is the ability to pay, not economic efficiency. As a result, this new variant of environmental standard setting will be another attempt to tax away quasi-rents, rather than an attempt to use resources efficiently.

3. Productivity Growth in Basic Industries

The engineering standards-setting process is inefficient since it allows political considerations to substitute for economic criteria in control decisions. In the preceding section I focused entirely upon the dissimilar costs of air-pollution removal across sources which results from federal new-source standards and state standards for existing sources. Given the extremely complicated approach of the Federal Water Pollution Control Act and the case-by-case approach of the NPDES permit system, there is little reason to believe that the results would be any different for water-pollution control.

The standards-setting process is not only inefficient in a static sense. Because of the manner in which it penalizes growing industries, it undoubtedly reduces capital formation in these industries and therefore slows down the growth in productivity that is embodied in new technology. To what extent this has actually happened may be difficult to tell because the policy has been in existence for a very short time. It would be necessary to estimate investment functions across industries and to test for the presence

[7] U.S. Environmental Protection Agency [1979].

TABLE 7

Productivity Changes in Pollution-Control-Affected Industries, 1958–1976[a]

Industry	SIC code	Pollution capital expenditures, 1973–1976 (million $)		Value-added 1976 (million $)	Average annual increase in output per employee-hour (%)			
		BEA Data	Census Data		1958–1970	1970–1976	1958–1973	1973–1976
Grain milling	204	—	129.2	6083	3.9[b]	3.1	3.3[b]	4.3
Pulp mills	2611	1860	327.6	9220.4	4.3	3.3	4.6	1.0
Paper mills	2621		908.8					
Paperboard mills	2631		519.3					
Building paper mills	2661		15.6					
Inorganic chemicals	281	2357	533.2	6164.7	4.3	1.8	4.4	−1.6
Plastics materials	282		437.8	6647.8	4.8	8.2	6.3	4.0
Industrial organic chemicals	286		996.5	11,348.5	6.5	3.1	7.1	−3.0
Miscellaneous chemicals	289		124.4	3119	1.9	3.8	2.4	3.3
Petroleum refining	2911	3902	1687.2	11,409.6	5.6	3.4	6.0	−1.0
Hydraulic cement	3241	n.a.[c]	267.8	1461.3	4.1	1.5	4.3	−2.4

	SIC							
Steel	331	1321	1462.8	17,273.9	2.2	2.4	3.1	−2.1
Copper, lead, zinc	3331,2,3	⎱ 1986	615.1	1051.2	1.8	3.2	2.7	0.3
Aluminum	3334	⎰	248.7	1465.9	3.9	0.9	3.5	−0.1
Total, above industries		11,426 (47.3%)	8,179.3 (64.5%)	75,245.3 (14.7%)	4.2	3.3	4.7	−0.2
Total, all manufacturing		15,824 (65.9%)	12,624.1 (100%)	511,470.9 (100%)	2.8	2.8	3.1	1.4
Total, all manufacturing less above industries		4,398 (18.2%)	4,444.8 (35.2%)	436,225.6 (85.3%)	2.6	2.7	2.8	1.6
Electric and gas utilities		6,897 (28.5%)	—	—	6.1	2.4	5.6	1.1
Above industries plus electric and gas utilities		18,323 (75.8%)	—	—	—	—	—	—
All industries		24,166 (100%)	—	—	—	—	—	—

[a] Source: U.S. Bureau of the Census, *Annual Survey of Manufactures, 1976, Industry Profiles*; Bureau of Economic Analysis, *Capital Expenditures by Business for Pollution Abatement*; Bureau of Labor Statistics, *Productivity Indexes for Selected Industries*.

[b] Series available only beginning with 1964.

[c] n.a. = not available.

of a shift in these functions due to environmental policy.[8] However, the timing and severity of environmental policies cannot be quantified easily. How does one include in an investment function the difficulties that the Clean Air Act Amendments create for finding new investment sites? Or how can the effects be discerned from the residuals of such equations when environmental policy has developed gradually over the 1970s—a period of two recessions, one bout of price controls, a commodity boom, and the most disruptive cartelization of a major world market in at least a century? In short, it is very difficult to reach global conclusions about the indirect effects of environmental policy upon productivity growth, effects created by a strong bias against growing, vital industries. In this section, I begin much more modestly: by examining differences in productivity growth among industries affected by environment policy.

Pollution-control costs in manufacturing are heavily concentrated in five basic industries: chemicals; paper; petroleum refining; copper; and steel. These five industries have contributed approximately 60% of all manufacturing capital outlays on pollution controls in the past few years. In the most recent year for which comprehensive data are available from the Census Bureau (1976), these industries, plus hydraulic cement, grain milling, and aluminum, accounted for less than 15% of value added in manufacturing but more than 67% of pollution capital spending. Given the additional fact that electric utilities account for nearly 30% of all pollution outlays by nonfarm private business, it is clear that a very small share of nonfarm private business is bearing the brunt of environmental policy.

Labor productivity data are available for all of the most severely affected industries, although the Bureau of Labor Statistics (BLS) does not publish several of the series because of statistical unreliability. Since pollution-control outlays began to grow rapidly in 1970, and since 1973 was a pivotal year in general productivity growth, I have divided available productivity series for all manufacturing, the most heavily affected manufacturing industries, and electric utilities into two sets of subperiods for comparison: 1958–1970 versus 1970–1976 and 1958–1973 versus 1973–1976. The starting point was chosen as 1958 simply because several series began in that year. The terminal date, 1976, is required because full 1977 data were not available when this study began.

In Table 7, the average rate of increase in output per employee-hour for each industry, for all manufacturing, and for all manufacturing less the most affected industries is presented for the two periods. Two important conclusions emerge from this tabulation. First, the rate of productivity increase in the most heavily affected industries was far above the manufacturing

---

[8] For an attempt to perform such an analysis see Council on Wage and Price Stability [1976].

average in the years prior to 1970. The average annual increase in productivity in all manufacturing was 2.8% in the 1958–1970 period while it averaged 4.2% (using 1976 value-added weights) for the 11 most affected industries.

Second, between 1970 and 1976, productivity in industries less affected by pollution controls increased to 2.7% per year, slightly more than the 2.6% achieved in the 1958–1970 period. On the other hand, the rate of productivity growth fell by 20% in the affected industries from 4.2% per year prior to 1970 to 3.3% after 1970. Breaking the 1958–1976 period at 1973 strengthens these conclusions. Productivity growth slows in the manufacturing industries not heavily affected by pollution-control spending—from 2.8% to 1.6% per year, but it falls drastically in the affected industries from 4.7 to −0.2% per year.

Similar results obtain for electric utilities. The BLS reports data for electric and gas utilities together, but this aggregate is dominated by the generation and distribution of electricity. Productivity growth began slowing measurably in 1970 and averaged only 2.4% annually from 1970 to 1976 as compared with 6.1% in the previous 12 years. The decline was even steeper after 1973, 1.1% per year as compared with 5.6% prior to 1973. The sharp rise in energy prices and the 1969–1970 and 1974–1975 recession might also have contributed to this deceleration in productivity, however.

These results support the political theory that pollution controls have been heaped disproportionately upon the high-productivity-growth industries. As we have seen, one of the industries that has demonstrated some acceleration in productivity growth since 1970—nonferrous metals—has been the beneficiary of more favorable treatment than the others most heavily affected—in large part because it was not prospering prior to 1970. But industries such as paper, chemicals, and refining were substantially outperforming the average manufacturing industry in productivity growth. As a result they were saddled with large pollution outlays, and they have shown sharp deceleration in productivity since 1970.

4. A Closer Examination of the Effect of Pollution-Control Expenditures

Pollution-abatement costs began to rise sharply about 1970. Unfortunately we have very poor data on abatement costs prior to 1973. Beginning with 1973, the Bureau of Economic Analysis (BEA) and the Bureau of the Census began to tabulate control costs collected in annual surveys of nonfarm business and manufacturing, respectively. Only the Census data contain noncapital operating costs; hence, they are likely to be more useful. Since

the most recent data available are for 1976, we are forced to use 1976 data
for further analysis.

To examine the effect of pollution-control costs on productivity growth
across industries, I selected a sample of three-digit and four-digit industries
for which the BLS calculates productivity indexes and which report pollution-
control operating costs of at least 1% of value added in 1976. The intersection
of these two sets includes 36 industries. Pollution operating costs include all
labor, material, and depreciation costs incurred in controlling air, water, and
solid-waste discharges. Since the sharp turning point in productivity growth
occurred in 1973—in part due to recession and energy dislocations—I attempt
to explain the growth in productivity from 1973 to 1976 by regressing an
index of output per employee-hour on deviations from trend in output,
projected productivity based upon 1960–1973 experience, and the ratio of
pollution-control outlays to value added. In order to explain the growth in
productivity from 1973 to 1976 across different industries, it is necessary to
correct for differences in underlying productivity trends across industries.
One method for doing this is to estimate an equation such as

$$(Q/L)_{1976} - (Q/L)_{1960}e^{16g} = F[(Q/Q^*)_{1976}, (POLL/VA)_{1976}], \quad (6)$$

where Q/L is output per employee-hour and g is the average annual rate of
growth in productivity between 1960 and 1973. The left-hand side is, therefore, the departure in 1976 productivity from its historical 1960–1973 growth
path. The independent variables are the ratio of actual industry output, Q, to
predicted output Q^*—assuming output had grown through 1976 at its 1960–
1973 average annual rate—and the ratio of pollution-control operating costs
to value added in the industry, POLL/VA, for the year 1976. Obviously,
productivity growth would be affected by cyclical swings in output, and the
inclusion of Q/Q^* represents an attempt to capture this effect. The variable
POLL/VA for 1976 alone is used because it should capture the cumulative
effect of depreciation charges from capital outlays made over a number of
years. These expenditures should reduce output per employee-hour if only
because the output of pollution control does not enter into the measurement
of output and because pollution-control operations require some labor. Just
as important, however, an effect on productivity is likely to be felt through
the process of capital formation. Capital outlays for pollution and strict
standards for new plants undoubtedly reduce investment in "productive"
capital that produces measured output Q.

For estimation purposes, Eq. (6) is transformed into (7) by simply moving
the trend projection of productivity to the right-hand side:

$$(Q/L)_{1976} = F\{[(Q/L)_{1960}e^{16g}], (Q/Q^*)_{1976}, (POLL/VA)_{1976}\}. \quad (7)$$

A linear form of (7) is estimated by ordinary least squares with the following results:

$$(Q/L)_{1976} = -62.25 + 1.0212(\widehat{Q/L})_{1976} + 65.61(Q/Q^*)_{1976}$$
$$\qquad\qquad\quad (12.28) \qquad\qquad\qquad (3.64)$$

$$-224.3(\text{POLL}/\text{VA})_{1976}, \qquad\qquad\qquad (8)$$
$$\quad (2.38)$$

with t statistics in parentheses and $R^2 = 0.825$, and where $(\widehat{Q/L})_{1976}$ is trend projected Q/L for 1976. All coefficients are statistically significant and of the expected sign. To place the size of the pollution-control coefficient in perspective, the elasticity of Q/L with respect to POLL/VA is -0.024. Thus, a 50% increase in pollution-control outlays in these industries would reduce output per employee-hour 1.2%, or about one-third of its average annual increase. This is a much more pronounced effect than Denison's estimate for the effect of environmental outlays on total factor productivity in non-residential business, but it is not strictly comparable. We have no disaggregated data on total factor productivity; hence I use only labor productivity as a dependent variable.[9]

The implications of Eq. (8) fade rapidly when another variable is included to capture the effect of the post-1973 meteoric rise in energy prices. This variable is $(\text{BTU}/\text{VA})_{1976}$, the ratio of *purchased* Btus of energy to value added. It and the pollution variable are highly correlated, with a zero-order correlation coefficient of 0.63. The resulting equation is

$$(Q/L)_{1976} = -63.50 + 1.036(\widehat{Q/L})_{1976} + 66.27(Q/Q^*)_{1976}$$
$$\qquad\qquad\quad (13.11) \qquad\qquad\qquad (3.88)$$

$$-0.7470(\text{POLL}/\text{VA})_{1976} - 0.9375(\text{BTU}/\text{VA}), \qquad R^2 = 0.829. \quad (9)$$
$$\quad (0.66) \qquad\qquad\qquad (2.16)$$

Thus it is not possible to identify pollution-control spending per se as the villain in the productivity decline if (9) is an accurate picture of reality. Pollution problems are heavily associated with energy use, but it appears to be energy use that is associated with productivity decline. Whether part of the explanation is the degree of pollution control required for heavy energy users cannot be determined from the ad hoc approach adopted here. A more comprehensive model is clearly required.

---

[9] Clearly, the specification of (7) for econometric estimation presents a variety of problems. Aside from problems of measurement error there is a serious question of whether or not the relationship between productivity and the independent variables can be assumed to be the same across all industries. The results should, therefore, be viewed tentatively.

One cannot deny that there is an opportunity cost for resources devoted to pollution control. If the full effect of such expenditures upon productivity were merely a reflection of these opportunity costs, one might expect that the effect would have been building slowly since 1970. On the other hand, if environmental expenditures and the associated restrictions upon new plant construction reduce capital formation and the embodiment of new knowledge in capital goods, the effect may be much larger. It might represent a large fraction of Denison's "residual." To test whether the decline in productivity growth, after correcting for changes in demand, has been accumulating gradually over the 1970–1976 period, it is necessary to examine the residuals from an equation relating productivity to output changes and a time trend.

Since productivity may be expected to vary cyclically, it is important to eliminate the effects of changes in demand before attempting to analyze the productivity decline in the affected industries. Unfortunately this is not easy, for two reasons: (1) any measure of short-term movements in industry output could be caused either by macroeconomic influences or by the decline in productivity we are trying to isolate; and (2) the effects of the business cycle upon productivity are subtle.

Productivity is likely to grow at less than normal rates when the economy is at full capacity and when it is in the early stages of recession. However, productivity will usually grow at above average rates during the early stages of a recovery from recession. In this paper I do not attempt to model the cyclical pattern of productivity. Instead, I use a measure of deviation from trend in output or of the potential–actual GNP gap as the correction for cyclical influences on productivity in each industry. Using the deviation from the historical output trend introduces the problem of failing to isolate cyclical influences from changes in underlying productivity trends that are themselves influencing output. The potential–actual GNP gap avoids this problem, but it is less precise as a measure of cyclical influences on a particular industry.

The equations estimated are of the form

$$\log(Q/L) = b_0 + b_1 \log(Q^a/Q^p) + b_2 \text{TIME} + u. \tag{10}$$

where Q/L is output per employee-hour and Q^a/Q^p is the ratio of actual to potential (or trend-projected) output. The latter variable is formed either by estimating the trend rate of growth in each industry from Federal Reserve Board (FRB) indexes of production or by using estimates of actual to potential GNP published by the Council of Economic Advisers in 1978.

Each equation is estimated for the period 1954–1976 or 1958–1976, depending upon data availability. Hildreth–Liu corrections for serial correlation are made where appropriate. The residuals from each equation for various subperiods since 1970 are reproduced in Table 8.

When we use the deviations from production trend as the cyclical variable, only four of the ten manufacturing industries show a productivity slowdown relative to all manufacturing for 1974–1976, but utilities show substantially larger negative residuals than all manufacturing. For 1976 alone, four of the ten manufacturing industries show larger residuals than all manufacturing, and utilities still remain below the manufacturing average. Unfortunately, these residuals probably understate the deviations in productivity from trend because part of the mystery of productivity decline is wrapped up in the output variable.

Substituting the actual–potential GNP ratio for deviation from industry output trend reduces the precision of fit somewhat and increases the size of the affected-industry residuals relative to the average for all manufacturing.

TABLE 8

Residuals from Productivity Equations (10)

		Cyclical variable				
		Deviation from FRB production index trends		Potential–actual GNP gap		
		Average residual		Average residual		
SIC code	Industry	1974–1976 (%)	Residual 1976 (%)	1971–1976 (%)	1974–1976 (%)	Residual 1976 (%)
204	Grain milling	−1.7	−0.4	−1.6	−1.8	−2.3
261–3	Pulp, paper, paperboard	+0.6	+0.7	+1.0	−0.7	+0.7
281	Inorganic chemicals	+0.9	−1.9	+0.9	+0.6	−1.9
282	Plastics materials	+2.7	+3.5	+2.5	+1.7	+3.8
286	Industrial organic chemicals	+0.6	+2.2	+1.3	−2.9	+0.4
291	Petroleum refining	−1.8	−4.9	−0.8	−2.7	−4.9
324	Hydraulic cement	−1.4	+1.9	−0.4	−3.2	−1.5
331	Steel	+1.7	+1.3	+1.7	+1.1	+1.6
3334	Aluminum	−1.9	−1.3	−1.9	−2.7	−1.9
335 (part)	Copper, lead, zinc	+1.8	+7.1	+1.4	0.0	+6.0
49 (part)	Utilities	−2.0	−1.7	−1.1	−1.3	−3.5
All manufacturing		−1.1	+1.6	+0.4	−0.2	+2.0

Six of the ten manufacturing industries show greater negative residuals over the 1974–1976 period than all manufacturing. The surprising feature of these results is the better-than-expected performance of manufacturing in general. This average -0.2 percentage point residual is far less than Denison's estimate of the decline in productivity growth. But utilities continue to perform badly. In short, productivity growth has been slowed more in pollution-control-affected industries than in the average industry, although this is hardly surprising. In the absence of total factor productivity data, and without a few more years of experience with large pollution-control outlays, it may be difficult to determine just how large this impact has been and whether the biases in standards setting have contributed importantly to the deceleration in productivity growth.

5. Conclusion

There can be little doubt that productivity has declined more sharply in pollution-control-affected industries than in others. Whether this is due to the severity of the pollution standards and the disincentives provided by environmental policy for new investment or to other factors such as slow recovery from the 1974–1975 recession and the energy crisis of 1973–1974 is difficult to say. Environmental policy has developed rapidly in the past few years, and its full effect upon investment decisions can hardly have been registered by 1976 or 1977. Lead times for new plants may be as much as five to ten years (and even more for nuclear power plants).

What is clear is that the political requirements for the growing maze of social regulation in general and environmental regulation in particular are not conducive to new investment. Therefore it seems likely that the embodiment of new technology will be impeded by government regulation and that productivity growth will be slowed by more than Denison's accounting for factor costs of control would suggest. By the time this antigrowth bias is recognized, however, basic industries will have adjusted to the imperatives of the policy and will resist vigorously any attempt to change them. The challenge for economists is to identify these effects and to suggest options that allow more efficient use of resources and more dynamic adaptation of capital to new technology.

ACKNOWLEDGMENTS

I am indebted to Robert Lawrence, Edward Denison, Arthur Okun, Thomas Cowing, Paul Portney, and a referee for valuable comments. In addition, helpful research assistance was provided by Arthur Kupferman, Lewis Alexander, and Karen Ostrow. Remaining errors and biases are my responsibility.

14

Motivations and Barriers to Superior Performance under Public Utility Regulation

Harry M. Trebing

Institute of Public Utilities
Graduate School of Business Administration
Michigan State University
East Lansing, Michigan

1. Introduction

There is a growing recognition that government regulation is a major determinant of industry performance. This is particularly evident in the public utility industries where much of the debate over regulatory reform, including deregulation, is premised on the belief that performance is significantly affected by government control of prices, earnings, and conditions of entry. Since productivity is widely accepted as an important measure of performance,[1] it is reasonable to expect that productivity will become an

---

[1] Performance in the public utility industries can be broadly defined as the attainment of efficiency and equity goals. Indeed, the objective of the so-called public-interest theory of regulation has always been to promote efficiency and equity by preventing monopolistic pricing practices, monopolistic restriction of output, and a monopolistic redistribution of income from the consumer to the firm. Performance in this paper will be identified primarily with static and dynamic efficiency. Equity objectives are more difficult to specify since they tend to vary on a case-by-case basis and are often highly judgmental. Where equity issues are particularly relevant, they will be treated directly.

369

integral part of any discussion of the adequacy and role of regulation. A review of changing patterns of productivity and the parallel patterns of regulatory action provides a helpful preface to an examination of the impact of commission practices on industry performance.

The pivotal years for changing patterns of performance in the public utility industries were 1968 and 1969. At that time the rate of growth in total factor productivity for the electric utilities flattened out and average price per kilowatt-hour began to rise, signaling an end to the secular trend that had prevailed from the turn of the century.[2] In natural gas production, the ratio of new findings to production fell below unity for the first time,[3] indicating that the era of abundant gas supplies, with additions to reserves greater than annual production, was closed. In telecommunications, the Carterfone decision (FCC [1968]) and the MCI decision (FCC [1969]) were manifestations of the impact of technological change on the structural, rate-making, and performance standards that had prevailed since World War I.[4]

In the era before 1968–1969, high rates of output growth, little cyclical variation in output, pervasive economies of scale, and above-average rates of investment in new plant and equipment produced average annual rates of growth in total factor productivity for communications, electricity, and gas that were well above those of the private domestic economy.[5] Furthermore, pricing policies facilitated these changes and even the Averch–Johnson effect could be construed as beneficial because it stimulated higher rates of capital formation, which were invariably associated with higher rates of technological advance.

While advocates of regulatory reform might have wished for a more aggressive form of public intervention, passive regulation was not an entirely detrimental influence on performance. A system of state regulation that was for the most part dormant could provide a positive inducement to perform-

[2] Total factor productivity and average price per kilowatt-hour data are contained in Stevenson ([1975], pp. 11–33). Also see Kendrick ([1975], pp. 302 *et seq.*).

[3] Although not a conventional productivity measure, the F/P ratio provides the best estimate of demand-supply relationships for new gas supplies. An F/P ratio of less than 1.0 means that net additions to reserves are less than net production on an annual nationwide basis. The ratios were: 1967: 1.1; 1968: 0.6; 1969: 0.4. Since that date, the ratios have averaged 0.3 while pipelines and distribution companies have experienced sharp curtailments and worsening capacity factors. Source of data: American Gas Association.

[4] In the Carterfone decision (FCC [1968]) and the MCI decision (FCC [1969]), the Federal Communications Commission opened the terminal equipment market and private line market to liberalized entry and competition. This marked a dramatic change in regulatory policy of foreclosing entry which had prevailed since the inception of common carrier regulation.

[5] In the period 1948–1966, total factor productivity in communications, electricity, and gas increased at 4–5% per year; the rate was 2.5% for the private domestic economy. See Kendrick [1975].

ance in the form of regulatory lag. Fixed output prices, reviewed only at infrequent intervals, provided management with an opportunity to capture the gains from efficiency until the infrequent rate case passed a portion of them forward to the consumer.

However, in the period after 1968–1969, a substantial reversal took place. Rates of productivity gain began to diminish, fuel costs rose dramatically, society demanded that social costs be internalized, and the promise of new technology diminished. Only in telecommunications did new technology suggest that some prices might continue to decline.

Government reacted to these pressures by modifying traditional forms of public utility regulation, introducing new rate-making concepts, and resorting to new forms of social intervention. Rate base regulation was modified to place greater emphasis on current costs rather than historic costs. Procedures for changing rates were also modified to permit the automatic pass-through of certain expenses without formal rate-making proceedings, and there was a strong move to substitute time-of-use rates for declining block rates. While many of these changes were beginning to take place at the state level, the passage of the National Energy Act in 1978 ensured that greater attention would be focused on the reassessment and revision of rate-making policies in the field of electric and gas regulation.

At the same time, the growth of consumer activism and increasing demands for environmental protection brought new pressures to bear on the regulatory process and industry performance. The steady increase in public utility prices stimulated many consumer advocates to insist upon greater protection for poor, elderly, and low-income consumers against the effects of rising energy prices. Similarly, consumer advocates argued for more stringent controls on the expenses, earnings, and pricing practices of the regulated firm. Sheltering selected consumer groups through programs of cross-subsidization, such as lifeline rates, and the imposition of tighter constraints on expenses and earnings, would have significant implications for efficiency. The creation of new agencies to promulgate standards to protect the environment under the Clean Air Act, the Federal Water Pollution Control Act, and the National Environmental Policies Act would likewise affect performance in the energy utilities.

In this paper we shall examine these forces in light of their effects on various forms of efficiency. The adequacy of current regulatory efforts to improve performance will also be evaluated, particularly in terms of the efforts of commissions to introduce modifications in traditional rate base regulation in order to give more weight to incentives and penalties as a means of stimulating greater efficiency. Finally, we shall set forth a series of recommendations designed to promote improved industry performance.

2. Barriers to Improved Performance

Rising costs and growing uncertainty in the era after 1968–1969 make it imperative that barriers to improved performance and greater efficiency be studied. This can be done by examining five areas in which public policy, regulatory response, and corporate power appear to converge and impede the attainment of greater efficiency. These include: (1) the inducement to overinvestment; (2) the incentives for X-inefficiency; (3) the frustration of performance gains associated with structural change and technological advance; (4) the pressures against attaining a least-cost solution to the pollution problem; and (5) the equity impasse.

2.1 The Inducement to Overinvestment

The pattern of investment in the public utility industries is particularly important because of the capital-intensive nature of these industries. Any significant divergence from an optimal expansion path will have serious consequences in terms of allocative inefficiency and diminished productivity.

At the present time, there are a number of incentives for overinvestment. These include the Averch–Johnson (A–J) effect, the normalization of taxes associated with accelerated depreciation, the investment tax credit, construction work in progress (CWIP) in the rate base, and various forms of guarantees designed to encourage new investment in high-cost projects.

It is difficult to estimate the A–J effect in the era after 1968–1969. Most of the empirical studies focus on an earlier period when the rate of return was greater than the cost of capital (as shown by market-to-book ratios for utility stocks, which often reached 2:1).[6] Spann [1974], Courville [1974], Peterson [1975], and Cowing [1978] found strong empirical support for the A–J effect, while Boyes [1973] found negligible support. The problem is whether conditions are conducive to the A–J effect at the present time. There still may be a strong incentive to camouflage excessive profits by inflating above-the-line expenses and the rate base, but there is no assurance that this will be reflected in the substitution of capital for labor and fuel.[7]

---

[6] The market-to-book value ratios for the public utilities are: 1965: 2.22, 1966: 1.89, 1967: 1.77, 1968: 1.61, 1969: 1.48, 1970: 1.17, 1971: 1.18, 1972: 1.07, 1973: 0.93, 1974: 0.60, 1975: 0.60, 1976: 0.67, 1977: 0.73. Source: Moody's *Public Utility Manual* [1978].

[7] Ironically, the most obvious source of excess profits at the present time may be those reforms introduced to make rates more accurately reflect current costs. The forecasted test year and marginal cost pricing provide the best examples. In the forecasted test year, realized revenues in excess of realized costs confront the firm with the prospect of excess earnings and a price reduction. This provides a powerful incentive to inflate both expenses and the rate base. The introduction of marginal cost pricing can also produce revenues substantially in excess of allowed operating revenues. If the marginal cost of new capacity to meet the peak exceeds

Furthermore, the rise in the cost of capital and the drastic decline in market-to-book ratios strongly suggest that pure A–J distortions may have diminished significantly.[8]

While there may be doubt about the current applicability of the A–J effect, there is little need to question whether the normalization of deferred taxes and the investment tax credit stimulate overinvestment. Normalization provides an interest-free loan to the firm, as well as an incentive to maintain a high level of new investment in order to delay the eventual payback period. The investment tax credit, on the other hand, provides a direct incentive for investment spending. Further, the ability of the state commissions to negate these incentives through a current-year flow-through of tax savings has been severely constrained by Congress.[9] Evidence of the extent to which the investor-owned utilities have availed themselves of these tax incentives can be seen by noting that federal income taxes as a percentage of operating revenues have declined dramatically: from approximately 15% during the early 1960s to 4.4% in 1975. The California Commission estimated that in the same year electric utilities collected $2.5 billion on a nationwide basis in federal income taxes while paying only $885 million to the Internal Revenue Service.

CWIP in the rate base provides another strong incentive for overinvestment. It allows the utility to earn a full return on plant under construction while at the same time suffering no penalty for construction delays or errors in forecasting. The result can be an assumed rate of return over a long gestation period even though the plant is neither operational nor revenue producing. In the earlier period, standard regulatory treatment called for capitalizing interest during construction and adding this amount to the rate base when the plant was placed in service. Virtually no commissions placed CWIP in the rate base. In contrast, by 1976, 15 state commissions permitted CWIP in the rate base and 21 others permitted the use of either CWIP or allowance for funds used during construction (AFUDC) or both,

---

average capacity costs (a reasonable assumption for the energy utilities), and if demand at the peak is inelastic and off-peak demand is elastic, then the introduction of marginal cost pricing (reflecting peak capacity and energy costs and off-peak energy costs) will yield total revenues greater than allowable operating revenues. The result will be an incentive to inflate average costs rather than face an overall rate reduction or a price reduction in inelastic markets.

[8] See Footnote 6.

[9] Section 167(1) of the Internal Revenue Code (passed as part of the Tax Reform Act of 1969) asserts that state regulatory authorities cannot flow through taxes deferred through the use of accelerated depreciation unless such a system of rate reduction was in use before the enactment of Section 167(1). Section 46(f) deals with the treatment of the investment tax credit (passed as part of the Revenue Act of 1971), and it asserts that state regulatory authorities cannot use the credit to reduce rates in the year in which the credits are generated, unless such a method was in use before passage of Section 46(f).

while only 14 used AFUDC alone.[10] Furthermore, there appears to be a tendency for regulatory resistance to CWIP to weaken as the size of the investment burden increases. To illustrate, the Federal Power Commission (FPC) initially confined CWIP to pollution-abatement costs and fuel-conversion costs.[11] In the Seabrook case, however, the administrative law judge permitted CWIP associated with general plant construction to be included in the rate base.[12]

A final direct inducement to overinvestment is the willingness of regulatory agencies to apply subtle forms of subsidization and loan guarantees to encourage investment. This can be illustrated by two examples. Between 1970 and 1975, the Federal Power Commission authorized the natural gas pipelines to make advance payments to the major oil companies in the amount of $2.7 billion to finance greater investment in the exploration and development of gas reserves. In reality, these were interest-free loans that the pipelines included in their rate base. Interestingly, a court-mandated examination revealed that while these funds were committed to new investment, they did not achieve the desired objective of eliciting more gas for the interstate market. As a consequence, the FPC abandoned the program.[13] Advance payments by distribution companies may still be authorized by state commissions.

An illustration of the potential use of loan guarantees to encourage over-investment is provided by the Great Plains Coal Gasification proposal (estimated to cost over $1.5 billion). This project is sponsored by five inter-state pipelines, which insist that the repayment of debt capital must be guaranteed by an assessment against their consumers in the event that the project fails. The repayment guarantee has the effect of shifting the risk of failure to the ratepayer. As a consequence, a bizarre proposal emerges in which a high-risk coal gasification project would be financed by 75% debt capital and the accompanying coal mine would be financed by 100% debt capital, even though its output is estimated to cost from $7.16 to $8.29 per thousand cubic feet at the plant site—a price that is approximately three times the price of new supplies of natural gas in the field. The proposal has been endorsed by the United States Department of Energy, but final approval

[10] See NARUC 1976 Annual Report [1977], Table 12, p. 409.

[11] Federal Power Commission [1976].

[12] Federal Energy Regulatory Commission [1979a].

[13] The District of Columbia Court of Appeals held that the Federal Power Commission had failed to analyze the extent to which advance payments produced additional supplies of gas for the interstate market. As a consequence of this decision, the FPC conducted a survey and concluded that advance payments did not achieve the desired objective. For example, only 13% of the proved offshore reserves could be said to have moved faster to the interstate market because of advance payments. The Commission announced that it would not approve additional advance payments after 31 December 1975. See Federal Power Commission [1975a].

by the Federal Energy Regulatory Commission (FERC) is still pending.[14]

In addition to the direct incentives for overinvestment, there are important indirect inducements to overinvestment that arise when regulation fails to recognize economic costs in establishing the rate base, earnings, and prices. One might assume that the growing acceptance of marginal cost pricing in electricity supply and increased emphasis on incremental pricing in gas markets would tend to prevent any weakening of price as a constraint on investment. However, the actual process of implementing pricing guidelines provides large areas for discretionary judgment where the effectiveness of price can be severely weakened. For example, there is no consensus as to the proper costing methodology for implementing marginal cost pricing in electricity supply. As a consequence, at least four distinct techniques have been promoted by consulting firms as methods for assigning costs to peak and off-peak periods. The ability to choose among these different costing methodologies provides a degree of latitude for those who would like to employ cost and price to promote their particular objectives.

There also appears to be a tendency on the part of commissions to moderate or temper the impact of price on peak-period customers. As an illustration, the New York Commission decided to reduce the demand charges assigned to peak rating periods in the Long Island Lighting Company case [1976].[15] The company found that when marginal costs were translated directly into demand charges, the result was a ratio of demand charges between peak and intermediate usage periods of approximately 20:1. The company's rate proposal set an 8:1 ratio for these charges, and the New York Commission finally adopted a 4:1 ratio. In part, the rationale for the reduction was tied to nonpeak related costs associated with the conversion of oil-fired generating capacity; nevertheless, concern over high peak prices appears to have been a dominant consideration.

Incremental pricing for high-cost supplemental gas supplies has not fared much better. Originally, the Federal Power Commission imposed incremental pricing on new, liquefied natural gas (LNG) facilities in order to introduce a market test for judging the feasibility of these investments. However, in a series of subsequent decisions, the Commission abandoned incremental pricing in favor of a rolled-in approach that averaged high-cost LNG with low-cost flowing gas, thereby seriously diluting the effectiveness

---

[14] An initial decision by the administrative law judge has rejected the Great Plains Gasification proposal largely because the judge believes that the risk should be borne by taxpayers at the national level rather than by the customers of the five sponsoring pipelines. In either case, the inducement to overinvest still exists. It should be noted that the proposal also requires that the high cost of coal gas be averaged in with the lower cost of flowing natural gas. See Federal Energy Regulatory Commission [1979a].

[15] New York Public Service Commission [1976].

of price as a constraint on new investment.[16] The Natural Gas Policy Act (1978) reintroduced incremental pricing for industrial boiler-fuel users in order to assign high-cost sources of gas directly to low-priority boiler-fuel users. This is, of course, a highly selective application of incremental pricing that applies only until the price of such gas reaches the price of fuel oil. After that point, rolled-in or average-cost pricing is reinstated. Applied in this fashion, incremental pricing constitutes virtually no constraint on new investment.

Another example of a weakened constraint that encourages overinvestment is regulatory treatment of the excess capacity problem. Commissions have yet to establish adequate criteria for reserve margins or levels of reliability so that the prospects for removing excess plant from the rate base are very remote. Hence, management errors resulting in overbuilding are not apt to be penalized. The remoteness of any form of penalty is further reinforced by the inability of commissions to develop and apply appropriate forecasting techniques as a test of the need for new investment in rate-making proceedings.[17]

There are, of course, countervailing pressures that tend to limit overinvestment. The movement away from the declining block rate structure should not be dismissed, nor should the convergence of the allowed rate of return and the cost of capital. The most interesting countervailing force is the factor bias induced by the fuel adjustment clause (FAC). FACs could presumably encourage the adoption of a more fuel-intensive rather than a more capital-intensive production process. There would be a strong incentive in the direction of the former in cases where the utility is vertically integrated or where FAC is based on a forecasted average test year, as in the case of California. Vertical integration would permit the firm to earn excessive profits through its affiliates while the forecasted test year would

---

[16] The FPC's changing position on incremental pricing versus rolled-in pricing can be traced through the following cases: Columbia LNG Corp., Opinion No. 622, 47 FPC 1624, 1641 (1972); Columbia LNG Corp., Opinion No. 622-A, 48 FPC 723, 729 (1972); Columbia LNG Corp. v. FPC, 491 F 2d 651 (5th Cir. 1974); Columbia LNG Corp., et al., Docket Nos. CP71-68, et al., Opinion No. 786 (January 21, 1977); Trunkline LNG Co., et al., Docket Nos. CP74-138, et al., Opinion Nos. 796 (April 29, 1977) and 796-A (June 30, 1977).

[17] As a result, regulatory agencies are confronted with the paradox of excess current capacity in electricity supply, on the one hand, and dire industry predictions of power shortages in the long run if new investment is not encouraged by increasing the rate of return and modifying environmental restrictions on licensing new plants. To illustrate, the National Electric Reliability Councils' Eighth Annual Review (1978) shows that summer peak loads, when compared to available capacity, yielded a very high nationwide reserve margin of 28% for 1978, and a forecasted reserve margin of 21% for 1982, yet the same report predicts shortages, curtailments, and the rationing of electricity if regulatory approval of new investment is not accelerated and overlapping jurisdictions eliminated. See National Electric Reliability Council [1978], pp. 2–3, 16–17, Appendix A-1, A-3.

lend itself to overcollection.[18] However, there is reason to believe that the factor bias stemming from FACs is weak. FACs are subject to change, several states have dropped such clauses, and the newer FACs have been modified to include thermal efficiency standards. (These will be discussed later.) Furthermore, Section 208 of the Public Utility Regulatory Policies Act of 1978 mandates a Federal Energy Regulatory Commission review of FACs every four years to monitor potential abuses, and to determine whether they encourage the efficient use of resources. Under these circumstances it is doubtful that a firm would make a long-run investment decision in favor of a fuel-intensive mix of inputs on the basis of current FACs.

On balance, strong motivations for overinvestment continue in the public utility industries. Although it is not possible to quantify the loss in efficiency associated with these allocative distortions, the inducement to inefficiency remains.[19]

2.2   X-Inefficiencies under Regulation

A second set of incentives for inefficiency arises because specific regulatory practices are conducive to internal slack and waste (i.e., X-inefficiency) within the operation of the regulated firm. The implications of rate base regulation for the promotion of X-inefficiency are well known and do not need elaboration. Similarly, FACs which provide for the rapid pass-through of increased fuel costs are also conducive to X-inefficiency.[20] In addition to removing the effect of regulatory lag, the simple adjustment clause places no penalty on poor purchasing policies, worsening heat rates, or the poor management and operation of generating units. The daisy-chain exposé and the Congressional hearings of 1975 provide ample evidence of these abuses.[21]

---

[18] The vertical affiliate problem arises primarily with captive coal mines and fuel supply affiliates. For a further discussion of supply affiliate and overcollection abuses, see report by the House Subcommittee on Oversight and Investigations [1975].

[19] Gollop and Karlson [1978b] tested empirically for FAC-induced inefficiencies. Unfortunately, they examined only the period 1970–1972; however, they did find evidence of X-inefficiencies but no discernible evidence of allocative inefficiency. Cowing and Stevenson [1978] have examined the allocative distortions inherent in automatic adjustment clauses and conventional regulation under various assumptions. They conclude that factor-input distortion is greater with higher rates of fuel price inflation, demand growth, and inelastic demand function. However, they made no empirical estimates of the magnitude of this distortion.

[20] At the present time, 43 states and the District of Columbia have FACs. In 1977, conventional rate increases by gas and electric utilities amounted to $2.4 billion; increases associated with FACs for these industries amounted to $1.4 billion. (See U.S. Senate [1979]).

[21] See note 19, above, U.S. House of Representatives [1975]. The daisy chain involved successive markups by suppliers of fuel oil for Florida utilities. The FACs apparently diminished the incentive of the utilities to curb such practices.

Of course, it must be emphasized that rapid cost increases that are far in excess of productivity gains must be corrected for by some form of automatic adjustment clause. Otherwise, the worsening financial position of the firm will cause the cost of capital to skyrocket. The challenge for regulation becomes one of designing an automatic adjustment clause which negates X-inefficiency. Less evident, however, is the inducement to X-inefficiency inherent in the growing campaign to give the consumer proper "price signals" by placing greater reliance on current costs. This shift in emphasis is accomplished by recourse to a forecasted test year, a year-end rate base, an increased allowance for attrition, CWIP, and FACs. All of these changes reduce the stimulus of a regulatory lag and have the effect of maintaining cost-plus regulation during a period of price inflation. A rough measure of the stimulus or pressure for internal efficiency associated with regulatory lag may be derived from the spread between the allowed and earned rate of return on equity capital after taxes. For 1975–1977, the average spread was 2.0 percentage points for electric utilities, 3.6 percentage points for gas utilities, and 1.4 percentage points for telephone companies.[22] Obviously, changes in rate base regulation that narrow the spread will tend to eliminate this pressure.

A final source of X-inefficiency stems from the lack of any regulatory penalty for mismanagement or excess capacity. In the case of the railroads, regulation required that the carriers maintain excess capacity and this was a contributing factor in bankrupting many of them. The situation is quite different in the case of the energy utilities. As an example, the need for natural gas pipelines to engage in curtailment resulted in excess transmission capacity; however, this redundant plant was not translated into a parallel reduction in the share-holders' return. The major interstate natural gas pipelines had virtually no curtailment problems in 1970, but by 1974–1975, net curtailment had risen to 13.6% of firm requirements. Despite this growth in curtailments, the year-end rate of return on common equity for the major pipelines increased from 12.1% in 1970 to 15.2% in 1974.[23] Rate base regulation tends to shift the burden of excess capacity forward to the consumer through higher average unit prices while maintaining the earnings level for the firm. Adjustment procedures such as the California Commission's Supply Adjustment Mechanism and similar volume variation adjustment proposals reinforce this outcome by ensuring that expense margins and earnings will be maintained in the face of declining output.[24]

[22] See NARUC *1977 Annual Report* [1978], Table 23, pp. 444–445.

[23] Federal Power Commission [1975].

[24] The Supply Adjustment Mechanism (SAM) was adopted by the California Commission in Decision No. 8835, 16 May 1978, Case Number 10261. SAM is applied to gas utilities and it permits the firm to adjust prices twice a year to maintain a Commission-approved expense

2.3 Dynamic Performance Benefits Forgone

Substantial performance benefits may be forgone as a result of regulatory policies and monopoly power that frustrate structural change and technological advance. Maintaining barriers to entry, permitting structural rigidities to remain intact, and foreclosing selected competitive pressures will inhibit new technology that could yield substantial savings. The effect of these practices can be seen by contrasting FPC–FERC policy toward the market structure of the energy utilities with that of the Federal Communications Commission (FCC) toward telephone common carriers.

FERC has generally followed a policy of voluntarism with respect to interconnection and coordination in bulk power supply. The Commission has no authority over retail rates. As a result, the initiative for developing pooling arrangements and other forms of coordination is entrusted to industry, with oversight, if any, exercised by regional reliability councils. Further, these reliability councils, which are composed of representatives from the major utilities, have little direct authority to promote coordination other than by moral suasion. Pooling and interconnection tend to move at a slow, evolutionary pace, and the initiative to develop an interconnected network for bulk power supply rests with the actions of individual firms and the degree to which they perceive such a network as yielding direct benefits to them. FERC is reluctant to mandate an expansion of interconnection or to impose new responsibilities on power pools.[25]

As a consequence of these policies, a good case can be made that the development of an interconnected coordinated network has lagged in the United States. The absence of such a network negates a number of significant opportunities for improving industry performance. For example, the greater the interconnected network, the greater the opportunity for the economic dispatch of generating units so as to apply the equimarginal principle in equalizing the fuel costs of operating all units. There could be major savings in fuel where underutilized base load units exist in one region, while less efficient cycling and peaking units are employed in other regions. Similarly, economic dispatch would permit the substitution of low-cost fuel for high-cost fuel and the conservation of oil. As a case in point, a Department of

---

spread between gross sales revenues and the cost of purchased gas—regardless of declining gas supplies or changing usage patterns. Thus, the company is assured that it will recover an established expense margin by raising prices twice a year despite declining sales. The Commission noted that SAM will reduce risk to the shareholders, and that this reduction will be considered in future rate proceedings. To date, there is no evidence that this has been expressly recognized by lowering the rate of return on equity.

[25] For a further discussion of Commission policy toward market structure variables, see Trebing [1977].

Energy (DOE) study of the southeastern region found that net savings in fuel costs of $8.5 billion and one billion barrels of oil would accrue over a ten-year period from such an interchange (after allowing for a $0.5 billion power loss in transmission and $2.5 billion in new transmission facilities). At present, transmission plant in this region is inadequate to achieve these objectives.[26]

Another potential benefit forgone is the ability to improve reliability while at the same time effecting significant savings through a reduction in standby capacity, spinning reserves, and improved maintenance scheduling. An interconnected network would also provide greater opportunity for minimizing the cost of expanding new generating plant. The DOE case study previously noted estimates that interconnection and coordination could save $1.5 billion in new capital expansion costs avoided in the South-eastern Electric Reliability Council region alone.[27]

Another illustration of a performance benefit forgone as a result of inadequate interconnection is the inability to choose between "coal-by-wire" (mine-mouth generation) versus load-center generation. A DOE study estimates that locating 28,000 MW along the Powder River, with four rights-of-way to deliver energy to the Midwest, would be 15% cheaper than the construction of the same generating capacity at load centers.[28]

A reluctance on the part of the major firms to engage in greater inter-connection or to permit unlimited entry into power pools may result from a desire to protect monopoly markets or from a desire to protect the he-gemony of the firm. It may also be argued that the failure to interconnect stems from the fact that the firm cannot capture all of the externalities or spillover benefits in the prices which it charges for transmission. Regardless of the cause, FERC policy together with the reluctance of the firms to move in the direction of greater coordination and interconnection appear to have denied the public significant performance benefits.

Regulatory policy in the electric utility industry contrasts sharply with that in telecommunications, where the FCC has aggressively promoted entry into the terminal equipment and specialized carrier markets. By relaxing barriers to entry, terminal development time dropped from 7–10 years to 10 months. At the same time, ownership options in terminal equip-ment have been broadened and competitors have brought forth new hard-ware, new features, new technology, smaller size, and lower maintenance costs. Competitive entry into the specialized carrier market has also resulted

[26] U.S. Department of Energy, National Power Grid Study, Chapter 5.
[27] Ibid.
[28] U.S. Department of Energy, National Power Grid Study, Chapter 6.

in a proliferation of voice–digital service offerings, greater consumer choice, and lower prices for point-to-point service. The impact of competition has even extended to the vertical affiliates of the telephone companies. Western Electric has dropped old equipment, cut prices, reduced cost, added new features, and shortened delivery time. However, it would be a mistake to assume that the creation of selective competitive pressures has proceeded without difficulty in telecommunications. The monopoly power of AT&T still remains to be reckoned with. Several firms have dropped out of the terminal equipment market, including RCA, GE, and Litton, while DATRAN was unable to meet AT&T price reductions in the specialized carrier field and therefore went bankrupt—even though these reductions were later found to be unlawful. Monopoly power still remains a major deterrent to efficiency despite the apparent tendency of Congress to favor substantial interstate deregulation (Trebing [1979]).

A final note on potential structural–technological benefits forgone raises the question of the source of research and development (R&D). In the past, the electric utilities purchased new technology from the electric equipment manufacturers. These manufacturers innovated by pioneering in the design and production of new equipment. In the 1970s, a new center for R&D was created in the form of the Electric Power Research Institute (EPRI). The counterpart of EPRI in the gas industry is the Gas Research Institute. These research organizations are funded by contributions from electric and gas utilities. Further, the same utilities occupy the majority of seats on the boards of directors of these research institutions. One can speculate whether this type of vertical integration is conducive to R&D programs that will create Schumpeterian "gales of creative destruction." This is a doubtful outcome since these institutions must be mindful of the source of their support. Equally important, it is reasonable to assume that such R&D programs will be much more conducive to fostering "hard path" solutions to the energy problem. The Colorado Commission has raised serious doubts whether this approach to R&D has produced demonstrable benefits for the consumer.[29]

---

[29] The Colorado Commission denied applications by four gas distribution utilities to pass through payments to GRI. The Commission denied the applications on the grounds that consumers will provide all of the funding for GRI without any reasonable assurance that they will derive significant benefits (such as lower operating expenses or a lower rate of return because of a decline in risk). The companies would have to make a demonstration of discernible benefits in a general rate proceeding. The reasonableness of interstate contributions to GRI is a matter for determination by FERC, not the Colorado Commission. See Colorado Public Utilities Commission, Decision No. C79-907, Application Nos. 31010, 31011, 31486, 31517, 14 June 1979.

2.4   Pressures against Attainment of Least-Cost Methods
of Pollution Abatement

A fourth area of potential inefficiency is associated with efforts to control air and thermal pollution in the electric utility industry. Critics can argue that much of the gain in performance in the electric utility industry in the era before 1968–1969 came because industry exploited free goods in the form of air and water. However, the attempts to control these abuses and to force the electric utilities to internalize social costs have produced a new set of biases that can affect industry efficiency and performance.

Antipollution legislation sets two contradictory forces in motion. On the one hand, the Clean Air Act and the Amendments of 1977 restrict the number of sites where large coal-fired generating plants can be located. This legislation, together with similar state siting laws, creates a bias in favor of overinvestment in large facilities. On the other hand, the cumulative interaction of state and federal antipollution legislation creates a degree of risk and uncertainty that provides an incentive for the firm to avoid large-scale investment in favor of a larger number of small plants with short gestation periods. This conflicting set of pressures will be discussed in greater detail.

Clean air standards emerge as a major factor limiting the number of sites. To meet national ambient air quality standards for pollutants (including sulfur dioxide and particulates), standards are imposed on a geographic basis. Where the level of pollutants has already reached maximum limits, special nonattainment areas are established. In order to build a large coal-fired generating plant in such an area, the utility must overcome a set of barriers that are virtually insurmountable. At the same time, a series of so-called "prevent significant deterioration standards" are imposed, which further restrict the number of available sites. According to one estimate, these two sets of restrictions foreclose building new large coal-fired plants in 20% of the land area of the nation.[30] Such limitations create a new scarce resource in the form of "allowable air pollution increments," which will become as crucial as water and fuel in locating new plants. The problem of plant location is further complicated by the large number of state siting commissions and thermal pollution standards associated with the Federal Water Pollution Control Act.

While the restriction on the number of sites may be conducive to over-investment, the proliferation of agencies at the state and federal levels administering pollution laws creates another set of incentives. The risk to the firm associated with the delay and uncertainty in establishing standards and obtaining final authorization will have an effect on the size of a project.

[30] U.S. Department of Energy, National Power Grid Study, Chapter 12.

It can be argued that large plants are vulnerable to delay,[31] to stringent environmental review, and to greater financial pressure, while less capital-intensive plants with shorter gestation periods involve less risk. If one accepts this argument, then there is a strong incentive to build small oil-fired plants that may be both counterproductive in terms of conserving oil and suboptimal in terms of efficiency. States typically do not limit technology in approving new plant construction, so the principal constraint would be the Power Plant Industrial Fuel Use Act of 1978. However, DOE is authorized to grant exceptions for the construction of new oil- and gas-fired plants.

Of course, one can also argue, conversely, that the complex licensing process and the long lead time create a bias in favor of overbuilding. In the absence of a series of case studies, it is difficult to determine what the net impact of the administrative process will be.

Many economists have argued that the problems associated with a command-control specification of output quality can be overcome by imposing effluent charges. The effluent charge would provide an incentive for the firm to select the least-cost method of reducing pollution in order to minimize the charge and increase profits. If no solution were possible, then the firm would attempt to shift the charge forward through a higher price, which would cause output to fall if demand were elastic. If the charge could not be shifted forward, then it would reduce profits, promote a reallocation of resources, and ultimately reduce output. However, rate base regulation introduces a special set of problems. If an effluent charge were introduced, the cost would be treated as a part of the cost of service and assessed against the consumer. There would be no effect on profits in the short run or in the long run. Hence there would be no profit incentive to select the most efficient method of curbing pollution. Nor would continued pollution depress profits and drive the firm out of the industry. The only constraint would be the effect of a price increase on sales in the retail market as the effluent charge or the cost of remedial measures were shifted forward to the consumer.

If no effluent charge were imposed and general pollution standards were established directly, the effect would still be the same. Abatement costs would be shifted forward to the consumer. Without a profit incentive, the corporate conscience would be the principal inducement to select the least-cost method of abatement. However, one can speculate that pollution abatement does provide an opportunity to inflate the rate base and camouflage excessive profits—particularly in light of FERC policy regarding CWIP in the rate base for pollution abatement. Under regulation, the consumers will bear all of the costs of pollution abatement. Moreover, they

---

[31] For example, there is no statute of limitations on challenges to an environmental-impact statement (EIS). Thus, an adverse judicial action on an EIS can stop a project in its tracks even though it is well along the way to completion.

will also bear the cost of errors and failures in judgment regarding the methods of pollution abatement.

In summary, efforts to control pollution in the electric utility industry will take place in a setting where restrictions on site availability, the risk of delay in the administrative process, and rate base effects will have a significant impact on the mix of inputs and the scale of plant selected. There is no assurance that such a selection process will choose either the least-cost method of abatement or the optimal size of plant.

2.5 Equity Considerations

There is little doubt that efficiency objectives must be tempered by equity considerations in the public utility industries. This has become increasingly apparent, since the burden of price increases falls heavily on the poor and the elderly (Palmer et al. [1976]). A further dimension of the equity problem has arisen as a result of growing concern over the fairness of the distribution of benefits and costs associated with new projects and new services.

Unfortunately, the regulatory response to equity–fairness problems seldom comes to grips directly with matters of income distribution or the benefits and costs of particular actions. Rather, the regulatory agency's perception of equity and fairness tends to create an additional set of barriers to the attainment of efficiency. As it emerges in practice, the regulatory concept of equity or fairness tends to average conflicting claims, roll-in different cost-of-service characteristics, and minimize direct harm to individual groups.[32]

The result is a tendency toward average cost pricing and a reluctance to translate operational failures, excess capacity, technological obsolescence or a loss in markets into capital losses for the firm. Such practices tend to negate the roles of price and markets as inducements to the promotion of greater efficiency. Instead, they introduce a degree of cross-subsidization that may serve as an impediment to the achievement of greater efficiency. We note in passing that Owen and Braeutigam [1978] argue that the major rationale for regulation is the desire on the part of Congress to reject efficiency-oriented solutions if these solutions impinge upon equity considerations. Russell and Shelton [1974] suggest that this concern for equity will create a permanent tendency to engage in cross-subsidization, higher prices in monopolistic markets, and prices below cost in favored markets.

[32] Classic illustrations of the regulatory reluctance to do direct harm to the firm can be found in the FCC's willingness to transfer TWX to Western Union, the continued depreciation of early transatlantic telephone cables, and the unwillingness of state and federal commissions to reduce the rate base in the face of excess capacity and poor performance records. Support for the latter policy is usually imputed to Justice Brandeis in Southwestern Bell Telephone Company v. Public Service Commission of Missouri, 262 U.S. 276 (1922).

Such practices undoubtedly extract a price in terms of efficiency forgone to achieve a rather ill-defined set of equity objectives. One cannot deny that there is an efficiency–equity tradeoff. What is regrettable is that the true equity objectives, primarily in the form of income distribution and the incidence of benefits and costs of particular actions, are seldom set forth with precision, with the result that the exact nature of the tradeoff remains unclear.

3. Improving Incentives for Efficiency

Most of the barriers to improved performance appear to be associated with government policies and practices and corporate power. The next logical question is whether current reforms, which are being initiated at the state and federal levels, will make a significant contribution toward eliminating these sources of inefficiency.

3.1 New Developments in Fuel Adjustment Clauses

The Public Utility Regulatory Policies Act of 1978 requires that FERC make a thorough review of FACs to determine whether they effectively provide incentives for the efficient use of resources. This study is to be made within two years of the enactment of the act, and every four years thereafter. It seems reasonable to assume that FERC's criteria for promoting efficiency will reflect the more recent efforts of the state commissions. There appear to be five features that characterize new thinking on the design of FACs.

First, some commissions have introduced a lagged recovery period. For example, Florida requires a two-month lag, and North Carolina a three-month lag. The intent appears to be to reintroduce regulatory lag as a stimulus for efficiency.

Second, two states (Michigan and South Dakota) have introduced a limited fuel expense recovery. A 90% recovery factor is applied, presumably as an incentive to promote more diligent policies regarding fuel procurement and utilization.

Third, a number of states have begun extensive FAC audits. These audits include a check of the utility's invoices, financial statements, inventory, and other documents needed to review the accuracy of a change in the fuel adjustment clause. Some commissions have gone further and investigated fuel procurement policies, while 13 state commissions audit fuel suppliers affiliated with jurisdictional electric utilities, 9 audit oil and gas exploration affiliates, and 11 audit coal-mining affiliates.

Fourth, there is a growing tendency to include purchased power in FACs as an incentive for the utility to use the least-cost source of power. The objective is to motivate the utility to purchase power when self-generation is more expensive.

Fifth, an increasing number of states have taken thermal efficiency into consideration in designing FACs. This typically involves the selection of an appropriate heat rate. The electric utilities prefer a fixed thermal-efficiency factor on the grounds that a fixed rate provides an incentive to the company to lower its heat rate. At present, six states use such a fixed heat rate. A variable heat rate, on the other hand, would tend to pass the benefits of increased thermal efficiency due to more efficient generation forward to the consumer. By employing a variable heat rate the commission uses a "stick" rather than a "carrot" to minimize fuel costs. Thirty-four states use a variable rate. Most interesting have been the "limit heat rate" (as introduced in Kansas) and the "target heat rate" (as introduced in Ohio). The limit heat rate is a maximum allowable figure, beyond which thermal efficiency decreases may be judged to be either outside the utility's control or due to imprudent management action. If the latter is the case, the commission will apply a limit value in the fuel adjustment clause. The target heat rate allows thermal efficiency to vary until a predetermined performance level is reached. If the heat rate exceeds this target (that is, thermal efficiency declines), then an FAC adjustment may be ordered. Thus, the Ohio Commission can disallow fuel costs due to a utility's failure to achieve a target level.

For the most part, the revisions in FACs are designed to tighten up the degree of laxity prevalent in the more simplified clauses and to emphasize penalties rather than incentives. A firm that has been extremely aggressive in locating and purchasing the lowest-cost fuel available would receive no particular advantage under these revisions. Indeed, the limited recovery factor would provide an incentive to inflate the base period fuel cost component. Nevertheless, these revisions do introduce a more stringent control over X-inefficiency. The introduction of target heat rates also provides a means whereby allocative distortions in favor of a fuel-intensive technology can readily be curbed.

Two additional variants of the fuel adjustment clause that tie FACs to capacity utilization should also be mentioned. The Connecticut Public Utility Control Authority sets target capacity factors for nuclear plants. If performance exceeds the target capacity factor, the FAC will allow an overrecovery of fuel costs. Conversely, a failure to meet the target introduces a penalty by the underrecovery of expenses.

The North Carolina Commission establishes a target nuclear plant capacity factor of 60%. A failure to achieve this target triggers a review of performance at the next semiannual fuel adjustment clause hearing. If management is at fault for the poor performance, an adjustment may be made disallowing a portion of the fuel costs.

3.2 Introducing Productivity Indexes

The introduction of total factor productivity (TFP) indexes as an integral part of the rate-making process constitutes another reform that should be evaluated. The Cost and Efficiency Revenue Adjustment Clause (CEAC), which will be discussed in the next section, and Bell Canada's performance studies [1974] have relied heavily upon TFP estimates. However, the former was not adopted, and the latter were submitted essentially as supplemental evidence. The forecasted test year provides one of the best illustrations of an effort to integrate TFP indexes into rate-making practice.

The New York Commission has been at the forefront in cases involving the use of TFP in estimating the forecasted test year. In the Consolidated Edison case [1979], the Commission designated a "Special Phase on Total Factor Productivity."[33] With respect to this phase, the administrative law judge concluded that TFP was highly arbitrary and difficult to predict. Further, he felt that the exercise of reasonable judgment regarding the rate of productivity was preferable to a mechanical reliance on TFP estimates. The Commission has not yet acted on this phase of the case. However, in the Long Island Lighting Company case [1979], the Commission found that TFP was too mechanical and that judgment was needed in making adjustments for productivity gains.[34]

The New York experience would seem to indicate that productivity will play an important role in rate-making decisions, but that its application is apt to reflect judgmental discretion rather than the direct introduction of TFP estimates. The difficulties of developing a generally acceptable measure of productivity and applying it to the regulated firm appear to be greater than one might have supposed. This conclusion is reinforced by the Massachusetts Commission's decision in the Boston Edison case [1979], in which the Commission expressed a strong interest in integrating productivity into the allowance for the rate of return on equity.[35] However, the Commission noted that acceptable estimates of productivity were still not available after five years of concern over the problem on the part of the agency and four rate cases.

[33] New York Public Service Commission [1979b].
[34] New York Public Service Commission [1979a].
[35] Massachusetts Department of Public Utilities [1979].

3.3 Comprehensive Modifications of Rate Base Regulation

In the 1920s, a number of efforts were made to develop innovative departures from conventional rate base regulation. The service-at-cost and sliding-scale plans represented such innovative approaches. Under a typical service-at-cost plan, surplus profits were placed in a reserve, to be drawn down when earnings levels were deficient. Sliding-scale plans, on the other hand, provided for a division of cost savings between the consumer and the investor.

In the post–World War II period, proposals to depart from the conventional revenue requirements formula were usually tied to inflation. The New Jersey Bell Company proposed a comprehensive adjustment clause that was approved by the New Jersey Commission in 1973. The clause permitted annual adjustments in prices based on changes in four components (wages and salaries, taxes other than federal income taxes, depreciation, and "other expenses"). The wage component was subject to a partial productivity offset (output per man-hour), and total increases were subject to a maximum rate of return constraint. The clause was upheld by the New Jersey Supreme Court in 1974, but the company has never chosen to implement the clause even though it filed two rate cases between 1974 and 1979. Apparently the company believes that the clause is not superior to conventional rate-making procedures in promoting its own objectives.

The Cost and Efficiency Revenue Adjustment Clause (CEAC) was perhaps the most sophisticated effort to modify traditional rate base regulation, tying the maintenance of past productivity performance to the full recovery of inflation-related costs. CEAC explicitly introduced a TFP measure that was lacking in the simple FAC. Also, CEAC broadened the base of costs to be considered so that cost increases incurred in one phase of an operation could be offset by productivity gains in another phase. Essentially, CEAC would permit the utility (Illinois Bell Telephone) to adjust prices on a monthly basis to recover one-half of the inflation-related cost increases. Recovery of the remaining one-half would be dependent on the firm's rate of TFP. A TFP rate equal to the company's historic TFP rate would allow complete recovery. The overall rate-of-return constraint would remain, so CEAC would not tie differential performance rates to a variable rate of return.

CEAC suffered from a number of serious flaws. The first was the assumption that the firm's past TFP record was optimal and that this would be an appropriate constraint on future X-inefficiency. Second, it must be assumed that the firm would start from an efficient base of operations. That is, there could be no significant cumulative past X-inefficiencies or a rate base that had already been inflated. Third, there was the question of whether CEAC provided a biased incentive in favor of short-term TFP gains at the expense of long-term gains. Such a bias in favor of short-term gains could be realized by simply deferring investment, to the long-term detriment of the consumer. Finally, the 50–50 split must represent an acceptable allocation of the burden of inflation between the consumer and the firm, recognizing that this is essentially an arbitrary judgment.

The Illinois Commission rejected CEAC in 1975, holding that

> the operation of the proposed CEAC formula would allow a very substantial portion of any increases in operating expense experienced by Bell to be recaptured by flow through to its customers without providing this Commission with an opportunity to fulfill its regulatory obligations by examination of such expenses in a retrospective and comparative manner and determine the reasonableness thereof. The implementation of the CEAC formula would be tantamount to an abdication of regulatory responsibilities.[36]

The New Mexico Commission introduced a rate-making methodology known as cost-of-service indexing (COSI) in 1975. Under COSI, the Public Service Company of New Mexico (PNM) applied for an adjustment in its rates on a quarterly basis in order to ensure that the return on equity stayed within a range of 13.5 to 14.5%. The spread was designed to offer an incentive to PNM to use efficient methods and improve its productivity. If the company earned more than 14.5%, a price reduction would be required. If it was below 13.5%, a price increase would be allowed. On 29 December 1978, the Commission concluded that COSI should not be terminated and that it would be reviewed again within two years.

In practice, COSI did permit PNM to maintain its bond rating and attract the necessary capital for a large expansion program. However, there was no agreement that the cost of capital was actually reduced as a result of COSI, nor was there any clear evidence that the productivity of the firm improved while the plan was in operation. Further, there was no indication that the plan reduced the burden on the staff and permitted the Commission to investigate problems of productivity and performance—freed from the burden of repeated rate filings. The latter, in part, accounted for the elimination of the quarterly adjustment in favor of an annual adjustment.

On balance, it is not unexpected that the New Mexico Commission was unable to discern a significant improvement under COSI. The plan provided

---

[36] Illinois Commerce Commission [1975], p. 7.

all of the inducements for X-inefficiencies associated with cost-plus regulation while eliminating the constraint of regulatory lag.[37] Further, it guaranteed a rate of return, and one can only speculate as to the degree of X-inefficiency that would have resulted had comparable plans been in effect throughout the nation during the 1970s. It is difficult to determine whether COSI was conducive to allocative distortions in favor of more capital expansion. During the hearing, the argument was raised that the company had an incentive to overexpand, but this was attributed to an imbalance between demand and energy charges so that peak consumption was relatively underpriced.

It is interesting to note that the shift from a quarterly to an annual adjustment has prompted PNM to argue that its return on equity capital should be 19–20% because of increased risk. This would yield one of the highest returns in the nation for an electric utility. It is equally interesting to note that the beta for PNM in the first quarter of 1979 was 0.75. The beta for Pacific Gas and Electric was 0.65, and for Southern California Edison 0.75. The latter reflect the stringent regulatory environment prevailing in California. If these measures of risk are accurate, COSI has had little impact on relative risk.[38]

An entirely different form of incentive plan was introduced in Michigan. The Michigan plan was composed of three parts: (1) a 90% FAC recovery; (2) a plant availability incentive that tied the level of plant availability to the return on equity; and (3) an incentive allowance for other operating and maintenance expenses (primarily wages). The plant availability incentive establishes a neutral range for plant available between 70.1 and 80%. Below 70% the return on equity would be reduced by 0.25%; between 80.1 and 85% it would be increased by 0.25%; and between 85.1 and 100% it would be increased by an additional 0.25%. Other operating and maintenance (O&M) expenses are tied to the Consumer Price Index (CPI). The annual pass-through of other O&M expenses is limited to the rate of increase in the CPI.

The Michigan plan has been applied to both Detroit Edison and Consumers Power. The initial results have been encouraging. In 1978, Detroit Edison was able to improve its plant availability from 71–72% to over 80%, and thereby earned the additional 0.25% return on equity. Consumers Power, on the other hand, was plagued by operational problems with its nuclear units and did not achieve the incentive return.

[37] During 1975–1979, the return on equity actually earned was above the 14.5% ceiling for only three quarterly periods (two in 1975–1979 and one in 1978), and within the permissible range for only one quarter (in 1978). This meant that PNM was free to increase prices and raise revenues each quarter from late 1976 through 1979—except for the one quarter in 1978 just noted. The permissible range was eliminated in 1979 and only the floor was retained.

[38] The beta for Arizona Public Service was also 0.75. All of the beta estimates were taken from *Value Line Investment Survey*, Part 3, Ratings and Reports, Edition 11, pp. 1600–1742, 16 March 1979.

The Michigan plan represents an innovative step forward, yet it is not free from infirmities. The shortcomings of a partial pass-through fuel clause have already been discussed. Tying incentives to plant availability may tend to bias management toward small-scale generation having a high level of reliability. While this would reduce the forced outage rate, it could also result in suboptimal additions to capacity and a reluctance to experiment or innovate.

Finally, there is no assurance that a CPI constraint would limit X-inefficiency insofar as other O&M expenses are concerned. Whether the Michigan plan will induce a bias in favor of capital inputs as opposed to labor and fuel inputs is difficult to forecast. The answer will probably depend upon the resource mix that yields the highest level of plant availability.

4. A Program for Reform

It is reasonable to assume that most of the reforms introduced by commissions will have some beneficial effects on performance. Modified FACs that place partial restrictions on pass-throughs or limits on deteriorating heat rates are certain to provide a strong stimulus for greater internal efficiency. Similarly, growing commission concern over the adequacy of performance by the regulated firm will serve to orient the attention of both commission staff and management toward the formulation of efficiency standards. The Michigan plan also appears to demonstrate that an incentive adjustment in the rate of return can serve to improve plant availability. One might even go so far as to argue that the New Mexico plan makes a contribution by demonstrating the fallacy of relaxing regulatory constraints without introducing a penalty for inefficiency.

Unfortunately, these reforms represent only a first step in the direction of improving regulation's ability to come to grips with performance problems. At least three issues remain to be resolved. These include: (1) the economic cost dilemma; (2) the development of a comprehensive system of incentives and penalties; and (3) an analysis of the contribution of changes in industry structure to improved performance.

Any effort to improve efficiency confronts a commission with a dilemma in dealing with the question of how to treat economic costs. If the agency fails to give weight to economic costs in establishing prices, it will provide a strong incentive for overinvestment. On the other hand, regulatory attempts to introduce current costs as a proxy for economic costs can result in incentives for X-inefficiency.The solution to this dilemma will require new regulatory techniques that reflect economic costs and identify economic rents. As currently practiced, the forecasted test year, the year-end rate base, FACs, indexing, and an allowance for attrition in the rate of return do not satisfy these requirements. The problem is further complicated by the need to develop techniques that better discern the impact of rates based on economic costs on different classes of customers.

The development of a comprehensive system of incentives and penalties for the regulated firm involves much more than the rigorous formulation of a model that maximizes some obscure welfare function. A workable system must prescribe a series of rewards for superior performance and penalties for inferior performance. The debate over the so-called incentive rate of return (IROR) for the Alaska Natural Gas Transmission System[39] provides an excellent example of the difficulties of determining what constitutes a premium for superior performance as well as a penalty for inferior performance. The imposition of a penalty also poses additional problems. Management will argue that the disallowance of expenses or a reduction in the rate of return will only worsen the prospects for improvement and it will take a great deal of regulatory fortitude to face the possibility that one's efforts to improve efficiency may force the firm into bankruptcy. The on-going performance problems confronting the Massachusetts Commission in regulating the Boston Edison Company, noted earlier, are ample proof that the development and application of appropriate penalties is not an easy task.

Furthermore, although efforts to measure productivity have made progress in recent years, much work remains to be done before effective interfirm comparisons can be made and differentials in performance can be imputed to factors over which management has reasonable control. Experience with TFP indexes demonstrates the difficulty of developing confidence in acceptable measures of productivity, while the deficiencies in the CEAC proposal reveal the infirmities of basing performance comparisons only on the firm's historic record.

Finally, there is the question of whether an incentive system can be designed that negates both the Averch–Johnson type of factor bias and the motivation to inflate the rate base to camouflage excessive earnings. One might assume that the removal of an upper limit on the rate of return would eliminate such behavior. However, this is a reasonable assumption only if the regulator is able to prescribe an acceptable standard for efficiency. Otherwise, the firm could either distort factor inputs or inflate the rate base and enjoy an excessive return on an ever-expanding base. In short, the introduction of an incentive system can only be effective if it is combined with adequate guidelines for judging efficiency and the establishment of an agreed-upon base for introducing such a system.

[39] Federal Energy Regulatory Commission [1979b].

However, no system of incentives and penalties would be conducive to achieving the type of dynamic performance benefits that could be expected if competition could be promoted in selected markets within the public utility industries. As noted earlier, the communications industry is replete with examples where competition in specific markets has produced substantial benefits. The problem becomes one of identifying and promoting such markets in electricity and gas.

The bulk power market provides an excellent opportunity to introduce greater competitive pressure via a change in industry structure. Free access to a comprehensive transmission network would maximize the number of potential buyers and sellers of power and increase the volume of energy transmitted over the network. This, in turn, would realize the substantial economies of scale inherent in extra-high voltage transmission. Creation of a competitive bulk power market would require that the network be given common carrier status and that a central authority be established to perform certain market-related functions, such as recording transactions, handling power transfers, and acting as a clearinghouse for payments.

The performance benefits could be substantial. Such a market could realize many of the dynamic performance benefits described earlier in the discussion of interconnection and regional power transfers. In addition, by expanding the scope of the bulk power market, firms would be better able to achieve high-capacity factors because surplus power could be sold expeditiously through the market. An increase in the total number of suppliers would also permit more efficient operation of existing generating plants in the short run by loading each unit to a point where the short-run marginal cost of producing the last kilowatt-hour was the same for all generating units. In the long run, the market would permit cost minimization by offering each firm the option of either contracting to buy power or building additional capacity. This choice would also greatly enhance the effectiveness of regulatory control of overinvestment and X-inefficiency since commissions could simply require that the utility select the least-cost option for meeting the growth in demand.

A competitive bulk power market would also create significant performance benefits in the area of pollution control. The individual firm would be under considerable pressure to select the least-cost method of pollution abatement since it would have to compete in selling the output of that plant. In addition, an effluent charge would achieve the desired effect under these circumstances. A greatly enhanced bulk power market would also provide the best opportunity for expanding the number of potential sites for locating new plants consistent with environmental constraints.

If concurrent advances can be made in each of these areas, the commission system will have taken a major step toward reconciling any inconsistencies between the function of regulation and the promotion of efficiency. Of course, a number of equity considerations will remain; however, commissions should find that many of the fairness judgments associated with regulatory treatment of individual expense and rate base items will disappear because of the new pressures for efficiency. Economic rents may also be diminished by these reforms. In essence, regulatory reform, improved performance, and greater competition should not be perceived as contradictory objectives, but rather as complementary ways to promote the public welfare.

References

Afriat, S. N. [1972]. Efficiency estimation of production functions, *Int. Econ. Rev.* **13**, 568–598.
Aigner, D. J., Lovell, C. A. K., and Schmidt, P. J. [1977]. Formulation and estimation of stochastic frontier production function models, *J. Economet.* **6**, 21–37.
Allen, R. C. [1981]. Accounting for Price Changes: American steel rails, 1879–1910, *J. Political Econ.* (forthcoming).
Allen, R. G. D. [1938]. "Mathematical analysis for economists." Macmillan, New York.
American Gas Association [1965]. "Gas Engineers Handbook." Industrial Press, New York.
American Medical Association [1976]. "Profiles of Medical Practice" (J. R. Cantwell, ed.), Center for Health Services Research and Development, American Medical Association, Chicago, Illinois.
American Medical Association [1978]. "Profiles of Medical Practice" (J. C. Gaffney, ed.), Center for Health Services Research and Development, American Medical Association, Chicago, Illinois.
American Telephone and Telegraph Company [1976]. An Econometric Study of Returns to Scale in the Bell System. Federal Communication Commission Docket 20003 (Fifth Supplemental Response), Bell Exhibit 60 (August).
Appelbaum, E. [1979]. Testing price taking behavior, *J. Economet.* **9**, 283–294.
Appelbaum, E., and Kohli, U. R. [1979], Canada-United States trade: Test for the small-open-economy hypothesis, *Canad. J. Econ.* **12**, 1–14.
Averch, H., and Johnson, L. [1962], Behavior of the firm under regulatory constraint, *Amer. Econ. Rev.* **52** (December), 1053–1069.
Bailey, E. E. [1973]. "Economic Theory of Regulatory Constraint." Heath, Lexington, Massachusetts.
Bailey, E. E., and Malone, J. C. [1970]. Resource allocation and the regulated firm, *Bell J. Econ. and Management Sci.* **1** (Spring), 129–142.
Baron, D. P. [1975]. A method for the measurement of hospital output, service intensity and costs, Health Management Research Discussion, Paper No. 75-3. Northwestern Univ., Evanston, Illinois.
Barten, A. P. [1969]. Maximum likelihood estimation of a complete system of demand equations, *Eur. Econ. Rev.* **1** (Fall), 7–73.
Batko, W. [1979]. Compliance in Truth-in-Lending, The Costs and Benefits of Public Regulation of Consumer Financial Services. Abt Associates, Cambridge, Massachusetts, NSF-C76-18548.
Battelle Memorial Institute, Columbus Laboratories [1976]. Probable Levels of R & D Expenditures in 1977 (December).

Baumol, W. J. [1977a]. On the proper cost tests for natural monopoly in a multiproduct industry, *Amer. Econ. Rev.* **67** (December), 809–822.

Baumol, W. J. [1977b]. "Economic Theory and Operations Analysis." Prentice-Hall, Englewood Cliffs, New Jersey.

Baumol, W. J., Bailey, E. E., and Willig, R. D. [1977]. Weak invisible hand theorems on pricing and entry in a multiproduct natural monopoly, *Amer. Econ. Rev.* **67** (June), 350–365.

Baumol, W. J., and Klevorick, A. K. [1970]. Input choices and rate-of-return regulation: An overview of the discussion, *Bell J. Econ. Management Sci.* **1** (Autumn), 162–190.

Bell Canada [1974]. Memorandum on Productivity, filed as Exhibit B-73-62 before Canadian Transport Commission.

Benston, G. J. [1972]. Economies of scale of financial institutions, *J. Money, Credit and Banking* **4** (May), 312–341.

Berndt, E. R. [1978]. Aggregate energy, efficiency, and productivity measurement, *Ann. Rev. Energy*, **3**.

Berndt, E. R., and Christensen, L. R. [1973], The translog function and the substitution of equipment, structures, and labor in U.S. manufacturing 1929–68, *J. Economet.* **1**, 81–114.

Berndt, E. R., and Jorgenson, D. W. [1975]. Energy, Intermediate Goods, and Production in an Inter-Industry Model of the U.S., 1947–1971, Paper delivered at the World Congress of the Econometric Society, Toronto, Canada.

Berndt, E. R., and Khaled, M. S. [1979]. Parametric productivity measurement and choice among flexible functional forms, *J. Political Econ.* **87** (December), 1220–1245.

Berndt, E. R., and Savin, N. E. [1975]. Estimation and hypothesis testing in singular equation systems with autoregressive disturbances. *Econometrica* **43**, No. 5-6, 937–957.

Berndt, E. R., and Wood, D. O. [1975a]. Technology, prices, and the derived demand for energy, *Rev. Econ. Statist.* **57** (August), 259–268.

Berndt, E. R., and Wood, D. O. [1975b]. Technical change, Tax Policy and the Derived Demand for Energy, unpublished manuscript, Department of Economics, Univ. of British Columbia, Vancouver, B.C., Canada.

Binswanger, H. P. [1974a]. A cost function approach to the measurement of elasticities of factor demand and elasticities of substitution, *Amer. J. Agr. Econ.* **56** (May), 377–386.

Binswanger, H. P. [1974b]. The measurement of technical change biases with many factors of production, *Amer. Econ. Rev.* **64** (December), 964–976.

Blackorby, C., Primont, D., and Russell, R. R. [1977]. On testing separability restrictions with flexible functional forms, *J. Economet.* **5**, 195–209.

Bower, B. T. [1975]. Studies of residuals management in industry, *in* "Economic Analysis of Environmental Problems" (E. S. Mills, ed.), pp. 275–324. National Bureau of Economic Research, New York.

Boyes, W. J. [1973]. Empirical and Theoretical Essays on the Averch–Johnson Model of a Regulated Firm, Dissertation, Claremont Graduate School.

Boyes, W. J. [1976]. An empirical examination of the Averch–Johnson effect, *Econ. Inquiry* **14** (March), 25–35.

Breyer, S. G., and MacAvoy, P. W. [1974]. "Energy Regulation by the Federal Power Commission." The Brookings Institution, Washington, D.C.

Callen, J. L. [1978]. Production, efficiency, and welfare in the natural gas transmission industry, *Amer. Econ. Rev.* **68** (June), 311–323.

Caves, D. W., and Christensen, L. [1980a]. The Relative Efficiency of Public and Private Firms in a competitive Environment: The Case of Canadian Railroads. *J. Political Econ.* **88** (October), 958–976.

Caves, D. W., and Christensen, L. R. [1980b]. Global Properties of Flexible Functional Forms, *Amer. Econ. Rev.* **70** (June), 422–432.

Caves, D. W., and Christensen, L. R. [1980c]. Multilateral Comparisons of Output, Input, and Productivity Using Superlative Index Numbers. Social Systems Research Institute. Paper No. 8008 (July). Univ. of Wisconsin, Madison, Wisconsin.

Caves, D. W., Christensen, L. R., and Swanson, J. A. [1980]. Productivity in U.S. Railroads, 1951–1974, *Bell J. Econ.* (Spring); 166–181; originally SSRI Workshop Paper 7820 (1978), Univ. of Wisconsin, Madison, Wisconsin.

Chenery, H. B. [1949]. Engineering production functions, *Quart. J. Econ.* **63** (November), 507–531.

Chenery, H. B. [1952]. Overcapacity and the acceleration principle, *Econometrica* **20** (January), 1–28.

Chiang, Wang, S. J. [1979]. The Structure of Cost and Technology of Regulated Common Carriers of General Commodities. MIT M. S. Thesis, Department of Civil Engineering.

Christensen, L. R., and Greene, W. H. [1976]. Economies of scale in U.S. electric power generation, *J. Political Econ.* **84** (August), 655–676.

Christensen, L. R., and Jorgenson, D. W. [1969]. The measurement of U.S. real capital input, 1929–1967. *Rev. Income and Wealth* Series 15, **14** (December), No. 4, 293–320.

Christensen, L. R., and Jorgenson, D. W. [1970]. U.S. real product and real factor input, 1929–1967. *Rev. Income and Wealth* Series **16** (March), 19–50.

Christensen, L. R., Jorgenson, D. W., and Lau, L. J. [1971]. Conjugate duality and the transcendental logarithmic function, *Econometrica* **39**, 255–256.

Christensen, L. R., Jorgenson, D. W., and Lau, L. J. [1973]. Transcendental logarithmic production frontiers. *Rev. Econ. Statist.* **55** (February), 28–45.

Christensen, L. R., Cummings, D., and Jorgenson, D. W. [1980], Economic growth, 1947–1973: An international comparison. in "*New Developments in Productivity Measurement and Analysis*" (J. W. Kendrick and B. N. Vaccara, eds.), Studies in Income and Wealth Vol. 44, pp. 595–691. Univ. of Chicago Press, Chicago, Illinois.

Christensen, L. R., Gollop, F. M., and Stevenson, R. E. [1980a]. Measuring Capital Input in the Electric Power Industry. Unpublished manuscript. University of Wisconsin.

Cookenboo, L., Jr., [1954]. Costs of operating crude oil pipelines, *Rice Inst. Pamphlet* **40** (April), 35–113.

Council on Wage and Price Stability [1976]. Price Increases and Capacity Expansion in the Paper Industry, Washington, D.C., December.

Council on Wage and Price Stability [1977] Prices and Costs in the United States Steel Industry, Report to the President, Washington, D.C., October.

Courville, L. [1974]. Regulation and efficiency in the electric utility industry, *Bell J. Econ. Management Sci.* **5** (Spring), 53–74.

Cowing, T. G. [1970]. Technical Change in Steam-Electric Generation: An Engineering Approach, unpublished PhD dissertation, Univ. of California, Berkeley, California.

Cowing, T. G. [1974]. Technical change and scale economies in an engineering production function: The case of steam electric power, *J. Ind. Econ.* **23** (December), 135–152.

Cowing, T. G. [1978]. The effectiveness of rate-of-return regulation: An empirical test using profit functions, in "Production Economics: A Dual Approach to Theory and Applications" (M. Fuss and D. McFadden, eds.). North-Holland Publ., Amsterdam. An earlier version of this paper [1975] appeared as a mimeo, State Univ. of New York at Binghamton.

Cowing, T. G. [1979]. Duality and the Estimation of a Restricted Technology, Working Paper 79-1, Department of Economics, State University of New York at Binghamton.

Cowing, T. G., and Stevenson, R. E. [1978]. Allocative Efficiency and Automatic Adjustment Clauses: A Theoretical Analysis, Working Paper 1-78-1. Graduate School of Business, Univ. of Wisconsin, Madison, Wisconsin. (January).

Davenport, E., Hansen, M., and Smith, K. R. [1975]. The Empirical Definition of "Role." Paper prepared for presentation at the Second Working Conference of the Efficient Health Manpower Utilization Project, Taos, New Mexico (June).

Davis, B. E., Caccappolo, G. J., and Chaudry, M. S. [1973]. An econometric planning model for American Telephone and Telegraph Company, *Bell J. Econ. Management Sci.* **4** (Spring), 29–56.

Denison, E. F. [1962]. The Sources of Economic Growth in the U.S. and the Alternatives Before Us, Supple. Paper No. 13. Committee for Economic Development, New York.

Denison, E. F. [1967]. "Why Growth Rates Differ: Post-War Experience in Nine Western Countries." The Brookings Institution, Washington, D.C.

Denison, E. F. [1972]. Some major issues in productivity analysis: An examination of estimates by Jorgenson and Griliches, *Surv. Current Business* **52**, Part II (May), 37–63.

Denison, E. F. [1974]. Accounting for United States Economic Growth, 1929 to 1969. The Brookings Institution, Washington, D.C.

Denison, E. F. [1978a]. Effects of selected changes in the institutional and human environment upon output per unit of input, *Surv. Current Business* **58** (January), 21–44.

Denison, E. F. [1978b]. The puzzling drop in productivity, *The Brookings Bull.* **15** (Fall) 10–12.

Denny, M., and Fuss, M. [1977]. The use of approximation analysis to test for separability and the existence of consistent aggregates, *Amer. Econ. Rev.* **67** (June), 492–497.

Denny, M., and Fuss, M. [1979]. On the Interpretation of Conventionally Measured Total Factor Productivity Indices, mimeo, Univ. of Toronto, Toronto, Canada.

Denny, M., Everson, C., Fuss, M., and Waverman, L. [1979]. Estimating the Effects of Diffusion of Technological Innovations in Telecommunications: The Production Structure of Bell Canada, paper presented at the Seventh Annual Telecommunications Policy Research Conf., April 29–May 1, 1979; forthcoming in the *Canad. J. Econ.*

Diamond, P., McFadden, D., and Rodriguez, M. [1978]. Measurement of the elasticity of factor substitution and bias of technical change, *in* "Production Economics: A Dual Approach to Theory and Applications" (M. Fuss and D. McFadden, eds.), Vol 2, pp. 125–148. North Holland Publ., Amsterdam.

Diewert, W. E. [1973]. Functional forms for profit and transformation functions, *J. Econ. Theory* **6**, 284–316.

Diewert, W. E. [1974]. Application of duality theory, *in* "Frontiers of Quantitative Economics" (M. D. Intriligator and D. A. Kendrick, eds.), Vol. II, pp. 106–171. North-Holland Publ., Amsterdam.

Diewert, W. E. [1976]. Exact and superlative index numbers, *J. Economet.* **4** May, 115–145.

Diewert, W. E. [1978a]. Superlative index numbers and consistency in aggregation, *Econometrica* **46**, 883–900.

Diewert, W. E. [1978b]. Duality Approaches to Microeconomic Theory, IMSSS Techn. Rep. 281, Stanford Univ., Stanford, California, October.

Diewert, W. E. [1980]. "Aggregation problems in the measurement of capital," *in* "The Measurement of Capital" (Dan Usher, ed.), Studies in Income and Wealth, Vol. 45, pp. 433–528. Univ. of Chicago Press, Chicago, Illinois.

Diewert, W. E., and Parkan, C. [1979]. Linear Programming Test of Regularity Conditions for Production Functions, Disc. Paper 79-01. Department of Economics, Univ. of British Columbia, Vancouver (January).

Divisia, F. [1926]. L'indice monetaire et la theorie de la monnaie. Societe Anonyme de Recueil Sirey, Paris.

Dixit, A. K. [1976]. "The Theory of Equilibrium Growth." Oxford Univ. Press, London and New York.

Dobell, A. R., Taylor, L. D., Waverman, L., Liu, T. H., and Copeland, M. D. G. [1972]. Communications in Canada, *Bell J. Econ. Management Sci.* **3** (Spring), 175–219.

Douglas, G. W., and Miller, J. C. [1974]. "Economic Regulation of Domestic Air Transport: Theory and Policy." The Brookings Institution, Washington, D.C.

Drechsler, L. [1973]. Weighting of index numbers in multilateral international comparisons, *Rev. Income and Wealth* **19** (March), 17–34.

Farrell, M. J. [1957]. The measurement of productive efficiency, *J. Roy. Statist. Soc.* Ser. A, **120**, 253–281.

Faulhaber, G. R. [1975]. Cross subsidization: Pricing in public enterprises, *Amer. Econ. Rev.* **65** (December), 966–977.

Feldstein, M. S. [1977]. Quality change and the demand for hospital care, *Econometrica* **45** (October), 1681–1702.

Fisher, F. M., and Shell, K. [1972]. "The Economic Theory of Price Indices." Academic Press, New York.

Friedlaender, A. F. [1978]. Hedonic costs and economies of scale in the regulated trucking industry, *in* "Motor Carrier Economic Regulation." Washington D.C. National Research Council.

Friedlaender, A. F., and Spady, R. H. [1979]. Equity, Efficiency and Resource Rationalization in the Rail and Regulated Trucking Industries, Final Report: Alternative Scenarios for Federal Transportation Policy, Massachusetts Institute of Technology, Center for Transportation Studies Rep. No. 79-4, (March).

Friedlaender, A. F., and Spady, R. H. [1980]. "Surface Freight Transport: Equity, Efficiency and Competition." MIT Press, Cambridge, Massachusetts.

Fuss, M., and Waverman, L. [1977]. Multi-Product Multi-Input Cost Functions for a Regulated Utility: The Case of Telecommunications in Canada, paper presented to the *NBER Conf. Public Regulation, Washington, D.C., December,* forthcoming in G. Fromm (ed.). "Studies in Public Regulation," MIT Press, Cambridge, Massachusetts.

Fuss, M., and McFadden, D. (eds.) [1978]. "Production Economics: A Dual Approach to Theory and Applications." North-Holland Publ., Amsterdam.

Gollop F. M. [1974]. Modeling Technical Change and Market Inperfections: An Econometric Analysis of U.S. Manufacturing, 1947–1973. Unpublished Ph.D. Dissertation, Harvard Univ., Cambridge, Massachusetts.

Gollop, F. M., and Jorgenson, D. W. [1979]. Sources of Productivity Growth in the Postwar U.S., Unpublished manuscript.

Gollop, F. M., and Jorgenson, D. W. [1980]. United States productivity growth by industry, 1947–1973, *in* "New Developments in Productivity Measurement and Analysis" (J. W. Kendrick and B. N. Vaccara, eds.), Studies in Income and Wealth, National Bureau of Economic Research. Univ. of Chicago Press, Chicago, Illinois.

Gollop, F. M., and Karlson, S. H. [1978a]. An Intertemporal Model of Behavior: The Regulated Monopolist, SSRI Workshop Paper 7812, Univ. of Wisconsin, Madison, Wisconsin.

Gollop, F. M., and Karlson, S. H. [1978b]. The impact of the fuel adjustment mechanism on economic efficiency, *Rev. Econ. Statist.* **60** (November), 574–584.

Gordon, R. J. [1965]. Airline costs and managerial efficiency, *in* "Transportation Economics," pp. 61–94. National Bureau of Economic Research, New York.

Gorman, W. M. [1968]. Measuring the quantities of fixed factors, *in* "Value, Capital and Growth: Papers in Honor of Sir John Hicks" (J. N. Wolfe, ed.), pp. 141–172. Aldine Publishing Co., Chicago, Illinois.

Greenbaum, S. I. [1967]. A study of bank costs, *Nat. Banking Rev.* **4** (June), 415–434.

Greenbaum, S. I., and Haywood, C. F. [1971]. Secular change in the financial services industry, *J. Money, Credit, and Banking* **3** (May), 571–589.

Griffin, J. M. [1977a]. Long-run production modeling with pseudo data: Electric power generation, *Bell J. Econ.* **8** (Spring), 112–127.

Griffin, J. M. [1977b]. The Econometrics of Joint Production: Another Approach, *Rev. Econ. Statist.* **59** (November), 389–397.

Griffin, J. M. [1978a]. Joint production technology: The case of petrochemicals, *Econometrica* **46** (March), 379–396.

Griffin, J. M. [1978b]. Psuedo-Data Estimation With Alternative Functional Forms, unpublished paper (November).

Griffin, J. M. [1979]. Statistical cost analysis revisited, *Quart. J. Econ.* **93** (February), 107–129.

Griliches, Z. [1963]. The sources of measured productivity growth: U.S. Agriculture, 1940–1960, *J. Political Econ.* **71** (August), 331–346.

Griliches, Z. [1964] Research expenditures, education, and the aggregate agricultural production function, *Amer. Econ. Rev.* **54**, 961–974.

Griliches, Z. [1967]. Production functions in manufacturing: Some preliminary results, *in* "The Theory and Empirical Analysis of Production" (M. Brown, ed.), NBER Studies in Income and Wealth, Vol. 31, pp. 275–322. Columbia Univ. Press, New York.

Guilkey, D. K., and Lovell, C. A. K. [1979]. On the flexibility of the translog approximation, *Internat. Econ. Rev.* **21** (February).

Hanoch, G. [1975]. The elasticity of scale and the shape of average costs, *Amer. Econ. Rev.* **65** (December), 956–965.

Hanoch, G., and Rothschild, M. [1972]. Testing the assumptions of production theory: A nonparametric approach, *J. Political Econ.* **80** (March/April), 256–275.

Hayashi, P. M., and Trapani, J. M. [1976]. Rate of return regulation and the regulated firm's choice of capital–labor ratio: Further empirical evidence on the Averch–Johnson model, *South. Econ. J.* **42** (January), 384–398.

Haywood, C. F. [1977]. Production of consumer financial services. Public Regulation of Financial Services, Costs and Benefits to Consumers: Phase I, Interim Report, Abt Associates, Inc., Cambridge, Massachusetts, NSF-C76-18548.

Haywood, C. F. [1979]. Regulation, structure, and technological change in the consumer financial services industry, The Costs and Benefits of Public Regulation of Consumer Financial Services, Abt Associates, Inc., Cambridge, Massachusetts, NSF-C76-18548.

Haywood, C. F., and McGee, L. R. [1969]. The Expansion of Bank Funds in the 1970's, Association of Reserve City Bankers, Chicago, Illinois.

Hazilla, M. [1978]. The Use of Economic Theory in Econometric Estimation: Inference in Linear Constrained Models, unpublished Ph.D. Thesis, State University of New York at Binghamton.

Heggestad, A., and Haywood, C. F. [1977]. The effect of market structure on competition and performance in the markets for consumer financial services, Public Regulation of Financial Services, Costs and Benefits to Consumers; Phase 1, Interim Report, Abt Associates, Inc., Cambridge, Massachusetts, NSF-C76-18548.

Hicks, J. R. [1939]. "Value and Capital." Oxford Univ. Press, London and New York.

Hughes, W. R. [1971]. Scale frontiers in electric power, *in* "Technological Change in Regulated Industries" (W. M. Capron, ed.), pp. 44–85. The Brookings Institution, Washington, D.C.

Hulten, C. R. [1973]. Divisia index numbers, *Econometrica* **41** (November), 1017–1026.

Hulten, C. R. [1975]. Technical change and the reproducibility of capital, *Amer. Econ. Rev.* **65** (December), 956–965.

Hulten, C. R. [1978]. Growth accounting with intermediate inputs, *Rev. Econ. Stud.* **45**, 511–518.

Hulten, C. R. [1979]. On the "importance" of productivity change. *Amer. Econ. Rev.* **69** (March), 126–136.

Humphrey, D. B., and Moroney, J. R. [1975]. Substitution among capital, labor and natural resource products in American manufacturing, *J. Political Econ.* **83** (February), 57–82.

Illinois Commerce Commission [1975]. Illinois Bell Telephone Company, Proposed Monthly Changes in Telephone Rates Applicable to All Exchanges of the Company due to Cost and Efficiency Adjustment Factor, Case No. 58916 (February 26).

Jensen, J. T., and Stauffer, T. R. [1972]. Implications of Natural Gas Consumption Patterns for the Implementation of End-Use Priority Programs, Report to the Office of the General Counsel, General Motors Co., by Arthur D. Little, Inc.

Jorgenson, D. W., and Griliches, Z. [1967]. The explanation of productivity change *Rev. Econ. Stud.* **34** (July), 249–283.

Jorgenson, D. W., and Griliches, Z. [1972]. Issues in growth accounting: A reply to Edward F. Denison, *Survey of Current Business* **52,** No. 5, Part II, 65–94.

Kalish, L., III, and Gilbert, R. A. [1973]. An analysis of efficiency of scale and organizational form in commercial banking, *J. Ind. Econ.* **21** (July), 293–307.

Kendall, M. G. [1948], "The Advanced Theory of Statistics." Griffin, London.

Kendrick, J. W. [1961]. "Productivity Trends in the United States." Princeton Univ. Press, Princeton, New Jersey.

Kendrick, J. W. [1973]. Postwar Productivity Trends in the United States, 1948–1969. National Bureau of Economic Research, New York.

Kendrick, J. W. [1975]. Efficiency incentives and cost factors in public utility automatic revenue adjustment clauses, *Bell J. Econ.* **6** (Spring), 299–313.

Kendrick, J. W., and Vaccara, B. N. (eds.) [1980]. "New Developments in Productivity Measurement and Analysis," Studies in Income and Wealth, National Bureau of Economic Research. Univ. of Chicago Press, Chicago, Illinois.

King, M. A. [1977]. "Public Policy and the Corporation." Wiley, New York.

Kmenta, J. [1971]. "Elements of Econometrics." Macmillan, New York.

Kmenta, J., and Gilbert, R. F. [1968]. Small sample properties of alternative estimators of seemingly unrelated regressions, *J. Amer. Statist. Assoc.* **63** (December), 1180–1200.

Kopp, R. J., and Smith, V. K. [1979]. The Perceived Role of Materials in Neoclassical Models of the Production Technology, Quality of the Environment Discussion Paper No. D-45, Resources for the Future (January).

Lau, L. J. [1974]. Comments on applications of duality theory, *in* "Frontiers of Quantitative Economics" (M. D. Intriligator and D. A. Kendrick, eds.), Vol. II, pp. 176–199. North-Holland Publ., Amsterdam.

Lau, L. J. [1976]. A characterization of the normalized restricted profit function, *J. Econ. Theory* **12,** 131–163.

Lau, L. J. [1978]. The Approximate Representation of Convex Technologies with Pseudo Data, unpublished paper (November).

Lau, L. J. [1979a]. On exact index numbers, *Rev. Econ. Statist.* **61** (February), 73–82.

Lau, L. J. [1979b]. On the Measurement of Raw Materials Inputs, paper presented at RFF–NSF Conference on Resource and Environmental Constraints to Economic Growth, San Francisco, California (February 12–13).

Leland, H. E. [1974]. Regulation of natural monopolies and the fair rate of return, *Bell J. Econ. and Management Sci.* **5** (Spring), 3–15.

Longbrake, W. A., and Haslem, J. A. [1975]. Productive efficiency in commercial banking, *J. Money Credit and Banking* **7** (August), 317–330.

MacAvoy, P. W., and Noll, R. [1973]. Relative prices on regulated transactions of the natural gas pipelines, *Bell J. Econ. and Management Sci.* **4** (Spring), 212–234.

Mandell, L. [1977]. Diffusion of EFTS among national banks, *J. Money Credit and Banking* **9** (May), 341–348.

Mangasarian, O. L. [1969]. "Nonlinear Programming." McGraw-Hill, New York.

Manne, A. S. [1961]. Capacity expansion and probabilistic growth, *Econometrica* **29** (October), 632–649.

Mantell, L. [1974]. An Econometric Study of Returns to Scale in the Bell System. Staff Research Paper, Office of Telecommunications Policy (February).

Marsden, J. R. Pingry, D. E., and Whinston, A. [1974]. Engineering foundations of production functions, *J. Econ. Theory* **9**, 124–140.

Marshall, A. [1949]. "Principles of Economics." 8th ed. Macmillan, New York.

Mason, J. [1977]. Innovation in the money system: EFTS and economic welfare, *Quart. Rev. Econ. Business* **17** (Winter), 43–55.

Massachusetts Department of Public Utilities [1979]. Investigation by the Department on Its Own Motion as to the Propriety of the Rates and Charges Set Forth in Schedules M.D.P.U. Nos. 389 to 410, Inclusive, Filed by the Boston Edison Company with the Department on March 16, 1979, to Become Effective April 1, 1979, D.P.U. 19991 (September 28).

May, J., and Denny, M. [1979]. Post-war productivity in Canadian manufacturing. *Canad. J. Econ.* **12**, 29–41.

McFadden, D. [1966]. Cost, Revenue and Profit Functions: A Cursory Review, Institute for Business and Economic Research, Working Paper 86, Univ. of California, Berkeley, California.

McFadden, D. [1978]. Cost, revenue, and profit functions, *in* "Production Economics: A Dual Approach to Theory and Applications" (M. Fuss and D. McFadden, eds.). North Holland Publ., Amsterdam.

Miki, R. T., and Humphrey, B. G. [1979]. Regulatory Budgeting and Public Decisions, unpublished paper, Office of Regulatory Economics and Policy, U.S. Department of Commerce (March).

Milton, H. S. [1972]. Cost-of-research index, 1920–1970, *Operations Res.* **20**, 1–18.

Moody's Investors Service, Moody's Public Utilities, various issues.

Mundlak, Y. [1961]. Empirical production functions free of management bias, *J. Farm Econ.* **43** (February), 44–56.

Mundlak, Y. [1964]. Transcendental multiproduct production functions, *Internat. Econ. Rev.* **5** (September), 273–284.

Mundlak, Y. [1978]. On the pooling of time series and cross section data, *Econometrica* **46** (January), 69–85.

Mundlak, Y., and Razin, A. [1969]. Aggregation, index numbers and the measurement of technical change, *Rev. Econ. Statist.* **51** (May), 166–175.

Nadiri, M. I. [1970]. Some approaches to the theory and measurement of total factor productivity: A survey, *J. Econ. Literature* **8** (December), 1137–1177.

National Academy of Sciences [1979]. Measurement and Interpretation of Productivity, Report of the Committee on National Statistics, Assembly of Behavioral and Social Sciences, National Academy of Sciences, Washington, D.C.

National Association of Regulatory Utility Commissioners [1975]. The Measurement of Electric Utility Efficiency, Washington, D.C.

National Association of Regulatory Utility Commissioners [1977]. 1976 Annual Report on Utility and Carrier Regulation, Washington, D.C.

National Association of Regulatory Utility Commissioners [1978]. 1977 Annual Report on Utility and Carrier Regulation, Washington, D.C.

National Commission on Electronic Funds Transfer [1978]. Final Report.

National Electric Reliability Council [1978]. 8th Annual Review, Princeton, New Jersey (August).

National Highway Carriers Directory, Inc. [1973]. National Highway and Airway Carriers and Routes, Buffalo Grove, Illinois.

National Petroleum Council [1967]. U.S. Petroleum and Gas Transportation Capacities, Washington, D.C.

National Research Council [1978]. Motor Carrier Economic Regulation, Washington, D.C.

New York Public Service Commission [1976]. Case No. 26887, Long Island Lighting Company, Electric Rates (December 16).

New York Public Service Commission [1979]. Case No. 27374, Long Island Lighting Company (April 27).

New York Public Service Commission [1979]. Case No. 27353, Consolidated Edison Company of New York, Special Phase on Total Factor Productivity. Administrative Law Judge Decision (May 16).

O'Donnel, J. P. [1973]. 16th annual report on pipeline installation and equipment costs, *Oil and Gas J.* (August), 69–74.

Ohta, M. [1974]. A note on the duality between production and cost functions: Rate of return to scale and rate of technical progress, *Econ. Stud. Quart.* **25** (December), 63–65.

Over, A. M., Jr. [1978]. On the Estimation of the Primary Care Production Function Where Output Is an Unobservable Variable. Unpublished doctoral dissertation, Univ. of Wisconsin, Madison, Wisconsin.

Over, A. M., Jr., and Smith, K. R. [1979]. The estimation of the ambulatory medical care technology where output is an unobservable variable, *J. Economet.* **13**.

Owen, B. M., and Braeutigam, R. [1978]. "The Regulation Game: Strategic Use of the Administrative Process." Ballinger Publ., Cambridge, Massachusetts.

Palmer, J. L., Todd, J. E., and Tuckman, H. P. [1976]. The distributional impact of higher energy prices: How should the Federal Government respond? *Public Policy* **24** (Fall), 545–568.

Panzar, J. C., and Willig, R. D. [1977]. Economies of scale in multi-output production, *Quart. J. Econ.* **91** (August), 481–493.

Peck, S. C. [1974]. Alternative investment models for firms in the electric utilities industry, *Bell J. Econ. Management Sci.* **5** (Autumn), 420–458.

Petersen, H. C. [1975]. An empirical test of regulatory effects, *Bell J. Econ.* **6** (Spring), 111–126.

Pondy, L. R., Jones, J. M., and Braun, J. A. [1973]. Utilization and productivity of the Duke Physician's Associate, *Socio-Econ. Planning Sci.* **7**, 327–352.

Redich, M. [1974]. Hospital Inflationary Mechanisms. Paper presented at the Western Economics Association Meetings, Las Vegas, Nevada, Revised version (October).

Reinhardt, U. E. [1975]. "Physician Productivity and the Demand for Health Manpower." Ballinger, Cambridge, Massachusetts

Richter, M. K. [1966]. Invariance axioms and economic indexes, *Econometrica* **34** (October), 739–755.

Roberts, P. O. [1977]. Some Aspects of Regulatory Reform of the U.S. Trucking Industry, MIT Center for Transportation Studies Rep. No. 77-1.

Rosenberg, L. C. [1963]. Natural Gas Pipeline Rate-Making Problems. Unpublished Doctoral Dissertation, Cornell Univ.

Ruff, L. E. [1978]. Federal environmental regulation, in U.S. Senate Committee on Governmental Affairs, Study on Federal Regulation, 95th Congress, 2nd session, (December), Vol. VI, Appendix p. 251.

Russell, C. S. [1973]. "Residuals Management in Industry." Johns Hopkins Univ. Press, Baltimore, Maryland.

Russell, C. S., and Vaughan, W. J. [1976]. "Steel Production: Processes, Products, and Residuals." Johns Hopkins Univ. Press, Baltimore, Maryland.

Russell, M., and Shelton, R. B. [1974]. A model of regulatory agency behavior, *Public Choice* (Winter), 47–62.

Rutledge, G. L. *et al.* [1978]. Capital expenditures by business for pollution abatement, 1973–77 and planned 1978, *Sur. Current Business* (June), 33–38.

Sadler, A. M., Sadler, B. L. and Bliss, A. A. [1975]. "The Physician's Assistant Today and Tomorrow," 2nd ed. Ballinger, Cambridge, Massachusetts.

Salter, W. [1960]. "Productivity and Technical Change." Cambridge Univ. Press, London and New York.

Sharkey, W. W., and Telser, L. G. [1978]. Supportable cost functions for the multiproduct firm, *J. Econ. Transportation* **18,** 23–37.

Shephard, R. W. [1953]. "Cost and Production Functions." Princeton Univ. Press, Princeton, New Jersey.

Shephard, R. W. [1970]. "Theory of Cost and Production Functions." Princeton Univ. Press, Princeton, New Jersey.

Sheshinski, E. [1971]. Welfare aspects of a regulatory constraint: Note, *Amer. Econ. Rev.* **61** (March), 175–178.

Silber, W. L. (ed.) [1975]. "Financial Innovation." Heath, Lexington, Massachusetts.

Smith, K. R., Over, A. M., Jr., Hansen, M. F., Golladay, F. L., Davenport, E. J. [1976]. Analytic framework and measurement strategy for investigating optimal staffing in medical practice. *Operations Res.* **24** (September–October), 815–841.

Smith, V. K., and Vaughan, W. J. [1979]. Strategic Detail and Process Analysis Models for Environmental Management: An Econometric Analysis. Unpublished paper. Resources for the Future, Washington, D.C. (February).

Snow, S. [1975]. Investment cost minimization for communications satellite capacity: Refinement and application of the Chenery–Manne–Srinivasan model, *Bell J. Econ.* **6** (Autumn), 621–643.

Snow, J. W. [1977]. The problems of airline regulation and the Ford Administration proposal for reform, *in* "Regulation of Passenger Fares and Competition Among the Airlines" (P. W. MacAvoy and J. W. Snow, eds.), pp. 3–40. American Enterprise Institute for Public Policy Research, Washington, D.C.

Solow, R. M. [1957]. Technical change and the aggregate production function, *Rev. Econ. Statist.* **39** (August), 312–320.

Spady, R. H. [1979]. "Econometric Estimation of Cost Functions for the Regulated Transportation Industries." Garland Publ., New York.

Spady, R. H., and Friedlaender, A. F. [1978]. Hedonic cost functions for the regulated trucking industry, *Bell J. Econ.* **9** (Spring), 159–179.

Spann, R. M. [1974]. Rate of return regulation and efficiency in production: An empirical test of the Averch–Johnson thesis, *Bell J. Econ. Management Sci.* **5** (Spring), 38–52.

Srinivasan, T. N. [1967]. Geometric rate of growth of demand, *in* "Investments for Capacity Expansion" (A. S. Manne, ed.). MIT Press, Cambridge, Massachusetts.

Star, S. [1974]. Accounting for the growth of output, *Amer. Econ. Rev.* **64** (March), 123–135.

Stevenson, R. E. [1975]. Productivity in the private electric utility industry, *in* "Public Utility Productivity" (W. Balk and J. Shafritz, eds.). New York State Department of Public Service, Albany, New York.

Stevenson, R. E. [1976]. Cost Functions of Regulated Firms, mimeo. Univ. of Wisconsin, Madison, Wisconsin.

Stevenson, R. E. [1980]. Measuring technological bias, *Amer. Econ. Rev.* **70** (March), 162–173.

Stiglitz, J. E. [1976]. The corporation tax, *J. Public Econ.* **5,** 303–312.

Sudit, E. F. [1973]. Additive nonhomogeneous production functions in telecommunications, *Bell J. Econ. Management Sci.* **4** (Autumn), 499–514.

Tinbergen, J. [1942]. Zur Theorie der Langfristigen Wirtschaftsentwicklung, *Weltwirtsch. Arch.* **55**, 511–549; translated as, On the theory of trend movements, *in* "Jan Tinbergen Selected Papers" (L. H. Klassen, L. M. Koych, and H. J. Witteveen, eds.), pp. 182–211. North-Holland Publ., Amsterdam, 1959.

Törnqvist, L. [1936]. The bank of Finland's consumption price index, *Bank of Finland Mon. Bull.* **10**, 1–8.

Trebing, H. M. [1977]. Broadening the objectives of public utility regulation, *Land Econ.* **53** (February), 106–122.

Trebing, H. M. [1979]. The Future of Telecommunications Regulation: Conflicting Signals, paper presented at the Annual Meeting of the Rocky Mountain Telephone Association (September 12).

Trinc's Transportation Consultants [1973]. Trinc's Blue Book of the Trucking Industry, Washington, D.C.

U.S. Bureau of Labor Statistics [1978]. Productivity Indexes for Selected Industries, U.S. Department of Labor, Bull. 2002 (September).

U.S. Civil Aeronautics Board [1976]. Productivity and Cost of Employment, System Trunks, Calendar Years 1974 and 1975 (September).

U.S. Civil Aeronautics Board [1977]. Aircraft Operating Cost and Performance Report, 11 (July).

U.S. Civil Aeronautics Board [1978]. "Handbook of Airline Statistics." U.S. Government Printing Office, Washington, D.C. (January).

U.S. Department of Commerce, Bureau of Economic Analysis [1978]. *Survey of Current Business.* U.S. Government Printing Office, Washington, D.C.

U.S. Department of Energy, National Power Grid Study, Preliminary Draft, Chapter 5, An Assessment of the Benefits of Fully Integrated Planning and Operation. Washington, D.C. (no date).

U.S. Department of Energy, National Power Grid Study, Preliminary Draft, Chapter 6, Coal-by-Wire, Washington, D.C. (no date).

U.S. Department of Energy, National Power Grid Study, Preliminary Draft, Chapter 12, Governmental Impediments to Electric System Efficiency through Integration, Washington, D.C. (no date).

U.S. Department of Labor, Bureau of Labor Statistics [1974]. Technological Change and Manpower Trends in Six Industries, Bulletin 1817. Government Printing Office, Washington, D.C.

U.S. Environmental Protection Agency [1978]. Standards of Performance for New Stationary Sources: Electric Utility Steam Generating Plants, September 5.

U.S. Environmental Protection Agency [1979]. Cost and Economic Impact Assessment for Alternative Levels of the National Ambient Air Quality Standards for Ozone, EPA-450/5-79-002 (February), C-2.

U.S. Federal Communications Commission [1968]. Use of the Carterfone Device in Message Toll Telephone Service, 13FCC 2d 420, Washington, D.C.

U.S. Federal Communications Commission [1969]. Re Application of Microwave Communications, Inc., for Construction Permits to Establish New Facilities in the Domestic Public Point to Point Microwave Radio Service at Chicago Illinois, St. Louis, Missouri, and Intermediate Points, Docket No. 16509, Decision (August 14), Washington, D.C.

U.S. Federal Energy Regulatory Commission [1979a]. Initial Decision, Public Service Company of New Hampshire, Docket No. EL 78-15 (January 26), Washington, D.C.

U.S. Federal Energy Regulatory Commission [1979b]. Initial Decision Denying, on the Financing Terms Proposed, Applications to Transport and Sell for Resale Mixed Coal–Natural Gas (June 5), Washington, D.C.

U.S. Federal Energy Regulatory Commission [1979c]. Order Setting Values for Incentive Rate of Return, Establishing Inflation Adjustment and Change in Scope Procedures, and Determining Applicable Tariff Provisions, Order No. 31, Docket No. RM 78-12 (June 8), Washington, D.C.

U.S. Federal Power Commission, Statistics of Interstate Natural Gas Pipeline Companies, various issues.

U.S. Federal Power Commission [1951–1976]. Statistics of Privately Owned Electric Utilities in the United States, 1950–1975. U.S. Government Printing Office, Washington, D.C.

U.S. Federal Power Commission [1951–1976]. Steam–Electric Plant Construction Costs and Annual Production Expenses, 1950–1975. U.S. Government Printing Office, Washington, D.C.

U.S. Federal Power Commission [1973]. "Performance Profiles: Private Electric Utilities in the United States, 1963–1970." U.S. Government Printing Office, Washington, D.C.

U.S. Federal Power Commission [1975a]. Requirements and Curtailments of Interstate Pipeline Companies Based on Form 16 Reports Required to be Filed on April 30, 1975, Washington, D.C.

U.S. Federal Power Commission (1975b). Order on Demand from Court Opinion Terminating Investigation and Terminating Advance Payment Program with Conditions, Docket No. R411 and RM 74-4 (December 31), Washington, D.C.

U.S. Federal Power Commission [1976]. Order Adopting in Part Construction Work in Progress Rulemaking and Terminating Proceedings, Order No. 555 (November 8), Washington, D.C.

U.S. House of Representatives [1975]. Report by the Subcommittee on Oversight and Investigations of the Committee on Interstate and Foreign Commerce, Electric Utility Automatic Fuel Adjustment Clauses, 94th Congress, 1st Session, Washington, D.C.

U.S. Senate [1977]. Report prepared for the Subcommittee on Inter-governmental Relations and the Subcommittee on Energy, Nuclear Proliferation and Federal Services, Committee on Government Affairs, Electric and Gas Utility Rate and Fuel Adjustment Clause Increases, 1977. 95th Congress, 2nd Session, Washington, D.C.

Usher, D. [1974]. The suitability of the divisia index for the measurement of economic aggregates, *Rev. Income and Wealth* **20,** 273–288.

Uzawa, H. [1964]. Duality principles in the theory of cost and production, *Internat. Econ. Rev.* **5,** 216–220.

Varian, H. R. [1978]. "Microeconomic Analysis." Norton, New York.

Vartia, Y. O. [1976]. Ideal log-change index numbers, *Scand. J. Statist.* **3,** 121–126.

Vartia, Y. O. [1978]. Fisher's five-tined fork and other quantum theories of index numbers, *in* "Theory and Economic Applications of Economic Indices" (W. Eichhorn, R. Henn, O. Opitz, and R. W. Shephard, eds.), pp. 271–295. Physica-Verlag, Würzburg.

Vinod, H. D. [1972]. Nonhomogeneous production functions and applications to telecommunications, *Bell J. Econ. Management Sci.* **3,** 531–543.

Wales, T. J. [1977]. On the flexibility of flexible functional forms: An empirical approach, *J. Economet.* **5,** 183–193.

Ward, J. H. [1963]. Hierarchical grouping to optimize an objective function. *J. Amer. Statist. Assoc.* **58,** 236–244.

Whitman, Requardt and Associates [1975]. The Handy–Whitman Index of Public Utility Construction Costs, Bulletin No. 100 supplemented to 1975. Whitman, Requardt and Associates, Baltimore, Maryland.

Wills, J. [1979]. Technical change in the U.S. primary metals industry, *J. Economet.* **10,** 85–98.

Woodland, A. D. [1976]. Modelling the Production Sector of an Economy: A Selective Survey and Analysis, Department of Economics Discussion Paper 76-21, Univ. of British Columbia, Vancouver, B.C., Canada.

Zajac, E. E. [1970]. A geometric treatment of Averch–Johnson's behavior of the firm model, *Amer. Econ. Rev.* **60,** 117–125.

Zajac, E. E. [1972]. Lagrange multiplier values at constrained optima, *J. Econ. Theory* **4,** 125–131.

Zellner, A. [1962]. An efficient method of estimating seemingly unrelated regressions and tests for aggregation bias, *J. Amer. Statist. Assoc.* **57,** 348–368.

Author Index

Numbers in italics refer to the pages on which the complete references are listed.

Subject Index

413

ECONOMIC THEORY, ECONOMETRICS, AND MATHEMATICAL ECONOMICS

Consulting Editor: Karl Shell

UNIVERSITY OF PENNSYLVANIA
PHILADELPHIA, PENNSYLVANIA

Edmund S. Phelps. Studies in Macroeconomic Theory, Volume 1: *Employment and Inflation.* Volume 2: *Redistribution and Growth.*

Marc Nerlove, David M. Grether, and José L. Carvalho. Analysis of Economic Time Series: *A Synthesis*

Thomas J. Sargent. Macroeconomic Theory

Jerry Green and José Alexander Scheinkman (Eds.). General Equilibrium, Growth and Trade: *Essays in Honor of Lionel McKenzie*

Michael J. Boskin (Ed.). Economics and Human Welfare: *Essays in Honor of Tibor Scitovsky*

Carlos Daganzo. Multinomial Probit: *The Theory and Its Application to Demand Forecasting*

L. R. Klein, M. Nerlove, and S. C. Tsiang (Eds.). Quantitative Economics and Development: *Essays in Memory of Ta-Chung Liu*

Giorgio P. Szegö. Portfolio Theory: *With Application to Bank Asset Management*

M June Flanders and Assaf Razin. Development in an Inflationary World

Thomas G. Cowing and Rodney E. Stevenson (Eds.). Productivity Measurement in Regulated Industries

Robert J. Barro (Ed.). Money, Expectations, and Business Cycles: *Essays in Macroeconomics*

In preparation

Giorgio Szegö (Ed.). New Quantitative Techniques for Economic Analysis